PHILLIPS PUBLISHING INC.
POTOMAC, MARYLAND

The Local Area Networking Sourcebook™

4th EDITION

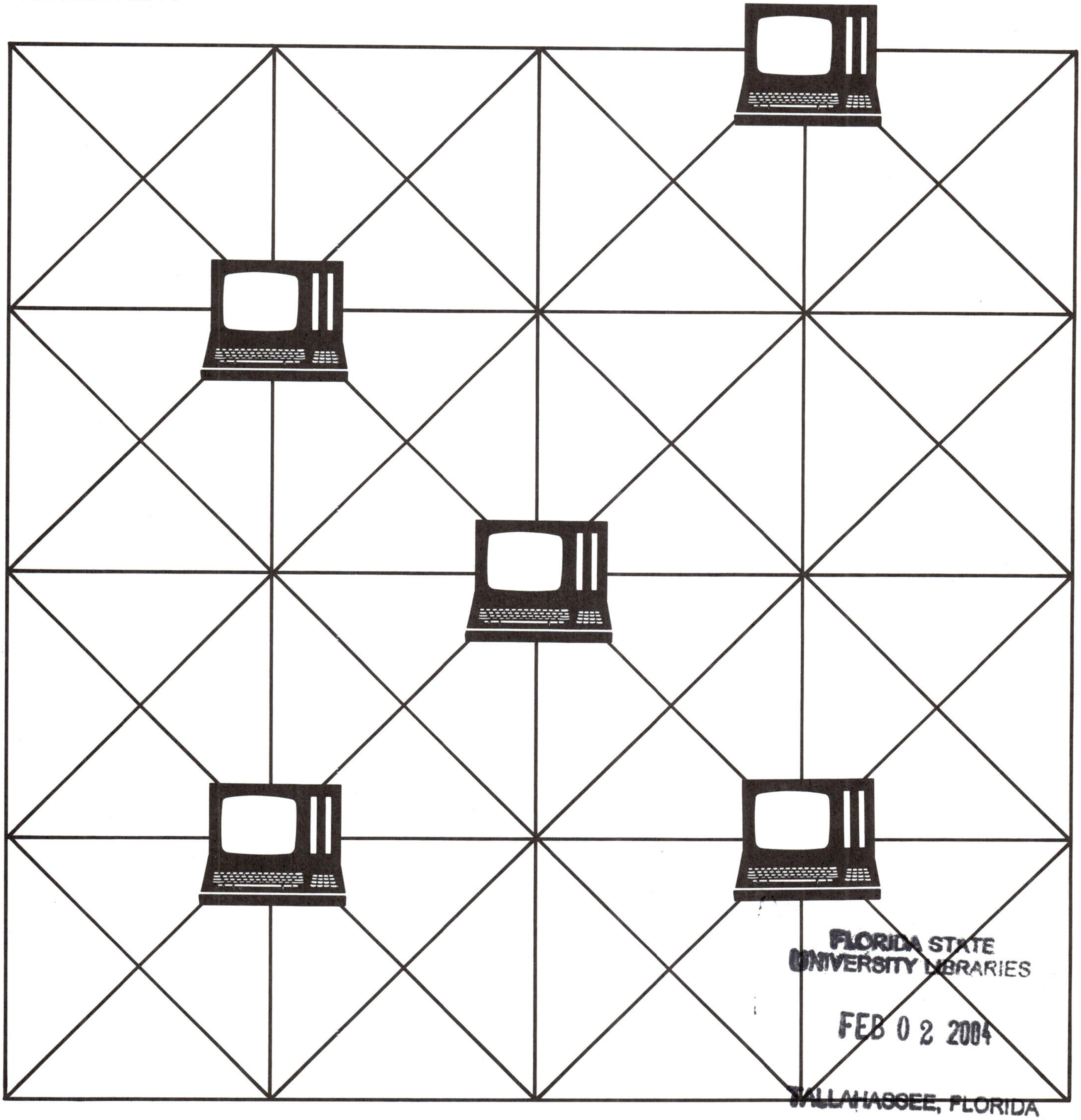

The Local Area Networking Sourcebook™

Editor	Dana M. Richens
Managing Editor	Mark R. Kimmel
Marketing Manager	Eric A. Cohen
Vice President, Publications	Ellen O. Hamm
Publisher	Thomas L. Phillips

Copyright © 1987
Phillips Publishing Inc.
7811 Montrose Road, Potomac, Maryland 20854
(301)340-2100; customer service (800)722-9000

Annual subscription rate $167. Please add $20 for shipment outside the United States.

ISBN 0-934960-32-1

Distributed outside of the U.S.A. and Canada by North-Holland—a Division of Elsevier Science Publishers BV. ISBN 0-444700-44-7. Contact Joop Dirkmaat, P.O. Box 1991, 1000 BZ, Amsterdam, The Netherlands (01)131-205-862-473

INTRODUCTION

The Local Area Networking Sourcebook, 4th Edition, provides a broad spectrum of information, ranging from company names, addresses and telephone/telex numbers to product and service descriptions and local area network profiles. Purchasing, sales, marketing, and other contact names are supplied in most cases.

All information in *The Local Area Networking Sourcebook, 4th Edition,* was furnished by the organizations listed and is believed to be accurate. Phillips Publishing Inc. cannot accept responsibility for inaccuracies or omissions.

Phillips Publishing Inc. also publishes *Data Channels, Outlook on IBM, Fiber Optics News, Outlook on AT&T, The Fiber Optics Sourcebook, The Satellite Directory, Telecommunications Regulatory Monitor,* and other newsletters and information services for the telecommunications industry.

If looking for a specific company, refer first to the company index that appears in the following pages. If seeking suppliers of a particular product or service, refer to the table of contents for the chapter most likely to contain that information.

Entries are grouped in chapters by major business area—e.g., local area networks, manufacturers and distributors, software, business and technical services, standards groups—and then alphabetically. At the beginning of each chapter, companies are cross-referenced by product or service.

A typical directory entry might include the following elements:

- Company name and principal mailing address
- Telephone, telex, TWX, and/or FAX number(s)
- Contact names and titles, including president, product manager, marketing director, product sales contact, public relations contact, and purchasing agent. Position titles are coded to reflect responsibilities—(PM) for product manager, (MD) for marketing director, (PSC) for product sales contact, (PR) for public relations contact, and (PA) for purchasing agent.
- Year founded and number of employees
- Branch offices and/or distributors. For companies with multiple branch offices and/or distributors, a representative sample of five locations has been listed.
- Description of products or services

Network provider entries are more extensive, but essentially follow the same format as that of other companies.

Organizations active in more than one major business area are listed accordingly in more than one chapter.

Refer to the appendix for LAN industry data.

SAMPLE ENTRY

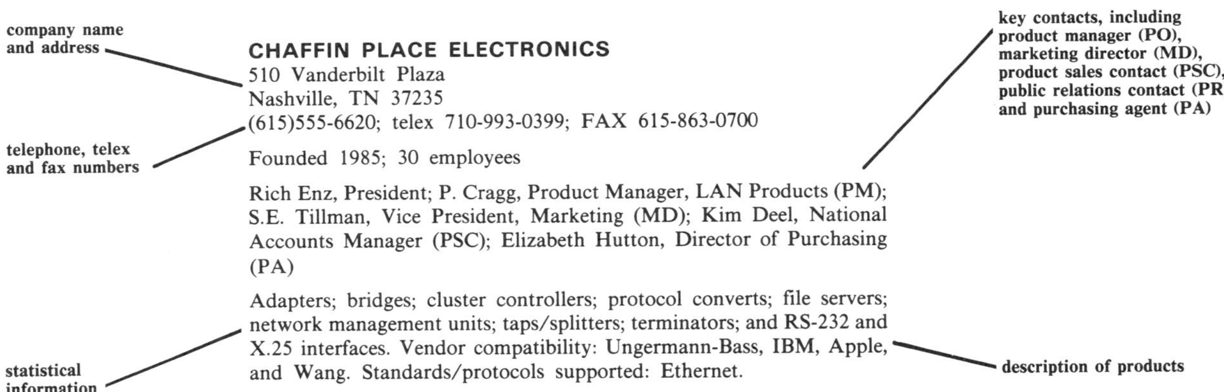

Contents

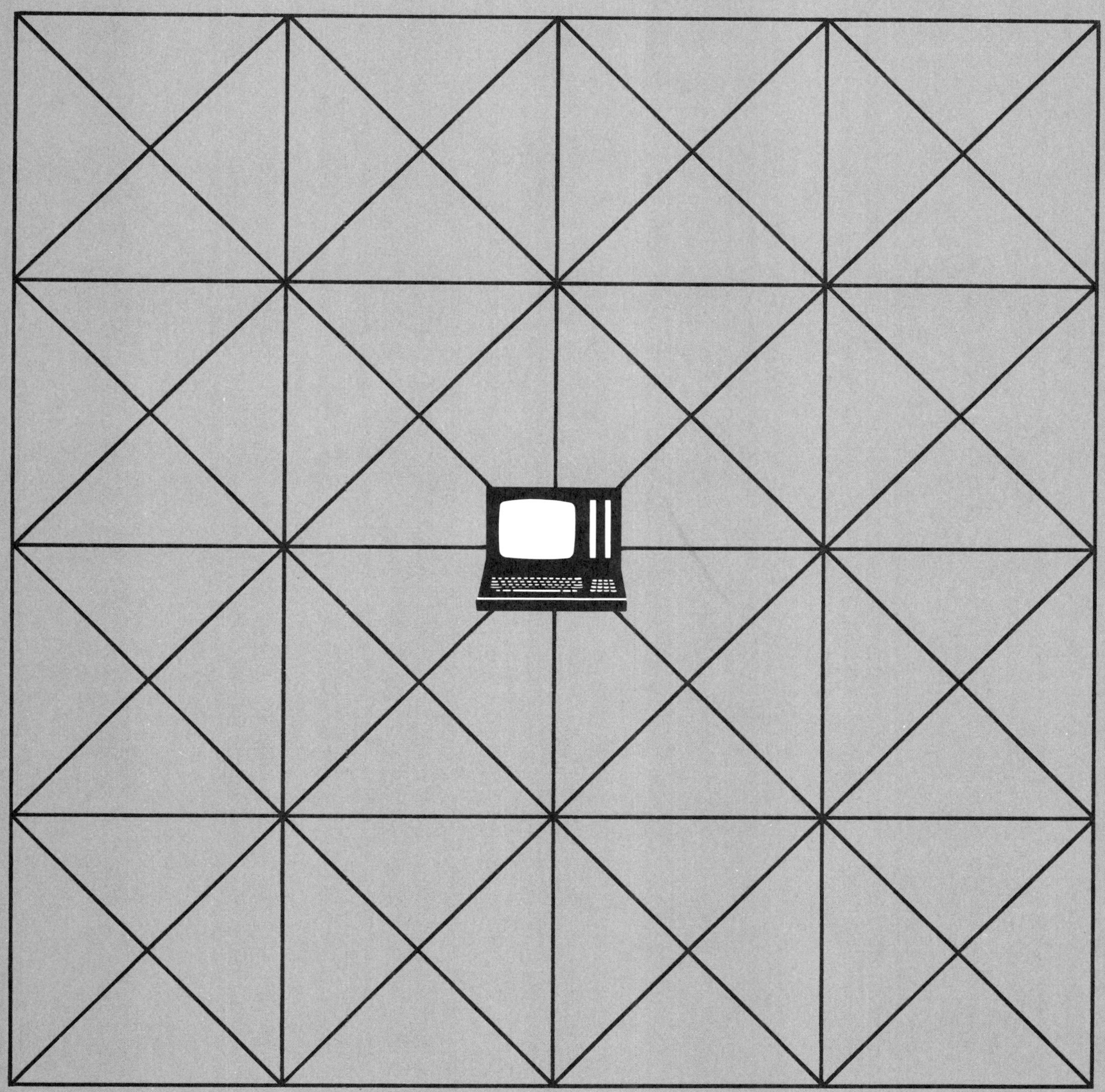

CONTENTS

Company Index

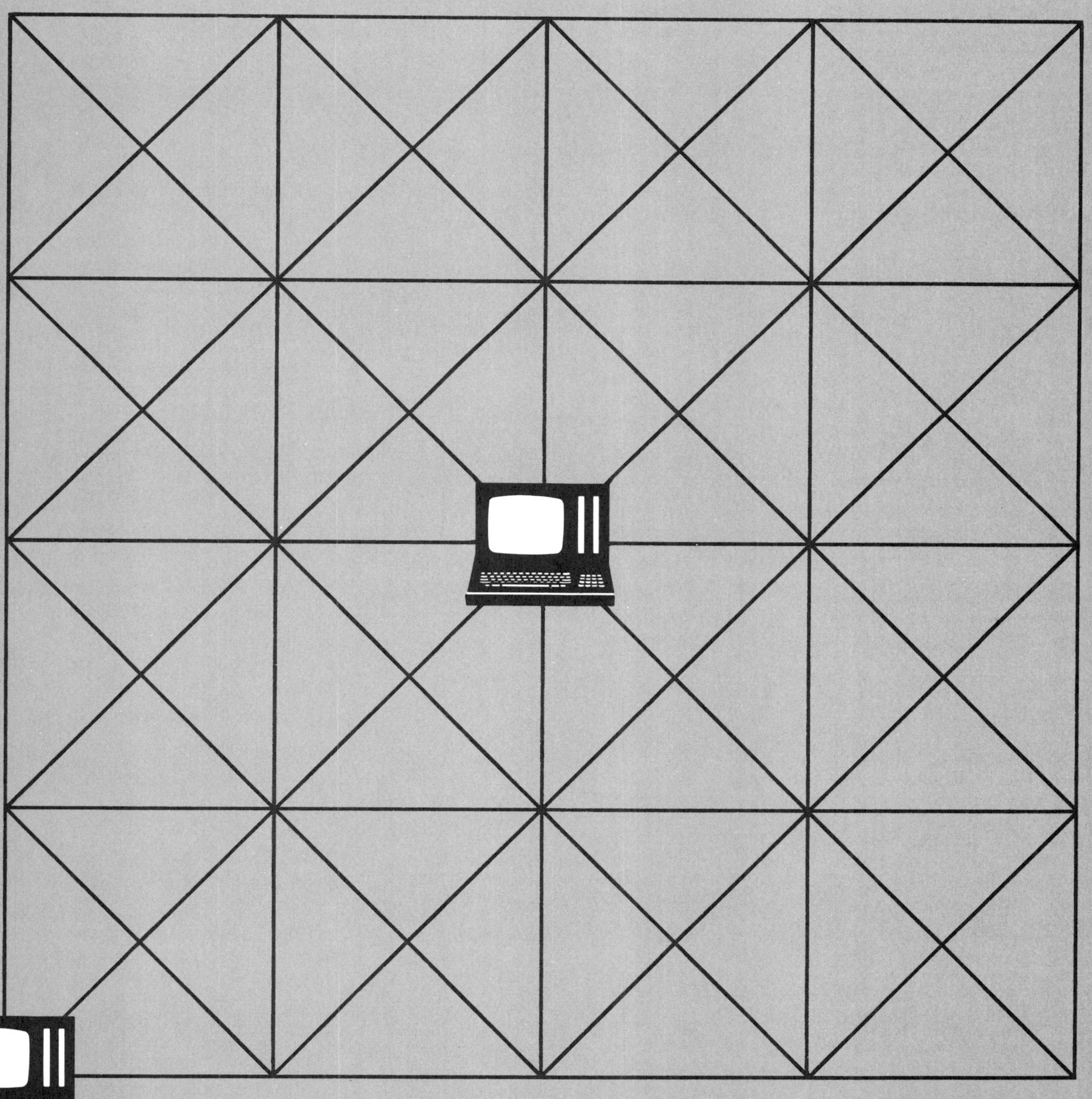

FIBER OPTICS SOURCEBOOK — ALL NEW SECOND EDITION

Table of Contents

Industry Overview and Forecast: Analysis of Current Industry Trends, Plus a Look at the Future

By Walter Morgan

- What was the progress in 1985?
- Installations - regional and national
- Networking
- Domestic vs. foreign suppliers
- Size of marketplace
- Network by network analysis
- Mergers and teams
- Aircraft uses
- Telecommunications security
- 1986 projections

Commercial Fiber Optics Networks

- Operational networks/long-haul and short-haul
- Planned networks/long-haul and short-haul
- Top 4 long-distance carriers
- Local bell operating companies
- Bypass carriers
- Independent telephone companies (Top 25)
- Interexchange carriers

Profiles of operational and planned fiber optics networks, including details on route miles, fiber miles, capacity, applications, areas served, route maps, and more.

Military Fiber Optics Projects

- Survey of military fiber networks under development

Manufacturers and Distributors

- Suppliers of cable, connectors, and other fiber optics products

Business and Technical Services

- Consultants, financial institutions, publishers, trade associations, research and development firms, engineering and technical consultants, system integrators, cable layers, and other providers of technical and business services

International Company Directory

- Listings of foreign companies in supplying fiber optics products and services

Glossary

Appendix

- Market Data
- Telephone Directory

Place your no-risk order for the new **Sourcebook** now. It's fast. It's easy. It's risk-free. It's a money-saver. But don't wait. Complete and mail the form below today! Or call, toll-free (800) 722-9000.

FIBER OPTICS SOURCEBOOK NO-RISK ORDER FORM

- ☐ **YES!** I need the Second Edition of the Fiber Optics Sourcebook. Please send __________ copy(ies) at $197 each and rush them to me via U.P.S. (Maryland residents, please add 5% sales tax.)
- ☐ Check enclosed for $__________. (Please add $4.50 for shipping and handling.)
- ☐ Bill me. (My order will be sent upon receipt of payment.)
- ☐ Bill my company. P.O. #__________. (My order will be sent upon receipt of payment.)
- ☐ Charge: ☐ VISA   ☐ MasterCard   ☐ American Express

Card No. _________________________________ Expiration Date _______________________

Signature _________________________________

Name _________________________________

Title _________________________________

Company _________________________________

Address _________________________________

City _______________ State __________ Zip __________

Phone (____) _________________________________

For faster service,
Call Toll Free
(800) 722-9000
TODAY!

Important Money-Back Guarantee

Order the new second edition of the Fiber Optics Sourcebook today, examine it for a full 15 days. If for any reason you're not satisfied that it is well worth it for you, just send it back to us for a **full, prompt refund.**

Please return to: **Fiber Optics Sourcebook**
Phillips Publishing, Inc.
7811 Montrose Road
Potomac, MD 20854

FD214

Local Area Networking: An Overview

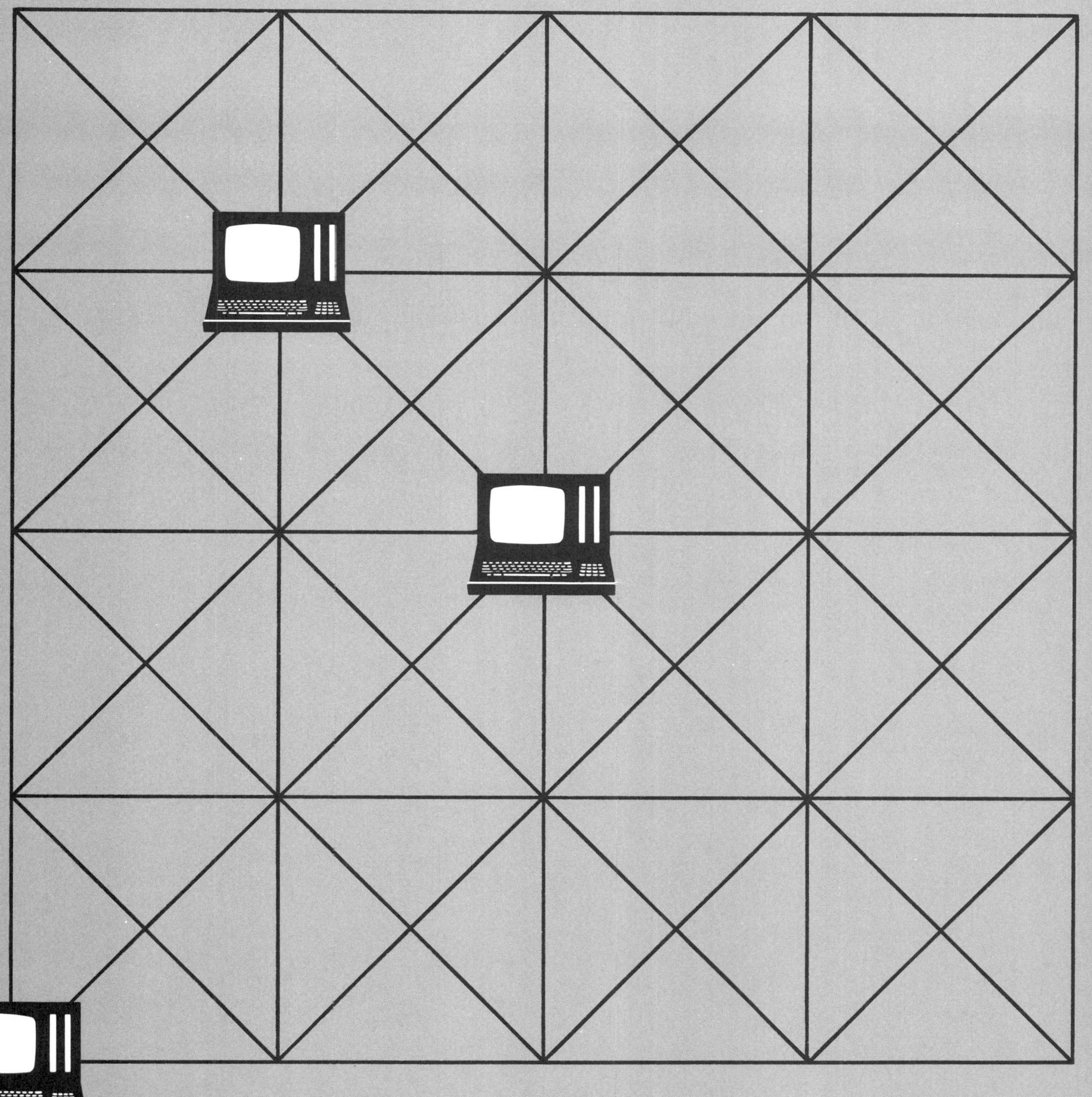

LOCAL AREA NETWORKING: AN OVERVIEW

Dana M. Richens

1970. The place: A typical corporate office in New York, Atlanta or Los Angeles. Inside, a financial officer anxiously awaits the arrival of critical data from the corporate marketing department. A week later, after a lengthy series of inter-office memos and numerous phone calls, the executive finally receives a packet containing the information he needs.

1986. The place: That same office in New York, Atlanta or Los Angeles. Inside, a financial officer, in need of current statistics from the marketing department, logs on to his desktop terminal, accesses the appropriate database and, within seconds, has all the marketing inormation he requires and more.

The executive of the 1980s has a distinct advantage over his counterpart of a decade ago. While "office automation" was the buzzword of the 1970s, it has been the technology of the 1980s that has introduced the local area network (LAN) as the means to interconnect the multitude of computers and devices developed and installed during the office automation era. And while the office scenarios above may be simplistic, the message is clear: the LAN has proved an effective and efficient means of satisfying the vast resource sharing and intrafacility communications requirements of the modern corporate, industrial or educational environment.

Gone are the days when a series of dumb terminals linked to a single mainframe comprised the bulk of a company's data processing system. Today, these terminals have been supplanted by minicomputers and PCs capable of transmitting electronic mail, accessing multiple databases and sharing other valuable information resources. And it is the LAN that has spurred such flexibility in short-haul data communications for banks, hospitals, offices, factories, municipalities, and universities alike.

But what makes the LAN different from other, more traditional, communications systems? An-swers to this question lie in the LAN's domain, speed, accuracy, distributed control, and consequent reliability.

Unlike a wide area network (WAN), the LAN is designed for use within a limited area, such as a campus, factory or office setting. Such geographic proximity among stations accounts for the high data rates achievable through LAN use, typically between 128 Kbps and 100 Mbps. The effectiveness of communications is also enhanced by the reduced error rate typical of local area networks, generally between 1×10^{-9} and 1×10^{-12}.

Another communications alternative, the private branch exchange (PBX), usually relies on a central switching unit to route information among stations. The LAN, on the other hand, is generally characterized by the absence of centralized control, thus si-destepping potential problems created by central controller malfunctions.

To create this decentralization of network control, most LANs feature either a bus, ring or tree node-connecting configuration, or topology, as shown below. The bus topology utilizes a single communication line to which all nodes are linked. The ring configuration is exactly as it sounds: each node is linked to two adjacent nodes, thus creating a ring-shaped network. The tree is a branching cable protruding from a headend that controls transmission frequency. The bus, ring and tree topologies are clearly designed for purposes of system decentralization. In contrast, a fourth topology, the star, is characterized by a central node, to which each peripheral node is linked.

This issue of network topology is only one of several features that distinguish local area networks. Another consideration is the transmission medium over which the LAN operates.

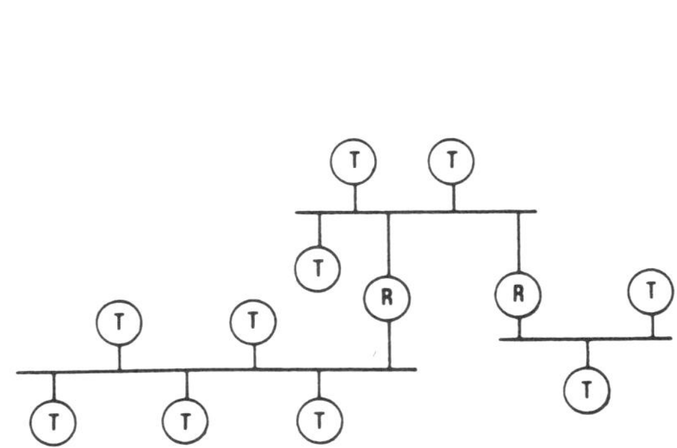

Bus network

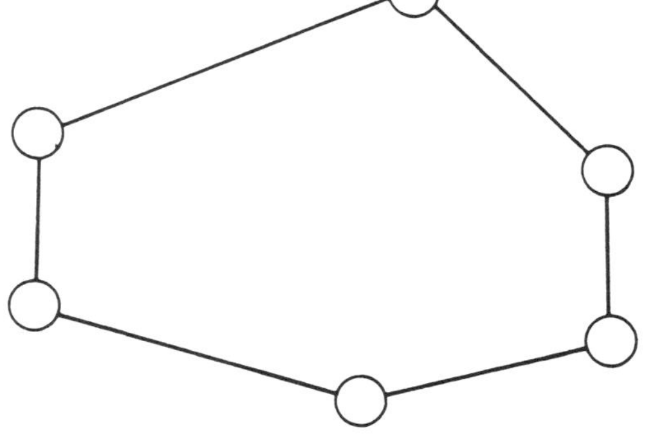

Ring network

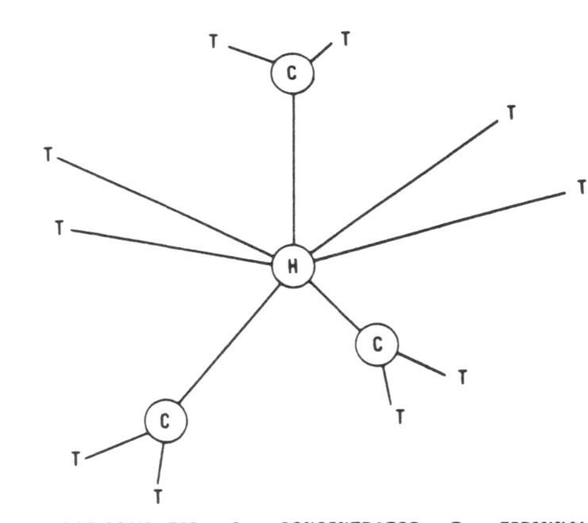

Star network

The least expensive medium and the easiest to install is the twisted wire pair, typically used in PBXs. This option, however, carries several disadvantages that tend to outweigh its cost savings. First, the wire pair is potentially the slowest of the available transmission mediums. In addition, it can be highly susceptible to electrical interference which increases a system's expected error rate. Finally, the twisted wire pair does not transmit well over long distances without the use of costly repeaters. But this distance restriction is not always a concern for LAN users, given the short sender-to-receiver distance that most LAN transmissions require.

A more popular transmission medium for LANs is coaxial cable. The most widely used medium for networking, the coaxial cable can accommodate transmission speeds of 10 Mbps. Several layers of metallic shielding and insulation surrounding the central electrical conductor provide substantial noise immunity and a reduced transmission error rate.

A third alternative is optical fiber. Fiber is recognized for its superior speed capabilities; small, lightweight cable; resistance to tapping and interference; and virtually unlimited bandwidth. Unfortunately, fiber is also noted for its expense and difficulty of installation.

Several other options for LAN use exist, including radio, microwave and infrared transmissions—the "wireless" LANs—but are generally either still in the conceptual stages or limited to experimental applications.

One LAN feature that must go hand-in-hand with a discussion of transmission media is transmission category. Baseband communications allow for a single digital transmission channel capable of carrying voice, image and data, but subject to distance restrictions. Baseband networks spanning several miles may require repeaters to regenerate attenuating signals.

In contrast, broadband systems can accommodate simultaneous transmission of numerous signals. Multiple channels, accessible through carrier modulation of amplitude (AM), frequency (FM) or phase (PM), can carry voice, data and video signals for distances of 10 miles, much farther than the domain of a typical LAN.

Early LANs, such as Ethernet, employed baseband coaxial able, thus encouraging many subsequent LAN vendors to adopt baseband cable as their preferred transmission hardware. However, a preference for broadband systems gradually emerged as end users became interested in the video potential of broadband systems, as well as their ability to accommodate the increase in data traffic associated with an expanding business. These users, mindful of their firms' future data communications needs, favored the expandability and high traffic capacity associated with broadband LANs. But this interest in broadband capabilities has been quelled somewhat by the introduction of the IBM Token-Ring, another baseband LAN. This recent product introduction has spawned a rejuvenation of support for baseband local area networks.

Finally, the access control method utilized by a given LAN is a fourth distinguishing network feature. To allow network devices to communicate with one another, some format must be used to coordinate traffic over the available transmission paths. Basically, this coordination may be achieved in one of two ways: stations may compete directly for channel access, or the network may require stations to take turns transmitting messages.

A contention network is one in which any station is free to transmit at any time, provided no other transmission is in progress. If another transmission is already underway, the network is considered busy, and a potential sender must wait until the network is idle to transmit. The carrier sense multiple access (CSMA) system is an example of such a contention format.

But just as northbound and westbound traffic can never simultaneously negotiate a four-way stop, so will a collision invariably follow if two or more contention network users concurrently initiate transmissions. To avoid the message garbling and time-consuming retransmission associated with undetected collisions, a more refined CSMA system may also make use of a collision detection (CD) feature. Collision detection serves to jam the system once a collision occurs, after which transmission is terminated. Each network interface unit involved in the collision then executes a unique, preassigned "back-off" interval, after which network access may be reattempted. The contention access method is simple and relatively inexpensive, but the transmission attempt/back-off/reattempt cycle characteristic of a CSMA/CD system is quite inefficient for a large network over which heavy traffic is anticipated and, consequently, the likelihood of collisions increased. For this reason, a noncontention access-control method such as token passing may be more practical for heavily congested networks.

In a token-passing network, no station may transmit unless it is in control of the token, a bit pattern that circulates around the network. When the free token arrives at a prospective sending station, it is loaded with data and sent along the network to its destination. Such a loaded token will not stop at any stations other than that of the message addressee. Once the message-bearing token reaches its destination, the data is copied and the token returned to the sender for rerelease. This token-passing method can be used over either the bus or ring network topology.

LAN INDUSTRY HISTORY

In terms of the evolution of the LAN industry, the 1980s thus far will be remembered as a muddle of announcements and non-announcements, multivendor joint agreements and incompatibilities and small vendors venturing into the LAN waters while leaving their launches tied to the IBM dock. But while IBM may be a determining force in local area networking, the company did not begin LAN product offerings until 1984.

It was actually a September 30, 1980, joint product announcement by DEC, Intel and Xerox that prompted early interest in the potential applications of local area networking. The DEC/Intel/Xerox Ethernet, Version 1.0, was the first LAN with wide commercial availability, and this early exposure quickly pushed Ethernet into the role of de facto industry standard.

As Corvus Systems, Wang Laboratories and a host of Silicon Valley firms—Apple, Bridge Communications and others—began to unveil their own LAN offerings, speculation naturally grew as to what role IBM would play in this budding communications field. In 1983, IBM eventually lent its seal of approval to the LAN concept by announcing preliminary plans for a token-ring network. The promised token ring, although not actually available at that time, soon became a de facto standard simply because it carried the endorsement of communications industry mogul IBM.

IBM's 1984 PC Cluster and PC Network introductions were seen by many as merely an appeasement for industry watchers still pressing for a tangible IBM contribution to local area networking. In October 1985, IBM announced a microcomputer networking segment of the actual token ring. The new piece, while incompatible with IBM's earlier PC Network, at least gave the industry its first taste of token ring networking, IBM style. More recent announcements by IBM have expanded the token ring's domain to include System/370 host processors and System/36 computers. Throughout the gradual evolution of its token ring, IBM has divulged enough technical specifics on the unrevealed portions of the network to allow competitors the opportunity to develop compatible products, thereby pushing the token ring further into the spotlight as an industry standard. Thus, as IBM announces each new LAN product, it is greeted with an array of new compatible devices from its competitors.

STANDARDS

This deadlock created by IBM's slowly evolving token ring network is a good example of the vital role of standards in the local area networking industry. For vendors to prosper, they must be able to offer products compatible with those of other major network manufacturers. Standardization gives industry vendors a better opportunity to market such products. In addition, standards allow end users a multivendor selection when implementing a network or expanding an existing one.

Nonproprietary standardization of local area networking has been spearheaded by two principal organizations: The International Organization for Standardization (ISO) with its United States representative, the American National Standards Institute, and the Institute of Electrical and Electronics Engineers Inc (IEEE). The ISO is responsible for the Open System Interconnection (OSI) Reference Model for data communications on which several other standards have been based. The OSI model is a seven-layer protocol, arranged according to complexity of system function, from the simple physical layer to the most complex application layer. One set of standards developed around the OSI Reference Model is the IEEE 802 Project. This set of LAN standards overlaps the physical and data link layers of the OSI Reference Model and includes specifications for token ring and token bus access methods, CSMA/CD and logical link control.

A third force in the area of standards development is the Consultative Committee on International Telephone and Telegraph (CCITT). A division of the United Nations' International Telecommunications Union, the CCITT is responsible for the X series and V series of data communications recommendations, including the well-known X.25 specification for DTE and DCE interface.

But the trends in LAN standardization are by no means limited to these third party organizations. As mentioned earlier, the IBM Token Ring has quickly become a de facto industry standard because of the principal role of IBM in the data communications field. Similarly, many vendors find confrmity to IBM's Systems Network Architecture or the Xerox Network System protocols an important feature when marketing network products. As end users seek to expand and interconnect their networks, the need for compatible devices also increases. Without adequate standardization, the development of hybrid systems and internetworks is restricted.

TRENDS

Where does local area networking go from here? What issues and trends will shape the movement of LANs into the 1990s? One developing area that will certainly expand the size and applications of LANs is internetworking. The existence of isolated LANs within an organization still leaves a void in corporate communications and resource sharing. Internetworking, or the connecting of two or more networks, allows devices on multiple LANs to interact, thus expanding overall productivity and efficiency. In fact, many industry watchers forecast the widespread adoption of a tri-level internetworking system. The first level would consist of intra-office LANs serving a very limited user group. The second level would link these separate office LANs into a more comprehensive intrabuilding system. Finally, these separate building networks could communicate via a multibuilding network made of fiber or some other high speed, high-traffic medium. Clearly, such a system would facilitate communications among all levels and departments of an organization.

But what happens when these multiple communications channels allow open accessibility to too much information? How does a corporate executive or a government security officer allow the free flow of information through a LAN while still protecting proprietary information? Local area networking and data security are diametrically opposite in function. Networking facilitates information flow; data security impedes it. Therefore, as local area networks open channel access to more and more users, stricter security must be imposed to protect sensitive data from both unauthorized network users and outside hackers. Available security measures include multiple, constantly changing passwords; file encrypting devices, designed to scramble a file and make it readable only to the user with the designated password; and card security, providing time windows that deny system access between certain predetermined hours. Security features were once offered as a purchasable option for local area networks, but because of the growing demand for data protection, such capabilities are now often built-in to a network as standard features.

Another issue that may expand the scope of the LAN industry is the Manufacturing Automation Protocol (MAP). First introduced by General Motors in the early 1980s, MAP is a multivendor industrial networking standard for factory-floor automation. Ultimately, MAP would facilitate plant management and plant-wide communications and allow more efficient use of technical resources, thereby significantly reducing production costs. Increased industry recognition of the MAP standard has spawned a variety of MAP pilot projects and joint corporate agreements, such as the IBM/Industrial Networking Inc. and DEC/Concord Data Systems Inc. ventures created to develop MAP-compatible products.

Accompanying MAP into the growing arena of LAN standards are the Technical and Office Protocols (TOP), developed by The Boeing Company. Like MAP, the objective of TOP is to make use of existing standards in establishing a uniform set of protocols. And while MAP is designed for factory-floor communications, TOP addresses general office applications.

Finally, the falling cost of fiber optic components and the rising awareness of the inherent advantages of fiber optics in telecommunications have made this transmission medium an increasingly popular alternative for local area networking. As a network or as a backbone for multiple subnetworks, the use of fiber optics allows high speed, high capacity transmissions without the need for repeaters. As end users realize the true cost effectiveness of fiber and as more standards, such as the ANSI Fiber Data Distributed Interface (FDDI), are established for this medium, the use of fiber optics in local area networking will be expanded.

Certainly other trends exist that do, or will, have an impact on the development of the LAN industry. And while local area networking has existed for years, a future of advanced technologies, broadened applications, newly recognized standards, falling costs, and heightened awareness of the productivity and efficiency associated with LANs points to an ever-increasing interest in, and implementation of, local area networks.

Articles

LOCAL AREA NETWORKS: TODAY'S INVESTMENT OPPORTUNITIES

Gordon B. Lamb

Each weekday morning as you enter your office, you walk to your CRT, flip the "on" switch and punch in your password. Next, you query the mainframe for any messages in your electronic mailbox and instruct the computer to print out these messages on your laser printer. You then head down the hall for your morning cup of coffee. Upon your return, your messages are printed and you are ready for the day's activities.

At 9:57 you are hard at work, when your pop-up alarm clock sets off an internal ring within your computer terminal and a message illuminates on the screen instructing you to switch to video channel 3 for a meeting of all department heads called by the company's president.

Three keyboard strokes puts the work you were doing into a special section of the mainframe's memory and puts you online with other staff members. The meeting begins at 10:00. You can see and hear each staff member as he or she speaks. Both audio and visual respond instantaneously to the human voice. When two or more participants speak at the same time, the screen splits like the old Lotus 1-2-3 window, with each speaker shown in a separate window! You're able to type your meeting notes directly into your own private memory bank as the meeting progresses. As you relax in your private office, you think back to the days when meetings took place around a conference table with each participant trying to outdo the other. Today you worked in your own office, conversing with other staff members via a fiber optic link to a centrally located mainframe computer which has been programmed to process and control all internal and external digital and analog information for the company.

Welcome to the age of local area networks (LAN). The above illustrates several aspects of an automated office environment where workstations are linked to one another and form a network. This network is able to handle many thousands of attached devices which come from many different manufacturers and in turn are connected to information sources coming from different computer vendors. The system can transport high-speed streams of digital information between nodes and through gateways which switch from one network protocol to another. Many of the components of this "office of the future" are here today and are in active use by many companies.

Herein lies an opportunity for those who wish to invest in the common stock of companies engaged in the development and maintenance of LANs. Opportunities exist in all facets from the architectural design of the network to the manufacture of the hardware and software that together make up the LANs.

And the market is growing. In its 1985 Annual Report, Fibronics International Inc. stated, "The market for LAN transfer and distribution systems worldwide was about $600 million in 1985. LAN installations are expected to grow to over $2 billion annually by 1990." This is rapid growth—the type of growth that will have a significant impact on the companies that are involved in the development of systems.

Today's investor has an opportunity to pick and choose the type of company in which to invest. Many large telecommunication giants such as AT&T, all the RBOCs and most of the independents such as Contel and Centel, plus ITT and Northern Telecom, are actively engaged in some aspect of LANs. At last count, the Directory of

Gordon B. Lamb is president of the Dividend/Growth Fund and the portfolio manager for its Laser & Advanced Technology Series. He also serves as president of American Investment Managers, the fund's investment manager.

Public High Technology Corporations published by American Investor Information Services showed over 250 companies involved in a wide variety of communication services and an additional 100 more that specialize in data communications—the key element of any LAN. Then you have the hardware manufacturers such as IBM, Data General, Hewlett-Packard, Control Data, and many more developing their on networks.

When a network is broken down into its component parts, an investor can begin to see just how specialized the manufacturing process can be. Each segment contains components that are available from numerous vendors. Some are part of an integrated system; other systems contain "stand-alone" equipment which may serve a single purpose. Other companies have set a goal of having every piece of communication equipment in an office or manufacturing facility communicate with others, regardless of that equipment's data rate, manufacturer or protocol.

One segment of the LAN market that has been of specific interest to individual and institutional investors is those companies that use fiber optics as the conduit through which data is channeled. By using fiber optic cable, designers of these networks have been able to develop greater transmission capacities. These newer fiber optic systems have many advantages over the older copper cable devices. Fiber cable is immune to hostile environments such as temperature and moisture. Installation costs are less due to the use of smaller size and lighter weight cable. Since the systems are usually entirely digital, they are suitable for the transmission of voice, video and data or a combination of all of these forms of communications.

During 1985 fiber optic stocks in many cases doubled in value only to fall back to their 1985 lows by early 1986. There are many reasons for this pullback, the main one being the disappointment of investors in the short-term lack of earnings. What many investors have not considered is the transition that the world economy is experiencing. For a number of years the United States and the industrialized nations of the world saw their economies driven by the forces of inflation. This started to change in

1982 when inflation began to settle down to the middle of the single digit range. For the period from the early 1970s to he early 1980s, companies were able to cover their inefficiencies and management blunders by raising prices.

This is no longer an option for manufacturers. In today's economic environment, price changes are more on the down side than up. In most cases, raw materials prices and interest rates are lower than they were just a year ago. Wages have also been steady.

All of this has affected those companies that normally would have spent millions of dollars to modernize and update their plants to meet the challenges of the future. Today, manufacturing plants are running at an average of 78 percent of capacity; therefore, management would be hard-pressed to justify the expansion of plant and equipment until such time as it becomes clear that the economy will again be growing at a rapid rate.

In addition to the transition from an inflationary economy to one of disinflation, the country still is lacking a comprehensive tax reform bill. When the managers of Ameiican industry have a depreciation schedule that they can count on for the future, capital spending will begin to increase.

Although the above factors may be negatives for the short-term performance of companies that are intimately involved in the development and maintenance of LANs, the long-term picture is extremely bright. There is no doubt that the use of centralized information processors is the way of the future. Whether people work at home or in the traditional office environment, workstations are here today and centralized access to and the retrieval of information in the form of video, data and voice will continue to be a growth industry.

Since there are so many investment opportunities within the component parts of a local area network, the best investment may well be a diversified portfolio of companies having some involvement with the total makeup of a LAN.

There are many excellent corporate candidates that could be considered as excellent long-term investments. To anchor the portfolio a purchase of shares of AT&T and IBM is a must. These two companies are now and will continue to be the giants of the communications and information gathering industries. Both are diversified companies which manufacture and develop the hardware and software that goes into systems.

Next we would add a fiber optic component by investing in two fiber optic companies. The first would be Artel Communications Corporation of Worcester, Massachusetts. This company is a manufacturer of fiber optic communication systems for computer graphics, video data and audio communications. Their key markets include CAD/CAM, telecommunications, process control, military, and broadcasting. Although Artel is a small company with total 1985 sales in the neighborhood of $6 million, the company's future is bright. Fibronics International Inc. should also be added to the fiber optic component of our portfolio. This company's products include optical fibers, fiber optic cable, optical components, electronics, and related software. Their area of expertise is on-premises communications involving data, voice and graphic information. The company has positioned itself in the high end of the LAN market. Their sales for the year ending December 31, 1985, exceeded $25 million.

Another company that should be included in this portfolio is 3Com Corporation of Mountain View, California. This company produces high performance LAN systems for 16- and 32-byte personal computers and workstations. These systems allow the high-speed communication of information among printers, disk drives, modems, and minicomputers and use Ethernet technology. The company's LANs provide personal computer communication compatibility among information processing devices from different vendors. The EtherSeries products are the leading Ethernet-based LANs for users of IBM Personal Computers, TI Professional Computers and their compatibles. EtherSeries is a family of integrated hardware and software network products that includes network adapters, network servers and network software based on MS-DOS and PC-DOS. Other products include Ethernet transceivers, Eth-

ernet controllers or multibus microcomputers and DEC minicomputers and network software for Unix computer systems. 3Com Corporation was scheduled to be merged with Convergent Technologies but the merger has been called off. This company's future is very bright.

Network Systems Corporation provides large commercial firms and government agencies with high-performance data communications equipment and software. Their HYPERchannel system permits high-speed communications among various computers and peripherals regardless of manufacturer. The company has recently introduced a lower-end 10 Mbps LAN, the Series B, which is receiving a lot of market interest.

Electronic messaging will become more and more a part of LANs. One company that should profit from integration of these messaging systems into a LAN will be VMX Inc. of Richardson, Texas. This company manufactures, markets and services a patented computer system which they call the Voice Message Exchange. As the company describes their system, "it allows a user to send, receive, reply to and redirect individual or group messages from any tone-signaling telephone in the world."

VMX Inc. has licensed their patent to several companies including NEC Corporation and Wang Laboratories Inc. They also have entered into a national distribution agreement with Xerox Corporation.

No portfolio would be complete without a Japanese manufacturer. We would therefore add NEC Corporation to the portfolio. This company is a leading manufacturer of communications equipment and systems, integrated circuits, computers, and industrial electronic systems.

These eight companies should all be considered long-term growth situations. AT&T and IBM are well-known. Both have been making money and paying dividends to their share holders for many years. NEC is a large company competing head to head with many of our U.S. companies. The remaining five portfolio choices are small companies, each with a specialized niche in the market. To realize the full potential of the earning power of these companies an investor must be patient. These companies will prosper over the next few years.

I NEED MORE COPIES OF:

The Local Area Networking Sourcebook, 4th Edition

_____ Please send me _____________ copies of
The Local Area Networking Sourcebook, 4th Edition

_____ I am enclosing my check for $167.00 each.*

_____ Please bill me.

_____ Standing order—5% discount: $159.

_____ I would like to pay by credit card.
Charge my Visa ☐, MasterCard ☐,
American Express ☐. My credit card number
is _______________________________
and the expiration date is _______________

Signature _______________________________

*(Please add $20.00 postage and handling per order for foreign shipment.)

**For faster service, order by phone:
(800) 558-8851**

____
Name

____
Company

____
Title

____
Address

____
City   State   ZIP

____
Phone

LA 252

- -

I'M NEW • I'VE MOVED
I WOULD LIKE TO BE LISTED IN:

The Local Area Networking Sourcebook, 5th Edition

_____ I'm new. Please send me a directory survey
for a FREE listing in **The Local Area
Networking Sourcebook,** 5th Edition

_____ I've moved. Please send me a directory survey
so my listing will be updated.

____
Name

____
Company

____
Title

____
Address

____
City   State   ZIP

____
Phone

- -

I WOULD LIKE TO ADVERTISE IN:

The Local Area Networking Sourcebook, 5th Edition

_____ Please send me information immediately.

____
Name

____
Company

____
Title

____
Address

____
City   State   ZIP

____
Phone

BUSINESS REPLY MAIL

FIRST CLASS PERMIT NO. 1429 POTOMAC, MD

POSTAGE WILL BE PAID BY ADDRESSEE

Phillips Publishing Inc.

7811 Montrose Road
Potomac, MD 20854

- -

BUSINESS REPLY MAIL

FIRST CLASS PERMIT NO. 1429 POTOMAC, MD

POSTAGE WILL BE PAID BY ADDRESSEE

Phillips Publishing Inc.

7811 Montrose Road
Potomac, MD 20854

- -

BUSINESS REPLY MAIL

FIRST CLASS PERMIT NO. 1429 POTOMAC, MD

POSTAGE WILL BE PAID BY ADDRESSEE

Phillips Publishing Inc.

7811 Montrose Road
Potomac, MD 20854

INTERCONNECTING LOCAL AREA NETWORKS

Lawrence J. Bolick

The personal computer (PC) population explosion of the early 1980s placed an important tool on many of America's desktops. For a time, however, the tools lacked convenient communications features and remained isolated. But, as interest in primary PC applications like word processing and spreadsheets grew, interest in sharing applications, files and output devices also grew. Vendors responded to the nascent market with a wide variety of local area networking (LAN) products. Administrators who had evaluated and recommended specific PC hardware and software for use in their organizations were confronted with a new set of abstruse decision criteria like medium type, medium access method and disk-sharing mechanism.

Even as these hurdles are being overcome and the number of LAN installations continues to grow, another obstacle is emerging. Though they have relieved personal computers of their isolation, many LANs are themselves isolated from each other. As users grow accustomed to the capabilities of communicating PCs, LAN interconnection will become an increasingly important topic.

The interconnection of LANs, though, is more complicated than the mere physical linkage of networks. Four issues are of special importance:

1. What level of security is acceptable in the interconnected environment and how can it be achieved? Data residing in departmental LANs that previously served a well-defined community of users could be accessible to a much broader audience after interconnection. If one or more of the interconnected networks allows access from public networks, the threat is even greater.

2. Is a "seamless" interconnection required and, if so, how can it be achieved? In many cases no uniform addressing scheme had been implemented over previously unconnected LANs, so interconnection must accommodate these duplicated addresses. Differences also may exist in file-locking mechanisms and in PC operating systems. A seamless interconnection would hide these distinctions from the user and make the interconnected networks appear as a single entity.

3. What flow and congestion control mechanisms would the interconnection provide? Without these controls, LANs with relatively high throughput rates can easily overwhelm those with lower throughput rates, thereby affecting the performance of the lower-speed LANs and arousing the ire of their users.

4. What network management capabilities would the interconnection provide? Network designers familiar with network management techniques on wide area networks know that the necessary procedures are fairly standard but are still not trivial. The addition of LANs, PCs and file servers makes fault detection and isolation, reconfiguration, traffic and reliability analyses, and the other aspects of network management even more omplex.

The interconnection of computer networks is not unknown, of course. The Defense Department's Arpanet began interconnecting research networks in the early 1970s, commercial SNA networks have been interconnected as a result of business mergers and commercial packet switching networks have been interconnected via the X.75 protocol standard.

LANs, too, have been interconnected to form larger networks. In the early 1980s, Xerox interconnected dozens of Ethernet LANs in its locations throughout the country to provide a standard electronic mail service throughout the company. Never-

Lawrence J. Bolick is a supervising consultant in the telecommunications consulting practice of the Management Consulting Services Division, Coopers & Lybrand, New York, NY.

theless, the interconnection of LANs has only recently become important to corporate America.

Three generic interconnection methods are available: bridge, router and gateway. A bridge connects similar networks at the data link layer of the Open System Interconnection (OSI) model by functioning as a store-and-forward device for packets traveling between the networks. By monitoring the addresses of the packets it receives, bridges can filter internetwork traffic by forwarding only those packets destined for devices on LANs other than the originating LAN. In this way, the interconnected networks avoid transmitting unnecessary packets outside the local domain. Bridges often are found in Ethernet environments in which the store-and-forward capability of the bridge can connect mulitple Ethernets and can serve to circumvent the 1.5-kilometer restriction on the length of the Ethernet bus.

A router connects networks that may differ at the data link level but are similar at the network and higher levels of the OSI model. Unlike bridges, which function at the data link level, routers operate at the network level. Because of the differences in the data link layers of the interconnected LANs, routers must accommodate differences in data link frame sizes. Consequently, the router may be required to split the original packets to accommodate smaller frame sizes on intermediate or destination LANs. Conversely, the router may construct larger packets for intermediate and destination LANs to take advantage of the efficiencies offered by larger frame sizes. The Defense Department's Transmission Control Protocol/Internet Protocol (TCP/IP) and the Xerox Network System (XNS) are examples of the protocol architectures used by routers.

A gateway connects networks with protocol architectures that may differ at all levels of the OSI model. The actual protocol conversion takes place in the application layer. Because of the greater complexity of gateways, this method often requires more resources than the previous two methods but, at the same time, can provide more local autonomy over each of the interconnected LANs. The interface by non-IBM vendors to IBM's Distributed Office Support System (DISOSS) for the transfer of documents between product lines is a recent example of a gateway.

Responding to the growing LAN interconnection market, vendors have begun to offer solutions based upon each of the three generic interconnection methods. Vitalink Communications Corporation, for example, offers an Ethernet bridge that conserves bandwidth on the LANs and their interconnection medium by filtering packets. Telephone system vendors like Intecom with its S/80 Private Branch Exchange (PBX) and AT&T with its Information Systems Network (ISN) data switch offer bridging capabilities that allow Ethernet-based, departmental networks to circumvent limitations on the length of the Ethernet bus.

Bridge Communications Inc. offers routers that interconnect Ethernet networks over a variety of media, including point-to-point links, packet networks and coaxial cable. Excelan, on the other hand, offers Ethernet routers to interconnect micro- and minicomputer systems based on operating systems like AT&T's Unix, DEC's VMS and RSX-11, and IBM's PC-DS.

Banyan Systems, a recent entrant into the LAN interconnection market, offers a gateway built around a file server. In addition to the transparent exchange of information among networks connected to the server, Banyan claims to offer electronic mail, host access, and consistent user and resource mnemonics throughout all interconnected LANs. And, in another portion of the LAN interconnection market, gateways to IBM's DISOSS have begun to appear since DISOSS emerged as the de facto standard for the format and transfer of office documents.

In spite of these and other products, the LAN interconnection market remains in a relatively nascent state. IBM's promised token ring LAN and its recent announcement of the peer-oriented Logical Unit 6.2 for its System Network Architecture (SNA) will spur development of a wide variety of new interconnection products in the next few years. The rapidly maturing OSI protocols will encourage even more products by the end of the decade.

Nevertheless, the roots of the future for LAN interconnection already exist. The wise manager will hone the skills needed for tomorrow on the products available today.

PC NETWORKING

Pete Maclean

OVERVIEW

The advent of local area networks for personal computers has changed the face of data processing considerably. Think back to The Way It Used To Be...a long, long time ago...January 1982. Big computers hosted throngs of users who accessed their powerful and expensive resources via plodding, dumb slavish terminals. Almost everything in the host was shared: the processor(s), the memory, the peripherals, the data, the hardware failures, the software crashes. Cumbersome operating systems exacted their toll for grudgingly extending a fair (or unfair) share of the machine to each user. Yet it's grand to have all that horsepower, enough torque to push you back in your seat. Personal computers, on the other hand, gave users the freedom to create powerful, personalized workstations, the autonomy to perform data processing at their desks, access to rafts of exciting personal productivity software, plus the ability to hook into the hosts, thanks to terminal emulation. Nevertheless, PCs are basically puny computers, which isolate their users in shuttered little worlds. Life with computers was a matter either of sharing too much when using a host, or sharing too little in the case of a PC.

There are some resources that demand to be shared: databases (within security bounds), application programs, electronic mail, and the services, if any, provided by operators (especially file back-up). Some things are best kept private: processors, memory, disk space, your personal way of doing things. Then came PC LANS, herding rogue PCs back from the brink of autocracy, roping them together into cooperative communities—in fact, bridging the best of both worlds (with a few exceptions, naturally).

Today's best PC networks are competitive in power with mainframes, but cheaper to buy, install and maintain. Mainframes, however, are not doomed to obsolescence. Not only will the tremendous investment in mainframe software ensure their longevity, but there are still three things which mainframes can handle better than PCs: number crunching, running huge programs and storing huge files. Most personal computers, notably IBM PCs and compatibles, are sadly lacking in memory capacity and therefore choke when asked to run applications which demand megabytes of code and working storage. Also, while gigabytes of disk can be added to these computers, it's difficult to make any single file larger than 32 Mb. Mind you, the next generation of PCs may stack up very differently in these respects.

PC LANs are finally coming of age. LAN quality and reliability are high. LAN products have been introduced or endorsed by such major U.S. vendors of personal computers as IBM, Apple, AT&T, and Zenith.

WHAT IBM IS UP TO

IBM came late to LANs (as it comes late to many new ideas) and then proceeded to set some industry standards: the NETBIOS, the first networking version of PC-DOS, and the token ring.

IBM's first LAN, PC Network, was undistinguished and now has few, if any, prospects for success. IBM is pushing it as the preferred network for small-scale installations, but customers seem to have more faith in the Token Ring. Although PC Network may be a white elephant, it remains historically important for two reasons. It established the IBM NETBIOS as the standard for software interfaces to LANs and introduced version 3.1 of PC-DOS,

Pete Maclean conducts seminars worldwide on PC communications and networking. A resident of San Francisco, Mr. Maclean also crafts software products and writes books.

which incorporated the locking mechanisms that allowed multi-user software to flourish. The Token Ring carries on the NETBIOS tradition and so, IBM promises, will any future IBM networks which are intended for PCs.

PC Network may receive continued support from IBM, but it seems unlikely that it will be developed any further. The network of the future is certainly the Token Ring. On the same day in October 1985 that IBM announced its first Token Ring products, many other vendors jumped on the bandwagon announcing compatible and add-on goodies. A steady flow of third party announcements has followed, confidence in the ring has grown and it seems safe to say that the Token Ring is already a standard—and was, perhaps, the only product to establish itself as a marketplace standard before it was even released.

IBM is following up with more and more Token Ring product announcements. The company held fast to the laudable "open architecture" approach adopted with its PC, in publishing the specifications for the network and by making available, through Texas Instruments, chip sets for building compatible interfaces. Many companies will choose the Token Ring both because of IBM's formidable clout and thanks to its potential to link up all major IBM computer systems from PCs to System/36s up through mainframes. Still, few companies will voluntarily become guinea pigs; although the Token Ring is built according to a solid standard (IEEE's 802.5), uses proven network software (an enhanced version of the program IBM sold for PC Network) and has been heavily tested at CERN (the European nuclear research establishment), it could still have teething problems.

OTHER LAN VENDORS

For linking non-IBM personal computers together, or networking IBM PCs to non-IBM hosts, plenty of other products can be recommended. Ethernet, the most famous LAN design, has not become a lion in the PC arena, which may seem surprising considering its prowess in so many others. Nevertheless, the extensive range of products made for Ethernet will undoubtedly secure for it a continued role in PC networking. In networks which tie PCs to DEC or Hewlett-Packard hosts, Ethernet remains most promising. Innovative development in this area is being pursued by many small start-up companies, to say nothing of major players like DEC, 3Com, Bridge Communications, and Excelan.

For small outfits which use only microcomputers, other networking options may hold great value. If a network accommodates all the PCs a company owns, performs well and has support from a reliable vendor, then it may prove superior to a Token Ring or an Ethernet, especially in terms of performance. For IBM PCs, NETBIOS compatibility may be regarded as a highly desirable feature. Products from Gateway Communications and Apple Computer shine here.

THE MARKETPLACE

PC networking has not yet taken off in the marketplace, but LAN products are selling briskly. PC LANs have reached a point of great strength today: the finest products on the market allow users to extract maximum performance from networked PCs. The only major weaknesses result from limitations inherent in the architectures and operating systems of PCs, problems which are magnified in network environments. I have already alluded to these in the case of IBM PCs: specifically, they are the restrictions on file size, to 32 MB, and program size, to about 600KB. (Methods of getting around these limitations exist, but most users cannot exploit them.) Multitasking operating systems for PCs also make LANs more viable.

NETWORK APPLICATIONS

Most organizations which install PC LANs do so in order to run multi-user applications. Many multi-user software products for PCs are old programs modified for LAN compatibility. An important example is Ashton-Tate's dBASE III PLUS, an edition of dBASE III containing several enhancements favoring a network environment. Usually, the only essential change required to convert a single- to a multi-user application is the addition of file/record-locking.

In the major application categories (database management, accounting, electronic mail), a wealth of products with support for networking have already appeared. In categories such as word processing and project management surprisingly few multi-user products are available, but enough probably exist for most users to find a suitable candidate. Source-code librarians and other exotic products may still be hard to find.

The majority of PC LAN users install them in order to run multi-user applications, but there are plenty of other reasons for networking PCs. Assembling a LAN with an SNA gateway, a shared protocol converter offering 3270 access to IBM mainframes, may cost little more than buying an individual emulator (of the IRMA type, for example) for each PC, yet provide considerably more power and room for expansion. Some small offices install cheap LANs just to facilitate file back-up, or to allow PCs to share printers or exchange files.

TRENDS

The latest developments in PC LANs include fault-tolerant file servers, dial-in access, standardization of network software, and direct connections to hosts.

Fault tolerance, pioneered in the world of mini-computers by Tandem and now offered by Novell and Nestar, employs duplicated components for redundancy. In one scheme, a network file server is provided with two identically written disks. If one disk fails, the other enables processing to continue with no interruption. Alternatively, an entire file server can be duplicated, thus affording protection against the failure of any single component.

Until recently, PCs had to be hardwired to LANs to make any use of them at all. Now, more and more vendors are providing network user capability to PCs which dial in through a standard modem link. Modem speeds limit the power of this feature, but it can be very convenient. While the LANs offered by some vendors include software to support dial-in, I have found that a "remote control" product, such as Meridian Technology's Carbon Copy,

often works better. Such packages allow a user at one PC to take control, through keyboard and screen, of another PC connected to the first by a telephone line. In a sense, these products permit two linked PCs to play the roles of terminal and (single-user) host.

When every LAN vendor offered a proprietary network operating system, there were big problems with application compatibility—to say nothing of the fact that many of them just weren't too good. Today we are seeing many vendors abandoning their own software in favor of one of a small group of popular systems. These are the IBM PC LAN Program, Microsoft's MS-NET, Novell's Advanced NetWare, and 3Com's 3+. The number of options is still a bit too large, even given that they are all converging on compatible application interfaces.

Despite high demand, there are rather few possibilities for connecting computers other than microcomputers directly to PC LANs. Yes, you can reach almost anything through some sort of gateway, but that tends to limit you to terminal-style links, with all the concomitant speed and reliability problems. Fortunately, much development is under way, and we have available, announced or rumored connections for DEC VAXen, HP-3000s, IBM Series/1s, System/36s and System/370 mainframes, as well as many Unix machines.

INTERNETWORKING

Just as PCs are enhanced by communication links to other computers, so do LANs become much more powerful when connected to other networks. Whereas PCs communicate using modems and 3270 emulators, LANs communicate through bridges and gateways. A bridge is a link between two LANs of the same kind. Gateways are portals between different networks. Sometimes the distinction between a bridge and a gateway is blurry; in practice, one term might suffice for both.

A bridge is typically a PC that is a member of two similar networks and passes data between them. It makes the two networks appear to any user to be unified. Why not just have one network, then?

Among other things, there may be more PCs than can be accommodated on a single network. This might be due either to a physical restriction on the number that can be connected or to performance limitations. One might bridge LANs installed in two departments of an organization to allow some cross-communication; or, when one LAN grows to a point where performance has begun to degrade, a partition, splitting it into two bridged networks, might be in order.

Most major networks provide bridging these days, but support is strong only for local bridges, links between pairs of LANs in the same location. A remote bridge, which would connect two geographically distant LANs, may be hard to find. Something of the same effect may be achieved by making a PC on one LAN a dial-in user on the other.

The most popular type of gateway connects a PC LAN to an IBM SNA network. The SNA gateway is usually a PC emulating an IBM 3274 cluster controller. This enables PCs on the network to perform 3270, and sometimes 3770, terminal emulation. The installation of a PC LAN with an SNA gateway permits both inter-PC communications and host access. And while that may be killing two birds with two stones, they can at any rate be cheaper than the cairn which would be required to provide host access alone with individual emulators.

Communication servers allow networked PCs to share a pool of asynchronous modems for dial-out use. They can be used with network-adapted versions of popular communications packages, such as Crosstalk and SmartCom. While properly called communication servers, they can also be regarded as asynchronous gateways.

INDUSTRY OUTLOOK

I believe that the key areas to watch are: token ring-compatible products, especially those providing links to non-IBM machines; multi-user applications; network management aids; remote bridging; low-coast/low-performance alternatives to the major LANs; and anything which enhances the performance, reliability, security, or capacity of file servers.

IBM will continue to lead the way as far as major hardware is concerned. Other vendors are certain to prosper in areas such as fault tolerance and gateway development. I do not want to guess who will win the battle of network operating systems.

Is 1986 truly going to be "the year of the LAN?" Or 1987? PC LANs are still expensive: costly to buy, to install and to manage. And most managers are scared of making a costly mistake. I predict that within a couple of years costs will be cut in half, standards will become clearer and LANs will boom.

FIBER OPTIC TRANSPORT IN LOCAL AREA NETWORKS

Richard A. Cerny

INTRODUCTION

It's a bit premature to mourn the death of coaxial cable, but signs indicate that its future is limited. In the face of new structure cabling systems that rely solely on the use of fiber optics and twisted wire pairs, coaxial cable appears destined to play only a limited role in local area network (LAN) wiring. This is due to the deliberate elimination of coax by such giants as AT&T and IBM, which have replaced it with a combination of fiber and wire for virtually all premises communications distribution—voice, data and video. In all probability, neither fiber nor wire alone could displace coax, but the marriage of the two diverse technologies presents a formidable challenge.

Fiber optic LANs are now being developed that ulitmately will replace coaxial cabling in CSMA/CD networks, token ring networks, IBM 3270 multiplexing and switch RS232-C data communications applications. Some intend to replace all of the above simultaneously on a broadband basis.

Fiber optics is one of those glamorous technologies that simultaneously inspires awe and fear in those individuals that stand to benefit from its implementation, but are not yet familiar with the fundamentals of the technology. To put it in its proper perspective, a large computer company takes the matter-of-fact approach that "fiber optics is just another transmission medium." Its use must be justified on an economical basis, using common sense evaluation techniques. Certain new trends in communications and computer processing appear to make fiber optics the emerging dominant communications medium. It's just another medium, but it's a medium that must be seriously considered when planning a local area network or premises distribution cabling system.

Richard A. Cerny is president of Trellis Communications Corporation, a fiber optics consulting firm in Salem, NH.

INDUSTRY BACKGROUND

The fiber optic communications industry is only about ten years old, but the concepts of optical communications and guided light transmission date back to the late 1800s. In 1966 theoretical analysis postulated that long-distance optical fiber transmission was feasible, given a suitably transparent glass. That "low loss" threshold of 20dB/km was reached in 1970 by Corning Glass Works, and the industry began deploying fiber optic transmission links in the late 1970s.

To date, most of the commercial activity has been in the long-distance, intercity telecommunications arena. That market is now well penetrated. Indeed, there may now even be an overabundance of long-haul fiber capacity. The next area to be addressed is the customer premises—building and campus—communications distribution market.

Many have predicted the widespread usage of fiber optics in data communications for years, initially for high-speed, mainframe-to-mainframe links. The idea was exciting. The execution was disappointing. Several manufacturers blamed the lack of standards as the reason for not following through, while others claimed the economics were not yet in favor of fiber optics.

Thus, what little market there was for short-haul fiber systems existed only for end-user "data links." Several smaller manufacturers offered a point-to-point product solution for transmission problems, like electromagnetic interference, communications security or ground loops. Today, however, the market for fiber optics in facilities cabling is poised for take-off.

Costs have declined, supply is abundant, standards have emerged and the technology finally has the sponsorship of the two largest players in the industry. The potential implications transcend what we currently refer to as "local area networks." All communications distribution is affected, not just the transmission of computer data.

WHAT IS FIBER OPTIC TRANSMISSION?

The term "fiber optcs" is used to describe the technology of transporting information by way of guided light waves in an optical fiber, in contrast to the conventional transmission of electrical signal energy on copper wires. Through the phenomenon of "total internal reflection," the glass fiber traps an entering beam of light from an optical source, such as a light-emitting diode (LED) or semiconductor laser diode, and guides this optical signal through the length of fiber to the detector at the far end. The fiber acts as an "optical waveguide," as Corning Glass Works called it, permitting the light to travel over very long distances, even around corners and bends.

The light signal flows only in the center portion (core) of the multilayer glass fiber, contained by the outer layer (cladding) of the fiber. The concept becomes very simple to envision when it is compared to water flowing through pipes. Like ordinary plumbing, the rate of flow (or power throughput) depends upon the power of the source, the efficiency of input coupling, the size of the pipe, the leakage at connectors and splices, the physical condition of the pipes, the lack of constrictions at the bends, and the output coupling efficiency. In fact, fiber optics have long been used for guiding light in noncommunications applications, such as medical illumination and image transmission. These lightguides are often referred to as "light pipes."

THE SYSTEM ELEMENTS

The basic fiber optic system consists of three elements: the transmitting source (transmitter), the receiving detector (receiver) and the interconnecting optical fiber cable.

The transmitter converts electrical communications signals to light signals through intensity (brightness) modulation of the LED or laser diode source, and launches the resultant signal into the end of the optical fiber. The fiber, perhaps one of several optical "conductors" in the cable structure, guides the light signal to the other end of the cable which may be only a few feet away or many miles away. At the far end, the receiver detects the optical signal and reconverts it to an electrical replica of the original electrical signal.

Since both the transmitter and receiver are active electro-optical devices, they often include a substantial amount of other electronic capabilities, such as self-testing, alarming, signal processing and electrical multiplexing. Bidirectional sets of digital data transmitters and receivers are commonly referred to as fiber optic "modems," since they both modulate and demodulate the signal from electrical-to-optical and back. Acting as a closed system, an optical modem set performs the same as a conventional limited distance wire modem. Only the performance capabilities differ.

THE DRIVING FORCES ARE ECONOMICAL

The driving force for fiber optics in long-haul telecommunications is strictly one of superior bandwidth-distance capacity, whereas in local premises applications there are a number of other issues that influence the economic equation. Clearly, the following well known technical advantages of fiber can have a great value to the user who faces specific transmission problems in the building/campus environment. However, for the technology to become a pervasive part of general building cabling, the economics have to prove in for the less troubled user. The cabling must have an intrinsically lower life cycle cost than alternative technologies, aside from all the other "nice-to-have" side benefits. Fiber optic transmission does.

There are many technical features of fiber optics that are cited as the rationale for using them for transmission, both for LANs and for long-haul, intercity communications. True, the benefits are virtu-

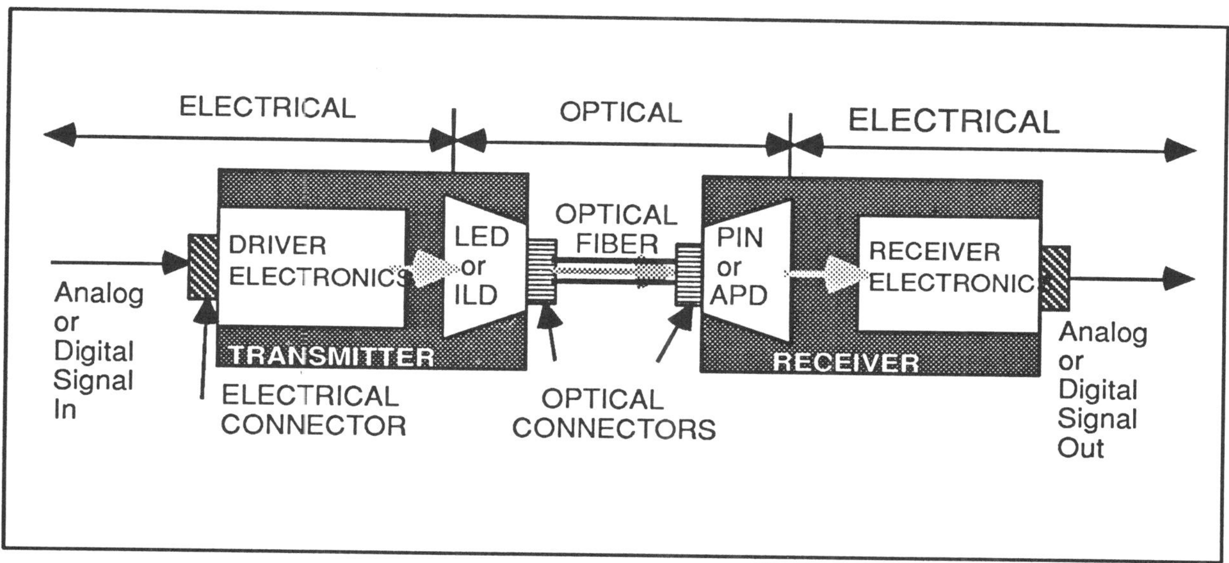

ally the same for both long- and short-distance transport, but the ecomonical reasons for using fiber differ greatly. Among the most often cited technical reasons for communicating with light are:

- longer distance capability—fiber optics allow signals to travel up to hundreds of miles without intermediate repeaters or signal boosting;

- wider bandwidth capacity—fibers can be unvirtually unlimited in their digital information carrying capacity. New laser transmission systems are transporting in excess of 1.5 Gbps (one and a half billion bits per second) over long distance telecommunications trunks;

- immunity to interference—fiber optic cables are totally non-inductive. They are not susceptible to electromagnetic interference (EMI), radio frequency interference (RFI), electromagnetic pulses (EMP), or crosstalk from adjacent power or communication lines. Even intentional "jamming" cannot disrupt the signals;

- absence of radiativity—fiber optic cables do not emanate electromagnetic fields at any frequency. They are often said to be ideal for secure communications by the military or other organizations that transmit sensitive information, since fiber cables are difficult to tap covertly without detection. Furthermore, new stringent

FCC regulations regarding cable radiation make fiber optics especially attractive, particularly at signal data rates above 1 Mbps;

- small size, low weight—fiber cables are much smaller than the equivalent copper cables, with as much as a 100-to-1 reduction in size and weight. Transportation, storage and installation costs can be lower. The substantial savings in (or recapture of) valuable conduit space can be greater than the first cost of the fiber cabling.

- absence of conductivity—optical fiber cables do not conduct electricity. Thus, they are often used to solve troublesome ground loop problems. As data rates increase, this benefit becomes an increasingly important consideration. Fiber optics also provide inherent protection against damage from nearby lightning strikes;

- intrinsic safety—fiber cables do not shock, short or spark. They do not cause fires, and can be routed through explosive atmospheres where conventional electrical cables cannot be allowed; and

- resistance to corrosion—fiber optic cables do not corrode even when installed directly in water. While outside plant wideband copper cables deteriorate over time from corrosion, prop-

APPLICATION	COAX	FIBER
Video Distribution	75Ω	62.5μ
Video Trunking (A2AT)	124Ω (bal)	62.5μ
IBM 3270	93Ω	62.5μ
IBM 5250	110Ω (bal)	62.5μ
CAD/CAM (IBM & CV)	75Ω	62.5μ
TTL DATA (Ethernet)	50Ω	62.5μ
WANG Broadband	75Ω (dual)	62.5μ

erly installed fiber cables maintain their transmission capacity indefinitely.

To date, the above advantages of fiber optics have been the basis for their limited penetration into local area communications. However, a much greater benefit is now about to drive their application in local area network cabling: the fact that fiber optic cables are universally transparent to any communication signal. That is, virtually any type of signal can be cleanly transported on fiber, without regard to signal bandwidth or the electromagnetic environment. Whereas nearly every data communications application utilizes a different type of copper cable, a planned combination of twisted-wire pairs and optical fiber replaces any and all of the specialized copper interconnects now in use. Take, for example, RS232-C wire pair cables. They are not compatible with the 93-ohm RG62 coaxial cables used on the IBM 3270 system. Neither is compatible with 75-ohm RG6 CAD/CAM cables or 50-ohm Ethernet cables. An optical fiber, with the appropriate transmitter/receiver combination, is capable of handling virtually any of these, and other, communications signal interfaces. This is the driving force for fiber optics in the LAN environment.

TRANSPARENCY IN PREMISES DISTRIBUTION CABLING

For this single reason of transparency, fiber optic transmission is central to the structured, uniform

cabling systems from AT&T and IBM. These companies view fiber optic and wire information transport as a "fourth building utility," similar to power, water and HVAC. They and other companies are aggressively marketing their cabling systems as a revenue generating adjunct to their mainstream businesses.

The problem of communications cabling management has become more severe and apparent with the divestiture of AT&T. Now the users have become responsible for the wiring within their own facilities. No longer can they rely upon the "telephone company" to specify, install and maintain wiring. Rather than treating the cabling as a service or hiddnn rental item, MIS directors and facilities managers now must address cabling as a large capital investment, one that has to be planned for and managed wisely.

With proper planning, the cabling system can act as a smooth running "organ," much like the circulatory system in the human body. Mismanaged, the cabling can become an expensive, haphazard mass of assorted, incompatible lines that clog the conduits and ceilings of the building facilities, hampering day-to-day operations and limiting the growth of information services.

The concept of a structured, uniform communications distribution cabling system appears to be logical and obvious, just like a planned community. However, just like most communities, when not properly managed the building cabling is installed only as needed at that moment. As personnel move to different offices, estimated at 50% per year relocation in most companies, new cable often has to be pulled to hook up the terminal at the new location. Often the old cable is abandoned, destined to corrode in the ceiling. One computer company estimates the cost of moving a terminal at about $3000, while the cost of reconfiguring a structured cabling system through fiber or wire cross-connects is about $750.

THE FIBER TYPES

Optical fibers are normally categorized by the type of refractive index profile their many layers of glass comprise. The two profile types in common use today are single-mode ad multimode.

As previously noted, every fiber has a central core glass, which carries the light signal, surrounded by an outer cladding glass, which entraps the light like an optical pipe wall. Most fiber types have an outer diameter of approximately 125 micrometers (0.005 inches), but the diameter of the transmitting core varies greatly. Single-mode fibers are distinguished by their very small core diameters (only 8 microns), whereas multimode fiber cores range from 50 to 100 microns in diameter.

Mode is a theoretical optics term that relates to the number of wavefronts (each characterized by a ray angle)that a fiber is capable of supporting or transmitting. The more modes a fiber supports, the more optical power the fiber can carry. Hwever, since rays traveling at different angles arrive at the far cable end at slightly different times, the more time dispersion the rays undergo. Thus, short pulses of light become longer, spread out pulses. Bandwidth suffers as a result.

Hence, one can see that the single-mode fiber suffers virtually no pulse broadening caused by time delays between mode delay time, since there is only one mode. The obvious drawback, however, is its very small core size, which makes connector and

splice alignment very critical and, therefore, expensive. Also, since the core is so small, the single-mode fiber requires a very small, high radiance emitting source, such as a laser diode or special LED to launch sufficient power into the 8-micron core. For this reason, single-mode fibers have been primarily limited to long distance telecommunications applications. Although single-mode fibers will become prevalent in high speed LANs, they have found little application to date in the local area network market.

The multimode fiber, on the other hand, is currently the workhorse of the short-distance communications market. The relatively large cores of these fibers make interconnection simple and inexpensive, and this is an important consideration in building cabling, which is quite connector-intensive. Inexpensive LED sources are used in multi-mode fiber modems, and the intermodal dispersion of these fibers is of small consequence over the short spans encountered in customer premises.

Within the category of multimode fibers, one could correctly further subdivide the types into graded-index and step-index. However, for practical purposes, step-index fibers are all but extinct due to their overwhelming bandwidth limitations. Therefore, it should be adequate to state that virtually all multi-mode fibers advocated by the large systems suppliers are of the graded-index type. Similarly, all further mention of multimode here will refer to the graded-index fiber.

So far, so simple. Two types of fibers: single-mode for long-distance telecommunications; multimode for campus and building communications. It becomes a bit more invloved, though, when the dynamics of commercial competition enter in.

As of this writing, AT&T and IBM are not in full agreement as to the geometric dimensions of the graded-index fibers they are promoting in their respective cabling systems. AT&T is uniformly advocating the "62.6-micron" fiber (62.5-micron core diameter/125-micron outer diameter) in its Premises Distribution System (PDS). This is the standard multimode fiber manufactured by AT&T Technologies. IBM, on the other hand, is split on its stance

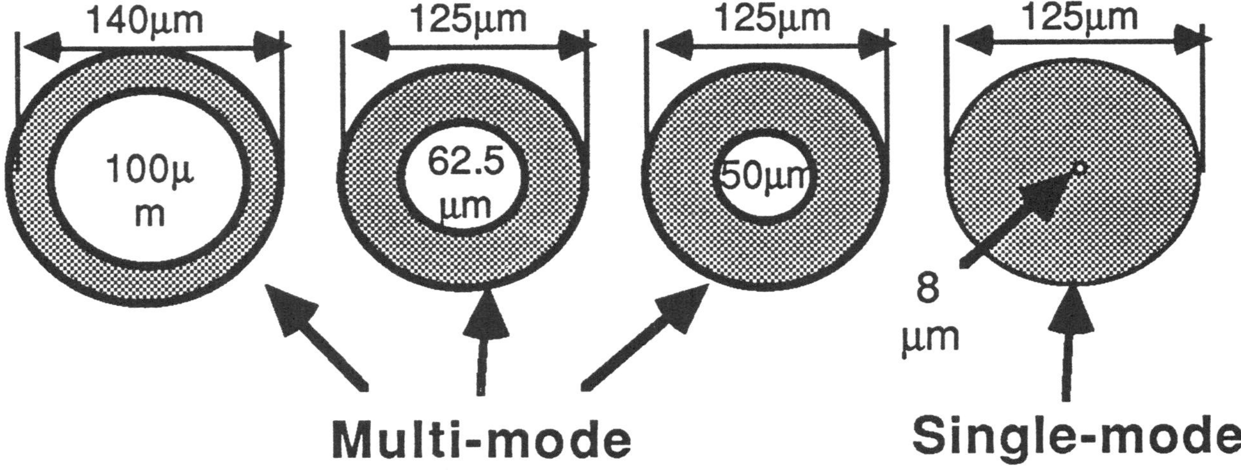

with respect to its fiber offerings. IBM in Pough-keepsie has introduced the same AT&T-style 62.5-micron fiber for its Channel Extender product line. However, IBM in Research Triangle Park has introduced a different, incompatible fiber for its IBM Cabling System , including the Token Ring fiber cable. This fiber is generally referred to as the "100-micron" fiber, and is the type manufactured by Corning Glass Works and promoted a the "Fat Fiber." Its dimensions are 100-micron core diameter/140-micron outer fiber diameter.

Further complicating things for the moment is the fact that several manufacturers of terminal equipment (modems, multiplexers and assorted "data links") are still supplying equipment designed to operate on the old "standard" fiber, the "50-micron" fiber (50-micron core/125-micron outer diameter). At one time this was the multimode fiber that both AT&T and Corning agreed upon, because it was used for long haul telecommunications before single-mode technology became technically and economically viable. Now, 50-micron fiber is nearly out of production, and terminal equipment suppliers are migrating toward interfacing to the 62.5-micron and/or 100-micron fibers.

THE EVOLUTION OF THE FIBER OPTIC "SYSTEM"

The very first fiber optic data communications products were simply called "data links." These ear-ly modules were nothing more than TTL-to-opical converters that were packaged in simple Pomona boxes. Data links evolved to fully-engineered RS232-C "modems," which included power supplies and the 25-pin connectors so that users could plug the unit directly to their terminals' data cable assemblies. Realizing that the fiber optic cable was under-utilized at 9600 baud, several firms introduced RS232-C multiplexers, which combined anywhere from eight to thirty-two channels of synchronous or asynchronous data for point-to-point transmission on a fiber pair (one fiber for transmit, one for receive). Soon new products evolved for interconnecting IBM 3270 terminals to the IBM 3274 controller, concentrating 32 channels of RG62 into one fiber pair. This was essentially the integration of a conventional coaxial multiplexer with an on-board fiber optic transmitter and receiver.

Other specialty transmission systems were introduced to take advantage of the niche opportunities on industrial and educational campuses. Some were digital data modems for IBM 3250 CAD/CAM, while others were wideband video systems. Combination video/audio systems were announced to solve the distance limitations of coaxial cable in television broadcasting and distribution. Other video/data systems were developed to transmit high resolution color computer graphics at rates beyond 100MHz.

Fiber optic systems aimed specifically at analog voice frequency applications have, for obvious reasons, been few. However, there have been several digital systems developed to transport T1 and T2 level PCM signals across campuses.

In the past couple of years several LAN suppliers have begun to use fiber optic systems as enhancements to their copper cable networks, typically as repeaters between distant nodes or network segments, and to solve specific noise or grounding problems in parts of the facilities. For instance, Ungermann-Bass offers an Ethernet fiber option, and Proteon offers a token-ring fiber option. Some fiber systems vendors have adapted conventional networks to fiber using different optical approaches. Codenoll offers a star-shaped 10-Mbps fiber optic Ethernet, while FiberCom offers a similar Ethernet in a ring configuration. Taking a more ambitious approach, Artel Communications, has introduced a 200-Mbps digital broadband network that is built around fiber backbones with copper and/or fiber optic branches.

THE FIBER OPTIC LAN CABLING

The fiber optic distribution system is made up of an assortment of cables. Each is made for a specific environment. Optically, they are all identical. All that changes is the cables' mechanical specifications, the size and fiber count (how many fiber conductors in the cable), and the jacketing material.

Riser cables run vertically through the building core, terminating at designated administrative distribution closets on each floor. A large number of fibers, say 72 or 144 fibers, are closely packed in a half-inch O.D. cable. Anywhere from two to twenty fibers are dropped off at each floor.

Lateral feeder cables run horizontally on each floor between the floor distribution closet and the individual work area's wall or floor socket. These UL-approved flame retardant cables are generally run in the air plenums, and typically contain from two to six fibers.

Work area cables run from the wall or floor socket to the user terminal or device. Normally a two-fiber ("duplex") design, this cable may resemble ordinary lampcord, or may be a flat cable specially designed to be laid under the carpet.

Campus cables are outside plant designs, either direct buried, conduit or aerial. These cables interconnect the various buildings within a campus environment, or serve in the user's other telecommunications bypass activities.

In many cases, the user will only integrate fiber into the riser and interbuilding sections of the network. For most low- to moderate-speed applications, conventional twisted wire pairs (either shielded or unshielded) will be adequate between the work area and the floor distribution closet. At the closet, fiber may be accessed through the use of a fiber optic concentrator, with vertical and interbuilding communications taking place on fiber optics.

ADMINISTRATIVE AND INTERCONNECTING HARDWARE

The key feature of a fiber optic LAN cabling system is its ability to deliver signals through a patch panel. Located, at minimum, in every floor closet and in the building's central equipment room, the fiber optic distribution panels are used as splice cases to split fibers out to the proper terminal equipment and, when an intermediate point of a fiber span, to act as full cross-connects and interconnects. Other administrative hardware include wall sockets, floor sockets and splice cases.

The cost of connectors, both in dollars and optical attenuation, is a major one in the local area network. In the electrical world, connector loss is a minor consideration, especially for voice frequency circuits. Thus, copper wire patching is routinely done without a great deal of thought given to the performance consequences. However, with fiber optic connectors careful planning must be made to maximize the administrative flexibility of the system while minimizing the number of physical fiber-to-fiber interconnections made.

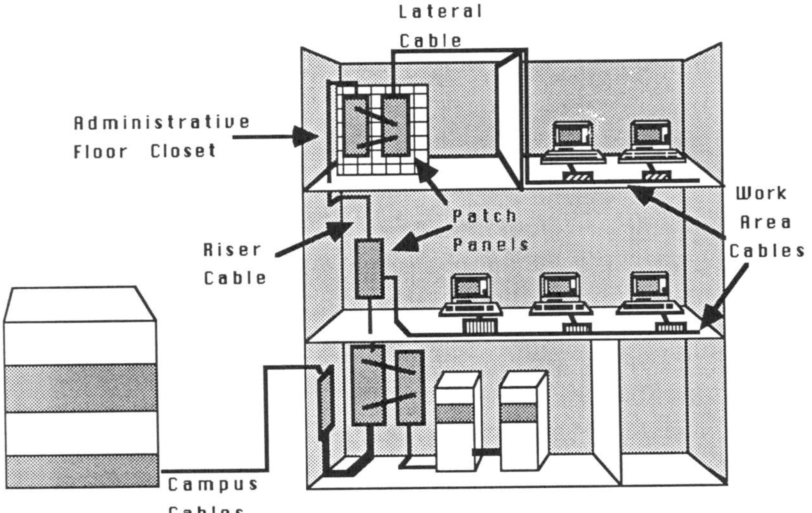

CONNECTOR STANDARDS

The industry is now in its third generation of optical connectors. The first generation was the optical SMA connector. Still in use by short distance optical modem manufacturers, the stainless steel SMA is a variation on the threaded sub-miniature type-A RF connector manufactured by companies such as Amphenol and AMP. Using precisely drilled holes in the ferrule (nose barrel), or a larger, less precise hole shimmed with four small drill rods in a cloverleaf pattern, the fiber is aligned concentrically and epoxied in place. A series of grind and polish steps smooth the perpendicular face of the fiber. Two funished ferrule ends then join to complete the interconnection.

The second generation of fiber connector is the molded "biconic" connector developed by AT&T. This self-aligning connector is used widely in the long haul telecommunications market, because its low coupling losses are suitable for even the precise core alignment required in single-mode fibers. Also manufactured under license by Dorran Phonotics Inc., the biconic connector (sometimes called the "Runge" connector after its designer) is used by AT&T in its outside plant cabling, and is specified by both the Poughkeepsie and RTP units of IBM.

The newest emerging standard in intrabuilding connectors is the AT&T-developed bayonet style connector known as the "ST" connector. Using powdered metallurgy and ceramics technologies, the ST connector is especially attractive due to its low cost, power coupling efficiency and repeatability. AT&T specifies the ST connector in its Premises Distribution System. Several second sources for this connector have been announced, including AMP Incorporated and Dorran Photonics.

OPTICAL COUPLERS

The optical coupler is essentially a means of passively splitting and/or combining power between fibers, resulting in a more efficient use of the installed fiber conductors. Optical couplers work on the principles that: (a)two light signals can pass in opposite directons on a single fiber wthout interfering with one another and, (b)different wavelengths (colors) of light can share the same fiber path without interference. In the first case, Y-splitters at each end of the fiber path are used to access the main fiber. In the second case, called wavelength division multiplexing (WDM), splitters are used in conjunction with narrowband color filters at the detector end to sort out and pass only the wavelength of interest from the appropriate LED or laser source (each source transmitting a different "color" of light).

Most commercial activity with couplers is in the long haul market where fiber conductors are a large

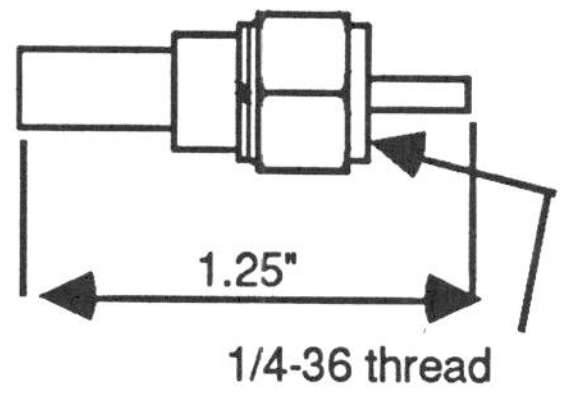

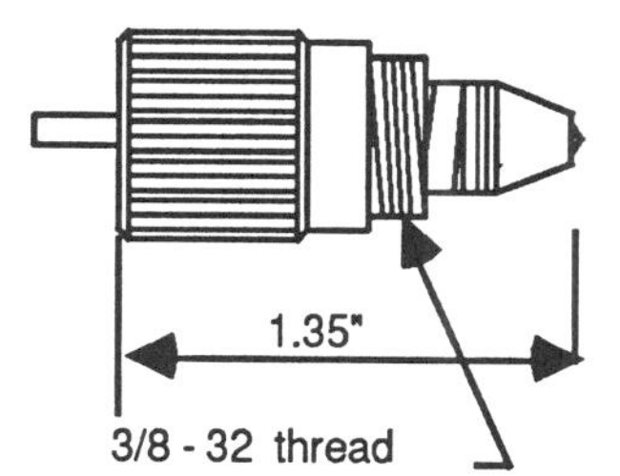

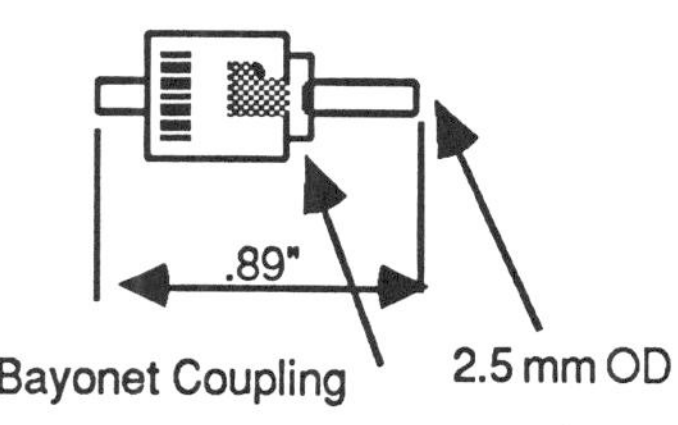

part of the system cost. Some limited activity is taking place in the LAN market, where couplers (as well as early versions of electromechanical fiber switches) are being explored as passive "taps" in bus topology networks. Because these individual Y-taps add significant optical loss on a linearly additive basis, a more accepted LAN coupler approach is to use a central N-port "star coupler", which effectively reduces the bus down to a single point, located at a convenient location like a floor closet. Such a coupler inserts one-time coupling loss on a logarithmic basis. The star coupler bus is the physical topology used by network suppliers like Ungermann-Bass for their CSMA/CD network segments.

WHEN A FIBER NODE FAILS

One criticism of this "star-hub" approach is that the coupler itself constitutes a potential single point of failure. Ring fiber configurations, on the other hand, rely on retransmission at each node using active taps, similar to broadband coaxial networks. Anticipating criticism regarding the potential reliability of cascaded active taps, several manufacturers promote the use of dynamically reconfigurable dual, redundant fiber rings. In this topology, every node contains two transmitter/receiver pairs, each operating on a different fiber in the reverse ring direction. Sensing a node malfunction, the nodes adjacent to the failed node reconfigure the ring from an "O-ring" to a "C-ring." Artel Communications

Corporation uses this approach for its 200 Mbps digital broadband network, and FiberCom uses this cabling approach for its 10 Mbps fiber Ethernet ring. One major advantage of fiber rings networks, in contrast to broadband coaxial networks, is that they are digitial. When a node is removed, inserted or changed, the fiber optic network does not have to be retuned as does the coax network, which is analog RF.

PATCHING FOR FIBER LANS

In setting up a fiber optic LAN one must decide what cable layout will be necessary both initially and as the network expands or changes. In most cases, some reconfiguration is inevitable, and it is most economical to insert those cable administration elements at the very beginning, rather than shutting down the network at a later date. One need not wire (or fiber) an entire building just to put a network on one floor. However, it is prudent to lay out the specific floor network in the same manner as the one into which it will likely evolve.

On coaxial cable a bus network, such as Ethernet, cable may meander through the ceiling. Every so often a new user attaches to the main cable near designated intervals. This presents a potential problem during system troubleshooting, however. Isolating network faults is a difficult, tedious job, often requiring large segments of the network to be shut

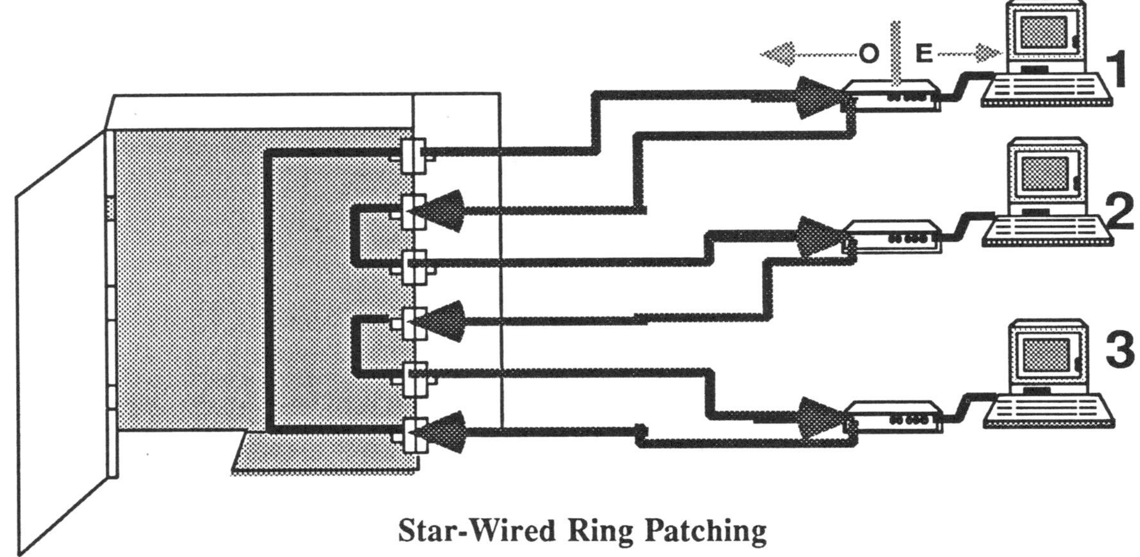

Star-Wired Ring Patching

down for extended periods of time. Many information systems managers now beieve that the optimum bus configuration approaches a pure "star wired" concept, with each user cable segment tying directly to the floor distribution closet. While this requires more cable and installation costs initially, the savings are realized in mean time to repair (MTTR).

Similarly, fiber optic LANs could conceivably be run in any number of physical configurations.

For the greatest flexibility in administration and troubleshooting, however, the "star wired" floor layout is considered most attractive. In such a fiber network, individual duplex fiber circuits are routed to each floor distribution closet, where patch panel administration takes place. There can be many variations on how the cable conductor channels are physically distributed, such as drops and splices in certain work areas.

"Star wiring" in this case denotes the general cable routing layout, not necessarily the patch panel interconnect scheme. Within the actual floor distribution patch panel, a wide variety of patching methods may take place. Point-to-point connections can be made for some application as simple as a TV camera to monitor.

Ring connections are made by looping through from port-to-port. Star connections can be made by utilizing a fiber optic star coupler, or by accessing a particular active device such as a data switch remote concentrator. Thus, while the floor ("horizontal" or "lateral") fiber cable layout continues to remain the same, various network (or other communications) applications can be transported on the cable, with the only cable changes being the way in which the patch panel connections are made.

THINGS TO COME

If the only use for fiber optics were as a direct replacement for coaxial cable and wire in today's low speed (< 10 Mbps) LANs, the technology's future would look awfully bleak. Such is not the case. As state earlier, the driving forces are economical. Not only does fiber save the incremental cabling expense during moves and equipment changes, it also offers more information transport for the buck.

In the long run, a 10-Mbps network probably will not be sufficient. Especially prevalent in graphics-oriented applications like CAD/CAM and image transfer, faster is better. Not just on the throughput speed, but on the certainty of access to the network without collisions or extensive delays. Recognizing the need for exploiting the bandwidth of fiber optics in LANs, the American National Standards Institute (ANSI) is working on a 100 Mbps "Fiber Data Distributed Interface" (FDDI) standard.

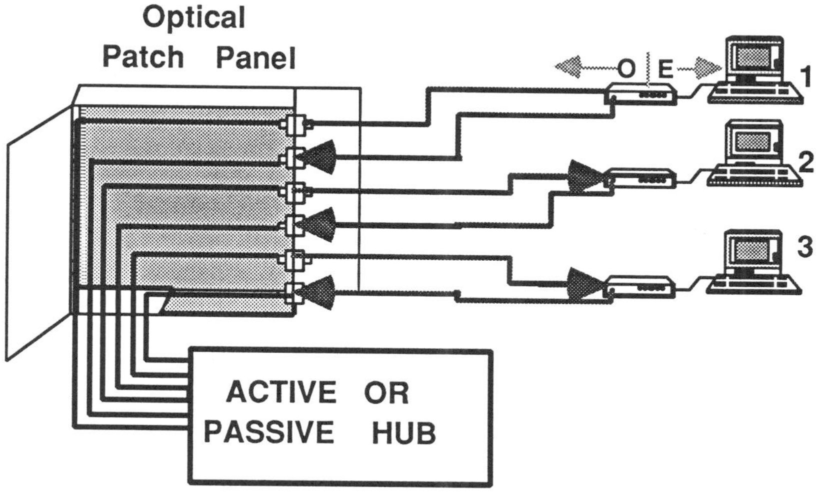

A Star Fiber Optic Bus or PBX Configuration

With the advent of such high speed LANs as FDDI and Artel's Fiberway, the argument for the use of single-mode fibers in customer premises becomes more compelling. The bandwidth capacity of single mode fibers will become required for near-gigabit LANs. While single-mode fiber cable costs are lower, however, the current cost of connectors and laser sources is significantly higher. These costs will have to come down dramatically before widespread intrafacility use of single-mode fiber cables creates a single, universal fiber standard for all communications applications.

It is not yet clear what impact emerging fiber LAN standards, such as FDDI, or other standards, such as ISDN, will play in the overall local area network market. However, its is clear that there is a need for a central cabling structure that will accommocdate all of today's information transport requirements, and be expandable to grow with the needs and standards of the future. It appears that fiber optics is the only technology than can meet these criteria. Since campus and building cabling represents suc a major capital investment, fiber optics deserves careful consideration.

Chapter 1 — Local Area Networks

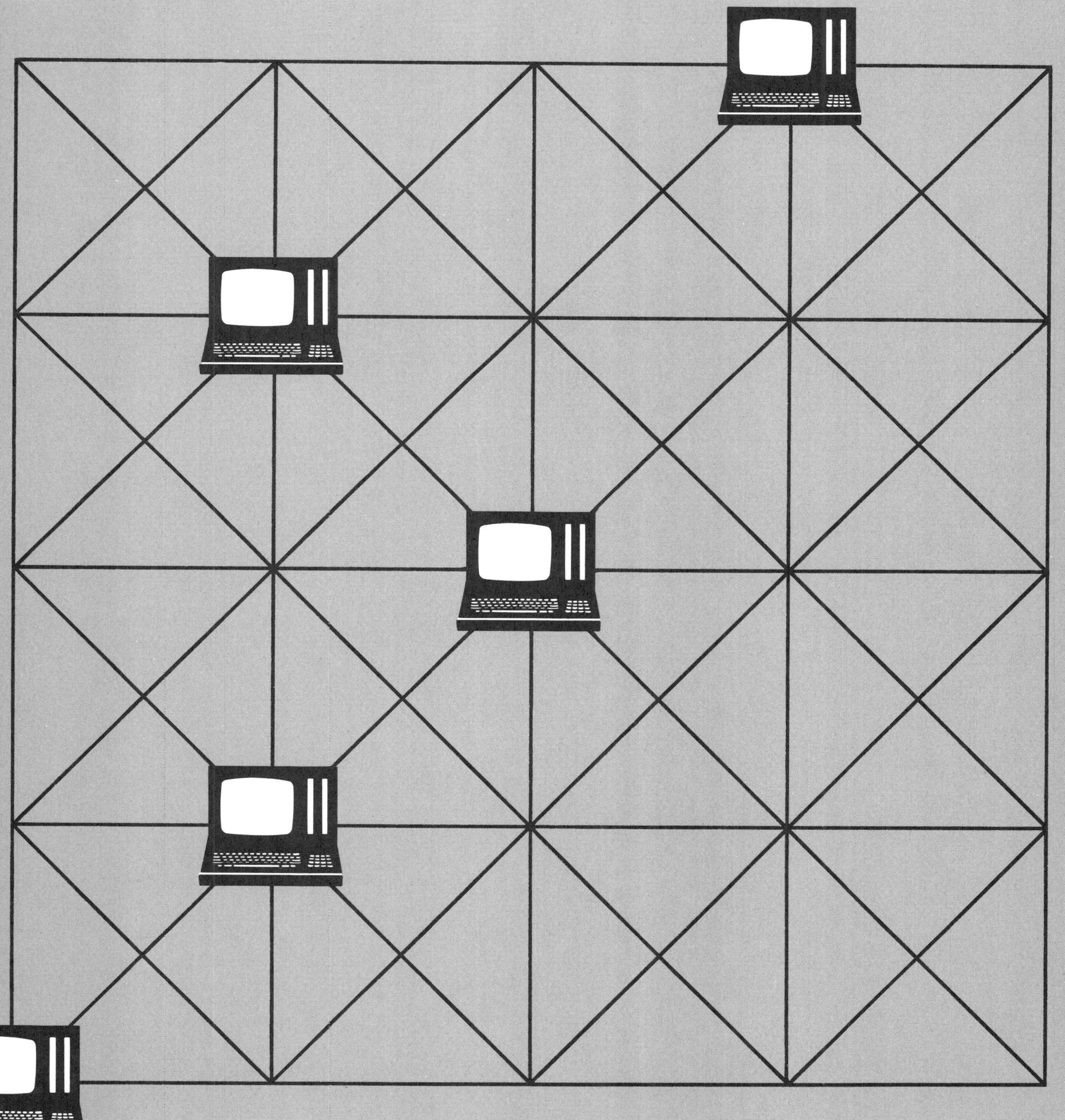

CHAPTER 1
LOCAL AREA NETWORKS

This chapter lists commercially available local area networks. The chapter is arranged alphabetically by system vendor; a network's name appears to the right of the name of its respective manufacturer.

Entries typically include company information as well as specific network information such as transmission medium, transmission speed, network topology, access method, and network standards/protocols supported. The amount of detail of each entry reflects the amount of information provided by each respective LAN manufacturer.

Networks are indexed by manufacturer in the matrix that precedes the entries. The matrix also classifies networks according to transmission category and medium, network topology and access method.

FUNCTION CODES

PM   Product Manager
MD   Marketing Director
PSC   Product Sales Contact
PR   Public Relations Contact
PA   Purchasing Agent

Company	Product	TRANSMISSION CATEGORY		TRANSMISSION MEDIUM					TOPOLOGY					ACCESS METHOD						
		baseband	broadband	baseband coaxial cable	broadband coaxial cable	twisted wire pair	optical fiber	other	ring	star	bus	tree	other	CSMA	CSMA/CD	CSMA/CA	polling	token passing	perfect scheduling	other
Adacom Corporation	3270 Local Distribution Network	✓		✓		✓	✓				✓						✓			
Allen-Bradley Company—Communications Division	VistaLAN/I		✓		✓													✓		
Allen-Bradley Company—Communications Division	VistaLAN/II	✓	✓	✓	✓													✓		
Allen-Bradley Company—Communications Division	VistaLAN/PC		✓								✓							✓		
Alpha Micro Systems	Alpha Net	✓			✓						✓							✓		
Altos Computer Systems	ENet	✓			✓						✓				✓					
Altos Computer Systems	Worknet II	✓				✓					✓							✓		
American Photonics Inc.	Ethernet	✓					✓				✓				✓					
Apollo Computer Inc.	Domain	✓			✓						✓				✓					
Apple Computer Inc.	AppleTalk	✓				✓					✓					✓				
Applitek Corporation	UniLAN	✓	✓		✓						✓				✓					✓
Artel Communications Corporation	FiberWay		✓				✓			✓					✓					
Asher Technologies Inc.	Quadnet VI	✓			✓						✓							✓		
Asher Technologies Inc.	Quadnet IX	✓				✓	✓			✓	✓							✓		
AST Research Inc.	AST-PCNet II	✓			✓						✓					✓				
AST Research Inc.	AST-Resource Sharing Network	✓				✓					✓					✓				
Astra Communications Inc.	AstraNet	✓	✓	✓							✓				✓					
Astrocom Corporation	XLAN	✓	✓	✓							✓				✓	✓				
AT&T Information Systems	Starlan	✓				✓				✓					✓					
AT&T Information Systems	Information Systems Network	✓				✓	✓				✓								✓	
Avatar Technologies Inc.	Alliance	✓								✓					✓					
Barrister Information Systems Corporation	Barrister/Net	✓		✓							✓						✓			
Basonje Systems	Trans-Net	✓			✓						✓							✓		
Bell Atlantic Network Services Inc.	C.O. LAN	✓				✓				✓									✓	
Braegen Corporation	ELAN	✓	✓	✓	✓	✓	✓				✓				✓					
Centram Systems West	TOPS	✓		✓		✓	✓				✓				✓					
Codenoll Technology Corporation	Codenet		✓			✓	✓	✓		✓	✓	✓			✓					
Codex Corporation	4000 Series LAN	✓	✓	✓	✓						✓				✓	✓				
Commtex Inc.	CX-80 Data Exchange Network	✓		✓							✓				✓					
Complexx Systems Inc.	XLAN	✓		✓	✓						✓				✓					
Computer Corporation of America	ProdNet	✓									✓				✓					
Computrol—A Division of Kidde Automated Syst.	Megalink	✓	✓	✓							✓				✓		✓	✓		
Corvus Systems Inc.	Omninet	✓				✓					✓				✓			✓		
Datapoint Corporation	ARC Net	✓			✓						✓				✓					
Davox Communications Corporation	DavoxNet	✓				✓				✓					✓					
The Destek Group	Desnet	✓				✓	✓			✓	✓				✓					
Develcon Electronics Limited	DevelNet	✓	✓	✓							✓							✓		
Develcon Electronics Limited	Lil'Net	✓		✓							✓							✓		
Digital Equipment Corporation	DECnet	✓		✓	✓	✓				✓					✓					
Digital Products Inc.	NetCommander	✓				✓				✓								✓		
Equinox Systems Inc.	Data PBX	✓		✓	✓					✓										✓
Excelan Inc.	EOS	✓		✓	✓						✓				✓					
FiberCom Inc.	WhisperNet	✓			✓	✓	✓			✓								✓		
FiberCom Inc.	WhisperRing	✓					✓		✓									✓		

cont.

Company	Product	TRANSMISSION CATEGORY		TRANSMISSION MEDIUM					TOPOLOGY					ACCESS METHOD					
		baseband	broadband	baseband coaxial cable	broadband coaxial cable	twisted wire pair	optical fiber	other	ring	star	bus	tree	other	CSMA/CD	CSMA/CA	polling	token passing	perfect scheduling	other
FiberLAN Inc.—A BellSouth-Siecor Company	TDM Ring		✓				✓		✓										✓
FiberLAN Inc.—A BellSouth-Siecor Company	Net 10		✓				✓			✓					✓				
Fortune Systems Corporation	Fortune:Link	✓		✓					✓	✓				✓			✓		
Fox Research Inc.	10Net	✓			✓				✓					✓					
Gandalf Data Inc.	PACX 2000	✓	✓	✓	✓	✓	✓	✓	✓	✓		✓							
Gateway Communications Inc.	G/Net	✓		✓					✓					✓					
Hancock Electronics	Cinchnet	✓		✓					✓						✓				
Hewlett-Packard	HP 9000 LAN	✓		✓							✓			✓					
IDEAssociates	IDEAnet																		
Infotron Systems	INX4400 Intelligent Network Exchange	✓	✓	✓					✓	✓				✓			✓		
IBM—Information Systems Group	Token-Ring Network	✓				✓			✓								✓		
IBM—Information Systems Group	PC Network		✓		✓						✓			✓					
International Electronics	M-Net	✓		✓							✓			✓					
KEE Inc.	KEE Net		✓		✓						✓	✓			✓				
Kimtron	K-Net	✓				✓					✓				✓	✓			
Lan-Tech	ELAN	✓				✓					✓				✓				
M/A-Com Telecommunications Inc.	IDX 3000 Local Communication Network	✓								✓									
Magnolia Microsystems Inc.	MAGNet	✓			✓				✓								✓		
Metapath Inc.	Metapath Distributed Data Switch	✓			✓				✓										✓
Modular Computer Systems Inc. (MODCOMP)	Maxnet		✓		✓						✓			✓					
Molecular Computer	System 16/300	✓			✓						✓			✓					
NBI Inc.	NBI Net	✓		✓							✓			✓					
NBI Inc.	Multinet	✓		✓							✓			✓					
Nestar Systems Inc.	PLAN 3000B	✓		✓							✓			✓					
Network Development Corporation	Device Network Architecture	✓				✓			✓						✓				
Network Systems Corporation	HYPERbus	✓		✓	✓						✓			✓					
Network Systems Corporation	HYPERchannel A	✓		✓	✓						✓			✓					
Network Systems Corporation	HYPERchannel B	✓		✓	✓	✓					✓			✓					
North Star Computers Inc.	Dimension	✓								✓								✓	
Northern Telecom Inc.	LANstar PC	✓								✓							✓		
Orchid Technology	PC Net	✓		✓						✓				✓					
Prime Computer Inc.	Ringnet	✓					✓		✓								✓		
Prime Computer Inc.	IEEE 802.3 LAN	✓		✓							✓			✓					
Proteon Inc.	ProNET-80	✓		✓		✓	✓		✓								✓		
Proteon Inc.	ProNET-4	✓		✓		✓	✓		✓								✓		
Proteon Inc.	ProNET-10	✓		✓		✓	✓		✓								✓		
Racore Corporation	LANpac		✓			✓				✓				✓					
Siecor Corporation	Fiber Optic Ethernet	✓					✓				✓		✓	✓					
Siemens Energy & Automation—Prog. Contr. Div.	Sinec L1 LAN	✓								✓						✓			
Siemens Energy & Automation—Prog. Contr. Di.	ControlNet	✓					✓			✓						✓			
Siemens Energy & Automation—Prog. Contr. Div.	Sinec H1 LAN	✓		✓						✓						✓			

cont.

Company	Product	TRANSMISSION CATEGORY		TRANSMISSION MEDIUM					TOPOLOGY					ACCESS METHOD						
		baseband	broadband	baseband coaxial cable	broadband coaxial cable	twisted wire pair	optical fiber	other	ring	star	bus	tree	other	CSMA	CSMA/CD	CSMA/CA	polling	token passing	perfect scheduling	other
Sunol Systems Inc.	Sun*Net	✓		✓							✓					✓				
SyFA Data Systems Corporation	SyFAnet		✓		✓						✓					✓	✓			
Syntrex Inc.	SynNet	✓		✓								✓			✓					
Sytek Inc.	System 6000		✓		✓							✓			✓					
Sytek Inc.	System 3000/7000		✓		✓							✓			✓					
Sytek Inc.	System 2000		✓		✓							✓			✓					
Tecmar Inc.	ELAN	✓		✓							✓				✓					
Tele-Engineering Corporation	Custom		✓		✓		✓		✓	✓	✓				✓					
Terminal Data Corporation	TermNET	✓				✓			✓									✓		
Texas Instruments—Data Systems Group	EtherSeries	✓		✓							✓				✓					
Tiara Computer Systems Inc.	TiaraLink	✓		✓		✓				✓						✓				
TRW Inc.—Information Networks Division	TRW Concept 2000	✓	✓	✓	✓						✓				✓		✓			
Ungermann-Bass Inc.	Optical Fiber Net/One		✓				✓			✓					✓					
Ungermann-Bass Inc.	Net/One Thin Coaxial Baseband	✓		✓							✓				✓					
Ungermann-Bass Inc.	Net/One Broadband		✓		✓						✓				✓					
Ungermann-Bass Inc.	Net/One Ethernet Baseband	✓		✓							✓				✓					
Ungermann-Bass Inc.	Intro/Net									✓								✓		
Wang Laboratories Inc.	WangNet/FastLAN		✓		✓					✓		✓			✓		✓	✓	✓	✓
Xerox Corporation	Xerox Communications 22(XC 22)	✓				✓					✓				✓					
Xerox Corporaton	Ethernet	✓		✓							✓				✓					
Xerox Corporation	Xerox Communications 24(XC 24)	✓		✓							✓				✓					
Xyplex Inc.	Xyplex System	✓		✓			✓	✓			✓				✓					
Zenith Electronics Corporation	Z-LAN 500		✓		✓						✓				✓					

ADACOM CORPORATION • 3270 LOCAL DISTRIBUTION NETWORK

8871 Bond, P.O. Box 14745
Overland Park, KS 66214
(913)888-4999; (800)232-2662; telex 510-601-5185 ADACOMM UD; FAX
913-888-7806

Moti Gura, President; Dan Cox, Director, Sales and Marketing (PM); Oscar Glottman, Vice President, Marketing (MD); Mike Holliger, Manager, Sales Support (PSC); Gina Owen, Marketing Manager (PR); Don Trotter, Chief Financial Officer (PA)

Founded 1985; 70 employees

Branch Offices and Distributors:
Adacom Corporation, Staten Island, NY (718)983-0500; Adacom Corporation, Coppell, TX (214)462-1772; Adacom Corporation, Westlake Village, CA (818)707-0941; CSI Systems Inc., Lexington, MA (617)863-0525; Glasgal Communications, Northvale, NJ (201)768-8082

3270 LDN is designed to connect hundreds of 3270 Type A coaxial devices throughout a multibuilding industrial, office, laboratory, or campus environment. Hundreds of terminals and printers can be distributed to nodes throughout many buildings within a 4.5-km radius of the computer center. Devices connected include mainframes, PCs and dumb terminals. Service contracts and instruction on network operation available.

• 3270 LOCAL DISTRIBUTION NETWORK TECHNICAL CHARACTERISTICS

Transmission category: baseband

Transmission mode: full duplex

Transmission medium: baseband coaxial cable, twisted wire pair, optical fiber

Topology: bus, IBM 3270

Access method: polling

Compatible operating systems: IBM 3270

ALLEN-BRADLEY COMPANY—COMMUNICATION DIVISION • VISTALAN/I

555 Briarwood Circle
Ann Arbor, MI 48104
(313)668-2500

Branch Offices and Distributors:
Allen-Bradley, San Diego, CA (619)292-4016; Allen-Bradley, Doraville, GA (404)455-7422; Allen-Bradley, Chicago, IL (312)922-9302; Allen-Bradley, Minneapolis, MN (612)781-3406; Allen-Bradley, Bloomfield, NJ (201)338-4600

VistaLAN/I is a distributed-intelligence network that serves as a high-speed communications medium for business data, manufacturing information, building security, energy management, and production or process control. Compatible with both dumb and intelligent terminals. Automatic shutoff feature keeps any one terminal from monopolizing the access token.

• VISTALAN/I TECHNICAL CHARACTERISTICS

Transmission category: broadband

Transmission speed: 2.5 Mbps

Access method: token passing

Maximum network length: 14 miles

• STANDARDS/PROTOCOLS SUPPORTED

Communications protocols: RS-232

ALLEN-BRADLEY COMPANY—COMMUNICATION DIVISION • VISTALAN/II
555 Briarwood Circle
Ann Arbor, MI 48104
(313)668-2500

Branch Offices and Distributors:
Allen-Bradley, San Diego, CA (619)292-4016; Allen-Bradley, Doraville, GA (404)455-7422; Allen-Bradley, Chicago, IL (312)922-9302; Allen-Bradley, Minneapolis, MN (612)781-3406; Allen-Bradley, Bloomfield, NJ (201)338-4600

VistaLAN/II is a MAP-compatible system that enables broadband connection of various devices as specified by IEEE 802.4, or to an 802.3 or Ethernet nework. Features include 4-, 8- and 16-port RS-232 terminal support and full network management support.

• VISTALAN/II TECHNICAL CHARACTERISTICS

Transmission category: baseband, broadband

Transmission medium: baseband coaxial cable, broadband coaxial cable

Transmission speed: broadband RS-232 server—19.2 Kbps maximum available for user connection, 10 Mbps backbone; baseband HDLC server—460 Kbps maximum available for user connection, 10 Mbps backbone

Maximum network length: 40 miles

• STANDARDS/PROTOCOLS SUPPORTED

Communications protocols: RS-232, HDLC, MAP, ISO, DOD

IEEE 802 standards: conforms to 802.3 and 802.4

ALLEN-BRADLEY COMPANY—COMMUNICATION DIVISION • VISTALAN/PC

555 Briarwood Circle
Ann Arbor, MI 48104
(313)668-2500

Branch Offices and Distributors:
Allen-Bradley, San Diego, CA (619)292-4016; Allen-Bradley, Doraville, GA (404)455-7422; Allen-Bradley, Chicago, IL (312)922-9302; Allen-Bradley, Minneapolis, MN (612)781-3406; Allen-Bradley, Bloomfield, NJ (201)338-4600

VistaLAN/PC is a hardware and software package that allows IBM PCs, XTs, ATs, and compatibles to interface directly with a broadband coaxial cable LAN. Communicates with any server on the network or bridged networks. Compatible with over 1200 true multi-user software programs. Bridge allows baseband Data Highway, 3Com, Orchid, Quadram, Corvus, and Sperry LANs to be tied into an Allen-Bradley LAN.

• VISTALAN/PC TECHNICAL CHARACTERISTICS

Transmission category: broadband

Transmission speed: 2.5 Mbps

Topology: bus

Access method: token passing

Compatible operating systems: Novell Advanced NetWare/IS, MS-DOS, PC-DOS

Gateways: SNA/SDLC

Maximum number of nodes: 255 nodes per channel

Maximum distance between nodes: 14 miles maximum network diameter

ALPHA MICRO SYSTEMS • ALPHA NET
3501 Sunflower Street
Santa Ana, CA 92704
(714)957-8500; TWX 910-595-2666

Richard Cortese, President; Gary Nelson (PM); Larry Meredith (MD); Dennis Trombley (PR)

Founded 1977; 500 employees

Branch Offices and Distributors:
Alpha Micro Systems, Reston, VA (703)689-0805; Alpha Micro Systems, Schaumburg, IL (312)397-1447; Alpha Micro Systems, Atlanta, GA (404)256-5943; Alpha Micro Systems, Santa Clara, CA (408)748-1602

Alpha Net is a baseband local area network connecting mainframes, minicomputers, PCs, dumb terminals, printers, modems, and disk drives. Runs on the Alpha Micro operating system. Service contracts, network installation, instruction on network operation, and network maintenance services available. First installed: 1984. Number installed: 500. Average number of stations per installation: 64.

• ALPHA NET TECHNICAL CHARACTERISTICS

Transmission category: baseband

Transmission mode: full duplex

Transmission medium: baseband coaxial cable

Transmission speed: 1 Mbps burst

Topology: bus

Access method: token passing with collision detection

Compatible operating systems: Amos

Gateways: proprietary

Maximum number of workstations per node: unlimited

Maximum number of nodes: 64

Maximum distance between nodes: 1200

Means of host interconnection: terminal ports

Network server: proprietary file server

Maximum number of file servers: 64

Disk backup: whole disk

Network operation during backup: yes

Site of network logic: central controllers

• STANDARDS/PROTOCOLS SUPPORTED

ALTOS COMPUTER SYSTEMS • ENET

2641 Orchard Parkway
San Jose, CA 95134
(408)946-6700; telex 184-815 ALTOS UT; FAX 408-434-0488

Dave Jackson, President; Russ Aldrich, Communications Marketing Manager (PM); Jeff Bork, Director, Systems Marketing (MD)

Founded 1977; 700 employees

ENet connects Altos 1086/2086 and 3068, and other systems that support Ethernet standards. Provides programmable interface for applications that require a high-speed link to Altos systems or other computer systems.

• ENET TECHNICAL CHARACTERISTICS

Transmission category: baseband

Transmission medium: baseband coaxial cable

Transmission speed: 10 Mbps

Topology: bus

Access method: CSMA/CD

Compatible operating systems: Unix, Xenix

Maximum number of nodes: 100

Maximum distance between nodes: 1000 meters total network length

• STANDARDS/PROTOCOLS SUPPORTED

Communications protocols: Ethernet, TCP/IP

IEEE 802 standards: conforms to 802.3

ALTOS COMPUTER SYSTEMS • WORKNET II

2641 Orchard Parkway
San Jose, CA 95134
(408)94-6700; telex 184-815 ALTOS UT; FAX 408-434-0488

Dave Jackson, President; Russ Aldrich, Communications Marketing Manager (PM); Jeff Bork, Director, Systems Marketing (MD)

Founded 1977; 700 employees

Worknet II is an IBM PC-compatible network that can support printers, modems and disk drives for use in an office environment. Transforms Xenix or Unix systems into a transparent distributed processing environment. Extends the file system hierarchy to include multiple systems across the network. With support for up to 30 machines, a single network can connect several hundred users. Service contracts and instruction on network operation available. First installed: 1983. Number installed: 2000. Average number of stations per installation: 4.

- ### WORKNET II TECHNICAL CHARACTERISTICS

Transmission category: baseband

Transmission medium: twisted wire pair

Transmission speed: .8 Mbps or 1.4 Mbps (software selectable)

Topology: bus

Access method: CSMA/CA

Compatible operating systems: Unix, Xenix

Gateways: SNA/SDLC, Ethernet, X.25, bisynchronous

Maximum number of workstations per node: 30

Maximum number of nodes: 30

Maximum distance between nodes: 1500 feet

Means of host interconnection: multiplexed interfaces

Network server: proprietary file server

Maximum number of file servers: 30

Disk backup: whole disk, partial disk

Network operation during backup: yes

Site of network logic: systems processor/operating system

- ### STANDARDS/PROTOCOLS SUPPORTED

Communications protocols: SNA, HDLC, asynchronous, RS-232, synchronous, bisynchronous, X.25, RS-422

ISO OSI Reference Model: conforms to level 1 (RS-422) and level 2

AMERICAN PHOTONICS INC. • ETHERNET

71 Commerce Drive, P.O. Box 289
Brookfield Center, CT 06805
(203)775-8950; telex 821-353

James E. Byrne, President; James R. Hickman (PM); James A. Walyus, Director of Marketing (MD); John T. Goehrke (PSC); Ellen L. Walyus (PR); Kathy Koziatek, Buyer (PA)

Founded 1981; 50 employees

Ethernet is a baseband system connecting mainframes, minicomputers, PCs, and dumb terminals for use in an industrial, office, laboratory, or campus environment. Compatible devices include Interlan terminal servers, DEC transceivers and bridges, Xerox workstations, and IBM PCs. Service contracts, network installation, instruction on network operation, and network maintenance services available. First installed: 1985.

• ETHERNET TECHNICAL CHARACTERISTICS

Transmission category: baseband

Transmission mode: full duplex, half duplex

Transmission medium: baseband coaxial cable, twisted wire pair, optical fiber

Topology: star

Access method: CSMA, CSMA/CD

Compatible operating systems: MS-DOS, CP/M, Unix

Gateways: Ethernet

Maximum number of nodes: 10,024

Maximum distance between nodes: 12,000 feet

Means of host interconnection: multiplexed interfaces, terminal ports

Site of network logic: terminal equipment

• STANDARDS/PROTOCOLS SUPPORTED

Communications protocols: bsynchronous, HDLC, asynchronous, RS-232, synchronous

IEEE 802 standards: conforms to 802.3

ISO OSI Reference Model: conforms to layer 1 (802.3)

APOLLO COMPUTER INC. • DOMAIN

330 Billerica Road
Chelmsford, MA 01824
(617)256-6600; TWX 710-343-6803; FAX 617-250-0183

Thomas Vanderslice, President; Michael Gallup, Product Marketing Director (PM); Edward Zander, Vice President, Marketing (MD); Angelo Guadagno, Vice President, North American Sales (PSC); Richard Germani, Directr of Purchasing (PA)

Founded 1980; 3400 employees

Domain is an open architecture system capable of supporting mainframes, superminis, PCs, printers, modems, disk drives, dumb terminals, and array processors in an engineering, technological or scientific environment. Features include network-wide demand paging. First installed: 1981. Number installed: 4000 workstations. Average number of stations per installation: 2-500.

• DOMAIN TECHNICAL CHARACTERISTICS

Transmission category: baseband

Transmission medium: baseband coaxial cable

Transmission speed: 12 Mbps network-wide communication

Topology: bus, ring

Access method: token passing

Compatible operating systems: Unix, Aegis (proprietary)

Gateways: SNA/SDLC, Ethernet, 3270 emulation, X.25

Maximum number of workstations per node: 1

Maximum distance between nodes: 1 km

Means of host interconnection: coaxial connectors

Network server: proprietary file server

Maximum number of file servers: unlimited

Disk backup: whole disk

Network operation during backup: yes

APPLE COMPUTER INC. • APPLETALK

20525 Mariani Avenue
Cupertino, CA 95014
(408)973-2042; telex 171-576; TWX 910-338-2054

John Sculley, President; William Campbell, Executive Vice President, Marketing and Sales (MD); Tom Marano, Vice President, Sales (PSC)

AppleTalk Personal Network is a PC LAN designed for the Macintosh office computers and related peripherals within a network diameter of 1000 feet. Connects up to 32 devices, with the computers and peripherals configured in any combination. First installed: 1985.

• APPLETALK TECHNICAL CHARACTERISTICS

Transmission category: baseband

Transmission medium: twisted wire pair

Transmission speed: 230.4 Kbps

Topology: bus

Access method: CSMA/CA

• STANDARDS/PROTOCOLS SUPPORTED

Communications protocols: SDLC

APPLITEK CORPORATION • UNILAN

107 Audubon Road
Wakefield, MA 01775
(617)246-4500; telex 510-600-1787; FAX 617-215-7340

Ashraf M. Dahed, President; David Kurtzer, Product Marketing Manager (PM); Gerald McDonald, Director of Marketing (MD)(PR); Tony Keyes, Director of Sales (PSC); Susan Fennel (PA)

Founded 1981; 82 employees

UniLAN is a 10-Mbps network with industrial, laboratory, campus, government, or military applications. Can support mainframes, minicomputers, PCs, dumb terminals, and printers. Utilizes UniLINK, Applitek's network access method. Service contracts, network installation, instruction on network operation, and network maintenance services available. First installed: 1984. Number installed: 75. Average number of stations per installation: 300.

• UNILAN TECHNICAL CHARACTERISTICS

Transmission category: baseband, broadband

Transmission mode: full duplex

Transmission medium: baseband coaxial cable, broadband coaxial cable, optical fiber

Transmission speed: 10 Mbps backbone; 1.544 Mbps maximum available for user connection; 10 Mbps burst

Topology: bus, tree

Access method: UniLINK

Gateways: SNA/SDLC, Ethernet, X.25, HDLC, T1

Maximum number of workstations per node: 32

Maximum number of nodes: unlimited

Maximum distance between nodes: unlimited

Means of host interconnection: terminal ports, DR11-W, high-speed RS-449, Ethernet, X.25

Site of network logic: bus/network interface units

• STANDARDS/PROTOCOLS SUPPORTED

Communications protocols: SNA/SDLC, bisynchronous, X.25, HDLC, asynchronous, RS-232, synchronous

IEEE 802 standards: conforms to level 1 (RS-232, RS-449, V.35, Milstd188), level 2 (UniLINK) and level 4 (Delta T)

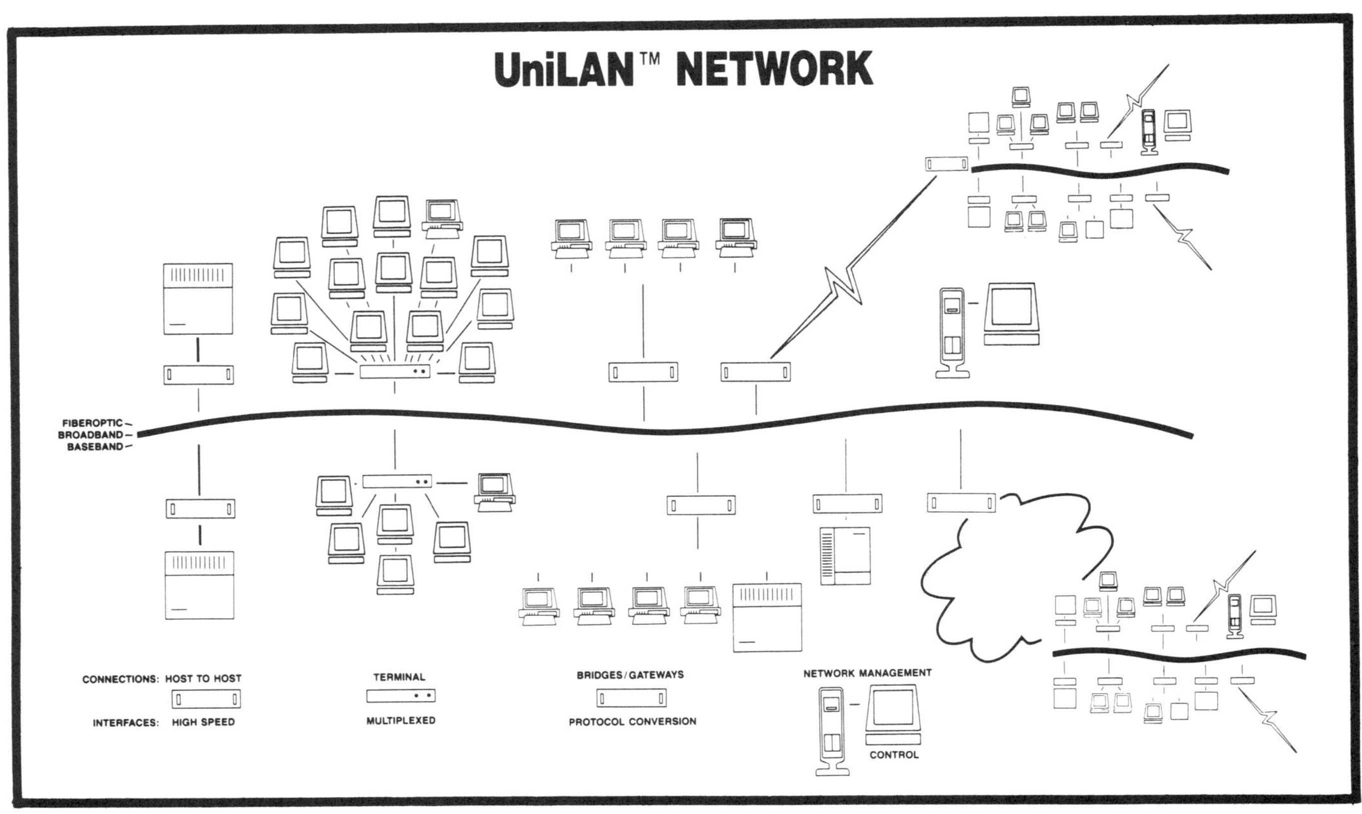

Figure 1

Courtesy Applitek Corporation

ARTEL COMMUNICATIONS CORPORATION • FIBERWAY

West Side Station, Box 100
Worcester, MA 01602
(617)752-5690; telex 940-103

Tad Witkowicz, President and Chief Executive Officer; Charles Brewer, Vice President, Sales (MD)(PSC); David B. Monk, Director of Corporate Communications (PR); George Koslosky, Purchasing Manager (PA)

Founded 1981; 80 employees

FiberWay is designed to connect minicomputers, PCs, dumb terminals, grahics workstations, and other LANs that already have file servers and other application software developed. FiberWay is designed for the industrial, laboratory or campus environment and can support any devices with IBM 3270, RS-232 or Ethernet interfaces. Configuration and maintenance software is provided for Fiberway through a microcomputer, which can be connected at any node. Service contracts, network installation and network maintenance services available. First installed: 1986. Average number of stations per installation: 6.

• FIBERWAY TECHNICAL CHARACTERISTICS

Transmission category: broadband

Transmission mode: full duplex

Transmission medium: optical fiber

Transmission speed: 200 Mbps backbone, maximum available for user connection

Topology: ring

Access method: token passing

Compatible operating systems: proprietary

Gateways: SNA/SDLC, Ethernet, RS-232

Maximum number of workstations per node: 32

Maximum number of nodes: 8

Maximum distance between nodes: 10,00 feet

Site of network logic: bus/network interface units, central controllers

• STANDARDS/PROTOCOLS SUPPORTED

Communications protocols: SNA/SDLC, asynchronous, RS-232, synchronous

IEEE 802 standards: conforms to 802.3

ISO OSI Reference Model: conforms to layers 1-3

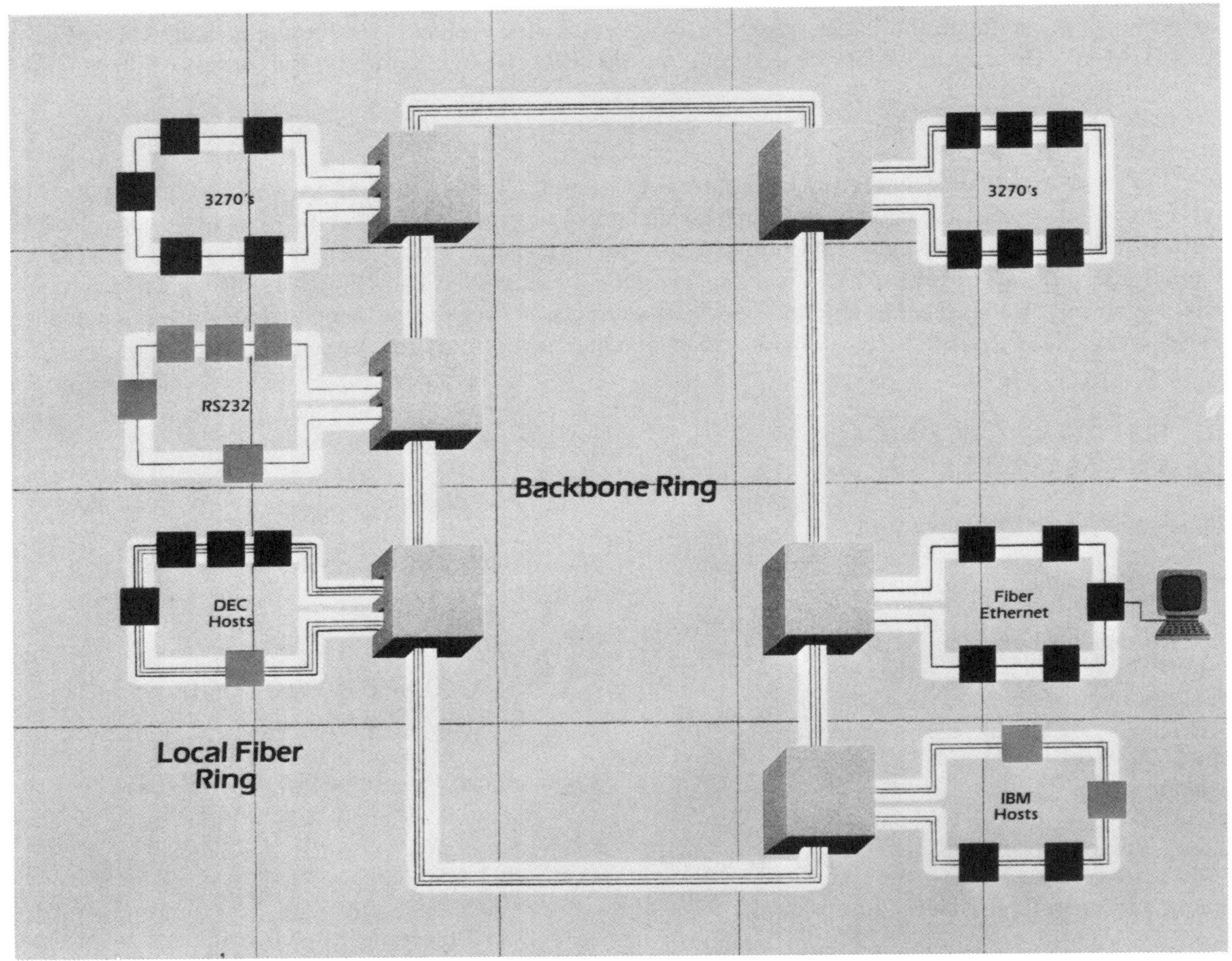

Figure 2

Courtesy Artel Communications Corporation

ASHER TECHNOLOGIES INC. • QUADNET VI

1009 Mansell Road
Roswell, GA 30076
(404)993-4590; FAX 404-642-1894

Wil Riner, President and Chief Executive Officer; Bruce Watson, Executive Vice President (MD); Robert Riner, Director of Sales (PSC); Margie Smith (PA)

Founded 1983; 40 employees

Branch Offices and Distributors:
Asher Technologies, Inc., New York, NY (212)938-1374; Asher Technologies, Inc., Irvine, CA (714)752-7703; Asher Technologies, Inc., San Mateo, CA (415)343-5231

Quadnet VI is a PC network designed for an office environment. The network will support printers, plotters, modems, disk drives, all PC and AT compatibles, and any LAN hardware that supports Novell Netware. Quadnet VI will also support any software compatible with IBM NETBIOS or Novell NetWare. Service contracts, network installation, instruction on network operation, and network maintenance services available. First installed: 1984. Number installed: 1500. Average number of stations per installation: 12.

• QUADNET VI TECHNICAL CHARACTERISTICS

Transmission category: baseband

Transmission medium: baseband coaxial cable

Transmission speed: 1.5 Mbps available for user connection

Topology: bus

Access method: CSMA/CA

Compatible operating systems: MS-DOS, Novell

Gateways: SNA/SDLC, X.25

Maximum number of workstations per node: 1

Maximum number of nodes: 255

Maximum distance between nodes: unlimited

Means of host interconnection: SNA gateways

Network server: multivendor file server, proprietary file server

Maximum number of file servers: unlimited

Disk backup: whole disk

Network operation during backup: yes

Site of network logic: bus/network interface units

• STANDARDS/PROTOCOLS SUPPORTED

Communications protocols: SNA/SDLC, X.25, asynchronous, synchronous, RS-232

IEEE 802 standards: conforms to 802.5

ASHER TECHNOLOGIES INC. • QUADNET IX

1009 Mansell Road
Roswell, GA 30076
(404)993-4590; FAX 404-642-1894

Wil Riner, President and Chief Executive Officer; Bruce Watson, Executive Vice President (MD); Robert Riner, Director of Sales (PSC); Margie Smith (PA)

Founded 1983; 40 employees

Branch Offices and Distributors:
Asher Technologies Inc, New York, NY (212)938-1374; Asher Technologies Inc., Irvine, CA (714)752-7703; Asher Technologies Inc., San Mateo, CA (415)343-5231

Quadnet IX is a PC network designed for an office environment. The network will support printers, plotters, modems, disk drives, all PC and AT compatibles, and any LAN hardware that supports Novell Netware. Quadnet IX will also support any software compatible with IBM NETBIOS or Novell NetWare. Service contracts, network installation, instruction on network opertion, and network maintenance services available. First installed: 1984. Number installed: 1500. Average number of stations per installation: 12.

• QUADNET IX TECHNICAL CHARACTERISTICS

Transmission category: baseband

Transmission medium: dual twisted wire pair, optical fiber

Transmission speed: 10 Mbps maximum available for user connection

Topology: star, ring

Access method: token passing

Compatible operating systems: MS-DOS, Novell NetWare

Gateways: SNA/SDLC, X.25

Maximum numbe of workstations per node: 1

Maximum number of nodes: 255

Maximum distance between nodes: unlimited

Means of host interconnection: SNA gateways

Network server: multivendor file server, proprietary file server

Maximum number of file servers: unlimited

Disk backup: whole disk

Network operation during backup: yes

Site of network logic: bus/network interface units

• STANDARDS/PROTOCOLS SUPPORTED

Communications protocols: SNA/SDLC, X.25, asynchronous, synchronous, RS-232

IEEE 802 standards: conforms to 802.5

Typical Quadnet VI Configuration

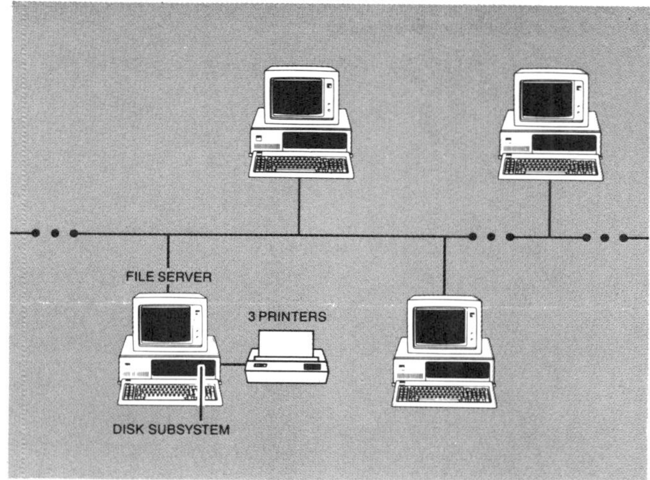

Figure 3

Courtesy Asher Technologies Inc.

Typical Quadnet IX Configuration

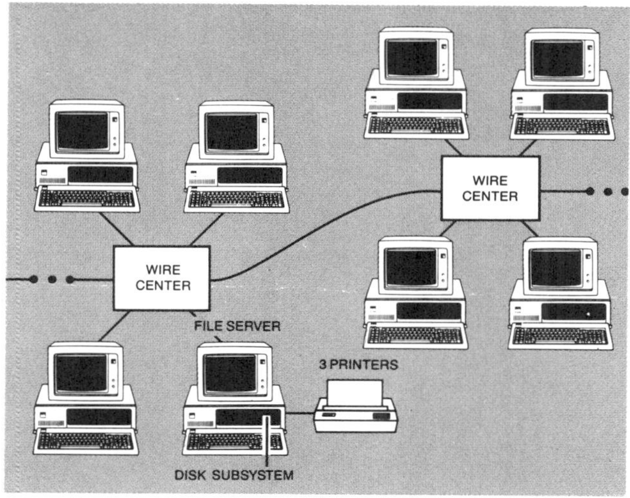

Figure 4

Courtesy Asher Technologies Inc.

AST RESEARCH INC. • AST-PCNET II

2121 Alton Avenue
Irvine, CA 92714
(714)863-1333; telex 753-699 ASTR UR; FAX 714-863-9478

Safi Qureshey, President; Mark Stieglitz, Director of LAN Products (PM)(MD); Ron Blaisdell, Director of Sales (PSC); Bob Maples, Manager, Public Relations (PR)

Founded 1980; 1000 employees

AST-PCNet II is a plug-in, twisted-pair LAN that enables the IBM PC, XT, AT, and compatibles to share resources. Network supports up to 32 PCs per 500-foot bus segment, extendable to 160 PCs over 2500 feet.

• AST-PCNET II TECHNICAL CHARACTERISTICS

Transmission category: baseband

Transmission medium: twisted wire pair

Transmission speed: 800 Kbps

Topology: bus

Access method: CSMA/CA

Compatible operating systems: PC-DOS 2.0/1, 3.0 and 3.1

Maximum number of workstations per node: 32 per bus segment

Maximum number of nodes: 5 bus segments

Maximum distance between nodes: 2500 feet total network length

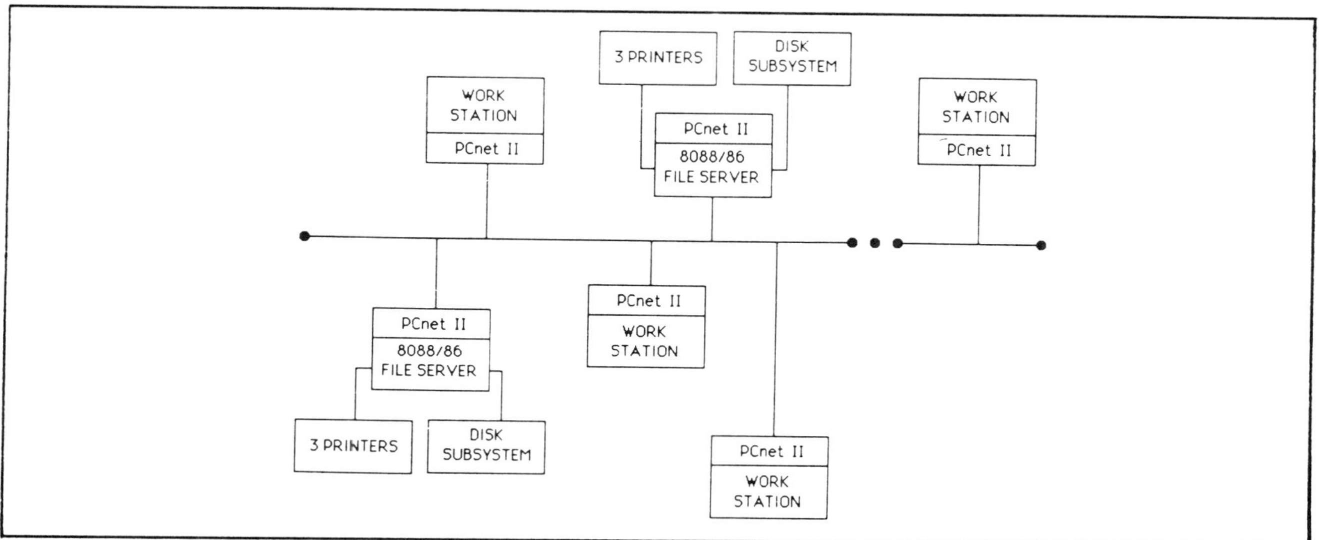

Sample AST PCnet II Topology

Figure 5

Courtesy Novell Inc.

AST RESEARCH INC. • AST-RESOURCE SHARING NETWORK

2121 Alton Avenue
Irvine, CA 92714
(714)863-1333; telex 753-699 ASTR UR; FAX 714-863-9478

Safi Qureshey, President; Mark Stieglitz, Director of LAN Products (PM)(MD); Ron Blaisdell, Director of Sales (PSC); Bob Maples, Manager, Public Relations (PR)

Founded 1980; 1000 employees

AST-Resource Sharing Network is a PC network designed for office use and capable of supporting IBM PCs, XTs, ATs, and compatibles and all MS-DOS peripherals. The LAN offers full IBM NETBIOS compatibility and supports Ashton-Tate, IBM and Microsoft software packages. Instruction on network operation available. First installed: 1985. Average number of stations per installation: 6.

• AST-RESOURCE SHARING NETWORK TECHNICAL CHARACTERISTICS

Transmission category: baseband

Transmission mode: half duplex

Transmission medium: baseband coaxial cable

Transmission speed: 5 Mbps maximum available for user connection

Topology: bus

Access method: CSMA/C

Compatible operating systems: MS-DOS

Gateways: SNA/SDLC, bisynchronous

Maximum number of workstations per node: 1

Maximum number of nodes: 64

Maximum distance between nodes: 1500 feet

Means of host interconnection: 3274 emulation

Network server: multivendor file server

Maximum number of file servers: 64

Disk backup: whole disk, partial disk

Network operation during backup: no

Site of network logic: terminal equipment, bus/network interface units

• STANDARDS/PROTOCOLS SUPPRTED

Communications protocols: SNA/SDLC, bisynchronous

ASTRA COMMUNICATIONS INC. • ASTRANET

329 North Bernardo
Mountain View, CA 94043
(415)960-1100

Andrew K. Ludwick, President and Chief Executive Officer

AstraNet extends the implementation of conventional, coaxial-based Ethernet to other physical media, including the IBM Cabling System and optical fiber. Modular design supports both under-carpet and air plenum installations. Supports over 250 workstations. First installed:86.

- **ASTRANET TECHNICAL CHARACTERISTICS**

Transmission medium: IBM Cabling System, optical fiber

Transmission category: baseband, broadband

Topology: star

ASTROCOM CORPORATION • XLAN

120 West Plato Boulevard
St. Paul, MN 55107
(612)227-8651; telex 297-421

Sidney N. Jerson, President (MD); John Sandberg , Vice President, Product Development (PM); Kent Johnson, Director of Sales (PSC); Janet Schmidt (PR); Jerry Fingal (PA)

Founded 1968; 200 employees

XLAN is a baseband bus network designed to connect mainframes, minicomputers, PCs, and dumb terminals in an industrial, office, laboratory, or campus environment. Service contracts, network installation and instruction on network operation available. First installed: 1984. Number installed: 50. Average number of stations per installation: 10.

• XLAN TECHNICAL CHARACTERISTICS

Transmission category: baseband

Transmission mode: full duplex

Transmission medium: baseband coaxial cable, twisted wire pair

Topology: bus

Access method: CSMA

Compatible operating systems: MS-DOS, Unix

Gateways: ASCII

Maximum number of workstations per node: 192

Maximum number of nodes: 64

Maximum distance between nodes: 16,000

Means of host interconnection: terminal ports

• STANDARDS/PROTOCOLS SUPPORTED

IEEE 802 standards: conforms to 802.4

ISO OSI Reference Model: conforms to levels 1-3

AT&T INFORMATION SYSTEMS • STARLAN

1 Speedwell Avenue
Morristown, NJ 07960
(201)898-3278

Charles Marshall, Chairman of the Board; Robert Casale, President, Marketing and Sales (MD)(PSC); Frank Vigilante, President, Product Management and Development (PM)

Founded 1983; 100,000 employees

Starlan is a departmental PC network featuring file sharing, file transfer, print sharing, and gateways. Service contracts, network installation, instruction on network operation, and network maintenance services available. First installed: 1984.

• STARLAN TECHNICAL CHARACTERISTICS

Transmission category: baseband

Transmission mode: full duplex, half duplex

Transmission medium: twisted wire pair

Transmission speed: 1 Mbps backbone

Topology: bus

Access method: CSMA/CD

Compatible operating systems: Unix, MS-DOS

Gateways: 802.3 standard

Maximum number of workstations per node: 1210

Means of host interconnection: multiplexed interfaces, terminal ports

Network server: multivendor file server, proprietary file server

Site of network logic: bus/network interface units

• STANDARDS/PROTOCOLS SUPPORTED

IEEE 802 standards: conforms to 802.3

AT&T INFORMATION SYSTEMS • INFORMATION SYSTEMS NETWORK

1 Speedwell Avenue
Morristown, NJ 07960
(201)898-3278

Charles Marshall, Chairman of the Board; Robert Casale, President, Marketing and Sales (MD)(PSC); Frank Vigilante, President, Product Management and Development (PM)

Founded 1983; 100,000 employees

Information Systems Network is a transport network allowing mainframes, minicomputers, PCs, dumb terminals, printers, modems, protocol converters, and Ethernets to be connected. Network market includes industrial, office, laboratory, campus, and LAN/WAN applications. Compatible devices include IBM PC/AT/XT, 3270 Series, 3705, and 3725; any asynchronous standard device; and Ethernet 802.3 running upper layer protocols of XNS, TCP/IP and 3BNet. Service contracts, network installation, instruction on network operation, and network maintenance services available. First installed: 1984.

• INFORMATION SYSTEMS NETWORK TECHNICAL CHARACTERISTICS

Transmission category: baseband

Transmission mode: full duplex, half duplex

Transmission medium: twisted wire pair, optical fiber

Transmission speed: 8.64 Mpbs backbone; 1 Mbps maximum available for user connection and burst

Topology: hierachical star

Access method: perfect scheduling

Compatible operating systems: MS-DOS

Gateways: SNA/SDLC, Ethernet

Maximum number of workstations per node: 1920

Maximum number of nodes: over 20

Maximum distance between nodes: unlimited; 2.9 km via fiber

Means of host interconnection: multiplexed interfaces, terminal ports

Disc backup: Winchester

Network operation during backup: yes

Site of network logic: central controllers

• STANDARDS/PROTOCOLS SUPPORTED

Communications protocols: bisynchronous, HDLC, asynchronous, RS-232, synchronous

AVATAR TECHNOLOGIES INC. • ALLIANCE

99 South Street
Hopkinton, MA 01748
(617)435-6872; telex 710-390-0375; FAX 617-435-6872

John A. Carr, President; Michelle Doyle, Vice President, LAN Development (PM); Neal Checkoway, Director of Marketing (MD); Richard Simpson, Vice President, Sales (PSC); David Conti, Public Relations Specialist (PR); Anita Lawler, Purchasing Manager (PA)

Founded 1981; 80 employees

Alliance is a complete networking system that allows IBM PC users to communicate with one another and to share peripherals and other resources such as printers, modems, mass storage devices, protocol converters, disk drives, and host computers. Alliance acts as a cluster controller situated at the center of a star configuration. Compatible with all IBM PCs and compatibles and any peripheral device with an RS-232 or RS-423 interface. Service contracts, instruction on network operation and network maintenance services available. First installed: 1986.

• ALLIANCE TECHNICAL CHARACTERISTICS

Transmission category: baseband

Transmission mode: full duplex

Transmission medium: twisted wire pair

Transmission speed: 115 Kbps maximum available for user connection

Topology: star

Compatible operating systems: MS-DOS

Maximum number of workstations per node: 1

Maximum number of nodes: 20 per cluster

Maximum distance between nodes: 1000 feet

Site of network logic: central controllers

BARRISTER INFORMATION SYSTEMS CORPORATION • BARRISTER/NET

One Technology Center, 45 Oak Street
Buffalo, NY 14203
(716)845-5010

Henry P. Semmelhack, President; E. Melvin (PM); H.J. Smith, Vice President, Marketing (MD); W.P. Mackey, Vice President, Sales (PSC); Ellen Duggan, Public Relations Specialist (PR); Ken Devantier, Purchasing Agent (PA)

Founded 1972; 400 employees

Barrister/Net is an office minicomputer network supporting the storage and spoolable devices of the individual network systems. Service contracts, network installation, instruction on network operation, and network maintenance services available. First installed: 1983. Number installed: 50. Average number of stations per installation: variable.

• BARRISTER/NET TECHNICAL CHARACTERISTICS

Transmission category: baseband

Transmission mode: half duplex

Transmission medium: baseband coaxial cable

Topology: bus

Access method: CSMA/CD

Compatible operating systems: MBOS (Multi-Function Barrister Operating System)

Gateways: Ethernet

Maximum number of workstations per node: 16

Maximum number of nodes: 50

Maximum distance between nodes: 164

Means of host interconnection: dedicated interface

Network server: proprietary file server

Maximum number of file servers: dependent upon number of systems on network

Disc backup: whole disk

Network operation during backup: yes

Site of network logic: central controllers

• STANDARDS/PROTOCOLS SUPPORTED

IEEE 802 standards: conforms to 802.3

ISO OSI Reference Model: conforms to layers 1 and 3

BASONJE SYSTEMS • TRANS-NET

138 Huron Street
Toronto, Ontario, M5T 2B2 CANADA
(416)598-7992; telex 06-963548 KAMPORT; FAX 16-593-7660

Allan Wong, President; James Kan (MD); K.T. Kan (PA)

Founded 1982

Trans-Net is a PC local area network system allowing sharing of hard drives, floppy drives, printers, modems, and other peripherals. Automatic error detection with capability to bypass a failed station without interrupting other workstations; transparency to DOS operating system. Designed for office, laboratory or campus environment. Compatible product vendors: IBM. Compatible software includes IBM PC Network Progam, Novell NetWare, and dBASE III PLUS. Service contracts, network installation, instruction on network operation, and network maintenance services available. First installed: 1986. Number installed: 200. Average number of stations per installation: 5-10.

- ### TRANS-NET TECHNICAL CHARACTERISTICS

Transmission category: baseband

Transmission mode: half duplex

Transmission medium: twisted wire pair

Transmission speed: 1 Mbps

Topology: bus

Access method: CSMA/CA

Compatible operating systms: MS-DOS

Gateways: SNA/SDLC with NETBIOS

Maximum number of workstations per node: 1

Maximum number of nodes: 255

Maximum distance between nodes: 4000 feet

Network server: multivendor file server, disk server

Maximum number of file servers: 100

Disk backup: whole disk

Network operation during backup: yes

Site of network logic: bus/network interface units

- ### STANDARDS/PROTOCOLS SUPPORTED

IEEE 802 standards: conforms to 802.3

ISO OSI Reference Model: conforms to layers 1-7

BELL ATLANTIC NETWORK SERVICES INC. • C.O. LAN

1310 North Courthouse Road
Arlington, VA 22201
(703)974-3000; TWX 703-975-3885

P.A. Campbell, President; B.T. Forrest, Product Manager (PM); Jeff McDermott, Assistant Vice President, Product Line Management (MD); M.E. Payne (PSC); Paul Wood, Media Relations Manager (PR)

Founded 1984; 70,000 employees

C.O. LAN is a central office-based LAN utilizing existing Centrex wiring for voice and data communications. Users communicate with other users or devices through virtual circuit switched connections. Applications include office, laboratory, campus, and general purpose environments. Network supports printers, modems, multiplexers, and all asynchronous RS-232C or RS-442 devices. Service contracts, network installation, instruction on network operation, and network maintenance services available. First installed: 1985. Number installed: 8. Average number of stations per installation: 300.

• C.O. LAN TECHNICAL CHARACTERISTICS

Transmission category: baseband

Transmission mode: full duplex

Transmission medium: twisted wire pair

Transmission speed: 19.2 Kbps maximum available for user connection

Topology: star

Access method: perfect scheduling

Gateways: X.25

Maximum number of workstations per node: unlimited

Maximum number of nodes: unlimited

Maximum distance between nodes: unlimited

Means of host interconnection: multiplexed interfaces, terminal ports, RS-232

Network server: multivendor file server

Maximum number of file servers: unlimited

Site of network logic: central controllers

• STANDARDS/PROTOCOLS SUPPORTED

Communications protocols: SNA/SDLC, bisynchronous, X.25, HDLC, asynchronous, RS-232, synchronous, and RS-442

ISO OSI Reference Model: conforms to layers 1 and 2

BRAEGEN CORPORATION • ELAN

525 Los Coches Street
Milpitas, CA 95035
(408)945-1900; TWX 910-338-7332

James Charnes, President; Bill Brown (PM); George Everhart (MD)(PR); Rem Smith (PSC)

Founded 1973; 300 employees

ELAN is a 1.5-Mbps LAN that can support mainframes, IBM PCs, XTs, ATs, and compatibles, 3287 type printers, JES output printers, and file servers. Suited for use in a variety of environments, including industrial, office, laboratory, campus, and hospital settings. Compatible software includes Novell Advanced Netware 286 and IBM PC Network Program. Service contracts, network installation, instruction on network operation, and network maintenance services available. First installled: 1983.

• ELAN TECHNICAL CHARACTERISTICS

Transmission category: baseband, transmittable to broadband

Transmission medium: baseband coaxial cable, broadband coaxial cable, twisted wire pair, optical fiber

Transmission speed: 1.5 Mbps backbone

Topology: bus, star

Access method: CSMA/CA

Compatible operating systems: MS-DOS

Gateways: SNA/SDLC, ASCII, Token Ring

Maximum number of workstations per node: 60

Maximum distance between nodes: 20,000 feet

Means of host interconnction: multiple 3270 controller, local and remote

Network server: multivendor file server

Maximum number of file servers: 60

Disk backup: whole disk

Network operation during backup: yes

• STANDARDS/PROTOCOLS SUPPORTED

Communications protocols: SNA/SDLC, bisynchronous, asynchronous, RS-232, synchronous

CENTRAM SYSTEMS WEST • TOPS

2372 Ellsworth Avenue
Berkeley, CA 94704
(415)644-8244; FAX 415-644-0267

Nat Goldhaber, President; Molly McCourt (PM); Jack Carroll (D); Kim Criswell (PSC)

Founded 1984; 20 employees

TOPS allows IBM PCs to become nodes on the AppleTalk network so that hard disk space and individual files can be shared between PCs, Macintoshes and LaserWriters on the network. Distributed-server architecture allows any computer on the network to become both a server device and a workstation. Macintosh requires no additional hardware; IBM PC requires AppleTalk board in expansion slot. First installed: 1986.

• TOPS TECHNICAL CHARACTERISTICS

Transmission category: baseband

Transmission medium: twisted wire pair

Transmission speed: .8 Mbps

Topology: bus

Access method: CSMA/CA

Compatible operating systems: MS-DOS, PC-DOS, Macintosh DOS, ProDOS, Unix

Maximum number of workstations per node: 32 users per bus

Maximum number of nodes: 254

Maximum distance between nodes: 2000 feet net length

Site of network logic: bus/network interface units

CODENOLL TECHNOLOGY CORPORATION • CODENET

1086 North Broadway
Yonkers, NY 10701
(914)965-6300; telex 646-159; FAX 914-965-6300

Michael H. Coden, President; Edwin Sakaguchi, Vice President, Sales and Marketing (MD)(PSC); John Mulvey (PA)

Founded 1980; 70 employees

Codenet is a fiber optic Ethernet connection supporting IBM PC, XT, AT, and compatibles. Various topologies supported by connecting Codenet transceivers to computer terminals through Codestar couplers.

• CODENET TECHNICAL CHARACTERISTICS

Transmission category: broadband

Transmission medium: optical fiber

Transmission speed: 10 Mbps

Topology: star, ring, bus, branching tree

Maximum number of nodes: 64

• STANDARDS/PROTOCOLS SUPPORTED

Communications protocols: Ethernet, NETBIOS, RS-232, RS-422

IEEE 802 standards: conforms to 802.3

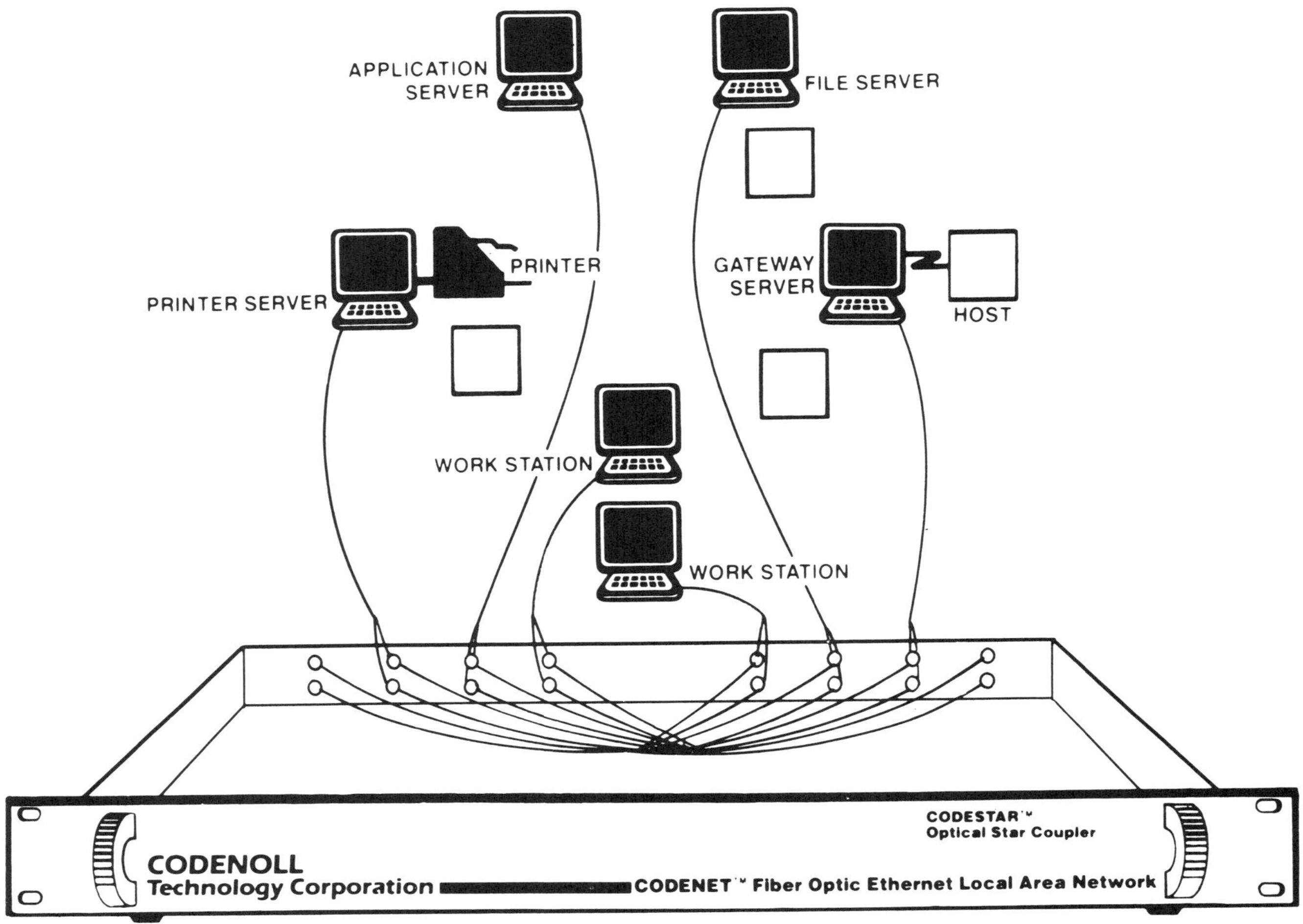

Figure 6

Courtesy Codenoll Technology Corporation

CODEX CORPORATION • 4000 SERIES LAN

20 Cabot Boulevard
Mansfield, MA 02048
(617)364-2000

John Pugh, General Manager, LAN Business Unit; Ralph Rio, Senior Product Manager (PM); Dennis Hawley, Director, LAN Marketing (MD); John Dimitruk, Director, LAN Sales (PSC)

Founded 1984; 140 employees, LAN Division
Codex 4000 Series LAN allows users to combine baseband and broadband technologies to create a network tailored to specific applications needs. Supports mainframes, PCs, dumb terminals, word processors, supermicros, minicomputers, modems, and disk drives for office, laboratory and campus applications. Service contracts and network installation available. First installed: 1984. Average number of stations per intallation: 200-400.

• 4000 SERIES LAN TECHNICAL CHARACTERISTICS

Transmission category: baseband, broadband

Transmission medium: baseband coaxial cable, broadband coaxial cable

Transmission speed: baseband, 10 Mbps; broadband, 5 Mbps

Topology: bus

Access method: baseband, CSMA/CD; broadband, CSMA

Compatible operating systems: MS-DOS, CP/M

Gateways: SNA/SDLC, Ethernet, X.25

Maximum distance of network: 500 meters

Maximum distance between nodes: baseband, 1.5 miles; broadband, 9 miles

Means of host interconnection: RS-232 terminal ports

Network server: multivendor file server

Network operation during backup: yes

• STANDARDS/PROTOCOLS SUPPORTED

Communications protocols: asynchronous, 2780/3780, 3270

IEEE 802 standards: conforms to 802.4 (baseband)

ISO OSI Reference Model: conforms to layer 2

COMMTEX INC. • CX-80 DATA EXCHANGE NETWORK

2411 Crofton Lane
Crofton, MD 21114
(301)721-3666

Donald W. Parker, President

Founded 1978; 76 employees

Cx-80 Data Exchange allows for the direct connection of a broad range of asynchronous data communications equipment such as ASCII terminals, IBM Type-A workstations, graphic stations, ASCII host interfaces, PCs, printers, plotters, modems, and mini- and microcomputer ports. Enables 5 to 25 ASCII devices to communicate with one or two IBM mainframes.

• CX-80 DATA EXCHANGE NETWORK TECHNICAL CHARACTERISTICS

Transmission category: baseband

Transmission medium: baseband coaxial cable

Transmission speed: 19.2 Kbps

Gateways: X.25

• STANDARDS/PROTOCOLS SUPPORTED

Communications protocols: bisynchronous, SNA/SDLC

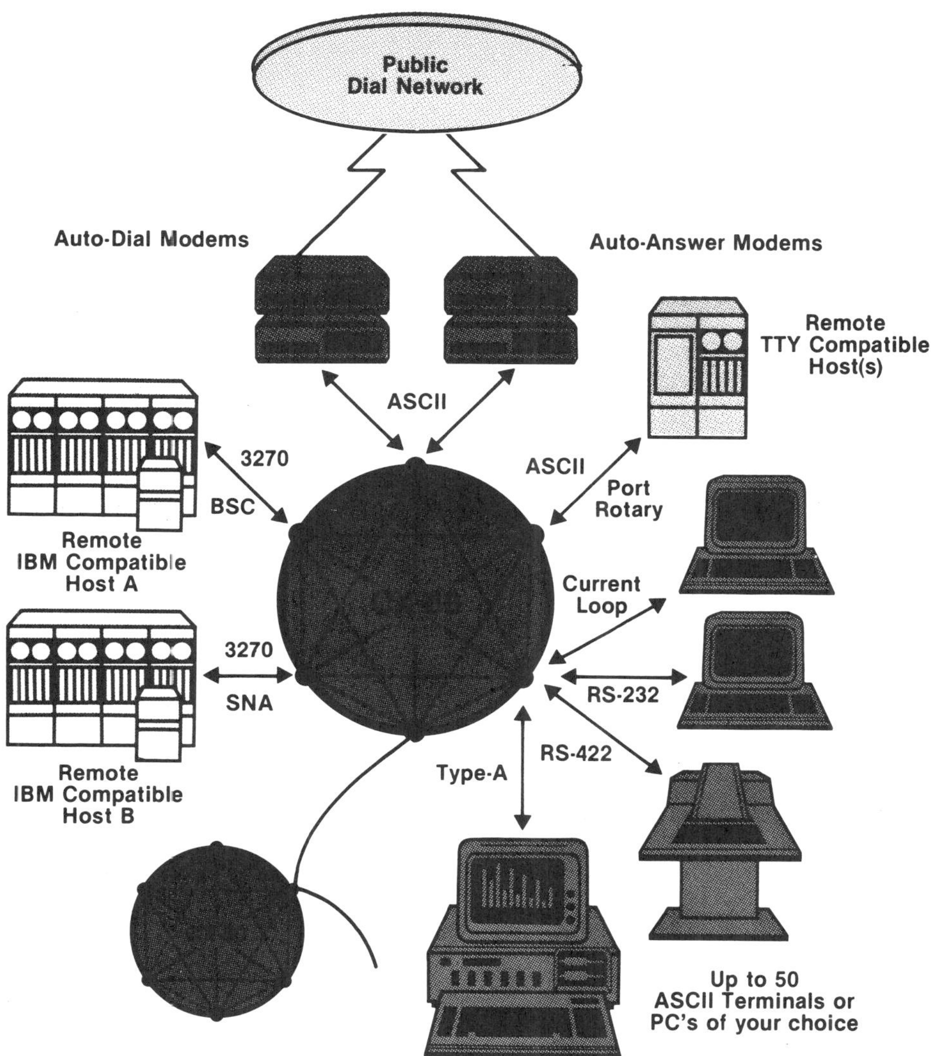

Cx-80 Data Exchange Network

Figure 7

Courtesy Commtex Inc.

COMPLEXX SYSTEMS INC. • XLAN

4930 Research Drive
Huntsville, AL 35805
(205)830-4310; telex 880-114

Sid Jerson, President; Byron Driver (PM); Kent Johnson (MD)(PSC); Janet Schmidt (PR); Dan Gaylean (PA)

Founded 1982; 200 employees

XLAN connects mainframes, minicomputers, PCs, dumb terminals, printers, and modems for industrial, office, laboratoy, or campus applications. Network will support any ASCII asynchronous devices. Compatible software includes Microstuf Crosstalk and Custom Software Remote Access. Service contracts, instruction on network operation and network maintenance services available. First installed: 1983. Number installed: 375. Average number of stations per installation: 25.

• XLAN TECHNICAL CHARACTERISTICS

Transmission category: baseband

Transmission mode: full duplex

Transmission medium: baseband coaxial cable, twisted wire pair

Transmission speed: 1 Mbps maximum available for user connection

Topology: bus

Access method: CSMA

Compatible operating systems: MS-DOS, CP/M, Unix

Maximum number of workstations per node: 3

Maximum number of nodes: 64

Maximum distance between nodes: 8000 feet, maximum cable distance

Means of host interconnection: multiplexed interfaces, terminal ports

Site of network logic: bus/network interface units

• STANDARDS/PROTOCOLS SUPPORTED

Communications protocols: asynchronous, RS-232

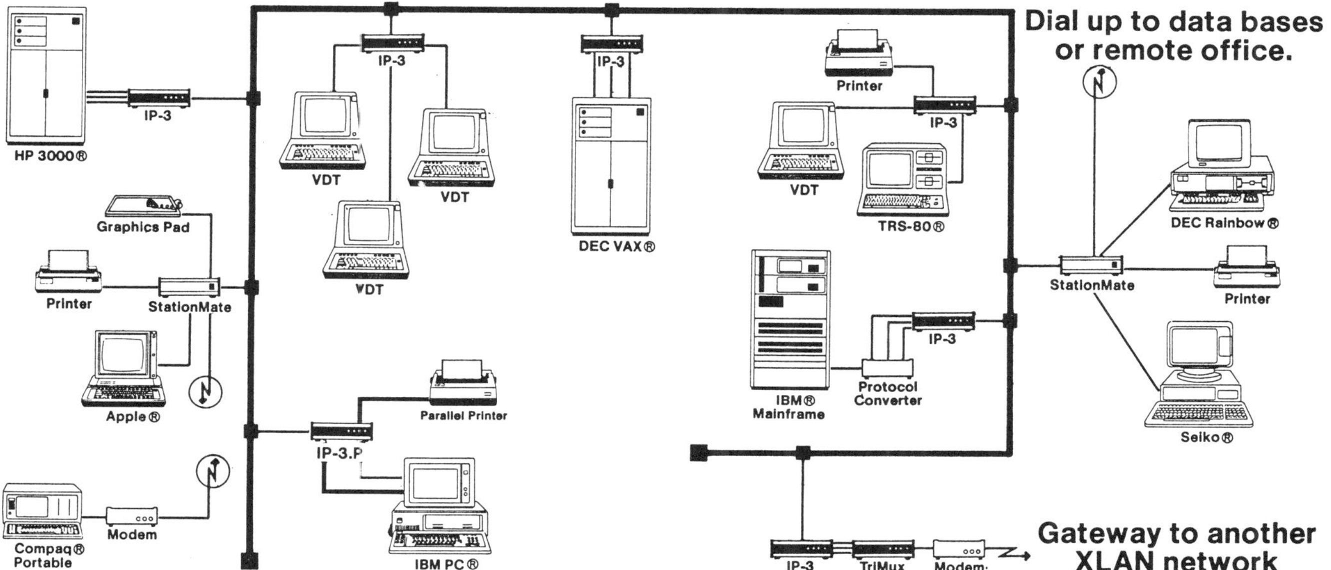

Complexx Systems Inc. XLAN

Figure 8

Courtesy Complexx Systems Inc.

COMPUTER CORPORATION OF AMERICA • PRODNET

4 Cambridge Center
Cambridge, MA 02142
(617)492-8860; telex 710-320-6479

Ken Draeger, Chief Executive Officer; Doug Miller (PSC), Director, Sales and Marketing (PM); John Donnelly, Vice President, Marketing (MD); Joanne Pickett (PR); Susan Pancreti (PA)

Founded 1965; 500 employees

ProdNet is a baseband LAN capable of connecting mainframes, minicomputers, PCs, and dumb terminals for use in industrial, office laboratory, or campus environments. Also supports printers, modems, disk drives, IRMA cards, SNA servers, and mouse. First installed: 1985. Number installed: 8. Average number of stations per installation: 100.

- **PRODNET TECHNICAL CHARACTERISTICS**

Transmission category: baseband

Topology: bus

Compatible operating systems: Port

COMPUTROL—A DIVISION OF KIDDE AUTOMATED SYSTEMS • MEGALINK

15 Ethan Allen Highway
Ridgefield, CT 06877
(203)544-9371; telex 643-358

Chuck Brewer, Vice President, Sales and Marketing (MD); Morton G. Scheraga (PSC)

Megalink is a complete industrial communications package—modems, DMA interfaces, software drivers, full documentation—in expandable modular design. Microprocessor-based with compact LSI design. High noise immunity and surge protection. Stand-alone interfaces and networking controllers support MBEbus, Q-bus, UNIbus, MULTIbus, CTIbus based processors, all on the same network. Service contracts, network installation and instruction on network operation available. First installed: 1973. Number installed: 30,000 nodes. Average number of stations per installation: 30.

• MEGALINK TECHNICAL CHARACTERISTICS

Transmission category: baseband, broadband

Transmission medium: baseband coaxial cable, broadband coaxial cable, optical fiber

Transmission speed: 2 Mbps, baseband; 1.544 Mbps, broadband; 10 Mbps, optical fiber

Topology: bus

Access method: polling, token passing, CSMA

Compatible operating systems: VMS, RT-11RRMX, RSX-11M/S

Maximum number of nodes: 100

Maximum distance between nodes: 50,000 feet

Means of host interconnection: bus interface cards

• STANDARDS/PROTOCOLS SUPPORTED

Communications protocols: SDLC/HDLC

IEEE 802 standards: conforms to 802.4

ISO OSI Reference Model: conforms to layer 1 (FSK 2.5 MHz) and layer 2 (SDLC/HDLC)

CORVUS SYSTEMS INC. • OMNINET

2100 Corvus Drive
San Jose, CA 95124
(408)559-7000; telex 278-976; FAX 408-559-5297

James L. Siehl, Predent; Bob Clark, Sales Manager, Distribution Division (PM); George McMurtry, General Manager, Distribution Division (MD); Dana Harrison (PSC); Norman Lombino, Manager, Corporate Public Relations (PR); Dean Personne, Purchasing Manager (PA)

Founded 1979; 350 employees

Branch Offices and Distributors:
   Compac Micro Electronics, Santa Clara, CA (408)720-0400; Com Systems, Dallas, TX (214)637-0061; Dataterm, Rochester, NY (716)381-7385; Trimarc Systems Inc., Rockville, MD (301)231-4991; LAN Distributing, Lawrence, MA (617)975-2000

Omninet is a 1 Mbps PC LAN designed for office, laboratory or campus use. Supports printers, disk drives and tape backups. Compatible devices include Apple IIe, Macintosh and MAC+; IBM PC, XT and AT; and DEC Rainbow. Service contracts, network installation and instruction on network operation available. First installed: 1981. Number installed: over 25,000. Average number of stations per installation: 10.

• OMNINET TECHNICAL CHARACTERISTICS

Transmission category: baseband

Transmission mode: full duplex

Transmission medium: twisted wire pair

Transmission speed: 1 Mbps maximum available for user connection

Topology: bus

Access method: CSMA

Compatible operating systems: MS-DOS, Constellation II, Novell Advanced NetWare

Gateways: SNA/SDLC

Maximum number of workstations per node: 64

Maximum distance between nodes: 4000 feet

Means of host interconnection: terminal ports

Network server: proprietary file server

Disk backup: whole disk

Network operation during backup: yes

• STANDARDS/PROTOCOLS SUPPORTED

Communications protocols: SNA/SDLC, asynchronous, RS-232

IEEE 802 standards: conforms to 802.3

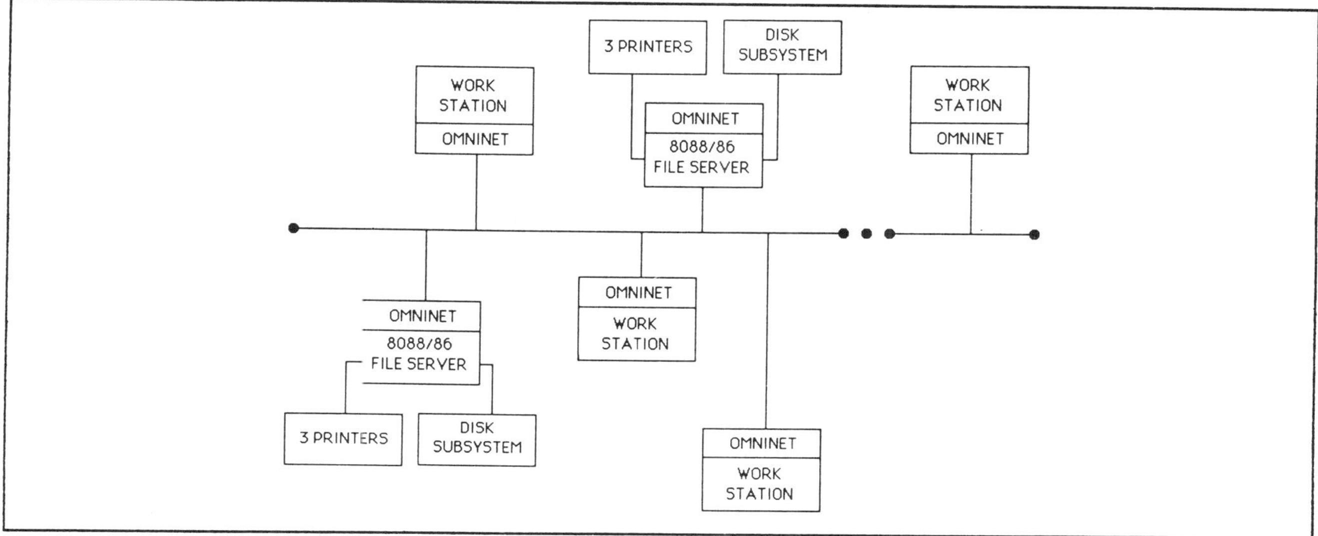

Sample OMNINET Topology

Figure 9

Courtesy Novell Inc.

DATAPOINT CORPORATION • ARCNET

9725 Datapoint Drive
San Antonio, TX 78284
(512)699-7151; telex 767-300

Ed Gistaro, President; Gary Maze (PM); Jim Rutledge (MD); Rose Mary Eash (PR)

Founded 1969; 4000 employees

ARCnet is a third generation system offering resource sharing, total functional independence, simplified programming, and easy access to all resources. Supports minicomputers, dumb terminals, printers, modems, disk drives, graphics terminals, and laser printers for office applications. Compatible vendors include Wang, Pro Computer and Nestar. Service contracts, network installation and instruction on network operation available. First installed: 1977. Number installed: over 5000.

• ARCNET TECHNICAL CHARACTERISTICS

Transmission category: baseband

Transmission medium: baseband coaxial cable, optical fiber

Transmission speed: 2.5 Mbps backbone, maximum available for user connection and burst

Topology: hybrid bus of stars acting as a logical ring

Access method: token passing

Compatible operating systems: Datapoint DOS; includes support for MS-DOS, CP/M, and Unix

Gateways: 3270

Maximum number of workstations per node: 6

Maximum network distance: 4 miles

Means of host interconnection: bus interface cards; 3270 BNC connectors

Network server: multivendor file server

Maximum number of file servers: 255

Disk backup: whole disk, partial disk

Network operation during backup: yes

• STANDARDS/PROTOCOLS SUPPORTED

Communications protocols: X.25, SNA, bisynchronous, 3270, Batch Burroughs, Univac Uniscope, Honeywell VIP and GRTs, CDC Batch

IEEE 802 standards: does not conform

DAVOX COMMUNICATIONS CORPORATION • DAVOXNET

4 Federal Street
Billerica, MA 01821
(617)667-4455; telex 510-1000-609; FAX 617-667-4433

Daniel A. Hosage, President; Michael Giltner (PM); Deirdre Searles (MD); Leonard Julius (PSC); Bill Bradley (PR); Luke Sabella, Controller (PA)

Founded 1981; 120 employees

DavoxNet is a proprietary office network capable of transmitting voice and data simultaneously over standard twisted pair telephone cable or over coaxial cable. Users can access their IBM 3270 network in SNA/SDLC or BSC, emulate a DEC VT-52, VT-100 or VT-220 terminal, or dial up to remote databases and timesharing services. Sold with Davox multifunction workstations and controllers. Connects mainframes, minicomputers, PCs, dumb terminals, line printers, dot matrix printers, letter-quality printers, and modems. Service contracts, network installation, instruction on network operation, and network maintenance services available. First installed: 1982. Number installed: 400. Average number of stations per installation: 15.

• DAVOXNET TECHNICAL CHARACTERISTICS

Transmission category: baseband

Transmission mode: half duplex

Transmission medium: baseband coaxial cable, twisted wire pair

Transmission speed: 400 Kbps backbone

Access method: proprietary

Compatible operating systems: mainframe operating systems

Gateways: SNA/SDLC, Ethernet, X.25

Means of host interconnection: multiplexed interfaces

Network server: proprietary file server, disk server

Maximum number of file servers: 1

Site of network logic: terminal equipment, central controllers

• STANDARDS/PROTOCOLS SUPPORTED

Communications protocols: SNA/SDLC, bisynchronous, X.25, asynchronous, RS-232, synchronous, TTY

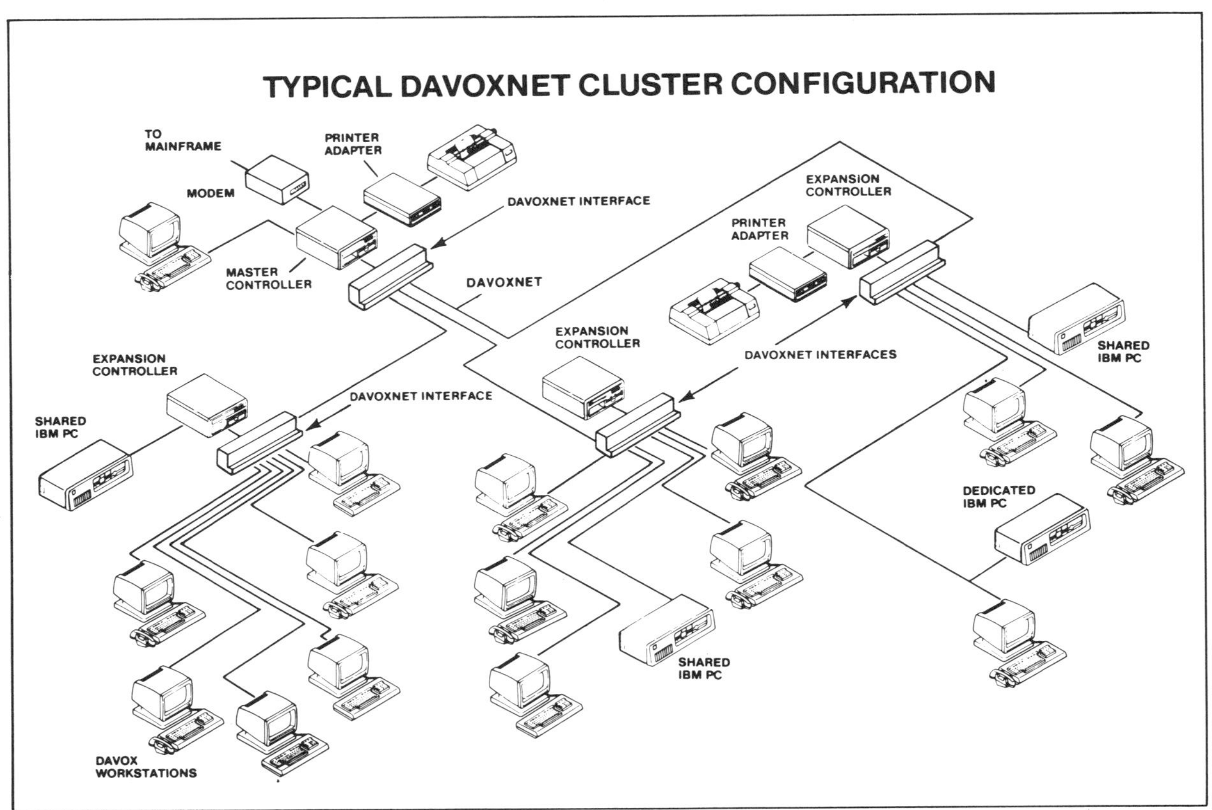

Figure 10

Courtesy Davox Communications Corporation

THE DESTEK GROUP • DESNET

830 East Evelyn Avenue
Sunnyvale, CA 94086
(408)737-7211

Tom McReynolds, President; Del Settle (PM)(MD)(PSC)(PR); Dennis Rieger (PA)

Founded 1981

Desnet is a multipurpose LAN connecting mainframes and PCs for industrial, office, laboratory, or campus applications. Also supports printers, modems and disk drives. Service contracts, network installation, instruction on network operation, and network maintenance services available. First installed: 1982. Number installed: over 1000. Average number of stations per installation: over 20.

• DESNET TECHNICAL CHARACTERISTICS

Transmission category: baseband, broadband

Transmission medium: baseband coaxial cable, broadband coaxial cable, twisted wire pair, optical fiber

Transmission speed: 2 Mbps

Topology: baseband, bus; broadband, tree or bus

Access method: CSMA/CD

Compatible operating systems: Magix

Maximum number of workstations per node: 1

Maximum number of nodes: 350

Gateways: SNA/SDLC, Ethernet

Means of host interconnection: terminal ports

Network server: multivendor file server, proprietary file server

Maximum number of file servers: 350

Disk backup: whole disk

Network operation during backup: yes

Site of network logic: bus/network interface units

• STANDARDS/PROTOCOLS SUPPORTED

Communications protocols: HDLC, asynchronous

IEEE 802 standards: conforms to 802.3, 802.4 and 802.5

ISO OSI Reference Model: conforms to layers 1, 2, 3, 5, and 7

DEVELCON ELECTRONICS LIMITED • DEVELNET

856 51st Street East
Saskatoon, Saskatchewan, S7K 5C7 CANADA
(306)933-3300; telex 074-2686

Founded 1974

Branch Offices and Distributors:
Develcon Electronics, Warminster, PA (215)443-5450

Develnet supports multiple host environments as well as a variety of terminals, PCs and intelligent workstations. Network can be built on any medium backbone, including line-of-sight mediums such as infra-red and low power microwave antennas. Flexible mesh topology allows any of the traditional topologies, or combination thereof, to be implemented as the network requires. Service contracts, network installation, instruction on network operation, and network maintenance services available. First installed: 1984. Average number of stations per installation: 500.

• DEVELNET TECHNICAL CHARACTERISTICS

Transmission category: baseband, broadband

Transmission medium: twisted wire pair, coaxial cable, optical fiber, infrared, low-power microwave

Transmission speed: 24 Mbps throughput

Topology: "mesh" topology

Compatible operating systems: proprietary

Gateways: SNA/SDLC, Ethernet, X.25

Maximum number of workstations per node: 240

Maximum number of nodes: 64

Maximum distance between nodes: unlimited

Site of network logic: central controllers

• STANDARDS/PROTOCOLS SUPPORTED

Communications protocols: SNA/SDLC, synchronous, X.25, bisynchronous

DEVELCON ELECTRONICS LIMITED • LIL'NET

856 51st Street East
Saskatoon, Saskatchewan, S7K 5C7 CANADA
(306)933-3300; telex 074-2686

Founded 1974

Branch Offices and Distributors:
Develcon Electronics, Warminster, PA (215)443-5450

Lil'Net is a data network allowing users to share computers, modems and other resources. Actually a sophisticated data PBX, the system allows up to 512 communications channels. Operator console gives manager complete network control.

• LIL'NET TECHNICAL CHARACTERISTICS

Access method: CSMA

Transmission speed: 9.83 Mbps aggregate throughput; 19.2 Kbps maximum available for user connection

DIGITAL EQUIPMENT CORPORATION • DECNET

146 Main Street
Maynard, MA 01754
(617)897-5111; telex 948-457; TWX 710-347-0212; FAX 617-493-8780

Kenneth H. Olsen, President; Peter Smith, Vice President, Product Applications Marketing (PM); John Shields, Vice President, Sales and Service, International (MD)(PSC); Ron Payne, Corporate Purchasing Manager (PA)

Founded 1957; 91,000 employees

DECnet is a baseband bus which can support mainframes, minicomputers, dumb terminals, and PCs for industrial, office, laboratory, and campus applications. Supports all Ethernet devices. Service contracts, network installation and instruction on network operation available. First installed: 1975. Number installed: 11,000. Average number of stations per installation: over 150.

• DECNET TECHNICAL CHARACTERISTICS

Transmission category: baseband

Transmission medium: baseband coaxial cable, twisted wire pair, optical fiber

Transmission speed: 10 Mbps

Topology: bus

Access method: CSMA/CD

Compatible operating systems: VAX/VMS, RSX-11M, RSTs/E, RT-11, Ultrix 32, PRO-350 PDS

Gateways: SNA/SDLC, Ethernet, X.25, DDCMP

Maximum number of workstations per node: over 128

Maximum number of nodes: 1024

Maximum distance between nodes: 9000 feet

Means of host interconnection: bus interface cards, RS-232 terminal ports, dedicated routers and severs

• STANDARDS/PROTOCOLS SUPPORTED

Communications protocols: X.25, DDCMP, Ethernet

IEEE 802 standards: conforms to 802.3

ISO OSI Reference Model: conforms to levels 1 and 2 (Ethernet, X.25, DDCMP)

DIGITAL PRODUCTS INC. • NETCOMMANDER

108 Water Street
Watertown, MA 02172
(617)924-1680; telex 312-345

Cornelius Peterson, President; Bill Pratt (PM); Janis Harvey (PSC); Marilyn Peterson (PR); Walter Kopek (PA)

Founded 1974; 40 employees

NetCommander is a smart asychronous PC network sub-LAN that provides port selection/contention management, printer sharing, electronic mail, file transfer, and data collection. A 4-, 7- or 16-port stand-alone unit, the NetCommander can be expanded by connecting ports to trunk lines between units. Typical application environments include data communications, manufacturing, process control/laboratory, minicomputer center, PC/micro center, and local work cluster. Instruction on network operation and network maintenance services available. First installed: 1984. Number of networks installed: 4000. Average number of stations per installation: 15.

• NETCOMMANDER TECHNICAL CHARACTERISTICS

Transmission category: baseband

Transmission mode: full duplex

Transmission medium: twisted wire pair

Transmission speed: 19.2 Kbps maximum available for user connection

Topology: star

Access method: polling

Compatible operating systems: MS-DOS, CP/M, Unix

Gateways: SNA/SDLC, Ethernet, X.25, HDLC

Maximum number of worksations per node: 30

Maximum distance between nodes: 200 feet

Means of host interconnection: terminal ports

Site of network logic: central controllers

• STANDARDS/PROTOCOLS SUPPORTED

Communications protocols: asynchronous, RS-232

EQUINOX SYSTEMS INC. • DATA PBX

12041 Southwest 144th Street
Miami, FL 33186
(305)255-3500; telex 153-893

Bill Dambrackas, President; Doug Noble, Marketing Manager (PM); Robert Gintz, Director of Marketing (MD); Mike Vidal, Telemarketing (PSC); Cathy Baldwin, Manager of Market Communications (PR); Rick Malinski, Supervisor, Purchasing (PA)

Founded 1983; 125 employees

Branch Offices and Distributors:
> Beta Distributors Inc., Englewood, CO (303)779-3604; Data Processing Sciences, Cincinnati, OH (513)961-0776; System Technology Associates, Houston, TX (713)440-8340; Teltone Corporation, Kirkland, WA (205)827-9626; W.C. Koepf Associates, Chagrin Falls, OH (216)247-5129

Data PBX supports mainframes, minicomputers, microcomputers and dumb terminals in an industrial, office, laboratory, or campus environment. Provides port sharing, access management, network control, and keyboard-controlled switching between host computers. Supports all devices with asynchronous RS-232C interfaces. Service contracts, network installation, instruction on network operation, and network maintenance services available. First installed: 1984. Number installed: 700. Average number of stations per installation: 250.

• DATA PBX TECHNICAL CHARACTERISTICS

Transmission category: baseband

Transmission mode: full duplex

Transmission medium: twisted wire pair

Transmission speed: 12 Mbps backbone and burst; 19.2 Kbps maximum available for user connection

Topology: star

Access method: TDM

Compatible operating systems: all operating systems

Gateways: via other vendors' PADs and protocol converters

Maximum number of workstations per node: 1320

Maximum number of nodes: 360

Maximum distance between nodes: 5000

Means of host interconnection: multiplexed interfaces, terminal ports

Site of network logic: central controllers

• STANDARDS/PROTOCOLS SUPPORTED

Communications protocols: asynchronous, synchronous

EXCELAN INC. • EXOS

2180 Fortune Drive
San Jose, CA 95131
(408)434-2300; telex 176-610; FAX 408-434-2310

C. Richard Moore, President; Jay Weil, Director of Product Marketing (PM); Subhash Bal, Vice President, Marketing (MD); Sue Johnson, Inside Sales Manager (PSC); Ellen Hodges, Marketing Communications Assistant (PR); VG Gupta, Materials Director (PA)

Founded 1982; 125 employees

EXOS (Excelan Open Systems) Product Family combines EXOS 200 Series software-compatible Ethernet front-end processors with protocol software to develop a complete communication subsystem that links multiple computers into a single, intergrated, distributed system. Each node requires an EXOS 200 Series intelligent Ethernet front-end controller; peripherals are accessible through host nodes. All EXOS 200 Seies processors are software compatible with each other and run the EXOS 8010 TCP/IP Protocol Package. Minicomputers, PCs and any Ethernet-TCP/IP devices can be connected for use in an office, laboratory, campus, or engineering environment. Service contracts, instruction on network operation and network maintenance services available. First installed: 1983. Number installed: 10,000 nodes.

• EXOS TECHNICAL CHARACTERISTICS

Transmission category: baseband

Transmission medium: baseband coaxial cable

Transmission speed: 10 Mbps backbone

Topology: bus

Access method: CSMA/CD

Compatible operating systems: MS-DOS, Unix, VMS, MicroVMS, RSX, DOS, Xenix

Gateways: SNA/SDLC, Ethernet, X.25, HDLC, others per Ethernet-TCP/IP specification

Maximum number of nodes: dependent on Ethernet-IEEE 802.3 specification

Maximum distance between nodes: dependent on Ethernet-IEEE 802.3 specification

Means of host interconnection: intelligent Ethernet front-end controller

Network operation during backup: yes

Site of network logic: bus/network interface units

• STANDARDS/PROTOCOLS SUPPORTED

Communications protocols: TCP/IP

IEEE 802 standards: conforms to 802.3

ISO OSI Reference Model: conforms to layers 1-2 (Ethernet/IEEE 802.3), layers 3-4 (TCP/IP) and layers 5-7 (FTP, TELNET, SMTP)

FIBERCOM INC. • WHISPERNET

P.O. Box 11966
Roanoke, VA 24022-1966
(703)342-6700; telex 883-099; FAX 345-4729

Dr. Albert D. Bender, President; Joseph A. Wiencko Jr., Manager, Adanced Programs (PM); Jack B. Freeman, Vice President, Business Development (MD) (PR); Herb Hawthorne, Product Sales Manager (PSC); Rick Haynes, Purchasing Agent (PA)

Founded 1982; 112 employees

Branch Offices and Distributors:
Data Express, Woodland Hills, CA (818)710-0344; FiberCom Inc., Newport Beach, CA (714)644-2252; FiberCom Inc., Wellesley, MA (617)239-8077; FiberCom Inc., Alexandria, VA (703)684-4453; ISC Communication Systems Corporation, Ridgewood, NJ (201)445-5210

WhisperNet is a fiber optic Ethernet that meets or exceeds Ethernet (Version 2.0) specifications and IEEE 802.3 standards. Supports mainframes, minicomputers, PCs, dumb terminals, printers, modems, and other devices with standard interfaces. Designed for industrial, office, laboratory, campus, or military applications. Can support all Ethernet Version 2.0 and IEEE 802.3 compatible devices. Network is transparent to all operating systems and can support many types of microcomputer communications software, including Microstuf, Microsoft and Hayes. Also available in a counter-rotating ring configuration which allows redundancy in the event of cable breakage. Service contracts, network installation, instruction on network operation, and network maintenance services available. First installed: 1986.

• WHISPERNET TECHNICAL CHARACTERISTICS

Transmission category: baseband

Transmission mode: full duplex

Transmission medium: optical fiber

Transmission speed: 10 Mbps

Topology: ring

Access method: CSMA/CD

Compatible operating systems: MS-DOS, CP/M, Unix

Gateways: SNA/SDLC, Ethernet, X.25, HDLC

Maximum number of workstations per node: 64

Maximum number of nodes: 1024

Maximum distance between nodes: 12,000

Means of host interconnection: multiplexed interfaces, terminal ports, Ethernet port

Network server: multivendor file server

Maximum number of file servers: 1024

Site of network logic: bus/network interface units

• STANDARDS/PROTOCOLS SUPPORTED

Communications protocols: SNA/SDLC, bisynchronous, X.25, HDLC, asynchronous, RS-232, synchronous, RS-422, IEEE 488

IEEE 802 standards: conforms to 802.3

ISO OSI Reference Model: conforms to layers 1 and 2 (Ethernet/802.3) and layers 3-7 (XNS or TCP/IP)

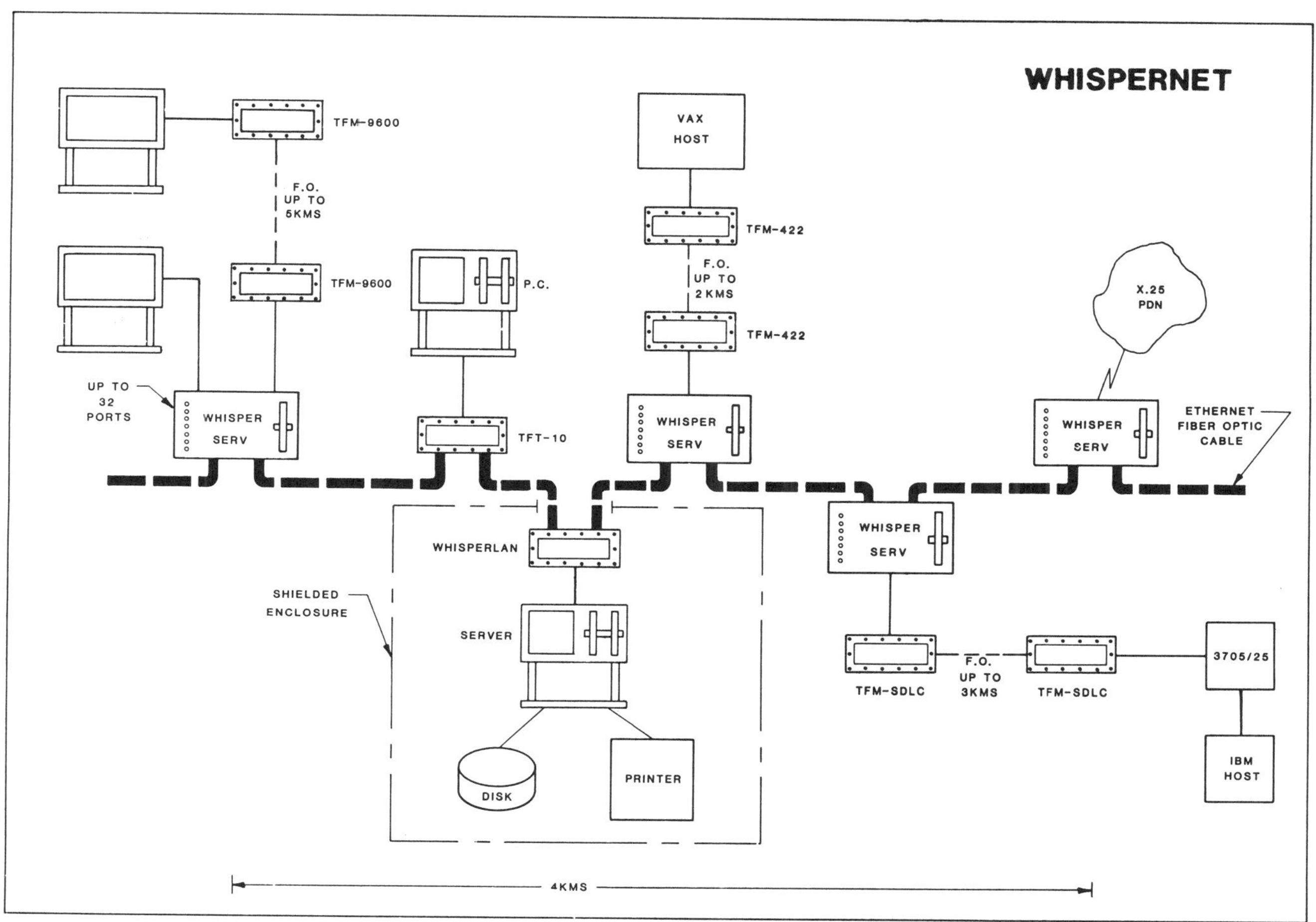

Figure 11

Courtesy FiberCom Inc.

FIBERCOM INC. • WHISPER RING

P.O. Box 11966
Roanoke, VA 24022-1966
(703)342-6700; telex 883-099; FAX 345-4729

Dr. Albert D. Bender, President; Mike Usberghi, Program Manager, Product Development (PM); Jack B. Freeman, Vice President, Business Develpment (MD)(PR); Herb Hawthorne, Product Sales Manager (PSC); Rick Haynes, Purchasing Agent (PA)

Founded 1982; 112 employees

Branch Offices and Distributors:
Data Express, Woodland Hills, CA (818)710-0344; FiberCom Inc., Newport Beach, CA (714)644-2252; FiberCom Inc., Wellesley, MA (617)239-8077; FiberCom Inc., Alexandria, VA (703)684-4453; ISC Communication Systems Corporation, Ridgewood, NJ (201)445-5210

WhisperRing is a multidrop token ring network. Supports mainframes, mincomputers, PCs, dumb terminals, printers, and any RS-422 devices. Designed for industrial, office, laboratory, campus, or military applications. Can also be configured in a point-to-point scheme. Software is resident in host and terminal. Service contracts, network installation, instruction on network operation, and network maintenance services available. First installed: 1986.

• WHISPER RING TECHNICAL CHARACTERISTICS

Transmission category: baseband

Transmission mode: full duplex

Transmission medium: optical fiber

Transmission speed: 2 Mbps backbone; 2 Mbps maximum available for user connection

Topology: ring, point-to-point

Access method: polling

Maximum number of workstations per node: 1

Maximum number of nodes: 16-100, depending upon configuration

Maximum distance between nodes: 6560 feet

Means of host interconnection: terminal ports, any RS-422 device

• STANDARDS/PROTOCOLS SUPPORTED

Communications protocols: RS-422

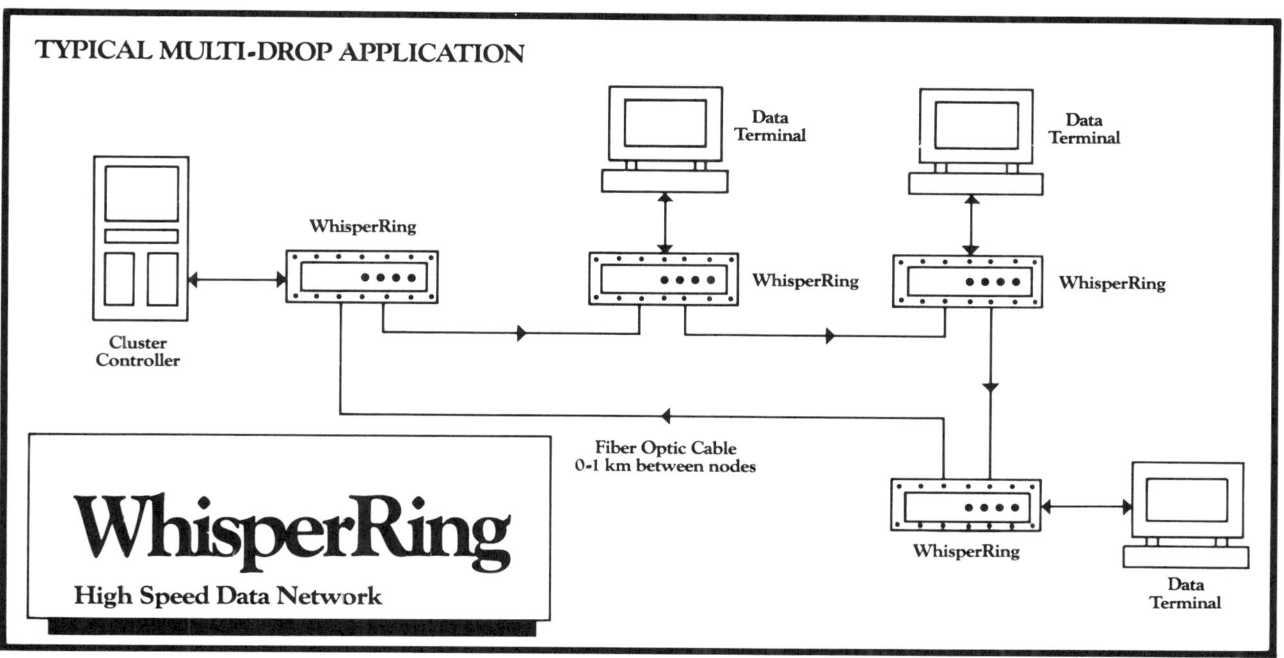

Figure 12

Courtesy FiberCom Inc.

Is your business in bypass? If so, do you know...

Who is using DTS? How is DTS being used? Where is DTS being used? Are you competitive? Are you reaching your markets? How can you tell?

Find out in The First DTS Market Survey

Volume I of the Bypass Opportunities Series

© 1986 by Phillips Publishing, Inc.

Bypassing the telephone company is blossoming into a $3 billion industry . . . 25% of all large businesses bypass and that number will rise to 50% by 1987. You, the bypass provider, have begun to target your market and scramble for a competitive position.

Now you can take advantage of a valuable new marketing information series that will help you thrive and survive in this competitive new bypass environment. Phillips Publishing, the leading publisher of telecommunications information, brings you the first in a comprehensive series of bypass surveys on digital termination systems (DTS) . . . private microwave . . . fiber optics, satellite . . . and more.

The *First DTS Market Survey* is a complete study of the DTS market. You find out *who* is using DTS. *How* DTS is being used. *Where* DTS is being used. *Why* DTS is being used.

THE FIRST DTS MARKET SURVEY—
A Valuable Marketing Tool

The *First DTS Market Survey* is your marketing information source on DTS bypass today. We've compiled, categorized, and published detailed marketing data from 70% of the DTS bypass providers currently on the air. What you get are 540 pages of figures you can put to good use in every phase of your marketing and strategic planning . . . broken down by company size and by SMSA and augmented by maps and charts.

Read them. Analyze them. And you'll come away with some startling insights into the nature of the bypass industry—and into the future. The *First DTS Market Survey* will help you:

- Discover profitable DTS market segments to target your sales efforts
- Identify potential DTS users by type of business
- Uncover lucrative service offerings
- Understand better the needs of your current DTS customers
- Assess strengths and growth potential of bypass industry
- Find out how much bypass diversification contributes to total revenues of DTS vendors
- Locate potentially profitable geographical areas of the country
- Understand the implications of potential FCC regulation on your market
- Discover lucrative DTS service mixes

No other volume gives you the figures you need to answer the toughest questions on how you're doing. And no other volume gives you figures you need to determine where you're going.

PHILLIPS PUBLISHING • 7811 MONTROSE ROAD • POTOMAC MARYLAND 20854

FIBERLAN INC.—A BELLSOUTH-SIECOR COMPANY • TDM RING
P.O. Box 12726
Research Triangle Park, NC 27709
(919)549-6551

F. Ray McDevitt, President; Nanita Vendrillo, Marketing Manager (MD)(PR)

TDM Ring is a voice/data transport system connecting multiple locations in a local communications network. Counter-rotating ring transmission links allow system to overcome failures at individual nodes or cable cuts without outage. Can be used as a PBX or LAN backbone for campus or high-rise applications.

- **TDM RING TECHNICAL CHARACTERISTICS**

Transmission category: broadband

Transmission medium: optical fiber

Topology: counter-rotating ring

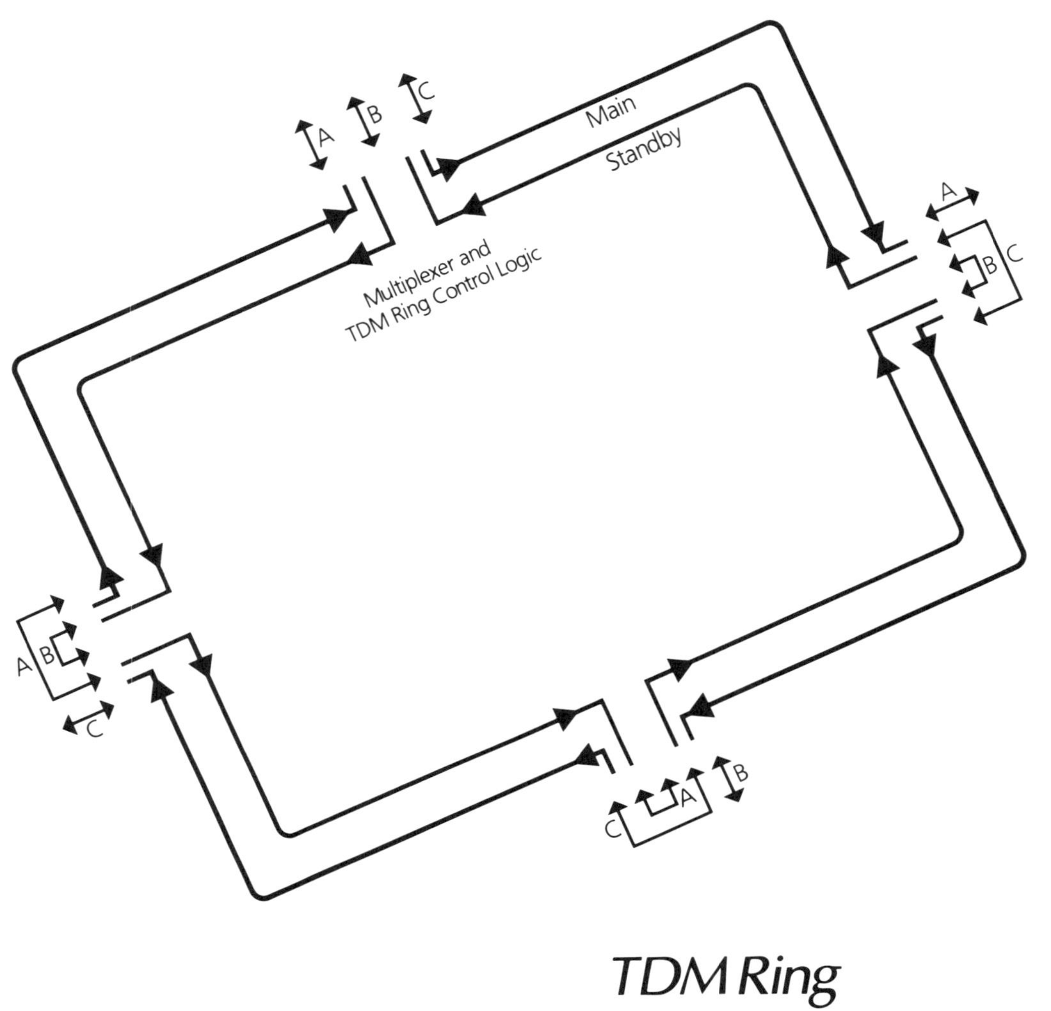

TDM Ring

Figure 13

Courtesy FiberLAN Inc. — A BellSouth-Siecor Company

FIBERLAN INC.—A BELLSOUTH-SIECOR COMPANY • NET 10

P.O. Box 12726
Research Triangle Park, NC 27709
(919)549-6551

F. Ray McDevitt, President; Nanita Vendrillo, Marketing Manager (MD)(PR)

NET 10 is a fiber optic Ethernet system that is completely compatible with coaxial Ethernets. System is connected through Fiber Optic Wiring Center using a star coupler, allowing the addition of nodes through a subordinate star coupler or by activating unused ports in the existing star. Can also serve as a fiber optic backbone for linking coaxial segments into a single network.

• NET 10 TECHNICAL CHARACTERISTICS

Transmission category: broadband

Transmission medium: optical fiber

Topology: star

Access method: CSMA/CD

• STANDARDS/PROTOCOLS SUPPORTED

IEEE 802 standards: conforms to 802.3

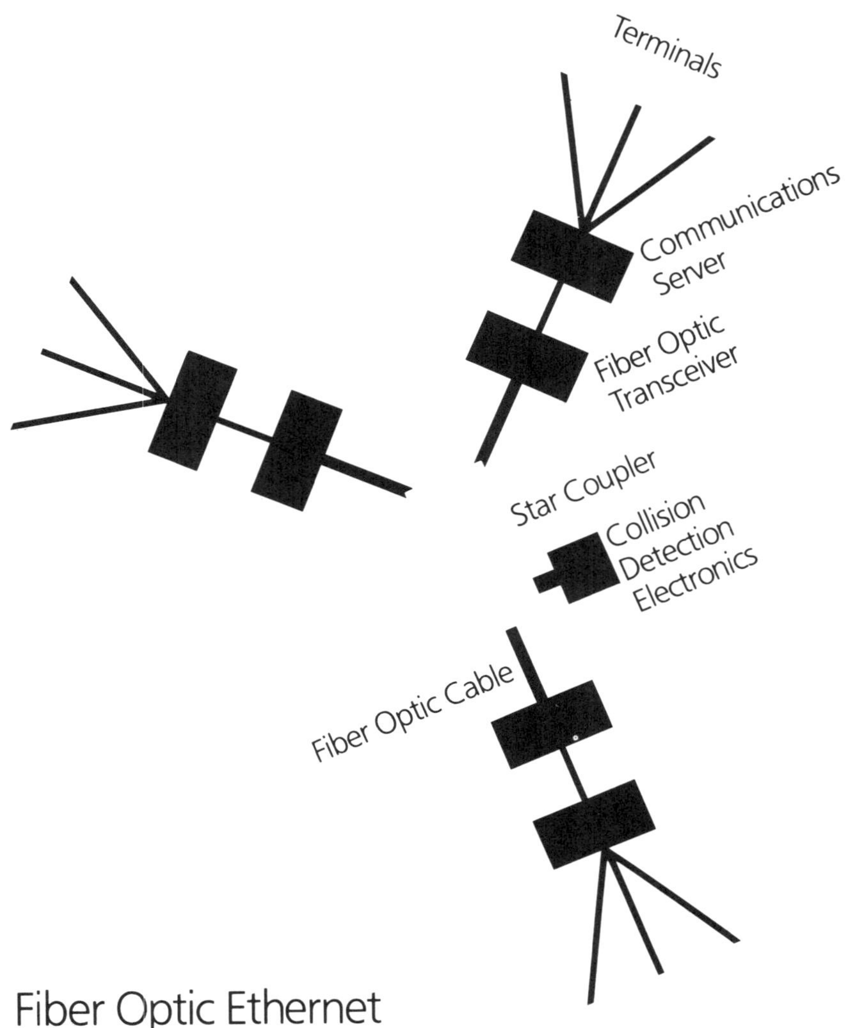

NET 10

Figure 14

Courtesy FiberLAN Inc. — A BellSouth-Siecor Company

FORTUNE SYSTEMS CORPORATION • FORTUNE:LINK

300 Harbor Boulevard
Belmont, CA 94002
(415)593-9000; telex 176-865

James Campbell, President; Bob Davis (PM); Paul Olin (PSC); Caroline Carnefix (PR); Jack Graham (PA)

Founded 1981; 260 employees

Fortune:Link is a combination of LAN hardware and software products that allow all FOR:PRO- and MS-DOS-based computers to communicate. Allows transparent sharing of information and peripherals, such as printers, tape drives and modems. Computer hubs are interconnected to form the network. Supports IBM PCs and compatibles. Suitable for use in professional offices and corporate departments.

• FORTUNE:LINK TECHNICAL CHARACTERISTICS

Transmission category: baseband

Transmission medium: baseband coaxial cable

Transmission speed: 2.5 Mbps

Topology: bus, tree

Access method: token passing

Compatible operating systems: MS-DOS, Unix, FOR:PRO

Maximum number of nodes: 255 computers

Maximum distance between nodes: 2000 feet

• STANDARDS/PROTOCOLS SUPPORTED

Communications protocols: XNS

FOX RESEARCH INC. • 10NET

7016 Corporate Way
Dayton, OH 45459
(512)433-2238; (800)358-1010; telex 650-207-9125; FAX 513-233-5805

Leo Kessler, President; Greg Goodall (MD); Dan Broussard (PSC); Sally Smith (PR); Gary Mercer (PA)

Branch Offices and Distributors:
ACS Telecomp, Lomita, CA (213)325-3055; System Solutions, Evanston, IL (312)864-2283; AT&D, Austin, TX (512)478-5795; Vitronix, Westboro, MA (617)366-1144; Computeach, Washington, DC (202)861-2602

10Net is an office PC LAN tat can support any PC-attachable serial, parallel or disk devices. Requires no dedicated server. Print spooling, electronic mail, interstation communication, electronic calendar, concurrency control, and electronic news included. Network supports all IBM-compatible PCs and IBM ATs. Network-compatible software vendors include Ryan-McFarland, Lotus and Ashton-Tate. 10-NET Training Program, an audio/visual aid for installing, configuring and maintaining the network, is also available. First installed:1984. Number installed: 7000. Average number of stations per installation: 7.

• 10NET TECHNICAL CHARACTERISTICS

Transmission category: baseband

Transmission medium: twisted wire pair

Transmission speed: 1 Mbps maximum available for user connection

Topology: bus

Access method: CSMA/CA

Compatible operating systems: MS-DOS

Gateways: SNA/SDLC, RS-232

Maximum number of workstations per node: 1

Maximum number of nodes: 32,000

Maximum distance between nodes: 10,000

Network server: multivendor file server; proprietary file server

Maximum number of file servers: unlimited

Disk backup: whole disk; partial disk

Network operation during backup: yes

Site of network logic: terminal equipment and bus/network interface units

• STANDARDS/PROTOCOLS SUPPORTED

Communications protocols: SNA/SDLC, bisynchronous, RS-232, asynchronous, synchronous

IEEE 802 standards: conforms to 802.3

ISO OSI Reference Model: conforms to levels 1 and 2 (802.3) and level 6 (DOS 2.0, 31, 3.2)

GANDALF DATA INC. • PACX 2000
1020 South Noel Avenue
Wheeling, IL 60090
(312)459-6630; TWX 910-651-4951

Alan Melkerson, President; Edward Milbury (PM); Howard Gunn (MD); Michael Salustri (PSC); Frank Connell (PA)

Founded 1970; over 1000 employees

Branch Offices and Distributors:
Gandalf Data Inc., Long Beach, CA (213)424-2258; Gandalf Data Inc., Atlanta, GA (404)447-5425; Gandalf Data Inc., Boston, MA (617)329-7630; Gandalf Data Inc., Dallas, TX (214)980-2690; Gandalf Data Inc., Washington, DC (301)421-1212

PACX 2000 is a floppy disk-based digital PBX that serves as the main data networking hub for interconnecting personal computers and terminals with a variety of data information resources. Connects mainframes, minicomputers and dumb terminals for industrial, office, laboratory, or campus applications. Service contracts, network installation and instruction on network operation available. First installed: 1971. Number installed: over 2000. Average numer of stations per installation: 300.

• PACX 2000 TECHNICAL CHARACTERISTICS

Transmission category: baseband, broadband

Transmission medium: baseband coaxial cable, broadband coaxial cable, twisted wire pair, optical fiber, microwave

Transmission speed: 19.2 Kbps asynchronous data rate

Topology: ring, star, tree

Gateways: SNA/SDLC, X.25, T1, bisynchronous, dial network

Maximum number of workstations per node: 896

Maximum number of nodes: 32

Maximum distance between nodes: unlimited

Means of host interconnection: RS-232 terminal ports, T-2 multiplexers, modems, statistical multiplexers, gateways

• STANDARDS/PROTOCOLS SUPPORTED

Communications protocols: SNA/SDLC, X.25, bisynchronous

IEEE 802 standards: does not conform

GATEWAY COMMUNICATIONS INC. • G/NET

16782 Redhill Avenue
Irvine, CA 92714
(714)261-0762; telex 509-264 GATEWAY COMM; FAX 714-261-6569

David S. McMaster, President (MD); Larry J. Stephenson, Executive Vice President (PM); Burt R. Ott, National Sales Manager (PSC); Mitch Barrie, Marketing Communications (PR); Dan Finley, Manager Manufacturing (PA)

Founded 1981; 35 employees

G/Net features support of both the IBM NETBIOS and NetWare network file server standards, coprocessor board at each workstation for fast network access, a piggyback diskless boot card for remote reset capabilities, a local bridge module linking G/Nets to each other, and a number of gateways to wide area networks and mainframe hosts. A baseband linear bus, G/Net is capable of linking mainframes, minicomputers, PCs, tape drives, printers, and disk subsystems in an industrial, office, laboratory, or campus environment. G/Net can also support dot-matrix and laser printers. Operates NetWare family of operating systems. Compatible device vendors include IBM, AT&T, Sperry, Xerox, and Zenith. Network installation and instruction on network operation available. First installed: 1983. Number installed: 10,000. Average number of stations per installation: 6.

• G/NET TECHNICAL CHARACTERISTICS

Transmission category: baseband

Transmission mode: half duplex

Transmission medium: baseband coaxial cable

Transmission speed: 1.43 Mbps, burst

Topology: bus

Access method: CSMA/CD, includes collision avoidance, positive acknowledgment, error correction, and detection

Compatible operating systems: MS/DOS, NetWare

Gateways: SNA/SDLC, asynchronous

Maximum number of workstations per node: 1

Maximum number of nodes: 255

Maximum distance between nodes: 4000 feet

Means of host interconnection: STD communication lines (RS-232)

Network server: multivendor file server (hardware); proprietary file server (software)

Maximum number of file servers: 64 with Advanced NetWare 286/G

Disk backup: varies with configuration

Network operation during backup: yes

Site of network logic: bus/network interface units

• STANDARDS/PROTOCOLS SUPPORTED

Communications protocols: SNA/SDLC, X.25, RS-232, asynchronous

ISO OSI Reference Model: conforms to layers 2 (customized HDLC)-5

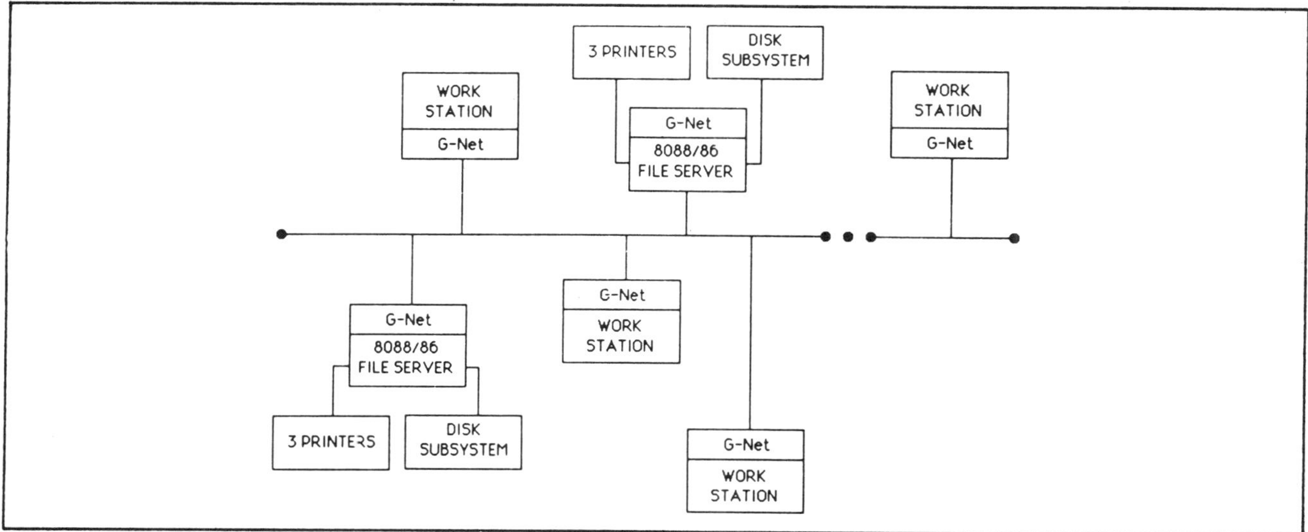

Sample G-Net Topology

Figure 15

Courtesy Novell Inc.

HANCOCK ELECTRONICS CORPORATION • CINCHNET

135 King Street, P.O. Box 557
Cohasset, MA 02025
(617)383-6610

Joyce Sturdy, President; David Sturdy (PM)(PA); Paula Dodrill (PSC)

10 employees

Cinchnet is an industrial network system providing access to other systems via RS-232 interface. First installed: 1982. Number installed: 50-100. Average number of stations per installation: 5 controllers.

• CINCHNET TECHNICAL CHARACTERISTICS

Transmission category: baseband

Transmission medium: twisted wire pair

Topology: bus

Access method: CSMA/CD

Maximum number of nodes: 125

HEWLETT-PACKARD • HP 9000 LAN

3000 Hanover Street
Palo Alto, CA 94304
(800)547-3400

John A. Young, President; Robert L. Puette, Vice President, Marketing (MD); Jim Arthur, Vice President, Sales and Director of U.S. Field Operations (PSC); David Kirby, Director of Public Relations (PR); Pete Hamilton, Marketing Manager (PA)

Founded 1939; 82,000 employees

HP 9000 is a high-performance LAN for HP 9000 Series 200/300/500 HP-UX systems supporting either IEEE 802.3 or Ethernet standards. Network capabilities include network file transfer, remote file access, link level access, remote process management, and interprocess communication.

• HP 9000 LAN TECHNICAL CHARACTERISTICS

Transmission category: baseband

Transmission medium: ThinLAN (RG58) or BackboneLAN cable

Transmission speed: 10 Mbps

• STANDARDS PROTOCOLS SUPPORTED

IEEE 802 standards: conforms to 802.3

ISO OSI Reference Model: conforms to layer 2 (LLA) and layer 7 (NFT, RFA, RPM, IPC)

IDEASSOCIATES INC. • IDEANET

29 Dunham Road
Billerica, MA 01821
(617)663-6878; telex 497-9780

Gautam Gupta, President; Nora Feldman Gildea, Director of Marketing (MD); James Bender, Vice President, Sales (PSC); Randi Cadigan, Marketing Communications Manager (PR)

Founded 1982; over 100 employees

IDEAnet is a combined hardware/software pckage that can link up to 20 users over coaxial cable. Compatible with the IBM PC, XT, AT, or portable. Advanced software features allow password protection, print spooling, file locking, and file sharing.

INFOTRON SYSTEMS CORPORATION • INX4400 INTELLIGENT NETWORK EXCHANGE

9 North Olney Avenue, Cherry Hill Industrial Center
Cherry Hill, NJ 08003
(609)424-9400; (800)257-8352; TWX 710-940-1247

James C. Hahn, President; John Reedich (PM); Ed DiMingo (MD); Steve Stewart, Vice President, Sales (PSC); Barry Cress (PR); Jack Campbell (PA)

Founded 1968; 1000 employees

INX4400 Intelligent Network Exchange is a disk-based electronic switching system that connects and controls access to data processing resources. The INX4400 may operate as a stand-alone system in a LAN environment or as a network control center monitoring the activity of devices connected to the INX4400. Devices can be connected to remote slaves in a ring network with segments as long as 2000 meters.

• INX4400 INTELLIGENT NETWORK EXCHANGE TECHNICAL CHARACTERISTICS

Transmission category: baseband, broadband

Transmission medium: twisted wire pair, optical fiber

Transmission speed: 35 Mbps

Topology: ring, bus

Infotron Systems INX4400 Intelligent Network Exchange

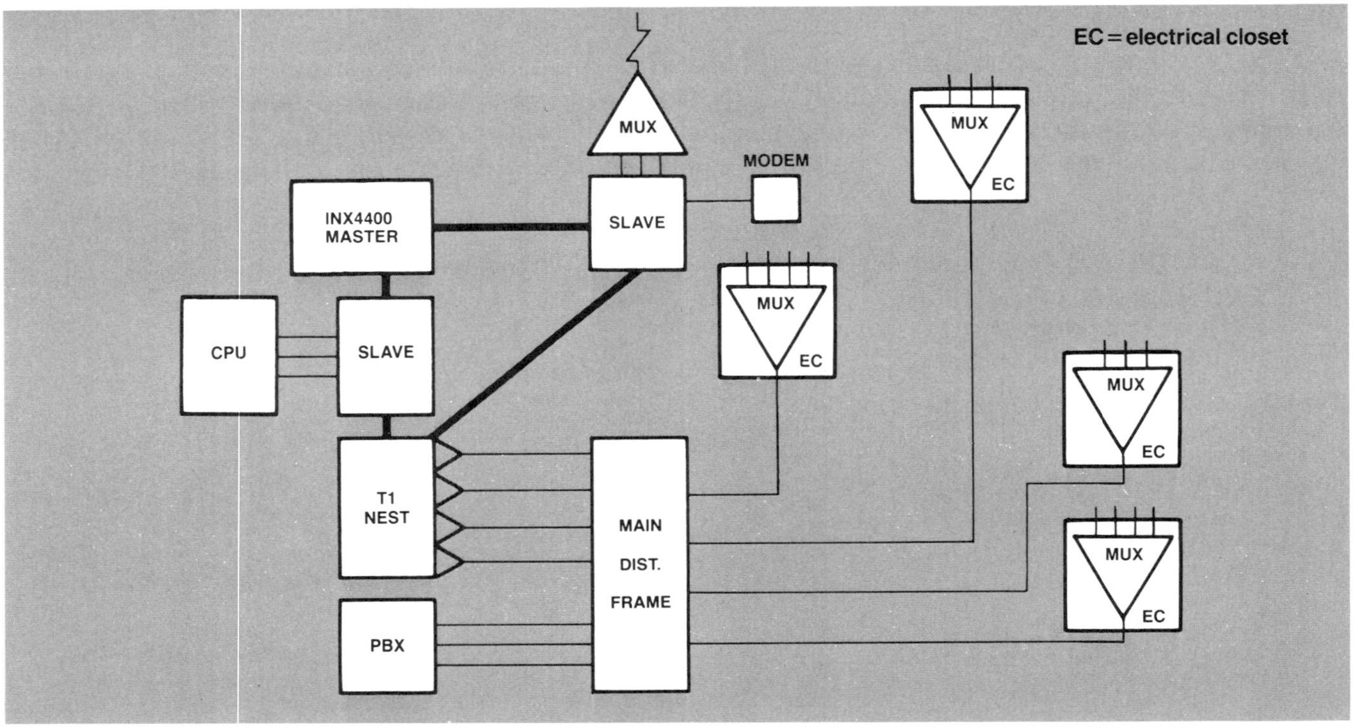

Figure 16

Courtesy Infotron Systems

INTERNATIONAL BUSINESS MACHINES—INFORMATION SYSTEMS GROUP o TOKEN-RING NETWORK

1 Corporate Park, 900 King Street
Rye Brook, NY 10573
(914)397-7806

John Akers, President; Richard H. Goldberg, Group Director, Telecommunications Marketing (MD)

Token-Ring Network is designed to connect information processing equipment within a building or in a campus environment. Will support IBM PC, XT, AT, and portable PC, printers, System/36 minicomputers, and System/370 mainframes (early 1987). May also be implemented using unshielded telephone twisted pair wiring. Connects up to 260 PCs using data-grade cable and up to 72 PCs with unshielded telephone cable. Ring-to-ring bridge can join multiple token rings to appear as a single network. First introduced: 1985.

- **TOKEN-RINGNETWORK TECHNICAL CHARACTERISTICS**

Transmission category: baseband

Transmission medium: twisted wire pair

Transmission speed: 4 Mbps

Topology: ring

Access method: token passing

Maximum distance between nodes: 2 kilometers network length

- **STANDARDS/PROTOCOLS SUPPORTED**

IEEE 802 standards: conforms to 802.5

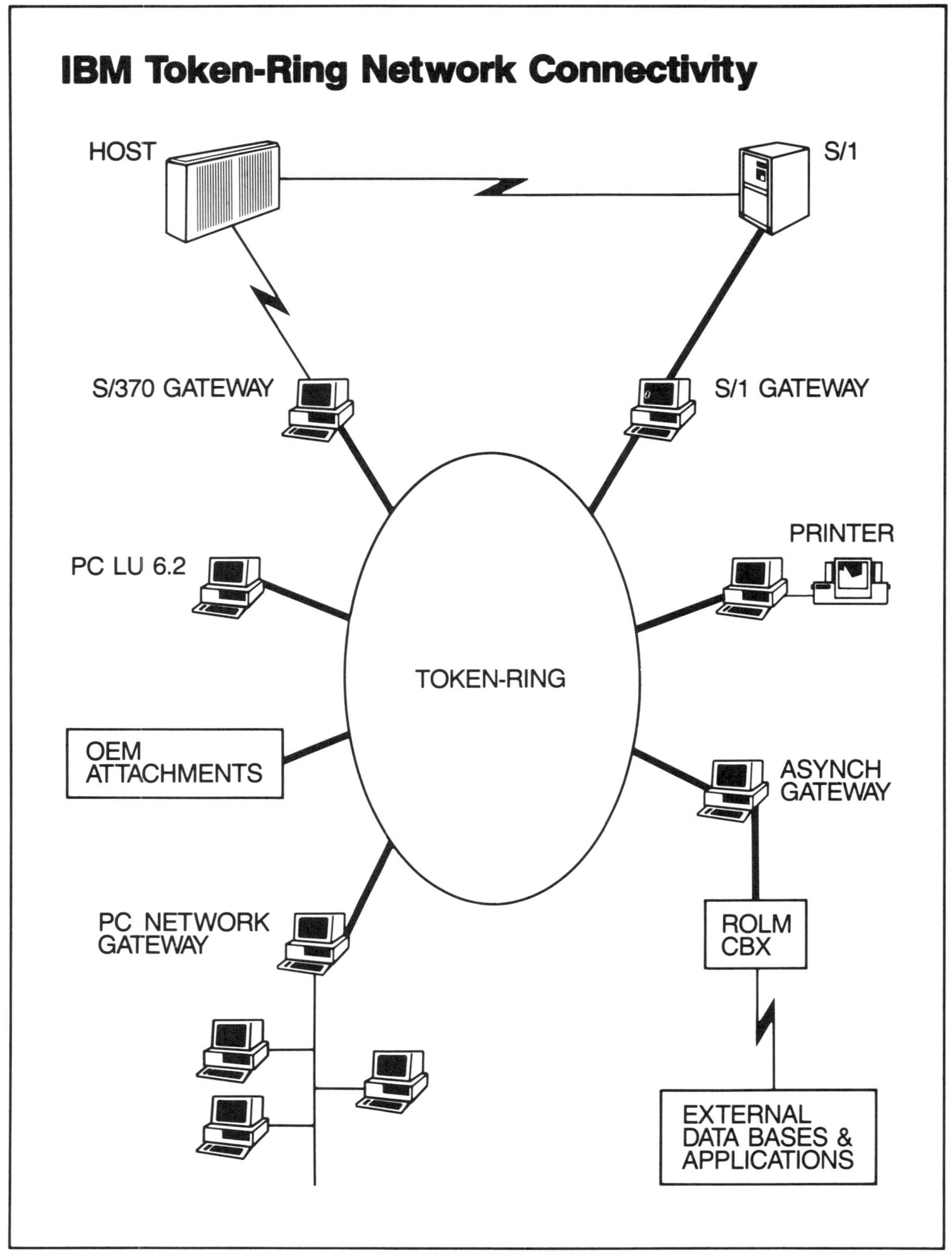

Figure 17

Courtesy IBM Corporation

INTERNATIONAL BUSINESS MACHINES—INFORMATION SYSTEMS GROUP • PC NETWORK

1 Corporate Park, 900 King Street
Rye Brook, NY 10573
(914)397-7806

John Akers, President; Richard H. Goldberg, Group Director, Telecommunications Marketing (MD)

PC Network is a hardware/software package linking up to 72 IBM PCs, XTs, AT, and portable PCs. Supports printers and fixed disk storage. Translator unit converts signals from transmit to receive frequencies and may attach to as many as eight PCs. Intended for applications requiring a peer-to-peer communications network among IBM PCs in a workgroup, department or small business.

• PC NETWORK TECHNICAL CHARACTERISTICS

Transmission category: broadband

Transmission medium: broadband coaxial cable

Topology: bus

Access method: CSMA/CD

Compatible operating systems: PC-DOS 3.1

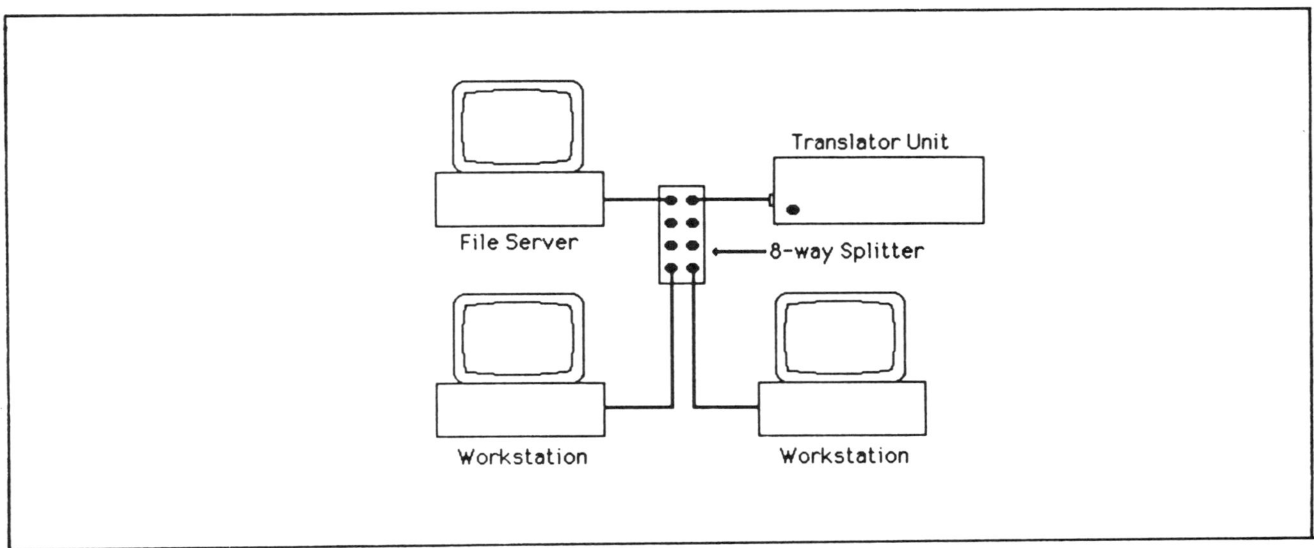

Sample IBM PC Network Topology

Figure 18

Courtesy Novell Inc.

INTERNATIONAL ELECTRONICS • M-NET

1518 East Broadway
Tuscon, AZ 85719
(602)622-7707; telex 383-754

Daniel J. Vance, President (PR); William Allaire, Vice President, Product Development (PM); Girish V. Shah, Vice President, Sales and Marketing (MD)(PSC); James J. Sheridan, Vice President, Operations (PA)

Founded 1980; 15 employees

M-Net is a networking solution for the integrated circuits manufacturer. M-Net device adapters allow the inclusion of all standard equipment used in the manufacturing and testing of ICs. Area host and LAN interfaces are connected using International Electronics' high-speed communications protocol, implemented on the IEEE 488 Bus (GPIB). Network-compatible software includes DECnet, RS/1, Datatrieve, Enhansys, Promis, and Comet. First installed: 1982. Average number of stations per installation: 15.

• M-NET TECHNICAL CHARACTERISTICS

Transmission category: baseband

Transmission mode: half duplex

Transmission medium: IEEE 488 baseband coaxial cable, twisted wire pair

Transmission speed: 250 maximum available for user connection; 250 Mbps burst

Topology: bus

Access method: polling

Maximum number of nodes: 60 per host

Maximum distance between nodes: unlimited

Means of host interconnection: DECnet

Network server: Proprietary file server

Maximum number of file servers: 1

Disk backup: whole disk, partial disk

Network operation during backup: yes

Site of network logic: bus/network interface units, central controllers

• STANDARDS/PROTOCOLS SUPPORTED

Communications protocols: IEEE 488

IEEE 802 standards: conforms to IEEE 488

ISO OSI Reference Model: conforms to layer 1 (IEEE 488)

KEE INC. • KEE NET

10727 Tucker Street
Beltsville, MD 20705
(301)595-4700; FAX 301-937-5205

Rool Matheson, President; Joe Greaney (PM); Pat Kelly (MD); Daniel Brigati (PSC); Kathleen Jausen (PR); Tom Blasek (PA)

Founded 1968; 75 employees

Kee Net is a multipurpose communications system that ties together mainframes, minicomputers, PCs, and dumb terminals for use in an industrial, office, laboratory, campus, or hospital environment. System also supports printers, modems and security devices. Service contracts, network installation, instruction on network operation, and network maintenance services available. First installed: 1980. Number installed: over 20. Average number of stations per installation: 300.

• KEE NET TECHNICAL CHARACTERISTICS

Transmission category: broadband

Transmission mode: full duplex

Transmission medium: broadband coaxial cable

Transmission speed: 2 Mbps backbone; 56 Kpbs maximum available for user connection

Topology: bus, tree

Access method: CSMA

Compatible operating systems: MS-DOS, Unix

Gateways: Ethernet, X.25, HDLC

Maximum number of workstations per node: 32

Maxium number of nodes: over 1000

Maximum distance between nodes: over 1000

Means of host interconnection: multiplexed interfaces, terminal ports

Network operation during backup: yes

Site of network logic: bus/network interface units

• STANDARDS/PROTOCOLS SUPPORTED

Communications protocols: SNA/SDLC, bisynchronous, X.25, HDLC, asynchronous, RS-232, synchronous

IEEE 802 standards: conforms to 802.2

ISO OSI Reference Model: conforms to layers 1-3

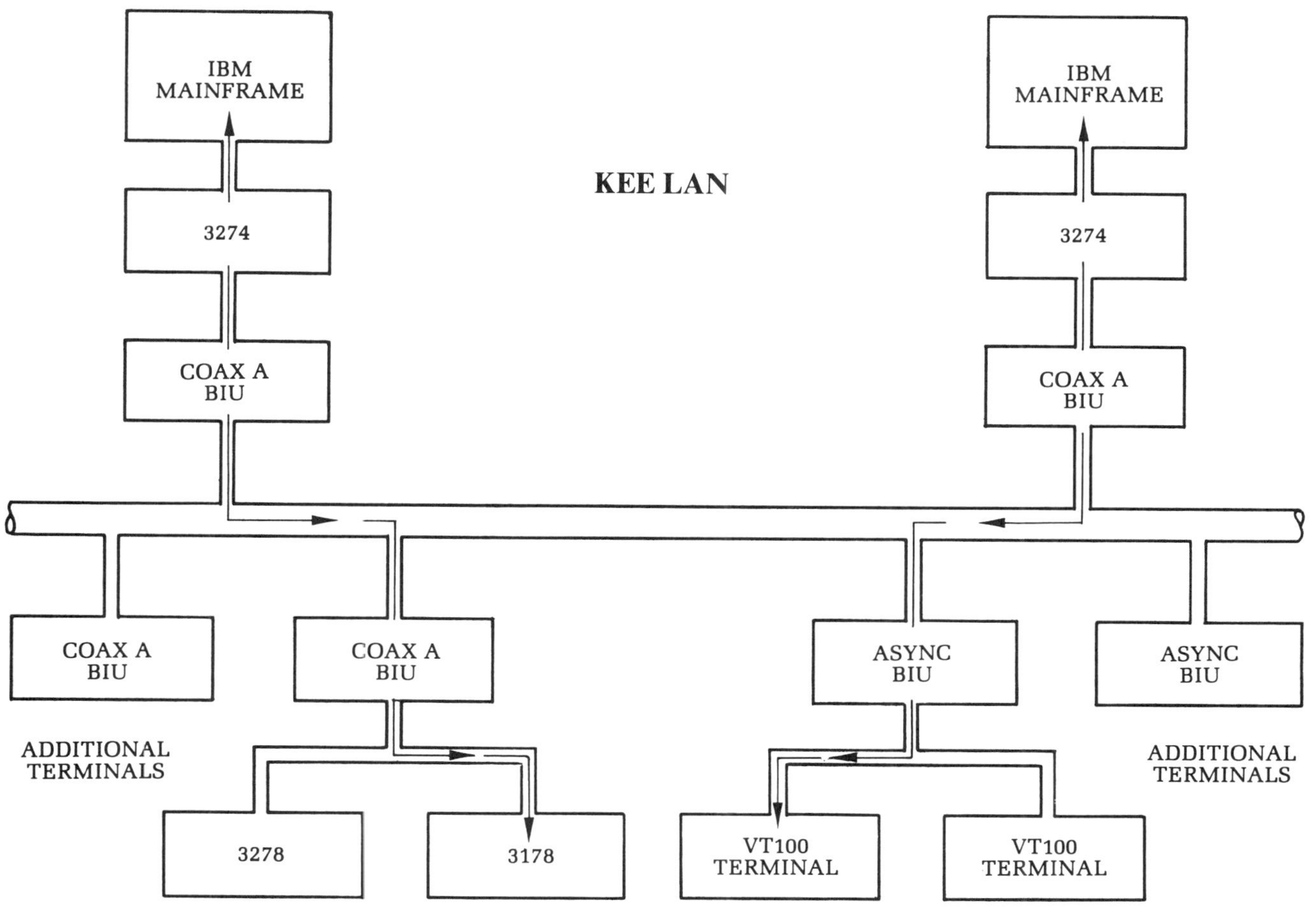

Figure 19

Courtesy KEE Inc.

KIMTRON • K-NET

1705 Junction Court, Building 160
San Jose, CA 95112
(408)436-6550; TWX 910-388-0237; FAX (408)436-1380

John Kim, President; Robert David, Director of Marketing (MD)(PSC)(PR); Harry Chai (PA)

Founded 1979; 60 employees

K-Net is an IBM compatible office PC network bus supporting up to 255 addressable users. Features include electronic mail, network data management and print spooling. Network is NETBIOS compatible. Service contracts and instruction on network operation available.

• K-NET TECHNICAL CHARACTERISTICS

Transmission category: baseband

Transmission medium: twisted wire pair

Transmission speed: 1 mbps backbone and maximum available for user connection

Topology: bus

Access method: CSMA, CSMA/CD

Compatible operating systems: PC-DOS, MS/DOS 2.0 and higher

Maximum distance between nodes: 4000 feet total network diameter

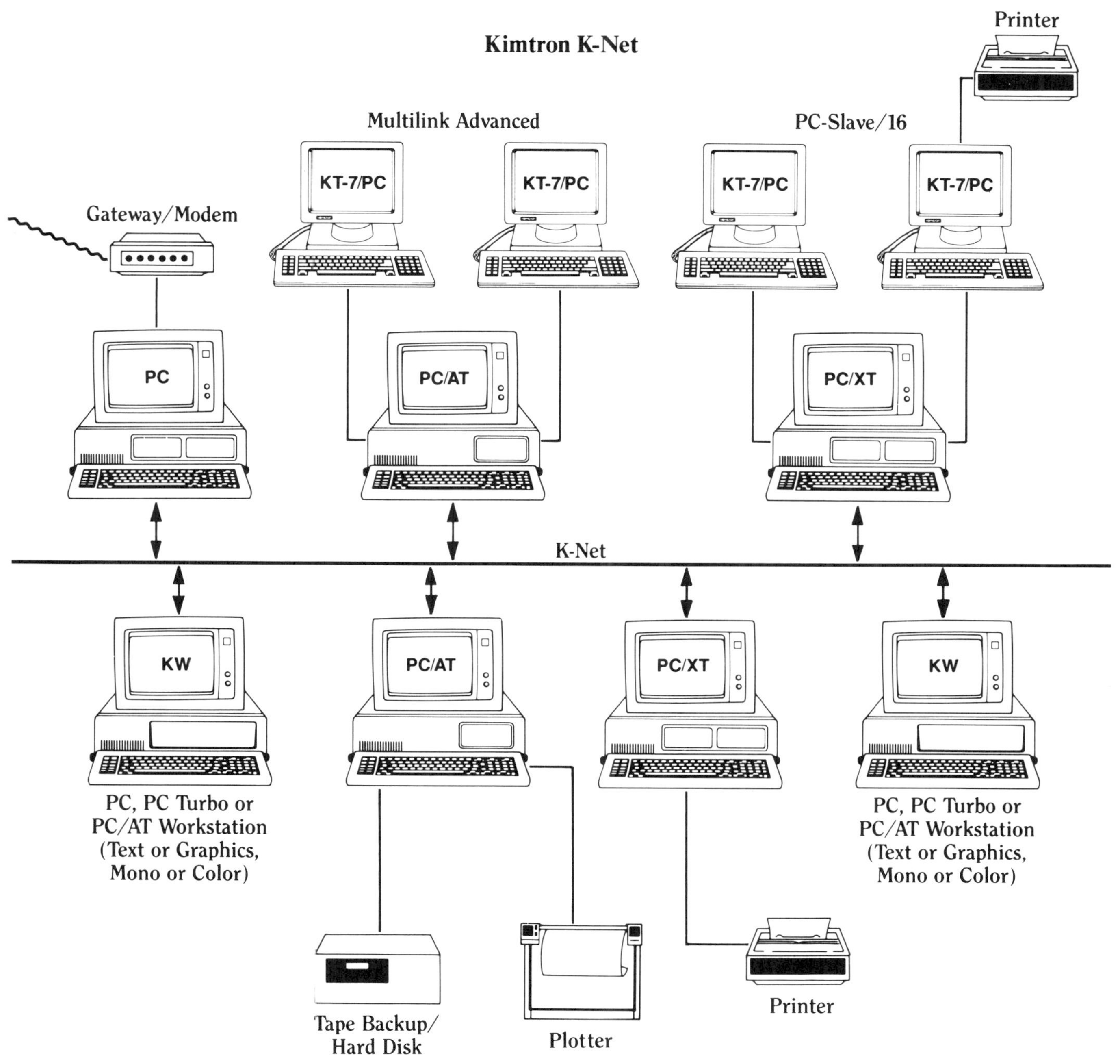

Figure 20

Courtesy Kimtron

LAN-TECH • ELAN
4501 North 22nd Street, Suite 220
Phoenix, AZ 85016
(602)955-7746

Randy Vogel, President; Bob Gabriel (PM)(MD)(SC)(PR)(PA)

5 employees

ELAN is an 880 Kbps PC LAN for educational applications. Network supports floppy drives, Xebec hard disks, modems, and printers. Service contracts, network installation, instruction on network operation, and network maintenance services available. First installed: 1983. Number installed: 400. Average number of stations per installation: 20.

• ELAN TECHNICAL CHARACTERISTICS

Transmission category: baseband

Transmission mode: half duplex

Transmission medium: twisted wire pair

Transmission speed: 880 Kbps burst

Topology: bus

Access method: CSMA/CA

Compatible operating systems: AppleDOS, ProDOS

Maximum number of workstations per node: 1

Maximum number of nodes: 128

Maximum distance between nodes: 1000 feet overall

Means of host interconnection: multiplexed interfaces

Network server: multivendor file server

Maximum number of file servers: 1

Disk backup: whole disk

Network operation during backup: no

Site of network logic: terminal equipment

• STANDARDS/PROTOCOLS SUPPORTED

Communications protocols: asynchronous

M/A-COM TELECOMMUNICATIONS INC. • IDX 3000 LOCAL COMMUNICATION NETWORK

10453 Roselle Street
San Diego, CA 92121
(619)453-7007; TWX 910-337-1277; FAX 619-457-0579

Judy Wheatley, Product Manager (PM); Robert A. Berlin, Director of Marketing (MD)(PSC); Julie Corrello Hotz, Marketing Specialist (PR)

Founded 1967; 1500 employees

The IDX 3000 Local Communication Network is a baseband star designed for industrial, office, laboratory, or campus use. Connects minicomputers, PCs, dumb terminals, and other peripherals, including any RS-232C devices. Service contracts, network installation, instruction on network operation, and network maintenance services available. First installed: 1982. Number installed: over 50. Average number of stations per installation: 1536.

• IDX 3000 LOCAL COMMUNICATION NETWORK TECHNICAL CHARACTERISTICS

Transmission category: baseband

Transmission mode: full duplex

Transmission medium: twisted wire pair

Transmission speed: 393 Mbps aggregate throughput

Topology: star

Compatible operating systems: Unix

Gateways: Ethernet, X.25

Maximum number of workstations per node: 3072

Maximum number of nodes: 1

Maximum distance between nodes: 5000

Means of host interconnection: multiplexed interfaces

Disk backup: whole disk

Network operation during backup: yes

Site of network logic: central controllers

• STANDARDS/PROTOCOLS SUPPORTED

Communications potocols: asynchronous, RS-232

MAGNOLIA MICROSYSTEMS INC. • MAGNET

2820 Thorndyke Avenue West
Seattle, WA 98199
(206)285-7266

Brad Gjerding (PM); Steve Posey, Marketing Manager (MD)

Founded 1978

MAGNet allows 8- and 16-bit microcomputers from different manufacturers to share networked resources, such as data files and printers. Designed for office, laboratory or campus use. Supports PC-bus computers, S100 bus computers and RS-232 terminals and printers. Service contracts, network installation, instruction on network operation, and network maintenance services available. First installed: 1981. Average number of stations per installation: 10.

• MAGNET TECHNICAL CHARACTERISTICS

Transmission category: baseband

Transmission mode: full duplex

Transmission medium: twisted wire pair

Transmission speed: 500 Kbps backbone

Topology: bus

Access method: token passing

Compatible operating systems: MS-DOS, CP/M

Maximum number of workstations per node: 1

Maxium number of nodes: 64

Maximum distance between nodes: 4000

Means of host interconnection: board

Network server: multivendor file server; proprietary file server

Maximum number of file servers: 63

Disk backup: partial disk

Network operation during backup: yes

Site of network logic: bus/network interface units

• STANDARDS/PROTOCOLS SUPPORTED

ISO OSI Reference Model: conforms to layer 7 (MS-DOS and CP/M)

METAPATH INC. • METAPATH DISTRIBUTED DATA SWITCH

222 Lincoln Centre Drive
Foster City, CA 94404
(415)345-7832; telex 280-2598

Bob Koontz, President; Gordon Orsborn (PM)(PSC)(PR); Robert Bauman (MD); Eli Torat (PA)

Founded 1983; 25 employees

Metapath Distributed Data Switch connects mainframes, minicomputers, PCs, and dumb terminals for industrial, office, laboratory, or campus use. Service contracts, network installation, instruction on network operation, and network maintenance services available.

• METAPATH DISTRIBUTED DATA SWITCH TECHNICAL CHARACTERISTICS

Transmission category: baseband with broadband option

Transmission medium: baseband coaxial cable

Transmission speed: 2 Mbps backbone; 20 Kbps maximum available for user connection and burst

Topology: bus

Access method: proprietary (similar to slotted ring)

Compatible operating systems: MS-DOS, CP/M, Unix

MODULAR COMPUTER SYSTEMS INC. (MODCOMP) • MAXNET

1650 West McNab Road
Fort Lauderdale, FL 33310
(305)974-1380; TWX 510-956-9414; FAX 305-977-1501

Gabriel Rosica, President; Jeanne Senatore, Senior Product Marketing Manager (PM)(MD)(PSC); Bob Turkovic, Manager, Public Relations (PR); Joe Ottaviano, Manager, Purchasing (PA)

Founded 1970; 850 employees

Branch Offices and Distributors:
  Modular Computer Systems Inc., Norcross, GA (404)662-8988; Modular Computer Systems Inc., Fort Lauderdale, FL (305)974-1380; Modular Computer Systems Inc., San Jose, CA (408)947-7440; Modular Computer Systems Inc., Houston, TX (713)333-3250; Modular Computer Systems Inc., Vienna, VA (703)442-8222

Maxnet is a broadband star network that connects minicomputers, printers, disk drives, and terminals in an industrial, laboratory or campus environment. Service contracts, network installation, instruction on network operation, and network maintenance services available. First installed: 1978. Number installed: 200. Average number of stations per installation: 20.

• MAXNET TECHNICAL CHARACTERISTICS

Transmission category: broadband

Transmission mode: full duplex

Transmission medium: broadband coaxial cable

Transmission speed: 56 Kbps backbone; 19.2 Kbps maximum available for user connection

Topology: star

Access method: polling

Compatible operating systems: Maxnet OS, MAX

Gateways: HDLC

Maximum number of workstations per node: 20

Maximum number of nodes: 100

Maximum distance between nodes: 5000 feet

Means of host interconnection: multiplexed interfaces

Network server: proprietary file server

Maximum number of file servers: 20

Disk backup: whole disk

Network operation during backup: yes

Site of network logic: central controllers

• STANDARDS/PROTOCOLS SUPPORTED

Communications protocols: bisynchronous, asynchronous, HDLC

IEEE 802 standards: does not conform

ISO OSI Reference Model: conforms to layer 1 (RS-232) and layer 2 (HDLC)

MOLECULAR COMPUTER • SYSTEM 16/300

1983 Concourse Drive
San Jose, CA 95131
(408)434-9500; telex 499-0791; FAX 408-434-9531

Frank Zurcher, President; Bill Heil (PM)(PR); Corinne Moore (MD); Barry Dearborn (PSC)

Founded 1981; 150 employees

Branch Offices and Distributors:
Crystal Computers, Lenexa, KS (913)541-1711; Cyber/Source, Southfield, MI (313)353-8660; Digital Solutions, Marietta, GA (404)955-4488; Emeritus, Fresno, CA (209)251-3525; Innes Systems, New York, NY (212)679-6180

System 16/300 is a PC LAN able to connect up to 16 network servers. Design to allow virtually unlimited growth in a typical office environment without the loss of power, storage or flexible options and upgrades. Network also supports IBM ATs and compatibles and up to 5 printers. Carries 7 RS-232 ports, which can be used to connect printers or modems. Compatible vendors: IBM, Compaq, Corona, Wyse, Epson, IDM, Texas Instruments, Zenith, and TeleVideo. Service contracts, network installation, instruction on network operation, and network maintenance services available. First installed: 1985. Number installed: 350. Average number of stations per installation: 6.

• SYSTEM 16/300 TECHNICAL CHARACTERISTICS

Transmission category: baseband

Transmission mode: full duplex

Transmission medium: twisted wire pair

Transmission speed: 3.2 Mbps internal bus; 800 Kbps on multidrop

Topology: star with multidrop on star legs

Access method: CSMA/CD

Compatible operating systems: Novell Advanced NetWare, supports DOS 2.1-3.1

Gateways: SNA/SDLC, Ethernet, X.25, HDLC, any other Advanced NetWare 2.0 file server

Maximum number of workstations per node: 8

Maximum number of nodes: 16 per server

Maximum distance between nodes: 1000 feet from last PC in multidrop chain to server

Means of host interconnection: terminal ports; 422 ports for PCs; RS-232 ports for modems and printers through interface card in PC

Network server: proprietary file server

Maximum number of file servers: 16

Disk backup: whole disk

Network operation during backup: no

Site of network logic: bus/network interface units

• STANDARDS/PROTOCOLS SUPPORTED

Communications protocols: SNA/SDLC, bisynchronous, X.25, HDLC, asynchronous, RS-232, synchronous

IEEE 802 standards: conforms to 802.2

ISO OSI Reference Model: conforms to layers 1-7

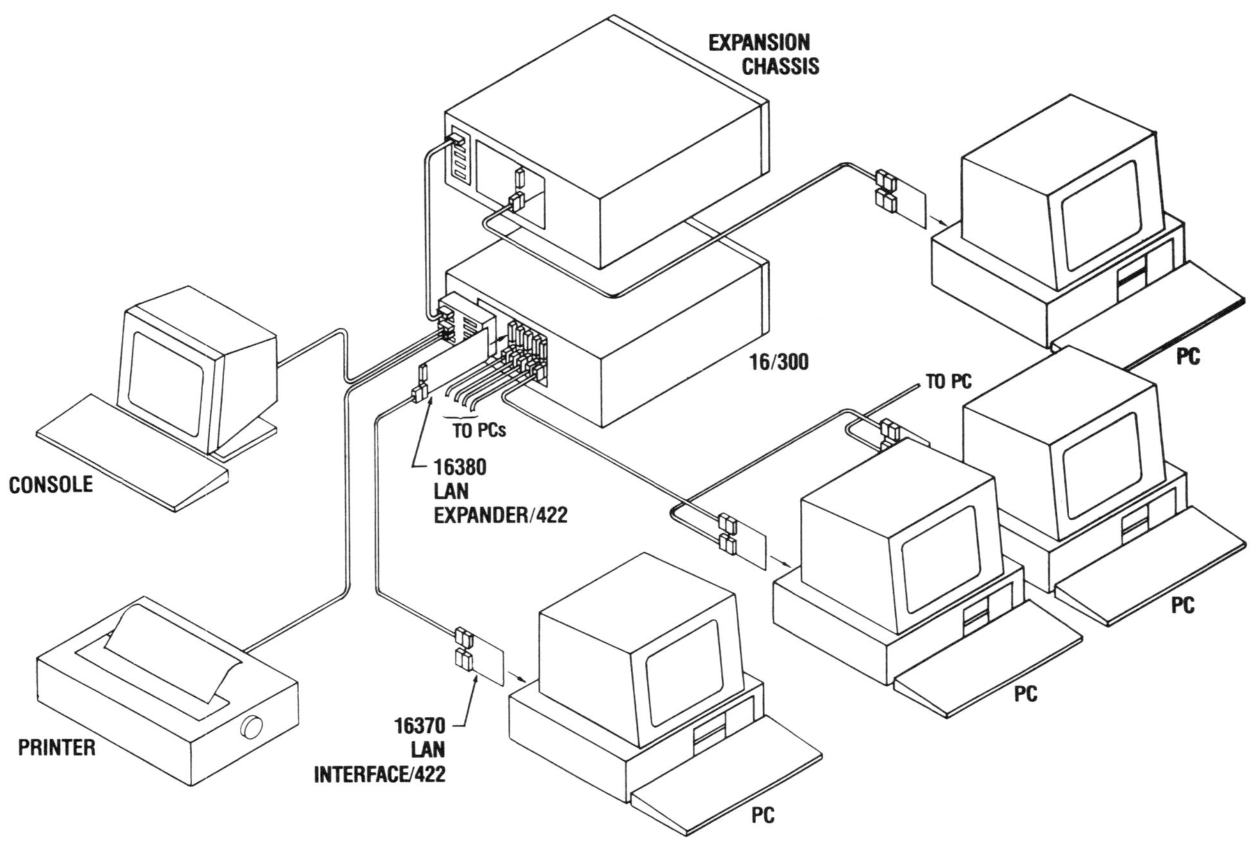

Molecular System 16/300

Figure 21

Courtesy Molecular Computer

NBI INC. • NBI NET

3450 Mitchell Lane, P.O. Box 9001
Boulder, CO 80301
(303)938-2705; telex 216-159 NBI UR

Thomas S. Kavanagh, President; Greg Flynn (PM); Robert Reid, Vice President, Marketing (MD); David Scott, Vice President, Direct Sales (PSC); Terri Douglas, Project Manager (PR); Ro Biegner, Purchasing Agent (PA)

Founded 1973; 3200 employees

NBI Net is an Ethernet-compatible LAN capable of connecting mainframes, minicomputers, PCs, and printers. Designed for office, laboratory or campus use, the network is IBM compatible and conforms to IEEE 802.3 and TCP/IP protocols. Supports virtual terminal emulation, file transfer and mail transfer. Service contracts, network installation, instruction on network operation, and network maintenance services available. First installed: 1985. Number installed: 22. Average number of stations per installation: 30.

• NBI NET TECHNICAL CHARACTERISTICS

Transmission category: baseband

Transmission medium: baseband coaxial cable

Transmission speed: 10 Mbps

Topology: bus

Access method: CSMA/CD

Compatible operating systems: VMS, MS-DOS, Unix

Gateways: SNA/SDLC

Maximum number of workstations per node: 50

Maximum number of nodes: 5 cable segments

Maximum distance between nodes: 1024 feet

Means of host interconnection: 802.3

Disk backup: whole disk, partial disk

Network operation during backup: yes

Site of network logic: bus/network interface units

• STANDARDS/PROTOCOLS SUPPORTED

Communications protocols: TCP/IP, FTP, Telnet

IEEE 802 standards: conforms to 802.3

ISO OSI Reference Model: conforms to layer 1 (CSMA/CD), layer 2 (Ethernet), layer 3 (IP), layer 4 (TCP), layer 5 (ARPA protocols), and layer 6 (ASCII)

NBI INC. • MULTINET

3450 Mitchell Lane, P.O. Box 9001
Boulder, CO 80301
(303)938-2705; telex 216-159 NBI UR

Thomas S. Kavanagh, President; Greg Flynn (PM); Robert Reid, Vice President (MD); David Scott, Vice President, Direct Sales (PSC); Terri Douglas, Project Manager (PR); Rob Biegner, Purchasing Agent (PA)

Founded 1973; 3200 employees

Multinet uses twisted pair cabling to create an IBM PC-compatible integrated office system. Allows use of existing PBX telephone wiring for connecting PCs to system. Additional devices supported include printers and modems.

• MULTINET TECHNICAL CHARACTERISTICS

Transmission category: baseband

Transmission medium: twisted wire pair

Transmission speed: 1 Mbps

Topology: bus

Compatible operating systems: MS-DOS

Maximum number of workstations per node: 8 per controller

Maximum number of nodes: 8 controllers

Maximum distance between nodes: 1000 feet from workstation to office link controller

Site of network logic: central controller

NBI Net

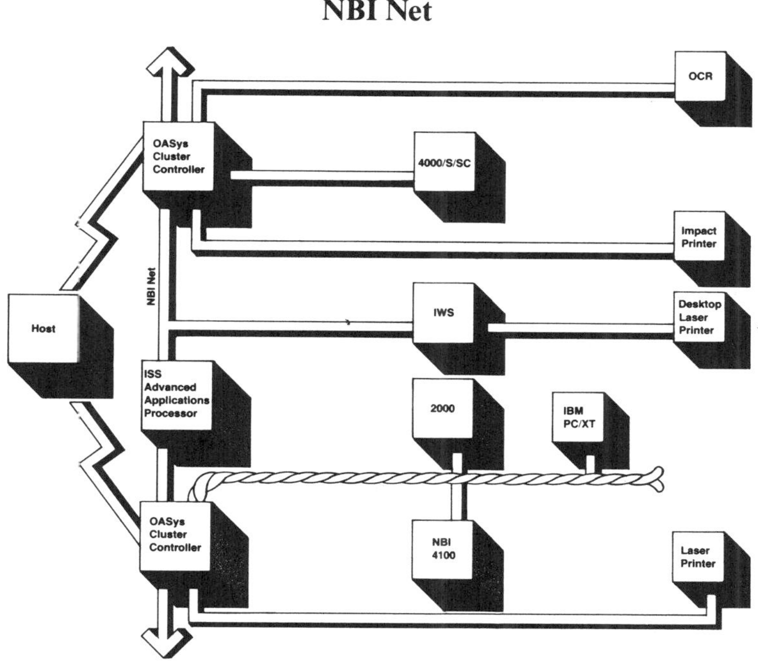

Figure 22

Courtesy NBI Inc.

NBI Multinet

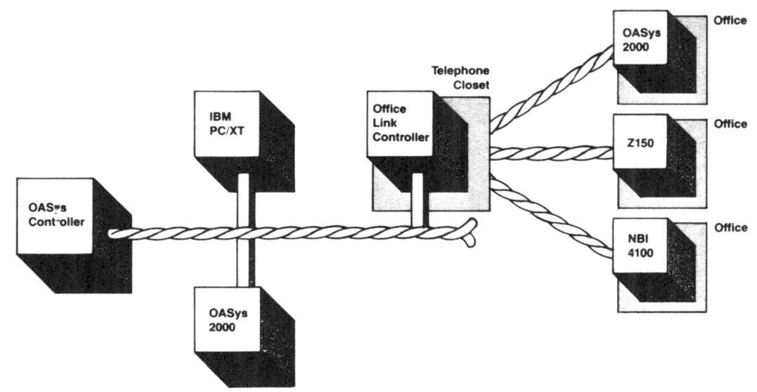

Figure 23

Courtesy NBI Inc.

NESTAR SYSTEMS INC. • PLAN 3000B

2585 East Bayshre Road
Palo Alto, CA 94303
(415)969-1777; telex 171-420 NESTAR PLA

Charles J. Hart, President; Ray M. Healy, Vice President, Sales and Marketing (MD)(PSC); Rose Ciank (PA)

Founded 1978; 100 employees

Plan 3000B is a set of LAN hardware and software for 10 IBM PCs, ATs, XTs, and compatibles. Designed to permit users with smaller network requirements to share data and programs with the same reliability and power as applied to large, complex networks. Features include password protection, sysem manager function and controlled access to files. Supports dumb terminals, printers, modems, and disk drives for industrial, office, laboratory, or campus applications. Service contracts, network installation and instruction on network operation available. First installed: 1982. Number installed: 1000. Average number of networks per installation: 10.

• PLAN 3000B TECHNICAL CHARACTERISTICS

Transmission category: baseband, broadband

Transmission medium: baseband coaxial cable, twisted wire pair, optical fi ber

Transmission speed: 2.5 Mbps

Topology: bus, star, arbitrary tree

Access method: token passing

Compatible operating systems: PC-DOS 2.1 and 3.0, Apple DOS, SOS, CP/M, proprietary

Gateways: SNA, Ethernet, bisynchronous, asynchronous

Maximum number of nodes: 255

Means of host interconnection: bus interface cards

Network server: proprietary file server

Maximum number of file servers: 254

Disk backup: intergrated streaming tape drive, whole disk

Network operation during backup: yes

• STANDARDS/PROTOCOLS SUPPORTED

Communications protocols: bisynchronous, asynchronous, XNS

IEEE 802 standards: does not conform

ISO OSI Reference Model: conforms to layers 1 and 2 (ARC Net), layers 3 and 4 (XNS) and layers 5, 6 and 7 (proprietary)

NETWORK DEVELOPMENT CORPORATION • DEVICE NETWORK ARCHITECTURE

81 Great Valley Parkway
Malvern, PA 19355
(215)296-7420; telex 910-350-6937 DNANET

Alan Laffkas, President; George Palmer, Executive Vice Prsident (PM); Bruce Quigley, Vice President, Marketing (MD)(PR); A. Tony Jacobs, National Sales Manager (PSC); Joanne Moore, Office Manager (PA)

Founded 1978; 15 employees

Device Network Architecture is a PC network designed for industrial, office, laboratory, or campus use. The network can support up to 5 printers/plotters as well as any disk drive which will operate on a stand-alone CPU. Service contracts, instruction on network operation and network maintenance services available. First installed: 1978. Number installed: 4000. Average number of stations per installation: 10.

- **DEVICE NETWORK ARCHITECTURE TECHNICAL CHARACTERISTICS**

Transmission category: baseband

Transmission mode: full duplex

Transmission medium: twisted wire pair

Transmission speed: 1 Mbps burst

Topology: star, multidrop

Access method: polling

Compatible operating systems: MS-DOS

Gateways: SNA/SDLC

Maximum number of workstations per node: 64

Maximum number of nodes: unlimited

Maximum distance between nodes: 5000 feet

Means of host interconnection: LAN host

Network server: multivendor file server

Maximum number of file servers: unlimited

Disk backup: whole disk

Network operation during backup: no

Site of network logic: terminal equipment

- **STANDARDS/PROTOCOLS SUPPORTED**

Communications protocols: asynchronous, synchronous, RS-232

ISO OSI Reference Model: conforms to layers 1-4

DNA™ *LOCAL AREA NETWORK*

Typical DNA™ System Configuration

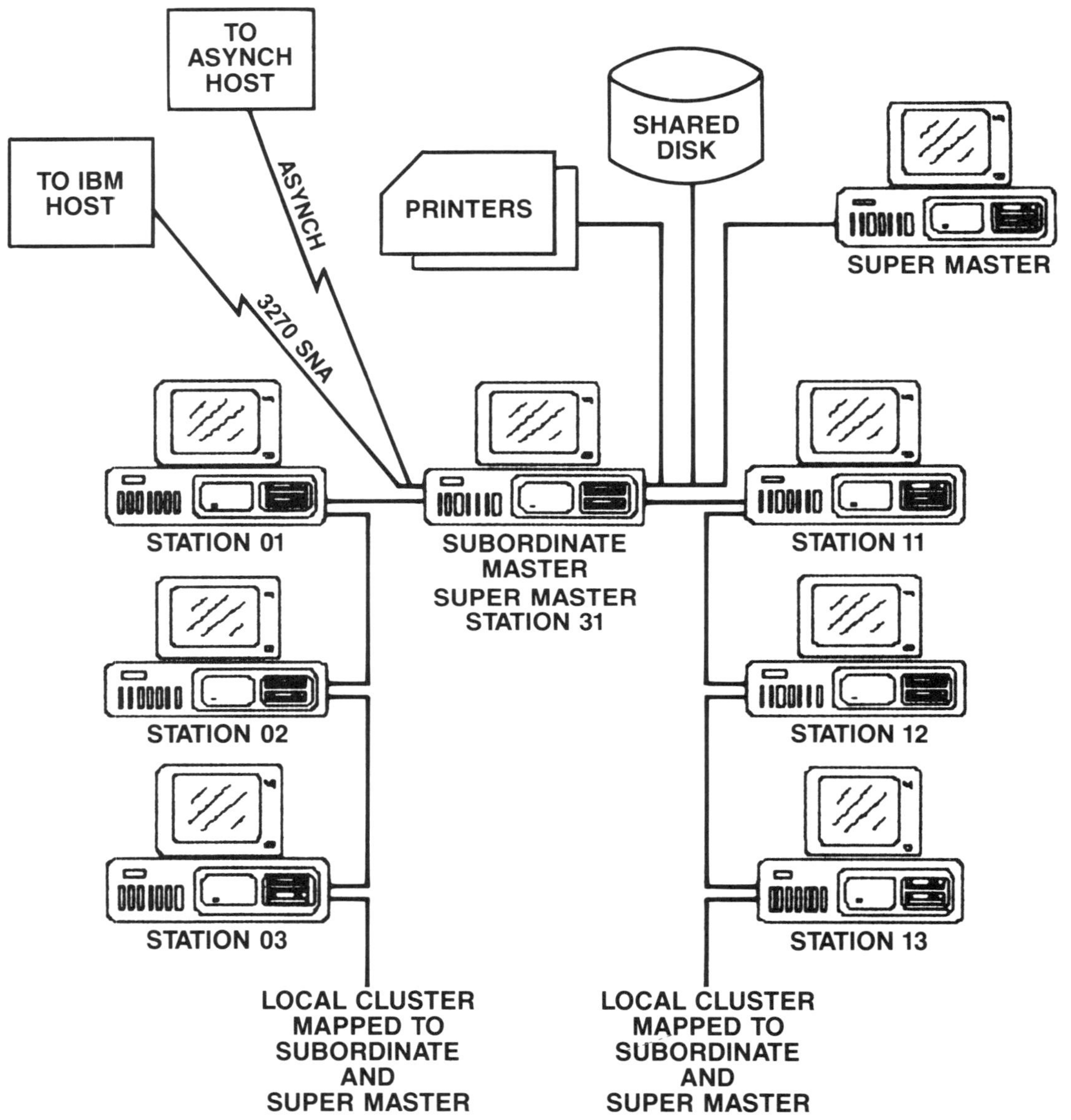

Figure 24

Courtesy Network Development Corporation

NETWORK SYSTEMS CORPORATION • HYPERBUS

7600 Boone Avenue North
Minneapols, MN 55428
(612)424-4888; telex 201-678; FAX 612-424-2853

Lyle D. Altman, President; Harold W. Durett, Vice President, Information Systems (PM); Mahlon L. Moore, Vice President, Marketing (MD); Robert Klein (PSC); Gerald Hoppe, Communications Manager (PR); Mike Finley (PA)

Founded 1974; 900 employees

Branch Offices and Distributors:
Network Systems Corporation, Los Angeles, CA (213)216-7009; Network Systems Corporation, Denver, CO (303)779-6996; Network Systems Corporation, New York, NY (212)269-3150; Network Systems Corporation, Dallas, TX (214)578-1554; Network Systems Corporation, Vienna, VA (703)281-0455

HYPERbus is a networking system designed to provide digital communications capability at the user level. Terminals and other devices connect to the bus by bus interface units, which function as intelligent transceivers. Can be directly integrated into the HYPERchannel network. Devices connected include RS-232 devices, 3270 terminals, workstations, PCs, minicomputers, mainframes, printers, modems, and disk drives. Designed for office, laboratory or campus environment. Service contracts, network installation, instruction on network operation, and network maintenance services available. First installed: 1982. Number installed: 75.

• HYPERBUS TECHNICAL CHARACTERISTICS

Transmission category: baseband

Transmission medium: baseband coaxial cable, twisted wire pair, optical fiber

Transmission speed: 10 Mbps backbone and maximum available for user connection

Topology: bus

Access method: CSMA/CA

Compatible operating systems: Netex (proprietary)

Gateways: proprietary

Maximum number of workstations per node: 16

Maximum number of nodes: 256

Maximum distance between nodes: 2400 feet

Means of host interconnection: RS-232 terminal ports

Site of network logic: bus/network interface units

• STANDARDS/PROTOCOLS SUPPORTED

Communications protocols: bisynchronous, asynchronous, synchronous, 3270, RS-232

IEEE 802 standards: does not conform

ISO OSI Reference Model: conforms to layers 1-5

NETWORK SYSTEMS CORPORATION • HYPERCHANNEL A

7600 Boone Avenue North
Minneapolis, MN 55428
(612)424-4888; telex 201-678; FAX 612-424-2853

Lyle D. Altman, President; Harold W. Durett, Vice President, Information Systems (PM); Mahlon L. Moore, Vice President, Marketing (MD); Robert Klein (PSC); Gerald Hoppe, Communications Manager (PR); Mike Finley (PA)

Founded 1974; 900 employees

Branch Offices and Distributors:
Network Systms Corporation, Los Angeles, CA (213)216-7009; Network Systems Corporation, Denver, CO (303)779-6996; Network Systems Corporation, New York, NY (212)269-3150; Network Systems Corporation, Dallas, TX (214)578-1554; Network Systems Corporation, Vienna, VA (703)281-0455

HYPERchannel A Series networks serve large, centralized computer centers, chiefly containing supercomputers and large mainframes with high-volume data communication needs. A Series networks support data transfers of up to 200 Mbps by using four HYPERchannel cables. Designed for office, laboratory or campus applications. Service contracts, network installation, instruction on network operation, and network maintenance services available. First installed: 1977. Number installed: over 800.

• HYPERCHANNEL A TECHNICAL CHARACTERISTICS

Transmission category: baseband

Transmission medium: baseband coaxial cable, optical fiber

Transmission speed: 50-200 Mbps backbone and maximum available for user connection

Topology: bus

Access method: CSMA/CA

Compatible operating systems: Netex (proprietary)

Maximum number of workstations per node: 16

Maximum number of nodes: unlimited

Maximum distance between nodes: 5000 feet

Means of host interconnection: RS-232 terminal ports

Site of network logic: bus/network interface units

• STANDARDS/PROTOCOLS SUPPORTED

Communications protocols: asynchronous, synchronous, RS-232, 3270

IEEE 802 standards: does not conform

ISO OSI Reference Model: conforms to layers 1-6

NETWORK SYSTEMS CORPORATION • HYPERCHANNEL B

7600 Boone Avenue North
Minneapolis, MN 55428
(612)424-4888; telex 201-678; FAX 612-424-2853

Lyle D. Altman, President; Harold W. Durett, Vice President, Information Systems (PM); Mahlon L. Moore, Vice President, Marketing (MD); Robert Klein (PSC); Gerald Hoppe, Communications Manager (PR); Mike Finley (PA)

Founded 1974; 900 employees

Branch Offices and Distributors:

Network Systems Corporation, Los Angeles, CA (213)216-7009; Network Systems Corporation, Denver, CO (303)779-6996; Network Systems Corporation, New York, NY (212)269-3150; Network Systems Corporation, Dallas, TX (214)578-1554; Network Systems Corporation, Vienna, VA (703)281-0455

HYPERchannel B Series products create networks that serve distributed computing environments using workstations, minicomputers and mainframes. Compatible vendors include IBM, DEC, Sperry, Honeywell, and Hewlett-Packard. Designed for office, laboratory or campus environments. Service contracts, network installation, instruction on network operation, and network maintenance services available. First installed: 1974. Number installed: 2100.

• HYPERCHANNEL B TECHNICAL CHARACTERISTICS

Transmission category: baseband

Transmission medium: baseband coaxial cable, twisted wire pair, optical fiber

Transmission speed: 10 Mbps backbone and maximum available for user connection

Topology: bus

Access method: CSMA/CA

Compatible operating systems: Netex (proprietary)

Gateways: none

Maximum number of workstations per node: 16

Maximum number of nodes: 16

Means of host interconnection: RS-232 terminal ports

Site of network logic: bus/network interface units

• STANDARDS/PROTOCOLS SUPPORTED

Communications protocols: bisynchronous, asynchronous, synchronous, RS-232

IEEE 802 standards: does not conform

ISO OSI Reference Model: conforms to layers 1-5

NORTH STAR COMPUTERS INC. • DIMENSION

14440 Catalina Street
San Leandro, CA 5536
(415)357-8500; telex 910-366-7001; FAX 415-895-1309

Bruce MacKay, President; Frank Marra, Vice President, Sales (PM); Brad West, Director, Marketing Services (PSC); Charles P. Almarez, Marketing Communications Coordinator (PR); Harry Moore, Senior Purchasing Agent (PA)

Founded 1976; 150 employees

Branch Offices and Distributors:
North Star Computers Inc., Marlton, NJ (609)596-2880; North Star Computers Inc., Dallas, TX (214)888-6017; North Star Computers Inc., Smyrna, GA (404)984-221; North Star Computers Inc., Bellevue, WA (206)454-9870

Dimension is a multi-user, multiprocessor IBM PC- and XT-compatible system that provides a separate processor for each of its 12 workstations. Dimension 1200 is designed for environments with large data storage requirements, while Dimension 300 is suited for small business needs. Service contracts, network installation, instruction on network operation and network maintenance services available. First installed: 1984. Number installed: 3000. Average number of stations per installation: 6.

• DIMENSION TECHNICAL CHARACTERISTICS

Transmission category: baseband

Transmission mode: half duplex

Transmission medium: not applicable

Transmission speed: 5.8 Mbps maximum available for user connection

Topology: star

Access method: interrupt driven

Compatible operating systems: MS-DOS, Novell NetWare

Gateways: SNA/SDLC, Ethernet, IBM Token Ring

Maximum number of workstations per node: 12

Maximum number of nodes: 1

Means of host interconnection: IBM bus

Network server: proprietary file server

Maximum number of file servers: unlimited; limited by gateway

Disk backup: whole disk, partial disk

Network operation during backup: no

Site of network logic: bus/network interface units

• STANDARDS/PROTOCOLS SUPPORTED

Communications protocols: SNA/SDLC, bisynchronous, X.25, HDLC, asynchronous, RS-232, synchronous; supported through interfaces

IEEE 802 standards: does not conform

ISO OSI Reference Model: does not conform

North Star Dimension

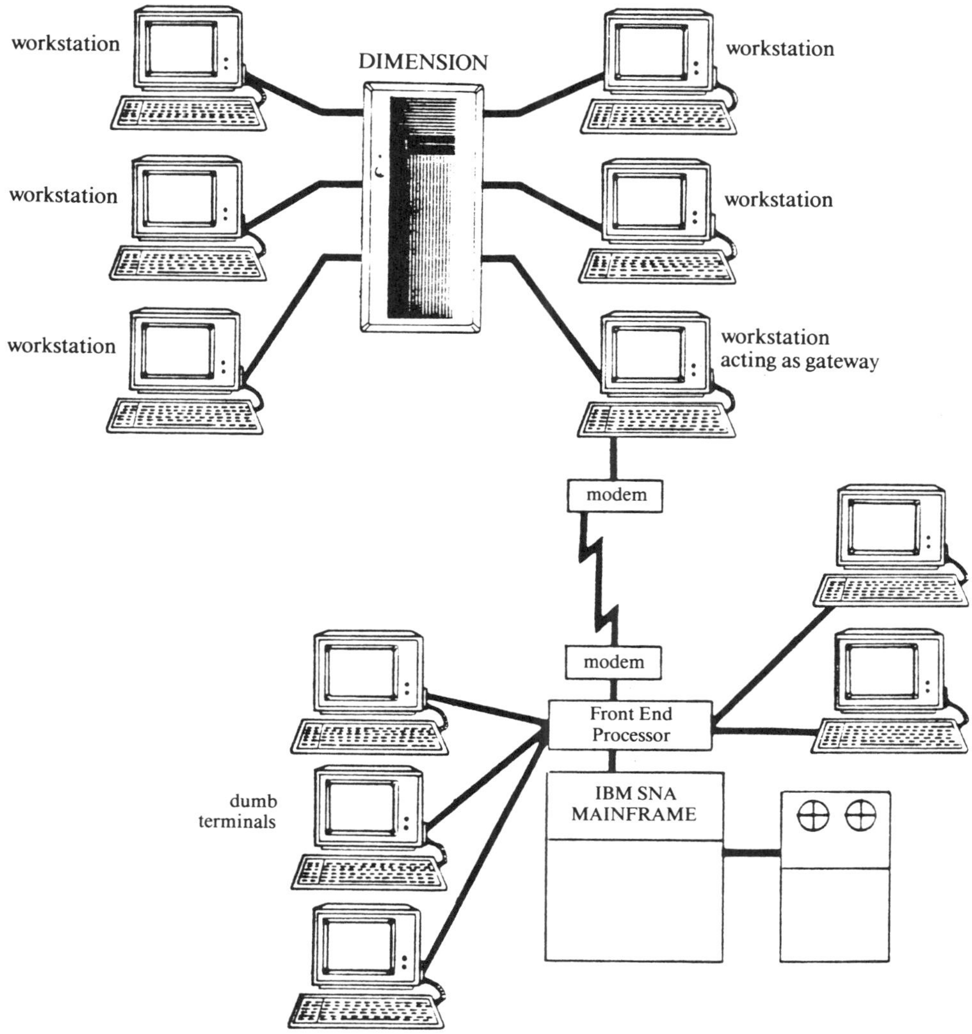

Figure 25

Courtesy North Star Computers, Inc.

NORTHERN TELECOM INC. • LANSTAR PC

2100 Lakeside Boulevard
Richardson, TX 75081
(214)437-8695; (800)328-8800; FAX 214-351-1142

Robert Potter, Group Vice President, Integrated Office Systems; Paul Masters, Product Manager (PM); Henry Theloosen, Director, Product Line Management (MD); Betsy Humber, Marketing Communications (PSC); Brian Murphy, Regional Manager, Public Affairs (PR)

Founded 1895; 22,000 U.S. employees

LANstar PC LAN links IBM PCs, XTs, ATs, and compatibles in the industrial, office, laboratory, or campus environment. Supports printers, disk drives and plotters. Compatible software includes Microsoft Networks and most PC-DOS compatible software. Service contracts, network installation, instruction on network operation, and network maintenance services available. First installed: 1985. Number installed: 7. Average number of stations per installation: 30.

• LANSTAR PC TECHNICAL CHARACTERISTICS

Transmission category: baseband

Transmission mode: full duplex

Transmission medium: twisted wire pair

Transmission speed: 40 Mbps backbone; 2.56 Mbps maximum available for user connection

Topology: star

Access method: perfect scheduling (grant/request)

Compatible operating systems: MS-DOS

Gateways: SNA/SDLC, Ethernet, X.25; all gateways via asynchronous terminal emulation

Maximum number of nodes: 1200

Maximum distance between nodes: 4000 feet

Means of host interconnection: multiplexed interfaces

Network server: disk server

Maximum number of file servers: 1200

Disk backup: whole disk, partial disk

Network operation during backup: yes

Site of network logic: terminal equipment

• STANDARDS/PROTOCOLS SUPPORTED

Communications protocols: SNA/SDLC, bisynchronous, X.25, HDLC, asynchronous, RS-232, synchronous, asynchronous packet (Northern Telecom)

IEEE 802 standards: conforms to 802.2

ISO OSI Reference Model: conforms to layer 1 (twisted wire pair), layer 2 (integrated voice/data), layers 3 and 4 (proprietary), layer 5 (MS Net/NETBIOS), layer 6 (MSNet), and layer 7 (redirector)

ORCHID TECHNOLOGY • PC NET

47790 Westinghouse Drive
Fremont, CA 94539
(415)490-8586; telex 70-289

Le Bui, President; Bill Berkman, Network Product Manager (PM); Sung R. Cho, Vice President, Marketing (MD); Alan Brudno, National Sales Manager (PSC); Jay Shotwell (PR);

Founded 1982; over 100 employees

Branch Offices and Distributors:
Crystal Computers, Lenexa, KS (913)541-1711; F.A. Components, Fort Wayne, IN (219)432-8540; Gates Distributing, Houston, TX (713)440-4444; Robec, Hopkinton, MA (617)435-9545; Softsel, Inglewood, CA (213)412-1700

PCNet is an office PC LAN which is capable of supporting all printers, modems, hard disks, plotters, terminal emulators, digitizers, light pens, and bar code readers. Compatible devices include Versaterm Systems-Versa Link, Techland Systems-Bluelink, CXI-Pecox Batway-16, Santa Clara Systems-PC terminal, and Novell servers. Compatible software includes Novell, Taurus or any software supporting DOS 3.1 locking calls. First installed: 1982. Number of networks installed: 15,000. Average number of stations per installation: 6.

• PC NET TECHNICAL CHARACTERISTICS

Transmission category: baseband

Transmission mode: full duplex

Transmission medium: baseband coaxial cable

Transmission speed: 1 Mbps burst

Topology: bus

Access method: CSMA/CD

Compatible operating systems: MS-DOS, Novell NetWare

Gateways: SNA/SDLC, X.25, HDLC

Maximum number of workstations per node: 1

Maximum number of nodes: 256

Maximum distance between nodes: 7000 feet

Means of host interconnection: terminal ports

Network server: disk server

Maximum number of file servers: 16

Disk backup: whole disk, partial disk

Network operation during backup: no

Site of network logic: bus/network interface units

• STANDARDS/PROTOCOLS SUPPORTED

Communications protocols: SNA/SDLC, bisynchronous, X.25, HDLC, RS-232, asynchronous, synchronous

IEEE 802 standards: not available

ISO OSI Reference Model: conforms to layers 1-7 (NETBIOS)

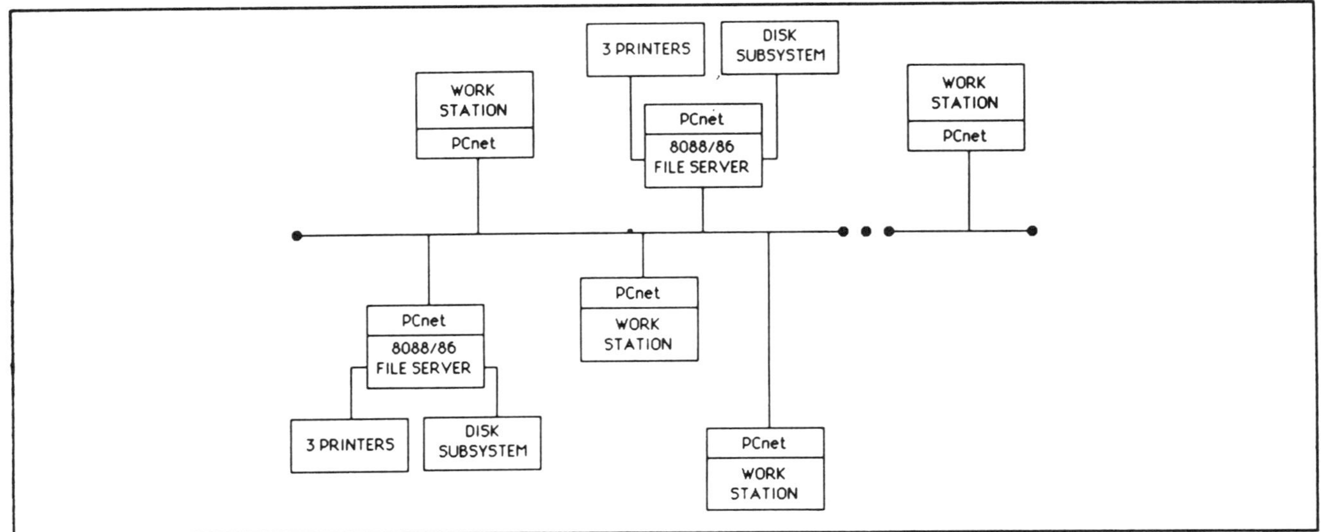

Sample Orchid PCnet Topology

Figure 26

Courtesy Novell Inc.

PRIME COMPUTER INC. • RINGNET

Prime Park
Natick, MA 01760
(617)655-8000; telex 174-170

Joe M. Henson, President and Chief Executive Officer; Wendy Wheeler, Vice President, Systems Marketing (MD)

Founded 1972; 8115 employees

Branch Offices and Distributors:
Prime Computer Inc., Parsippany, NJ (201)993-8400; Prime Computer Inc., Oak Brook Terrace, IL (312)953-9250; Prime Computer Inc., Woodland Hills, CA (818)992-8633

Ringnet connects mainframes, minicomputers, dumb terminals, printers, modems, and disk drives for industrial, office, laboratory, or campus applications. Service contracts, network installation and instruction on network operation available. First installed: 1974.

• RINGNET TECHNICAL CHARACTERISTICS

Transmission category: baseband

Transmission medium: shielded twisted wire pair, optical fiber

Transmission speed: 8 mbps

Topology: ring

Access method: token passing

Compatible operating systems: PRIMOS (proprietary)

Gateways: x.25

Maximum number of nodes: 128 hosts

Maximum distance between nodes: 750 feet

Means of host interconnection: bus interface cards, RS-232 terminal ports, proprietary

• STANDARDS/PROTOCOLS SUPPORTED

Communications protocols: x.25, bisynchronous, hdlc

IEEE 802 standards: does not conform

ISO OSI Reference Model: conforms to layers 1-3 (x.25) and layers 4 and 5 (proprietary)

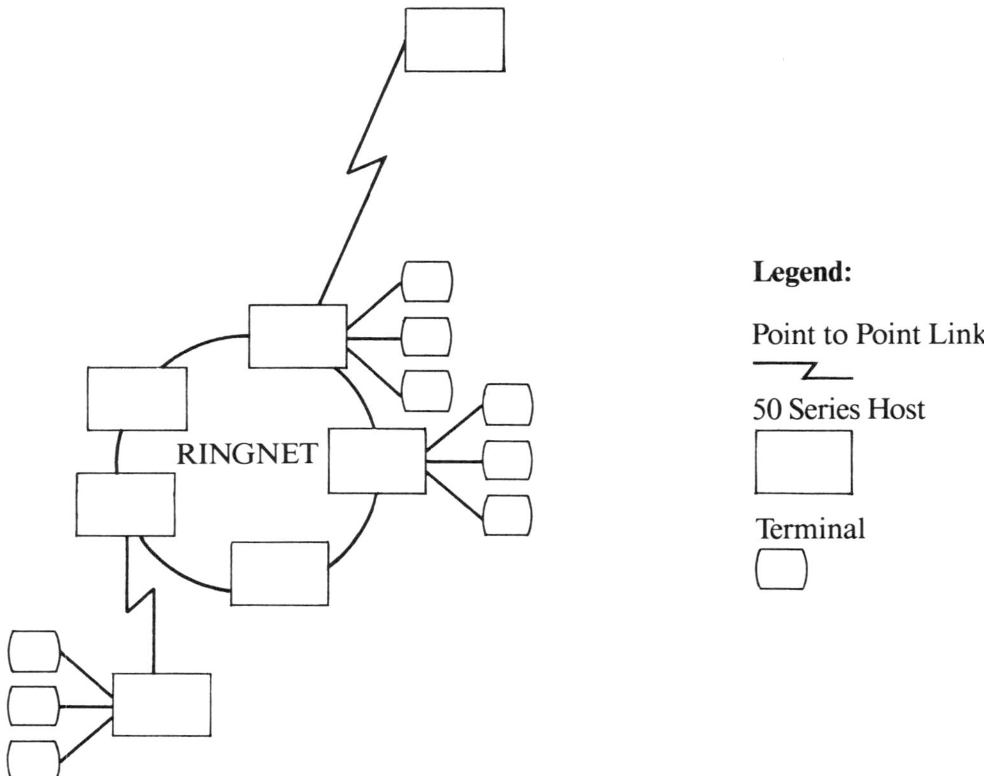

Figure 27

Courtesy Prime Inc.

PRIME COMPUTER INC. • IEEE 802.3 LAN
Prime Park
Natick, MA 01760
(617)655-8000; telex 174-170

Joe M. Henson, President and Chief Executive Officer; Wendy Wheeler, Vice President, Systems Marketing (MD)

Founded 1972; 8115 employees

Branch Offices and Distributors:
Prime Computer Inc., Parsippany, NJ (201)993-8400; Prime Computer Inc., Oak Brook Terrace, IL (312)953-9250; Prime Computer Inc., Woodland Hills, CA (818)992-8633

IEEE 802.3 LAN connects minicomputers for industrial, office, laboratory, or campus applications. Peripherals supported via minicomputers. First installed: 1979. Number installed: 1500. Average number of stations per installation: 5 minicomputers; 100 terminals.

• IEEE 802.3 LAN TECHNICAL CHARACTERISTICS

Topology: bus

Access method: CSMA/CD

Maximum number of nodes: 1024

Maximum distance between nodes: 2.5 kilometers

• STANDARDS/PROTOCOLS SUPPORTED

IEEE 802 standards: conforms to 802.3

IEEE 802.3 Bus Topology

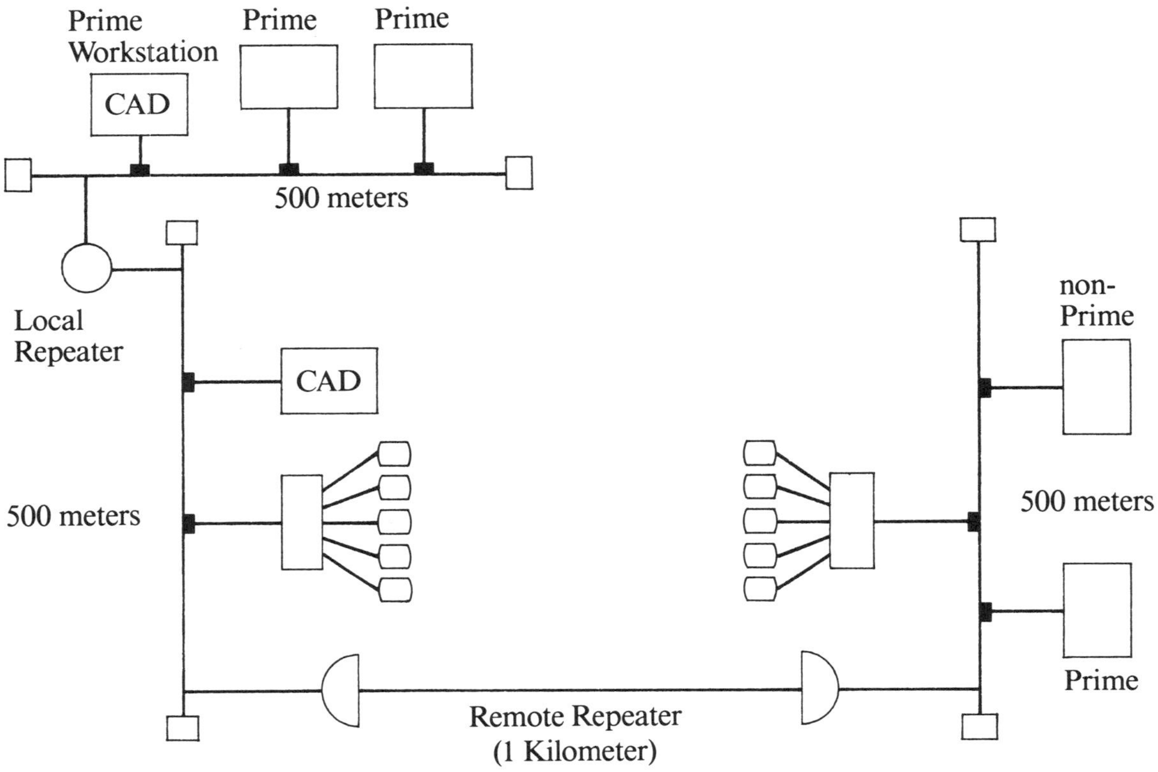

Figure 28

Courtesy Prime Inc.

PROTEON INC. • PRONET-80

4 Tech Circle
Natick, MA 760
(617)655-3340; telex 928-124; FAX 617-651-1612

Fran Scricco, President; John Shriver (PM); Tony Bolton (MD); Pat Lally (PSC); Nancy Krakora (PR); Ron Warwick (PA)

Founded 1972; 250 employees

Branch Offices and Distributors:
> Proteon Inc., Malvern, PA (215)648-3826; Proteon Inc., Vienna, VA (703)821-6980; Proteon Inc., New York, NY (212)971-9020; Proteon Inc., Framingham, MA (617)626-2330; Proteon Inc., Englewood, CO (303)740-6689

ProNET-80 is a modular design with the flexibility to be used as a backbone network for several slower LANs, as a transport mechanism for complex graphic images and as a superfast host-to-host network for minicomputers. Connects mainframes, minicomputers, PC, dumb terminals, printers, modems, and disk drives for industrial, office, laboratory, or campus applications. Service contracts, network installation, instruction on network operation, and network maintenance services available. First installed: 1985.

• PRONET-80 TECHNICAL CHARACTERISTICS

Transmssion category: baseband

Transmission mode: full duplex

Transmission medium: shielded twisted wire pair, optical fiber

Transmission speed: 80 Mbps backbone, maximum available for user connection and burst

Topology: star-shaped ring

Access method: token passing

Compatible operating systems: MS-DOS, Unix, Novell NetWare, Banyan VINES, VM/SP, VAX/VMS

Gateways: SNA/SDLC, Ethernet, HDLC, T2, high-speed asynchronous, Arpanet 1822, DECnet, other ProNET LANs.

Maximum number of workstatiss per node: 1

Maximum number of nodes: 240 hosts per network segment

Maximum distance between nodes: 5000 feet

Means of host interconnection: bus-to-bus

Network server: multivendor file server

Disk backup: whole disk, partial disk

Network operation during backup: yes

Site of network logic: bus/network interface units

• STANDARDS/PROTOCOLS SUPPORTED

Communications protocols: SNA/SDLC, HDLC, asynchronous, RS-232, synchronous

ISO OSI Reference Model: conforms to layers 1-3

PROTEON INC. • PRONET-4

4 Tech Circle
Natick, MA 01760
(617)655-3340; telex 928-124; FAX 617-651-1612

Fran Scricco, President; John Shriver (PM); Tony Bolton (MD); Pat Lally (PSC); Nancy Krakora (PR); Ron Warwick (PA)

Founded 1972; 250 employees

Branch Offices and Distributors:
Proteon Inc., Malvern, PA (215)648-3826; Proteon Inc., Vienna, VA (703)821-6980; Proteon Inc., New York, NY (212)971-9020; Proteon Inc., Framingham, MA (617)626-2330; Proteon Inc., Englewood, CO (303)740-6689

ProNET-4 is a 4 Mbps LAN that is fully compliant with the IEEE 802.5 standard and IBM Token Ring implementation. Supports mainframes, minicomputers, PCs, workstations, and peripherals. Can be implemented using standard IBM wiring scheme. Service contracts, network installation, instruction on network operation, and network maintenance services available.

• PRONET-4 TECHNICAL CHARACTERISTICS

Transmission category: baseband

Transmission mode: full duplex

Transmission medium: shielded twisted wire pair, optical fiber

Transmission speed: 4 Mbps backbone, 3.6 Mbps maximum available for user connection; 4 Mbps burst

Topology: star-shaped ring

Access method: token passing

Compatible operating systems: MS-DOS, Unix, Novell NetWare, Banyan VINES

Gateways: SNA/SDLC, Ethernet, HDLC, T1, high-speed asynchronous, Arpanet 1822, DECnet, other ProNET LANs

Maximum number of workstations per node: 1

Maximum number of nodes: 260 per segment

Maximum distance between node: 15,000

Means of host interconnection: bus-to-bus

Network server: multivendor file server

Disk backup: whole disk, partial disk

Network operation during backup: yes

Site of network logic: bus/network interface units

• STANDARDS/PROTOCOLS SUPPORTED

Communications protocols: SNA/SDLC, HDLC, asynchronous, RS-232, synchronous

IEEE 802 standards: conforms to 802.5

ISO OSI Reference Model: conforms to layers 1-3

PROTEON INC. • PRONET-10
4 Tech Circle
Natick, MA 001760
(617)655-3340; telex 928-124; FAX 617-651-1612

Fran Scricco, President; John Shriver (PM); Tony Bolton (MD); Pat Lally (PSC); Nancy Krakora (PR); Ron Warwick (PA)

Founded 1972; 250 employees

Branch Offices and Distributors:
> Proteon Inc., Malvern, PA (215)648-3826; Proteon Inc., Vienna, VA (703)821-6980; Proteon Inc., New York, NY (212)971-9020; Proteon Inc., Framingham, MA (617)626-2330; Proteon Inc., Englewood, CO (303)740-6689

ProNET-10 is a token-passing, star-shaped ring that allows for a combination of wiring options including shielded twisted wire pair, fiber, infrared link, and microwave link. Devices connected include mainframes, minicomputers, PCs, dumb terminals, printers, modems, and disk drives. Designed for office, industrial, educational, institutional, and campus environments. "Universal Bus" interface provides a building block for proprietary interfaces. Service contracts, network installation, instruction on network operation, and network maintenance services available. First installed: 1981.

• PRONET-10 TECHNICAL CHARACTERISTICS

Transmission category: baseband

Transmission mode: full duplex

Transmission medium: shielded twisted wire pair, optical fiber, microwave

Transmission speed: 10 Mbps backbone, maximum available for user connection and burst

Topology: star-shaped ring

Access method: token passing

Compatible operating systems: MS-DOS, Unix, NetWare, Banyan VINES, VMS, VM/SP

Gateways: SNA/SDLC, Ethernet, HDLC, T1, high-speed synchronous, Arpanet 1822, DECnet, other ProNET LANs.

Maximum number of workstations per node: 1

Maximum number of nodes: 255 hosts per network segment

Maximum distance between nodes: 15,000 feet

Means of host interconnection: bus-to-bus

Network server: multivendor file server

Disk backup: whole disk, partial disk

Network operation during backup: yes

Site of network logic: bus/network interface units

• STANDARDS/PROTOCOLS SUPPORTED

Communications protocols: SNA/SDLC, HDLC, asynchronous, RS-232, synchronous

ISO OSI Reference Model: conforms to levels 1-3

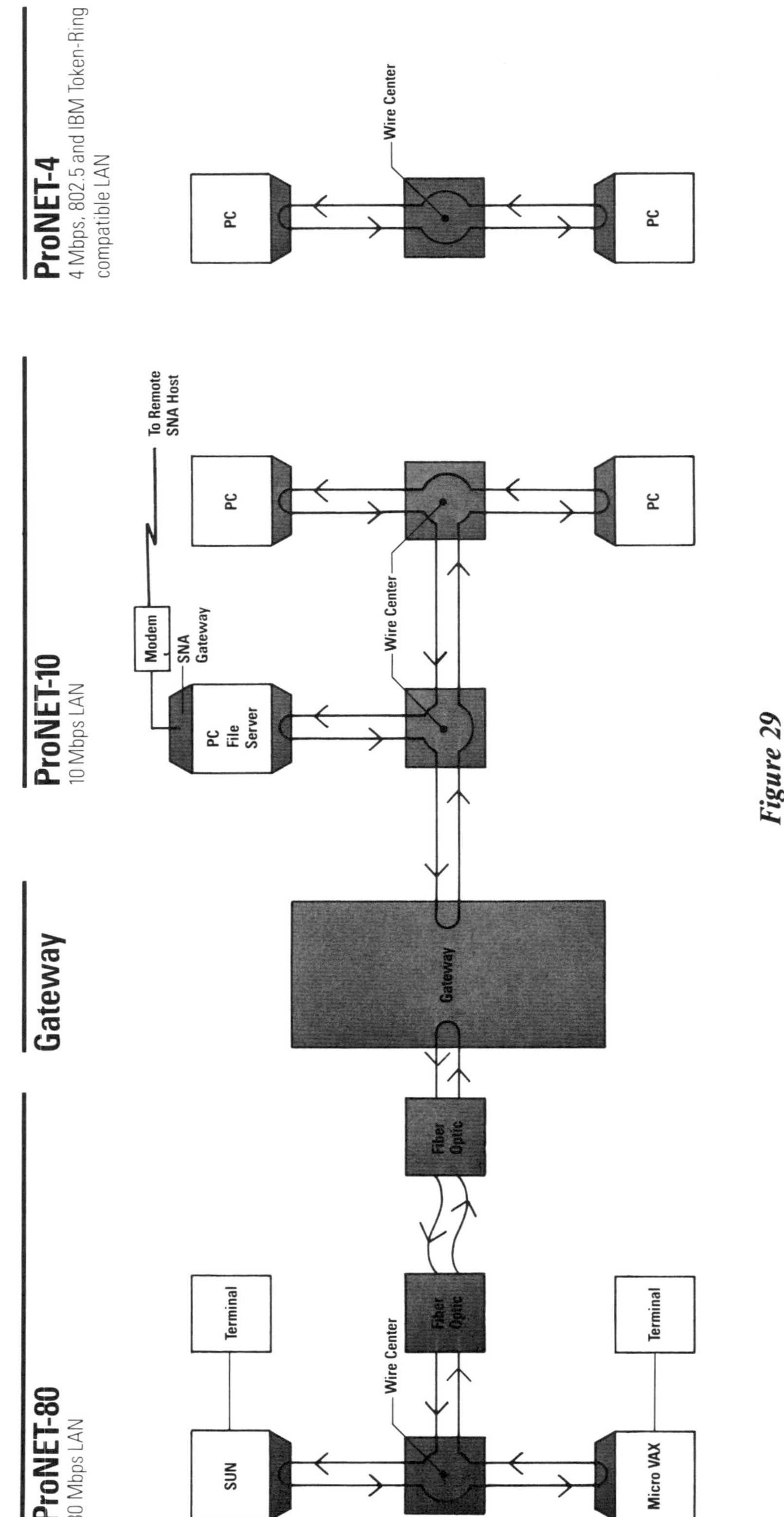

Figure 29

146

RACORE CORPORATION • LANPAC

10 Victor Square
Scotts Valley, CA 95066
(408)438-7255; telex 453-003; FAX 408-438-0937

John LaPorta, President; Bill Klaus (PM)(MD)(PSC)(PR)(PA)

Founded 1983; 41 employees

LANpac is a networking product connecting mainframes, minicomputers, PCs, and dumb terminals for industrial or office use. Service contracts, network installation, instruction on network operation, and network maintenance services available.

• LANPAC TECHNICAL CHARACTERISTICS

Transmission category: broadband

Transmission medium: broadband coaxial cable

Transmission speed: 2 mbps backbone, maximum available for user connection and burst

Topology: ring

Access method: token passing

Compatible operating systems: MS-DOS

SIECOR CORPORATION • FIBER OPTIC ETHERNET

99 T.W. Alexander Drive
Research Triangle Park, NC 27709
(919)549-6571; telex 216-910; FAX 919-541-9034

Charles Wakeman, President; Ghias Massarani, Director, Electro-Optic Products (PM); Jay Cunningham (MD); Bruce Stadler (PSC); Lois Boynton (PR)

Founded 1977; 900 employees

Fiber Optic Ethernet can be used as a fiber optic backbone LAN interconnecting multiple Ethernet segments. Star Wiring Center houses a star coupler or star coupler monitor and provides for interconnection and reconfiguration of nodes. Supports mainframes, minicomputers, PCs, and dumb terminals for industrial, office, laboratory, or campus applications. Compatible with Ethernet and IEEE 802.3 specifications. Service contracts, network installation, instruction on network operation, and network maintenance services. First installed: 1983. Number installed: over 100. Average number of stations per installation: 100.

• FIBER OPTIC ETHERNET TECHNICAL CHARACTERISTICS

Transmission category: baseband

Transmission medium: optical fiber

Transmission speed: 10 Mbps backbone and maximum available for user connection

Topology: star, point-to-point

Access method: CSMA/CD

Compatible operating systems: MS-DOS, CP/M, Unix

Gateways: Ethernet

Maximum number of workstations per node: 100

Maximum number of nodes: 1024

Maximum distance between nodes: 2500 meters

Means of host interconnection: multiplexed interfaces

Maximum number of file servers: 1024

Disk backup: whole disk

Network operation during backup: yes

Site of network logic: bus/network interface units, central controllers

• STANDARDS/PROTOCOLS SUPPORTED

Communications protocols: Ethernet

IEEE 802 standards: conforms to 802.3

SIEMENS ENERGY & AUTOMATION INC.—PROGRAMMABLE CONTROLS DIVISION
• SINEC L1 LAN

10 Technology Drive, Centennial Park
Peabody, MA 01960
(617)532-6720; telex 928-160

Ray Leveille, Vice President and General Manager; R.L. Bailey, Vice President, Sales and Marketing; Ken Appel, Manager, Marketing Communications (MD); Tom Varney (PR)

Founded 1984

Branch Offices and Distributors:
> Siemens-Allis Automation Inc., Buffalo, NY (716)834-3817; Siemens-Allis Automation Inc., Houston, TX (713)681-5001; Siemens-Allis Automation Inc., Dallas, TX (214)247-4481; Siemens-Allis Automation Inc., Santa Ana, CA (714)979-6600; Siemens-Allis Automation Inc., Plymouth Meeting, PA (215)825-2120

Sinec L1 is an industrial LAN that allows the transmission of data from one programmable controller to another via the network bus. A production line with a number of manufacturing islands can be implemented with this network just as easily as a communications network for production statistics. Provides interrupt capability. Devices connected include PCs, programmable controllers and modems. Compatible devices: IBM PC, Industrial Grade 5531 and XT computers. Network compatible with IBM software. Service contracts, network installation, instruction on network operation, and network maintenance services available. First installed: 1985. Average number of stations per installation: 10.

• SINEC L1 LAN TECHNICAL CHARACTERISTICS

Transmission category: baseband

Transmission mode: full duplex

Transmission medium: twisted wire pair

Transmission speed: 9.6 Kbps backbone, maximum available for user connection and burst

Topology: bus

Access method: polling

Compatible operating systems: CP/M

Maximum number of workstations per node: 1

Maximum number of nodes: 31 including master programmable controller

Maximum distance between nodes: 31 miles

Means of host interconnction: terminal ports

Site of network logic: bus/network interface units, central controllers

• STANDARDS/PROTOCOLS SUPPORTED

Communications protocols: AS 511 (Siemens) with BCC, RS 485

IEEE 802 standards: conforms to 802.3

SIEMENS ENERGY & AUTOMATION INC.—PROGRAMMABLE CONTROLS DIVISION
• CONTROLNET

10 Technology Drive, Centennial Park
Peabody, MA 01960
(617)532-6720; telex 928-160

Ray Leveille, Vice President and General Manager; R.L. Bailey, Vice President, Sales and Marketing; Ken Appel, Manager, Marketing Communications (MD); Tom Varney (PR)

Founded 1984

Branch Offices and Distributors:
Siemens-Allis Automation Inc., Buffalo, NY (716)834-3817; Siemens-Allis Automation Inc., Houston, TX (713)681-5001; Siemens-Allis Automation Inc., Dallas, TX (214)247-4481; Siemens-Allis Automation Inc., Santa Ana, CA (714)979-6600; Siemens-Allis Automation Inc., Plymouth Meeting, PA (215)825-2120

ControlNet is a high-speed, token-access industrial network that allows multiple S5-115Ls to communicate. Devices connected include PCs, programmable controllers, printers, modems, disk drives, and any serial ASCII device. Compatible devices include IBM PC, Industrial Grade 5531 and XT computers. Compatible software includes U.S. Data Factory Link. Service contracts, network installation, instruction on network operation, and network maintenance services. First installed: 1983. Average number of stations per installation: 4.

• CONTROLNET TECHNICAL CHARACTERISTCS

Transmission category: baseband

Transmission medium: triaxial cable

Transmission speed: 1 Mbps backbone; .7 Mbps maximum available for user connection and burst

Topology: bus

Access method: token passing

Compatible operating systems: MS-DOS

Gateways: all IBM PC gateways

Maximum number of workstations per node: 2

Maximum number of nodes: 254

Maximum distance between nodes: 5000 feet

Means of host interconnection: terminal ports, IBM network module (NI-2)

Network server: disk server

Maximum number of file servers: 254

Network operation during backup: yes

Site of network logic: central controllers

• STANDARDS/PROTOCOLS SUPPORTED

Communications protocols: ISA 802.4

IEEE 802 standards: conforms to 802.4

ISO OSI Reference Model: conforms to layer 1 (Manchester) and layer 2 (token passing)

SIEMENS ENERGY & AUTOMATION—PROGRAMMABLE CONTROLS DIVISION • SINEC H1 LAN

10 Technology Drive, Centennial Park
Peabody, MA 01960
(617)532-6720; telex 928-160

Ray Leveille, Vice President and General Manager; R.L. Bailey, Vice President, Sales and Marketing; Ken Appel, Manager, Marketing Communications (MD); Tom Varney (PR)

Founded 1984

Branch Offices and Distributors:
   Siemens-Allis Automation Inc., Buffalo, NY (716)834-3817; Siemens-Allis Automation Inc., Houston, TX (713)681-5001; Siemens-Allis Automation Inc., Dallas, TX (214)247-4481; Siemens-Allis Automation Inc., Santa Ana (714)979-6600; Siemens-Allis Automation Inc., Plymouth Meeting, PA (215)825-2120

Sinec H1 uses a segmented bus architecture based on Ethernet. Compatible with the Manufacturing Automation Protocol, H1 can work and communicate with all other MAP-compatible devices and systems. Network connects PCs, dumb terminals and programmable controllers for industrial or office applications. First installed: 1985.

• SINEC H1 LAN TECHNICAL CHARACTERISTICS

Transmission category: baseband

Transmission mode: serial

Transmission medium: baseband coaxial cable

Transmission speed: 10 Mbps backbone and maximum available for user connection; 1.2 Mbps burst

Topology: bus

Access method: CSMA/CD

Compatible operating systems: CP/M

Gateways: Ethernet, X.25

Maximum number of workstations per node: 1

Maximum number of nodes: 1024 feet

Maximum distance between nodes: 1.5 miles, with remote repeater

Means of host interconnection: terminal ports

Network server: proprietary file server

Site of network logic: bus/network interface unit, central controllers

• STANDARDS/PROTOCOLS SUPPORTED

Communications protocols: X.25

IEEE 802 standards: conforms to 802.3

ISO OSI Reference Model: conforms to layer 1 (802.3), layer 2 (CSMA/CD with CRC check) and layer 3 (X.25)

SUNOL SYSTEMS INC. • SUN*NET

1177 Quarry Lane
Pleasanton, CA 94566
(415)484-3322; telex 703-175

Robert McCullough, President; Robert Morten (MD); Virginia Wurts (PSC); Ginger Crocker (PR); Jessie Velasquez (PA)

Founded 1983; 20 employees

Sun*Net is a PC network compatible with over 20 different microcomputers, including Apricot, Apple, DEC Rainbow, IBM PC/XT/AT, Macintosh, Compaq, and Wang. Networks up to 16 microcomputer users and 7 different operating systems. Designed for industrial, office, laboratory, and campus environment. Can work simultaneously with other LANs on the same Sunol disk drive. Service contracts, network installation, instruction on network operation, and network maintenance services available. First installed 1983. Number installed: 4600. Average number of stations per installation: 10.

• SUN*NET TECHNICAL CHARACTERISTICS

Transmission category: baseband

Transmission medium: baseband coaxial cable

Topology: bus

Access method: polling

Compatible operating systems: MS-DOS, CP/M, Unix, Xenix, MAC, ProDOS, Pascal, DOS 3.3

Gateways: Ethernet, IBM PC Network, AppleTalk, AST PC Net, Novell

Maximum number of workstations per node: 64

Maximum number of nodes: 8

Maximum distance between nodes: 100 feet

Means of host interconnection: multiplexed interfaces

Network server: proprietary file server, disk server

Disk backup: whole disk, partial disk

Network operation during backup: no

Site of network logic: bus/network interface units

• STANDARDS/PROTOCOLS SUPPORTED

Communications protocols: asynchronous

SYFA DATA SYSTEMS CORPORATION • SYFANET

1311 North Plano Road
Richardson, TX 75081
(214)783-0993; FAX 214-783-2334

Robert M. Parker, President; Jack D. Lindt, Vice President, Sales and Marketing (PSC)

Founded 1985; 107 employees

SyFAnet is an office LAN system capable of connecting minicomputers, PCs and dumb terminals. The network can support 300/600/1000 LPM printers, a variety of asynchronous and bisynchronous modems, 1600 BPI tape drive, and 36, 86, 80, 160, and 340 MB disk drives. Compatible devices include IBM PC/XT/AT units. Service contracts, network installation, instruction on network operation, and network maintenance services available. First installed: 1983. Number installed: 48. Average number of stations per installation: 40.

• SYFANET TECHNICAL CHARACTERISTICS

Transmission category: broadband

Transmission mode: full duplex

Transmission medium: broadband coaxial cable

Transmission speed: 3 Mbps backbone; 19.2 Kbps maximum available for user connection; 3 Mbps burst

Topology: bus

Access method: CSMA/CA

Compatible operating systems: MS-DOS, CP/M, proprietary

Gateways: SNA/SDLC, X.25

Maximum number of workstations per node: 8

Maximum number of nodes: 64

Maximum distance between nodes: 3000 feet

Means of host interconnection: multiplexed interfaces

Network server: proprietary file server

Maximum number of file servers: 15

Disk backup: whole disk

Network operation during backup: yes

Site of network logic: bus/network interface units

• STANDARDS/PROTOCOLS SUPPORTED

Communications protocols: SNA/SDLC, bisynchronous, X.25, asynchronous, RS-232, synchronous

SYNTREX INC. • SYNNET

246 Industrial Way West
Eatontown, NJ 07724
(201)542-1500; (800)526-2829; TWX 710-722-6604; FAX 201-542-1980

Jim Bruno, President; Joan Grayken (PM)(PSC); Grace Carr (MD); Don Balelli (PR); Harry Tonks (PA)

Founded 1980; 550 employees

SynNet connects up to 15 Syntrex Gemini, Polaris or Virgo systems, allowing users in an office setting to share documents, personal computing files and other resources such as laser printers, tape drives and modems. User access is automatic by specifying the name of a remote document, file or peripheral. Service contracts, network installation, instruction on network operation, and network maintenance services available.

• SYNNET TECHNICAL CHARACTERISTICS

Transmission category: baseband

Transmission medium: baseband coaxial cable

Transmission speed: 10 Mbps backbone, maximum available for user connection and burst

Topology: non-rooted tree

Access method: CSMA/CD

Compatible operating systems: SOS (Syntrex Operating System)

Maximum number of workstations per node: 14

Maximum number of nodes: 15

Maximum distance between nodes: 1700 feet

Means of host interconnection: Ethernet interface board on fileroom node

Network server: multivendor file server

Disk backup: whole disk

Network operation during backup: yes

Site of network logic: bus/network interface units

• STANDARDS/PROTOCOLS SUPPORTED

Communications protocols: SOS proprietary

IEEE 802 standards: conforms to 802.3

ISO OSI Reference Model: conforms to layers 1-4

SYTEK INC. • SYSTEM 6000

1225 Charleston Road
Mountain View, CA 94043
(415)966-7400; telex 276-572 SYTEK UR

L. George Klaus, President; Suri Harish, Director of Product Marketing (PM); Joseph Seidler, Vice President, Product Marketing (MD); Jeff Wilbur, Headquarters System Engineer (PSC); Stuart McFaul, Manager of Public Relations (PR); Jeanne Blackmore, Purchasing Manager (PA)

Founded 1979; 500 employees

Branch Offices and Distributors:
Sytek Inc., San Jose, CA (408)275-9860; Sytek Inc., Itasca IL (312)250-0057; Sytek Inc., Bethesda, MD (301)530-5100

System 6000 products network IBM PCs, ATs, XT, and compatibles with the capacity to support PC networks of up to 1000 nodes. Supports printers and disk drives. Compatible with IBM PC Network and any NETBIOS-compatible software package. Service contracts, network installation, instruction on network operation, and network maintenance services available. First installed: 1984. Number installed: over 1000. Average number of stations per installation: 50.

• SYSTEM 6000 TECHNICAL CHARACTERISTICS

Transmission category: broadband

Transmission mode: full duplex, half duplex

Transmission medium: broadband coaxial cable

Transmission speed: 2 Mbps backbone

Topology: branching tree

Access method: CSMA/CD

Compatible operating systems: MS-DOS, Unix, any NETBIOS-compatible operating system

Gateways: SNA/SDLC, X.25, Sytek Systems 2000 and 3000/7000

Maximum number of workstations per node: 1

Maximum number of nodes: over 1000

Maximum distance between nodes: 6 miles

Means of host interconnection: terminal ports

Network server: multivendor file server

Maximum number of file servers: unlimited

Disk backup: whole disk, partial disk

Network operation during backup: yes

Site of network logic: bus/network interface units

• STANDARDS/PROTOCOLS SUPPORTED

ISO OSI Reference Model: conforms to layer 1 (broadband RF cable), layer 2 (Link Access Protocol), layer 3 (Packet Transport Protocol), layer 4 (Reliable Stream Protocol, Datagram Transport Protocol), layer 5 (Session Management Protocol, Name Management Protocol, User Datagram Protocol Diagnostics and Monitoring Protocol)

SYTEK INC. • SYSTEM 3000/7000

1225 Charleston Road
Mountain View, CA 94043
(415)966-7400; telex 276-572 SYTEK UR

L. George Klaus, President; Suri Harish, Director of Product Marketing (PM); Joseph Seidler, Vice President, Product Marketing (MD); Jeff Wilbur, Headquarters System Engineer (PSC); Stuart McFaul, Manager of Public Relations (PR); Jeanne Blackmore, Purchasing Manager (PA)

Founded 1979; 500 employees

Branch Offices and Distributors:
Sytek Inc., San Jose, CA (408)275-9860; Sytek Inc., Itasca IL (312)250-0057; Sytek Inc., Bethesda, MD (301)530-5100

System 3000 includes devices for IBM 3270 networking that allow access to or from other IBM equipment and asynchronous hosts and devices. System 7000 products are devices for IBM 3270 netwoking that support IBM device-to-controller connections. Systems support mainframes, minicomputers, PCs, dumb terminals, and any RS-232 device, including printers, modems and test equipment. Compatible with IBM 3270 family. Service contracts, network installation, instruction on network operation, and network maintenance services available. Number of networks installed: over 1000.

- ## SYSTEM 3000/7000 TECHNICAL CHARACTERISTICS

Transmission category: broadband

Transmission mode: full duplex, half duplex

Transmission medium: broadband coaxial cable

Transmission speed: 128 Kbps backbone; 2.34 Mbps maximum available for user connection

Topology: branching tree

Access method: CSMA/CD

Compatible operating systems: MS-DOS, Unix, any NETBIOS-compatible operating system

Gateways: Sytek System 6000

Maximum number of workstations per node: 16

Maximum number of nodes: 65,534

Maximum distance between nodes: 70 miles

Means of host interconnection: terminal ports

Network server: multivendor file server

Maximum number of file servers: unlimited

Disk backup: whole disk, partial disk

Network operation during backup: yes

Site of network logic: bus/network interface unit

SYTEK INC. • SYSTEM 2000
1225 Charleston Road
Mountain View, CA 94043
(415)966-7400; telex 276-572 SYTEK UR

L. George Klaus, President; Suri Harish, Director of Product Marketing (PM); Joseph Seidler, Vice President, Product Marketing (MD); Jeff Wilbur, Headquarters System Enginer (PSC); Stuart McFaul, Manager of Public Relations (PR); Jeanne Blackmore, Purchasing Manager (PA)

Founded 1979; 500 employees

Branch Offices and Distributors:
Sytek Inc., San Jose, CA (408)275-9860; Sytek Inc., Itasca IL (312)250-0057; Sytek Inc., Bethesda, MD (301)530-5100

System 2000 is the next-generation LocalNet product family with enhancements for operation in large networks. Supports mainframes, minicompouters, PCs, dumb terminals, and any RS-232 devices, including printers, modems and test equipment. Suitable for industrial, office, laboratory, or campus applications. Service contracts, network installation, instruction on network operation, and network maintenance services available. First installed: 1981 (LocalNet/20). Number installed: over 1000. Average number of stations per installation: 250.

• SYSTEM 2000 TECHNICAL CHARACTERISTICS

Transmission category: broadband

Transmission mode: full duplex, half duplex

Transmission medium: broadband coaxial cable

Transmission speed: 128 Kbps backbone; 19.2 Kbps maximum available for user connection

Topology: branching tree

Access method: CSMA/CD

Compatible operating systems: MS-DOS, Unix, any NETBIOS-compatible system

Gateways: linking between distinct cable systems; Sytek System 6000

Maximum number of workstations per node: 32

Maximum number of nodes: 65,534

Maximum distance between nodes: 70 miles

Means of host interconnection: terminal ports

Network server: multivendor file server

Maxim number of file servers: unlimited

Disk backup: whole disk, partial disk

Network operation during backup: yes

Site of network logic: bus/network interface modems

• STANDARDS/PROTOCOLS SUPPORTED

Communications protocols: asynchronous, bisynchronous, RS-232, synchronous

ISO OSI Reference Model: conforms to layer 1 (broadband RF cable), layer 2 (Link Access Protocol), layer 3 (Packet Transport Protocol), layer 4 (Reliable Stream Protocol), and layer 5 (Session Management Protocol)

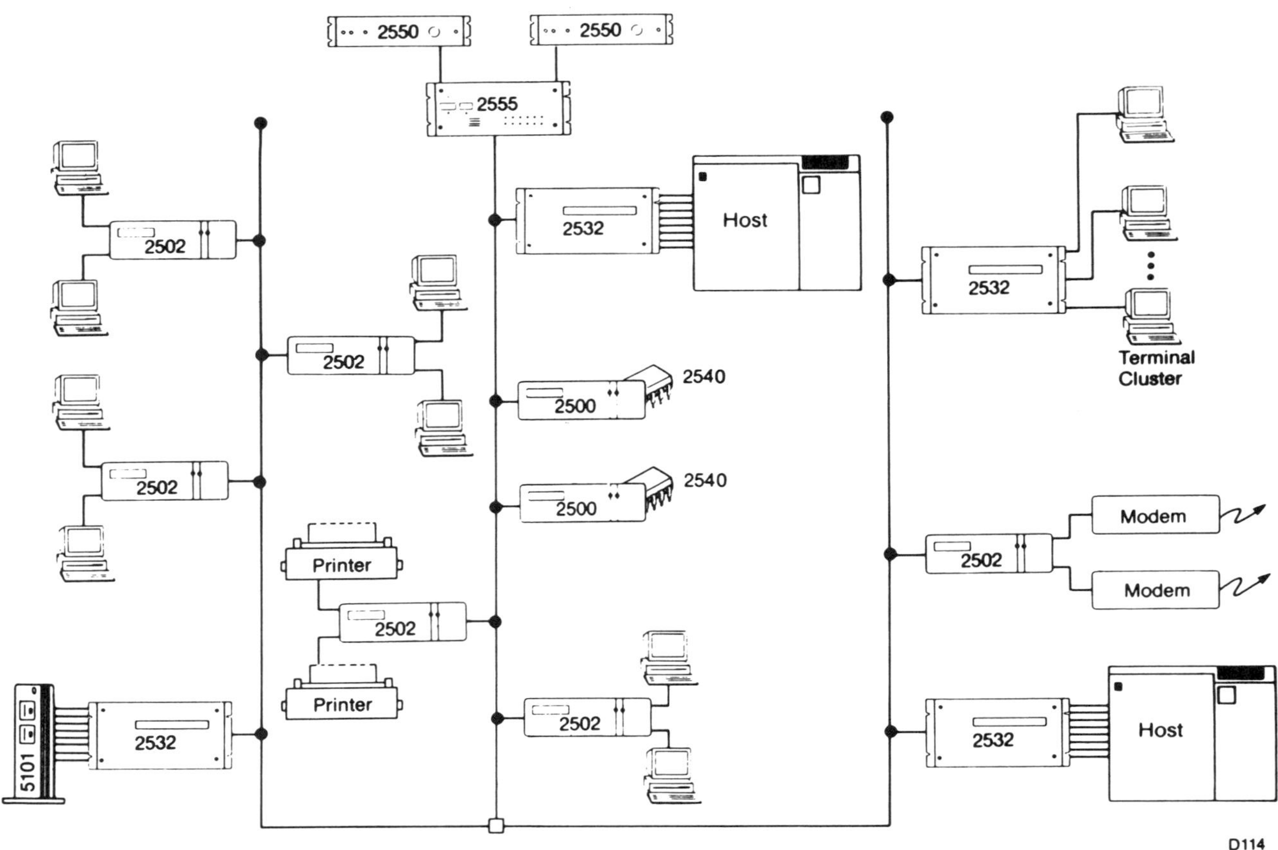

Representative Network Configuration

Figure 30

Courtesy Sytek Inc.

TECMAR INC. • ELAN

6225 Cochran Road
Solon, OH 44139
(216)349-1009; telex 466-692; FAX 216-349-0851

Martin Alpert, President; Rick Dorman, Vice President, Marketing (MD); John Purner, Vice President, Sales (PSC)

Founded 1974; 300 employees

ELAN is an office PC network capable of supporting all IBM PC/XT/AT compatibles, printers, disk drives, and the Phonegate. Instruction on network operation available.

- **ELAN TECHNICAL CHARACTERISTICS**

Transmission category: baseband

Transmission mode: full duplex

Transmission medium: baseband coaxial cable

Transmission speed: 10 Mbps burst

Topology: bus

Access method: CSMA/CD

Compatible operating systems: MS-DOS

Gateways: Ethernet

Maximum number of workstations per node: 1

Maximum number of nodes: 300

Maximum distance between nodes: 100 feet

Network server: proprietary file server

Maximum number of file servers: 1 per workstation

Disk backup: whole disk, partial disk

Network operation during backup: yes

Site of network logic: terminal equipment

- **STANDARDS/PROTOCOLS SUPPORTED**

Communications protocols: RS-232

IEEE 802 standards: conforms to 802.2 and 802.3

ISO OSI Reference Model: conforms to layer 1 (Ethernet)

TELE-ENGINEERING CORPORATION • CUSTOM

3 Speen Street, Suite 230
Framingham, MA 01701
(617)875-3137; FAX 617-788-0324

E.O. Tunmann, President; Gary Cooper (PM)(PSC)(PR); Victor Colantonio, Director of Marketing (MD); Alan Burt, Purchasing Agent (PA)

Founded 1973; 54 employees

Custom LAN is a fiber network connecting mainframes, minicomputers, PCs, dumb terminals, and gateways for industrial, office, laboratory, campus, government, and military applications. Service contracts, network installation, instruction on network operation, and network maintenance services available. First installed: 1980. Number installed: 100. Average number of stations per installation: 500.

• CUSTOM TECHNICAL CHARACTERISTICS

Transmission category: broadband

Trasmission mode: full duplex

Transmission medium: broadband coaxial cable, optical fiber

Topology: ring, star, bus

Access method: CSMA/CD, polling, token passing

Gateways: SNA/SDLC, Ethernet, X.25, HDLC

Maximum number of workstations per node: 8000

Maximum number of nodes: unlimited

Maximum distance between nodes: unlimited

Means of host interconnection: multiplexed interfaces, terminal ports, fiber

Maximum number of file servers: unlimited

Network operation during backup: yes

Site of network logic: bus/network interface units

• STANDARDS/PROTOCOLS SUPPORTED

Communications protocols: SNA/SDLC, bisynchronous, X.25, HDLC, asynchronous, RS-232, synchronous

IEEE 802 standards: conforms to 802.2-802.6

ISO OSI Reference Model: conforms to layers 2-4

TERMINAL DATA CORPORATION • TERMNET

15733 Crabbs Branch Way
Rockville, MD 20855
(301)921-8282

Len Titlebaum, President (PM); Mark Titlebaum (MD); James Odom (PSC); Barbara Miller (PA)

Founded 1970; 16 employees

TermNET is an office or campus LAN capable of connecting minicomputers, PCs, dumb terminals, printers, modems, and disk drives. Service contracts, network installation, instruction on network operation, and network maintenance services available. First installed: 1986. Average number of stations per installation: 6.

• TERMNET TECHNICAL CHARACTERISTICS

Transmission category: baseband

Transmission medium: twisted wire pair

Transmission speed: 1 Mbps backbone and maximum avilable for user connection

Topology: ring

Access method: polling

Compatible operating systems: MS-DOS

Gateways: RS-232 serial

Maximum number of workstations per node: 1

Maximum number of nodes: 256

Maximum distance between nodes: 100 feet

Means of host interconnection: terminal ports

Network server: disk server

Maximum number of file servers: 1 per station

Disk backup: whole disk

Network operation during backup: yes

• STANDARDS/PROTOCOLS SUPPORTED

Communications protocols: RS-232

IEEE 802 standards: conforms to 802.2

TEXAS INSTRUMENTS—DATA SYSTEMS GROUP • ETHERSERIES

P.O. Box 809063
Dallas, TX 75380-9063
(214)995-2011; telex 73-324; TWX 910-867-4702

Jerry R. Junkins, President; Walden C. Rhines (PM); Liston M. Rice, Vice President (MD); Den Hiser, Manager, Corporate Material (PA)

Founded 1930; 77,872 employees

EtherSeries is a family of hardware and software networking products for interconnecting TI Professional Computers and IB PCs into a resource-sharing local area network. Conforms to IEEE Ethernet standard. Servers include disk, print and electronic mail.

• ETHERSERIES TECHNICAL CHARACTERISTICS

Transmission category: baseband

Transmission medium: standard or thin Ethernet cabling

Transmission speed: 10 Mbps maximum available for user connection

Topology: bus

Access method: CSMA/CD

Maximum number of workstations per node: 100 computers per cable segment

Maximum number of nodes: 10 cable segments

Maximum distance between nodes: 1640 feet maximum network length

TIARA COMPUTER SYSTEMS INC. • TIARALINK

2685 Marine Way
Mountain View, CA 94043
(415)965-1700; telex 499-6251; FAX 415-965-2677

Thomas G. Hong, President; William Y. Terrill, Director of Product Marketing (PM); Mike Paul, Vice President, Marketing and Sales (MD); Sally Johnson, Manager, Marketing Communications (PR); Robert Kong, Director of Manufacturing (PA)

Founded 1985; 35 employees

Branch Offices and Distibutors:
Vitek Corporation, San Marcos, CA (619)744-8305; OnSite Business Systems; Ann Arbor, MI (214)634-3403; Access Data, Westchester, NY (401)434-0550; Computer Power, Jacksonville, FL (904)350-1400; Systems House, Vienna, VA (703)845-7770

TiaraLink is a PC network designed for office use. Offers true shared files throughout network. Operating system allows every station to function as shared file server or to have a network printer attached. The network will support printers, disk drives and modems. Software vendor compatibility: Software Connections. Instruction on network operation available. First installed: 1983. Number installed: 2500. Average number of stations per installation: 1.

• TIARALINK TECHNICAL CHARACTERISTICS

Transmission category: baseband

Transmission mode: full duplex

Transmission medium: baseband coaxial cable, optical fiber

Transmission speed: 2.5 Mbps maximum available for user connection

Topology: physical, distributed starburst; logical, bus

Accss method: token passing

Compatible operating systems: MS-DOS

Gateways: SNA/SDLC, X.25

Maximum number of workstations per node: 1

Maximum number of nodes: 255

Maximum distance between nodes: 20,000

Means of host interconnection: hubs

Network server: disk server

Maximum number of file servers: 255

Site of network logic: bus/network interface units

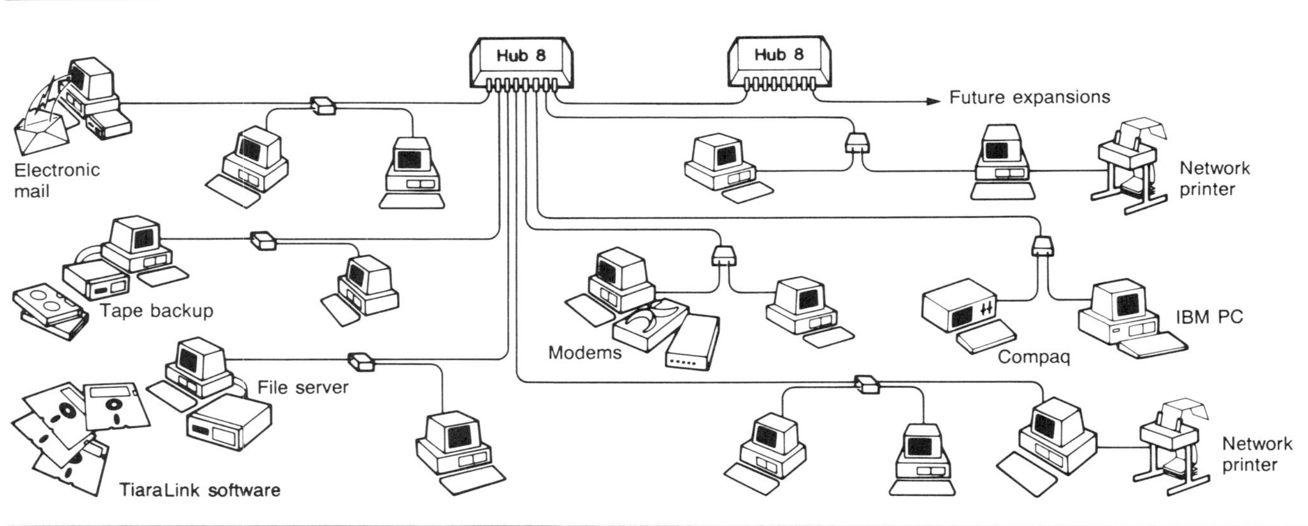

Figure 31

Courtesy Tiara Computer Systems Inc.

TRW INC.—INFORMATION NETWORKS DIVISION • TRW CONCEPT 2000

23800 Hawthorne Boulevard
Torrance, CA 90505
(213)373-911; FAX 213-375-5805

J. Edward Snyder, General Manager; John Cahill, Manager, Marketing Planning (PM); Bronson Purdy Jr., Director of Marketing (MD)(PSC); Jeanne Jalan, Manager, Marketing Communications (PR)

Founded 1985; 100 employees

Branch Offices and Distributors:
> TRW Information Networks Division, Chicago, IL (312)693-7730; TRW Information Networks Division, East Brunswick, NJ (201)238-1300; TRW Information Networks Division, Boston, MA (617)229-5809; TRW Information Networks Division, Arlington, VA (703)276-5100; Arc Associates, Westlake, OH (216)835-2055

TRW Concept 2000 consists of a family of LAN products for linking mainframes, minicomputers, microcomputers, and dumb terminals for use in an office, laboratory or campus environment. The network can also support printers, modems and disk drives. The backbone of TRW's Concept 2000 product line is a broadband LAN along which a number of asynchronous and synchronous devices, 3270 terminals, video units, and departmental baseband networks can be connected. Service contracts, network installation, instruction on network operation, and network maintenance services available. First installed: 1974. Number installed: 70. Average number of stations per installation: 1000.

• TRW CONCEPT 2000 TECHNICAL CHARACTERISTICS

Transmission category: baseband, broadband

Transmission mode: full duplex

Transmission medium: baseband coaxial cable, broadband coaxial cable

Transmission speed: up to 10 Mbps, backbone

Topology: bus

Access method: CSMA, CSMA/CD, token passing

Compatible operating systems: MS/DOS, Unix, VAX-VMS, IBM-OS

Gateways: SNA/SDLC, Ethernet, X.25, HDLC

Maximum number of workstations per node: 32

Maximum number of nodes: over 1000

Maximum distance between nodes: 10 miles

Means of host interconnection: multiplexed interfaces, terminal ports

Network server: multivendor file server

Maximum number of file servers: unlimited

Disk backup: whole disk, partial disk

Network operation during backup: yes

Site of network logic: bus/network interface units

• STANDARDS/PROTOCOLS SUPPORTED

Communications protocols: SNA/SDLC, X.25, asynchronous, synchronous, bisynchronous, HDLC, RS-232

IEEE 802 standards: conforms to 802.2, 802.3

ISO OSI Reference Model: conforms to layer 1 (802.3); layer 2 (802.3); layer 3 (XNS, TCP/IP, SDLC); layer 4 (XNS, TCP/IP, SDLC); layer 5 (XNS, TCP/IP, SDLC); layer 6 (XNS, TCP/IP, SDLC); and layer 7 (XNS, TCP/IP, SDLC)

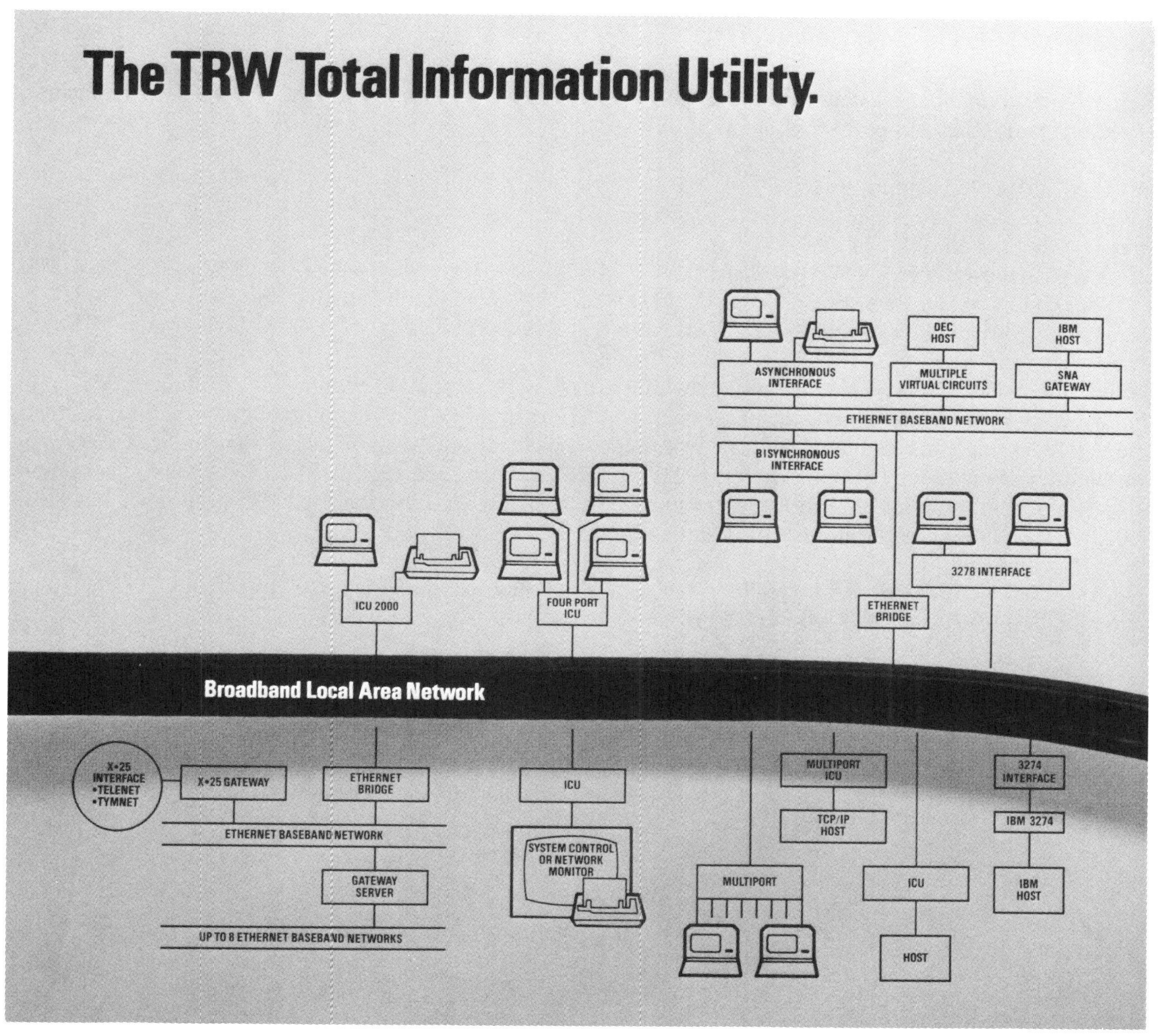

Figure 32

Courtesy TRW Inc., Information Networks Division

UNGERMANN-BASS INC. • OPTICAL FIBER NET/ONE

3900 Freedom Circle
Santa Clara, CA 95054
(408)496-0111

Ralph K. Ungermann, President; Cliff Rudolph, Vice President, Sales and Marketing (MD); Peter Kirschner, Director, Marketing Support (PSC)

Founded 1979; 700 employees

Branch Offices and Distributors:
Ungermann-Bass Inc., Newport Beach, CA (714)955-1414; Ungermann-Bass Inc., Dallas, TX (214)385-7090; Ungermann-Bass Inc., Chicago, IL (312)882-6885; Ungermann-Bass Inc., St. Louis, MO (314)532-9366; Ungermann-Bass Inc., New York, NY (212)466-1763

Optical Fiber Net/One combines high bandwidth with long link capabilities to allow attachment of a large number of devices on a single channel. Star coupler provides multiple access and broadcast functions compatible with a multiple-access bus. Conforms to Ethernet specifications (version 1.0) in that the transceiver-to-station interface is exactly the same as the coaxial system. Service contracts, network installation, instruction on network operation, and network maintenance services available. First installed: 1984. Number installed: 400. Average number of stations per installation: 12.

• OPTICAL FIBER NET/ONE TECHNICAL CHARACTERISTICS

Transmission category: broadband

Transmission medium: optical fiber

Transmission speed: 10 Mbps

Topology: star

Access method: CSMA/CD

UNGERMANN-BASS INC. • NET/ONE THIN COAXIAL BASEBAND

3900 Freedom Circle
Santa Clara, CA 95054
(408)496-0111

Ralph K. Ungermann, President; Cliff Rudolph, Vice President, Sales and Marketing (MD); Peter Kirschner, Director, Marketing Support (PSC)

Founded 1979; 700 employees

Branch Offices and Distributors:
Ungermann-Bass Inc., Newport Beach, CA (714)955-1414; Ungermann-Bass Inc., Dallas, TX (214)385-7090; Ungermann-Bass Inc., Chicago, IL (312)882-6885; Ungermann-Bass Inc., St. Louis, MO (314)532-9366; Ungermann-Bass Inc., New York, NY (212)466-1763

Net/One Thin Coaxial Baseband is especially suited for the networking of personal computers. Network repeater units can connect baseband segments of thin coaxial cable, Ethernet coaxial cable, and fiber optic cable to form complex topologies of dissimilar baseband media. Transceivers are Ethernet version 1.0 compatible. Service contracts, network installation, instruction on network operation, and network maintenance services available.

• NET/ONE THIN COAXIAL BASEBAND TECHNICAL CHARACTERISTICS

Transmission category: baseband

Transmission medium: RG 58 A/U coaxial cable

Transmission speed: 10 Mbps

Topology: bus

Access method: CSMA/CD

Maximum distance between nodes: 400 meters

UNGERMANN-BASS INC. • NET/ONE BROADBAND

3900 Freedom Circle
Santa Clara, CA 95054
(408)496-0111

Ralph K. Ungermann, President; Cliff Rudolph, Vice President, Sales and Marketing (MD); Peter Kirschner, Director, Marketing Support (PSC)

Founded 1979; 700 employees

Branch Offices and Distributors:
Ungermann-Bass Inc., Newport Beach, CA (714)955-1414; Ungermann-Bass Inc., Dallas, TX (214)385-7090; Ungermann-Bass Inc., Chicago, IL (312)882-6885; Ungermann-Bass Inc., St. Louis, MO (314)532-9366; Ungermann-Bass Inc., New York, NY (212)466-1763

Net/One Broadband can support up to five CATV channels operating at 5 Mbps each. Fully operable with video, voice and additional data. Allows mainframes, minicomputers, cameras, PCs monitors, terminals, modems, and printers, to be connected on a single cable over a large geographic area for industrial, office, laboratory, or campus applications. Adheres to EIA and IEEE 802 guidelines for broadband LANs. Service contracts, network installation, instruction on network operation, and network maintenance services available. First installed: 1982. Number installed: 400. Average number of stations per installation: 12.

• NET/ONE BROADBAND TECHNICAL CHARACTERISTICS

Transmission category: broadband

Transmission medium: broadband coaxial cable

Transmission speed: 5 Mbps

Topology: bus

Access method: CSMA/CD

Compatible operating systems: MS-DOS, Unix, CP/M

Gateways: SNA/SDLC, X.25, HDLC

Maximum number of nodes: 1500

Maximum distance between nodes: 52,800 feet

Means of host interconnection: bus interface cards, RS-232 terminal ports, IEEE 488, V.35

Network server: multivendor file server

Maximum number of file servers: 20

• STANDARDS/PROTOCOLS SUPPORTED

Communications protocols: X.25

Net/One Thin Coaxial Baseband

Single Cable Segment Configuration

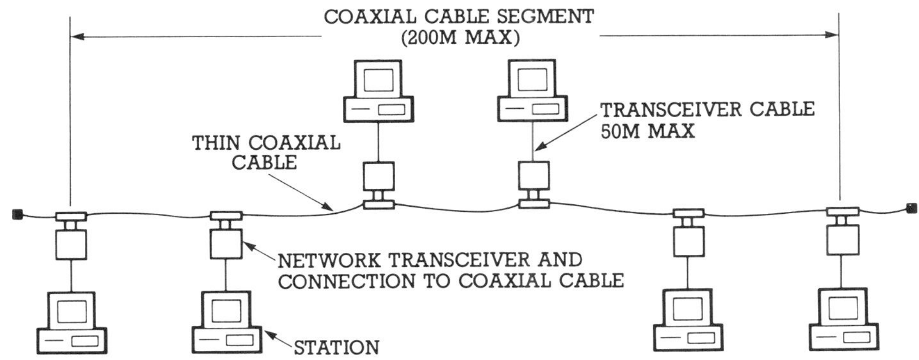

Net/One Thin Coaxial Baseband

Figure 33

Courtesy Ungermann-Bass Inc.

Net/One Broadband Network

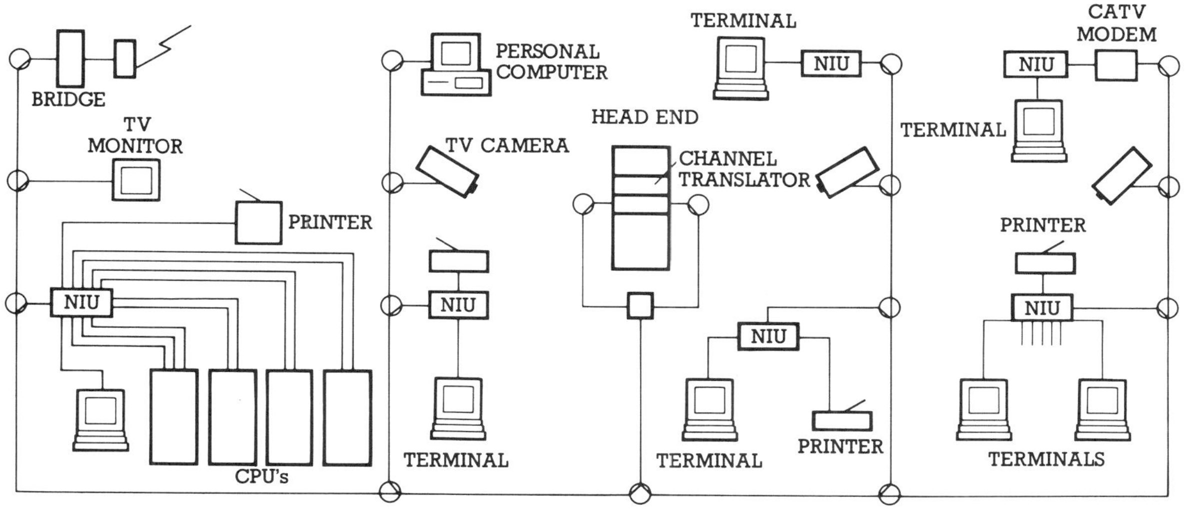

Figure 34

Courtesy Ungermann-Bass Inc.

UNGERMANN-BASS INC. • NET/ONE ETHERNET BASEBAND

3900 Freedom Circle
Santa Clara, 95054
(408)496-0111

Ralph K. Ungermann, President; Cliff Rudolph, Vice President, Sales and Marketing (MD); Peter Kirschner, Director, Marketing Support (PSC)

Founded 1979; 700 employees

Branch Offices and Distributors:
Ungermann-Bass Inc., Newport Beach, CA (714)955-1414; Ungermann-Bass Inc., Dallas, TX (214)385-7090; Ungermann-Bass Inc., Chicago, IL (312)882-6885; Ungermann-Bass Inc., St. Louis, MO (314)532-9366; Ungermann-Bass Inc., New York, NY (212)466-1763

Net/One Ethernet Baseband provides a communications facility for high-speed, reliable data exchange among computers and other digital devices located within a moderate-sized geographic area. Fully compatible with Ethernet version 2.0 and IEEE 802.3. Supports thousands of vendor independent devices. Passive transmission medium allows adding and deleting nodes without network downtime. Service contracts, network installation, instruction on network operation, and network maintenance services available. First installed: 1980. Number installed: 400. Average number of stations per installation: 12.

• NET/ONE ETHERNET BASEBAND TECHNICAL CHARACTERISTICS

Transmission category: baseband

Transmission medium: baseband coaxial cable

Transmission speed: 10 Mbps

Topology: bus

Access method: CSMA/CD

Compatible operating systems: MS-DOS, CP/M, Unix

Gateways: SNA/SDLC, X.25, HDLC

Maximum number of workstations per node: 24

Maximum distance between nodes: 2900 meters

Means of host interconnection: bus interface cards, RS-232 terminal ports, IEEE 488, V.35

Network server: multivendor file server

Maximum number of file servers: 20

• STANDARDS/PROTOCOLS SUPPORTED

IEEE 802 standards: conforms to 802.3

ISO OSI Reference Model: conforms to layers 1 and 2 (Ethernet), layer 3 (XNS) and layers 4-6 (proprietary)

Net/One Ethernet Baseband

SINGLE ETHERNET CABLE SEGMENT CONFIGURATION

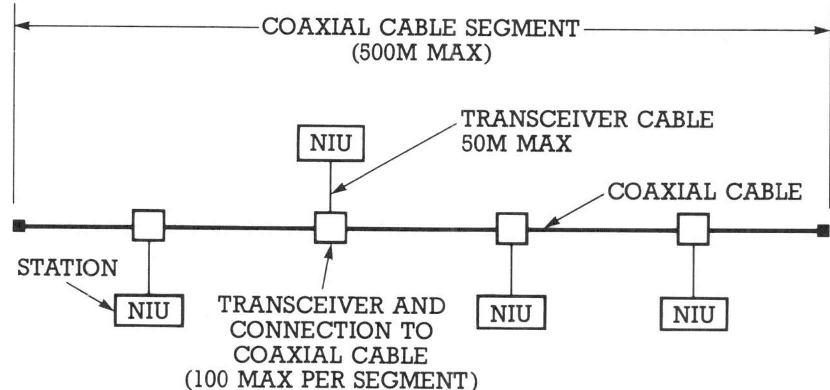

MULTIPLE ETHERNET CABLE SEGMENT CONFIGURATION

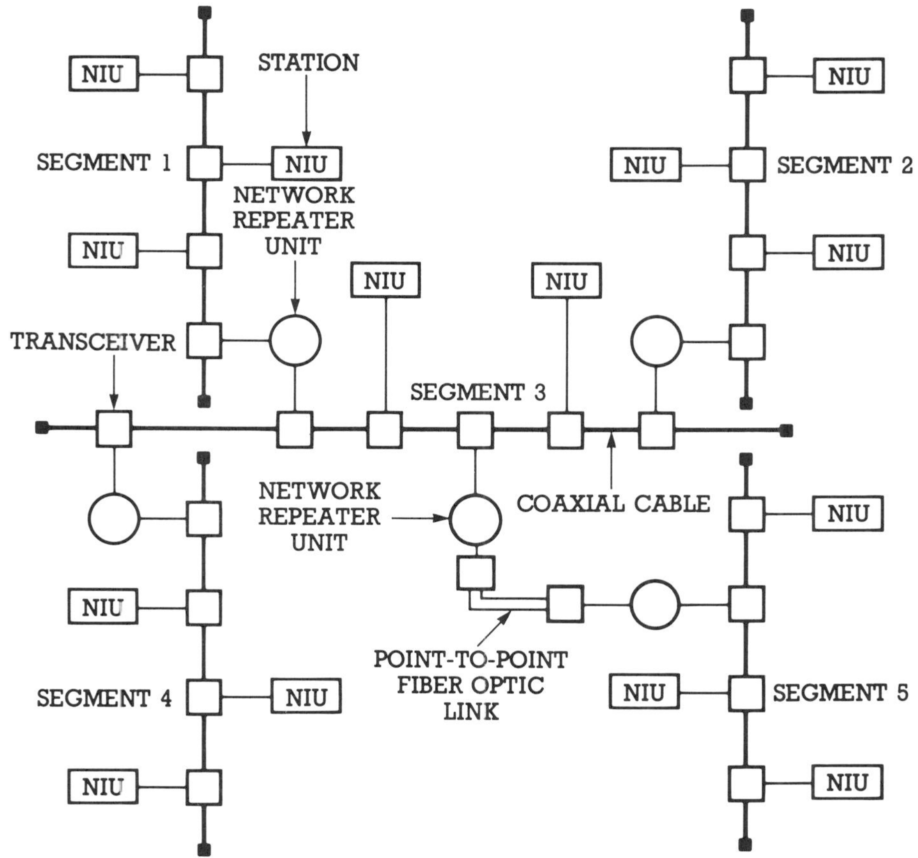

Figure 35

Courtesy Ungermann-Bass Inc.

UNGERMANN-BASS INC. • INTRO/NET

3900 Freedom Circle
Santa Clara, CA 95054
(408)496-0111

Ralph K. Ungermann, President; Cliff Rudolph, Vice President, Sales and Marketing (MD); Peter Kirschner, Director, Marketing Support (PSC)

Founded 1979; 700 employees

Branch Offices and Distributors:
Ungermann-Bass Inc., Newport Beach, CA (714)955-1414; Ungermann-Bass Inc., Dallas, TX (214)385-7090; Ungermann-Bass Inc., Chicago, IL (312)882-6885; Ungermann-Bass Inc., St. Louis, MO (314)532-9366; Ungermann-Bass Inc., New York, NY (212)466-1763

Intro/Net is an a IEEE 802.5 network that is compatible with the IBM Token-Ring implementation. Provides connectivity for asynchronous devices, the IBM 3270 product family and IBM PC, XT, AT, and compatibles. Includes full support for the IBM NETBIOS interface. Service contracts, network installation, instruction on network operation, and network maintenance services available.

• INTRO/NET TECHNICAL CHARACTERISTICS

Transmission speed: 4 Mbps

Topology: logical ring, physical star

Access method: token passing

Compatible operating systems: MS-DOS, PC-DOS 3.1

• STANDARDS/PROTOCOLS SUPPORTED

IEEE 802 standards: conforms to 802.5

Net/One Token Ring Intro/Net System

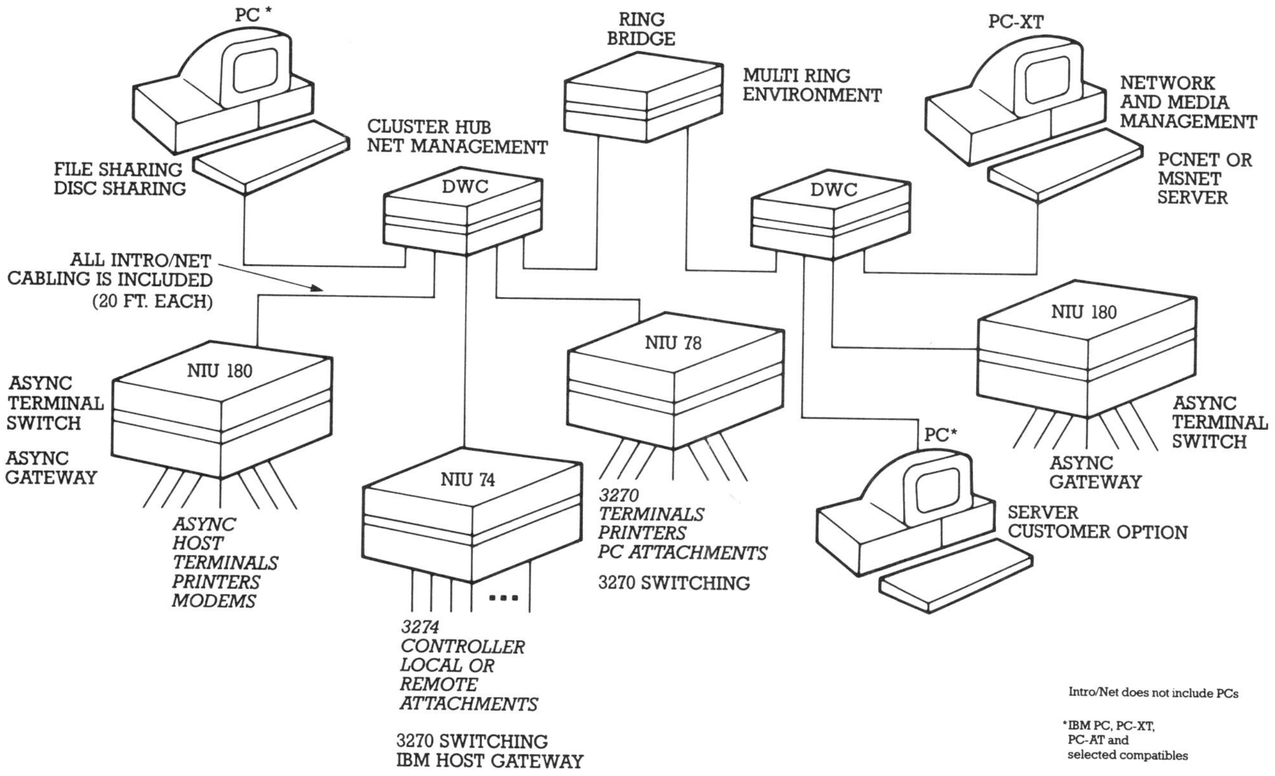

Figure 36

Courtesy Ungermann-Bass Inc.

WANG LABORATORIES INC. • WANGNET/FASTLAN

One Industrial Avenue
Lowell, MA 01851
(617)459-5000; telex 947-421; TWX 710-343-6769

Dr. An Wang, President; Stephen Young, WangNet Product Manager (PM); Ed Powers, Senior Public Relations Specialist (PR)

Founded 1951; 30,000 employees

Branch Offices and Distributors:
Wang Laboratories Inc., San Francisco, CA (415)956-7077; Wang Laboratories Inc., Chicago, IL (312)329-1530; Wang Laboratories Inc., Boston, MA (617)720-5700; Wang Laboratories Inc., New York, NY (212)599-3454; Wang Laboratories, Rosslyn, VA (703)243-4700

WangNet is a dual cable, broadband radio-frequency communications medium for the concurrent exchange of data, text, graphics, electronic mail, and video information. FastLAN is a modular WangNet that utilizes the WangNet as a distribution trunk, thus creating a single integrated network. Devices connected include mainframes, minicomputers, PCs, dumb terminals, asynchronous terminals, intelligent terminals, printers, modems, disk drives, and video cameras. Other compatible devices: 802.3 compatible equipment via Medium Access Unit; RS-232C compatible asynchronous devices via Shared Interconnect Modem Service; IBM 3278 display stations, 3287 printers, and 3289 printers via CMUX; and IBM PCs, PC-XTs and PC-ATs via PC-Net Adapter. Designed for office, laboratory or campus setting. Network supports both Wang-developed and industry-standard network interface devices. Service contracts, network installation, instruction on network operation, and network maintenance services available. First installed: 1981. Number installed: 1500. Average number of stations per installation: 130.

• WANGNET/FASTLAN TECHNICAL CHARACTERISTICS

Transmission category: broadband

Transmission mode: full duplex

Transmission medium: broadband coaxial cable

Transmission speed: 10 Mbps backbone; 4.27 Mbps maximum available for user connection

Topology: branching tree

Access method: CSMA, modified token passing, CSMA/CD, polling, frequency division multiplexing, CATV (for video)

Compatible operating systems: MS-DOS, CP/M, Unix

Gateways: SNA/SDLC, Ethernet, X.25, HDLC, asynchronous, bisynchronous

Maximum number of workstations per node: 30,000 (Wang Band)

Maximum number of nodes: varies according to application

Maximum distance between nodes: 8 cable miles

Means of host interconnection: multiplexed interfaces, terminal ports

Network server: multivendor file server, proprieary file server

Maximum number of file servers: varies with application

Disk backup: whole disk

Network operation during backup: yes

Site of network logic: bus/network interface units, central controllers

- ## STANDARDS/PROTOCOLS
  SUPPORTED

Communications protocols: SNA/SDLC, bisynchronous, X.25, HDLC, asynchronous, RS-232, synchronous

IEEE 802 standards: conforms to 802.3

ISO OSI Reference Model: conforms to layers 1-4

Multiple FASTLANS

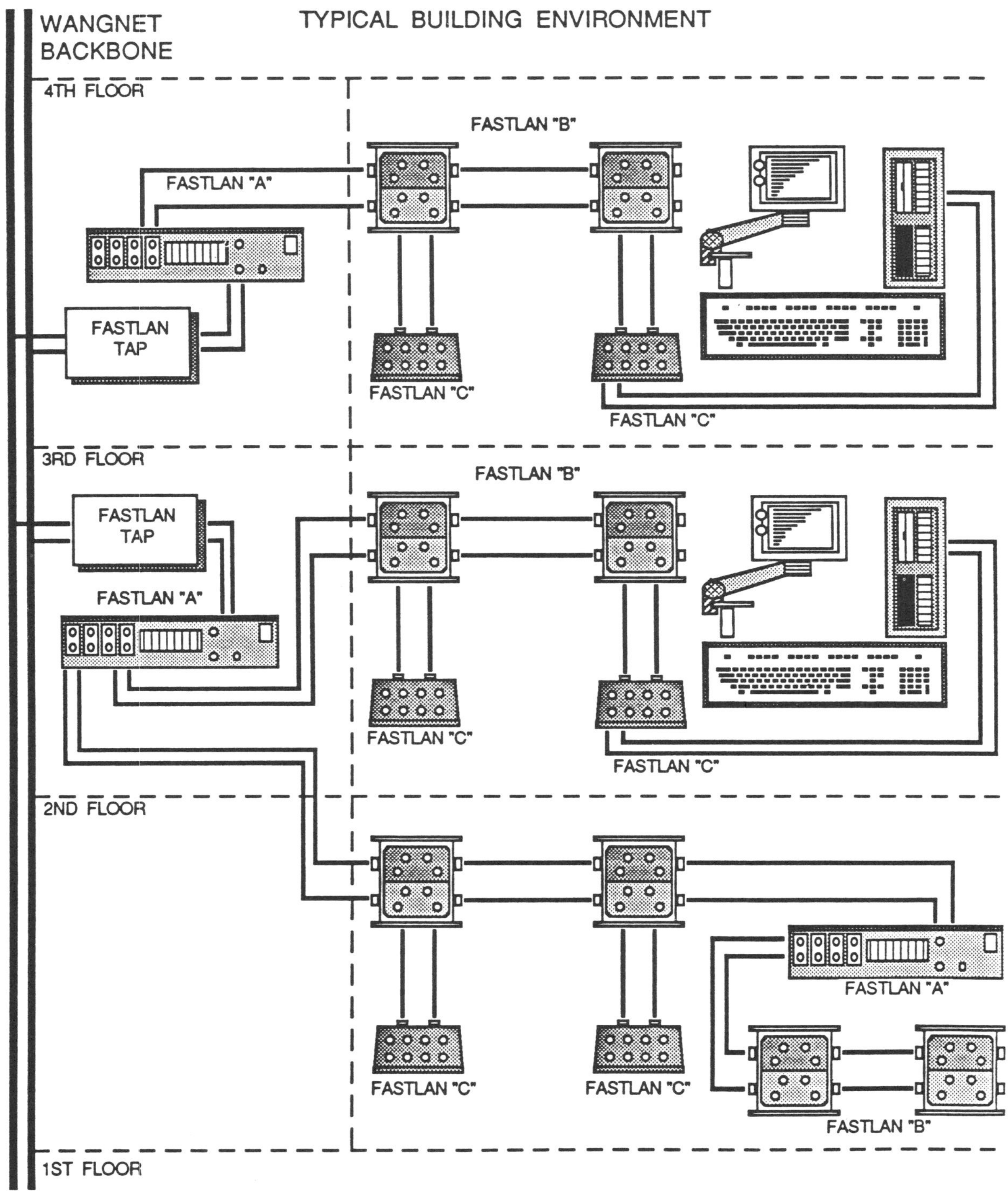

Figure 37

Courtesy Wang Laboratories Inc.

XEROX CORPORATION • XEROX COMMUNICATIONS 22 (XC 22)

Xerox Square
Rochester, NY 14644
(716)423-4828

David T. Kearns, President; Dan Minchen (PSC); Frank D. Steenburgh, Vice President, Information Systems Marketing (PSC)

Founded 1906; 103,500 employees

Branch Offices and Distributors:
Xerox Corporation, New York, NY (212)916-2300; Xerox Corporation, Arlington, VA (703)527-6400; Xerox Corporation, Atlanta, GA (404)255-5550; Xerox Corporation, Irvine, CA (714)660-0136; Xerox Corporation, Oakland, CA (415)430-3600

Xerox Communication 22 is a PC office network that runs over standard twisted-pair telephone wire. Utilizes STARLAN network technology. Network supports all Xerox printers used on 6060 workstations, as well as most printers with standard, parallel and serial interface. Network compatible with IBM PC/XT/AT and their compatibles and all MS-DOS 3.1 software written for the IBM PC Network and Token Ring Network. Service contracts, network installation, instruction on network operation, and network maintenance services available. First installed: 1986.

• XEROX COMMUNICATIONS 22 (XC 22) TECHNICAL CHARACTERISTICS

Transmission category: baseband

Transmission medium: twisted wire pair

Transmission speed: 1 Mbps maximum available for user connection; 1 Mbps burst

Topology: bus

Access method: CSMA/CD

Compatible operating systems: MS-DOS

Maximum number of workstations per node: 1

Maximum number of nodes: 200

Maximum distance between nodes: 17 miles

Network server: multivendor file server

Maximum number of file servers: 200

Site of network logic: terminal equipment

• STANDARDS/PROTOCOLS SUPPORTED

IEEE 802 standards: conforms to 802.3

ISO OSI Reference Model: conforms to layer 1 (802.3 and CSMA/CD) and layer 7 (file sharing, printer sharing, messaging, and support of DOS 3.1 applications)

XEROX CORPORATION • ETHERNET

Xerox Square
Rochester, NY 14644
(716)423-4828

David T. Kearns, President; Dan Minchen (PSC); Frank D. Steenburgh, Vice President, Informatin Systems Marketing (PSC)

Founded 1906; 103,500 employees

Branch Offices and Distributors:
Xerox Corporation, New York, NY (212)916-2300; Xerox Corporation, Arlington, VA (703)527-6400; Xerox Corporation, Atlanta, GA (404)255-5550; Xerox Corporation, Irvine, CA (714)660-0136; Xerox Corporation, Oakland, CA (415)430-3600

Ethernet is a local communications network that connects office equipment to form an integrated office system of professional workstations, PCs, word processors, electronic files, laser printers, and scanners. May also be implemented with thin-cable Ethernet (RG-58). Adopted by more than 300 vendors as a networking standard. Selected in 1982 as a standard by the IEEE and European Computer Manufacturers' Association. First introduced: 1979. Number installed: 35,000.

• ETHERNET TECHNICAL CHARACTERISTICS

Transmission category: baseband

Transmission medium: baseband coaxial cable, thin Ethernet

Transmission speed: 10 Mbps maximum available for user connection; 10 Mbps burst

Topology: unrooted tree

Access method: CSMA/CD

Gateways: SNA, X.25

Maximum number of nodes: 1024 (30 for thin Ethernet)

Maximum distance between nodes: 1.5 miles

• STANDARDS/PROTOCOLS SUPPORTED

IEEE 802 standards: conforms to 802.3

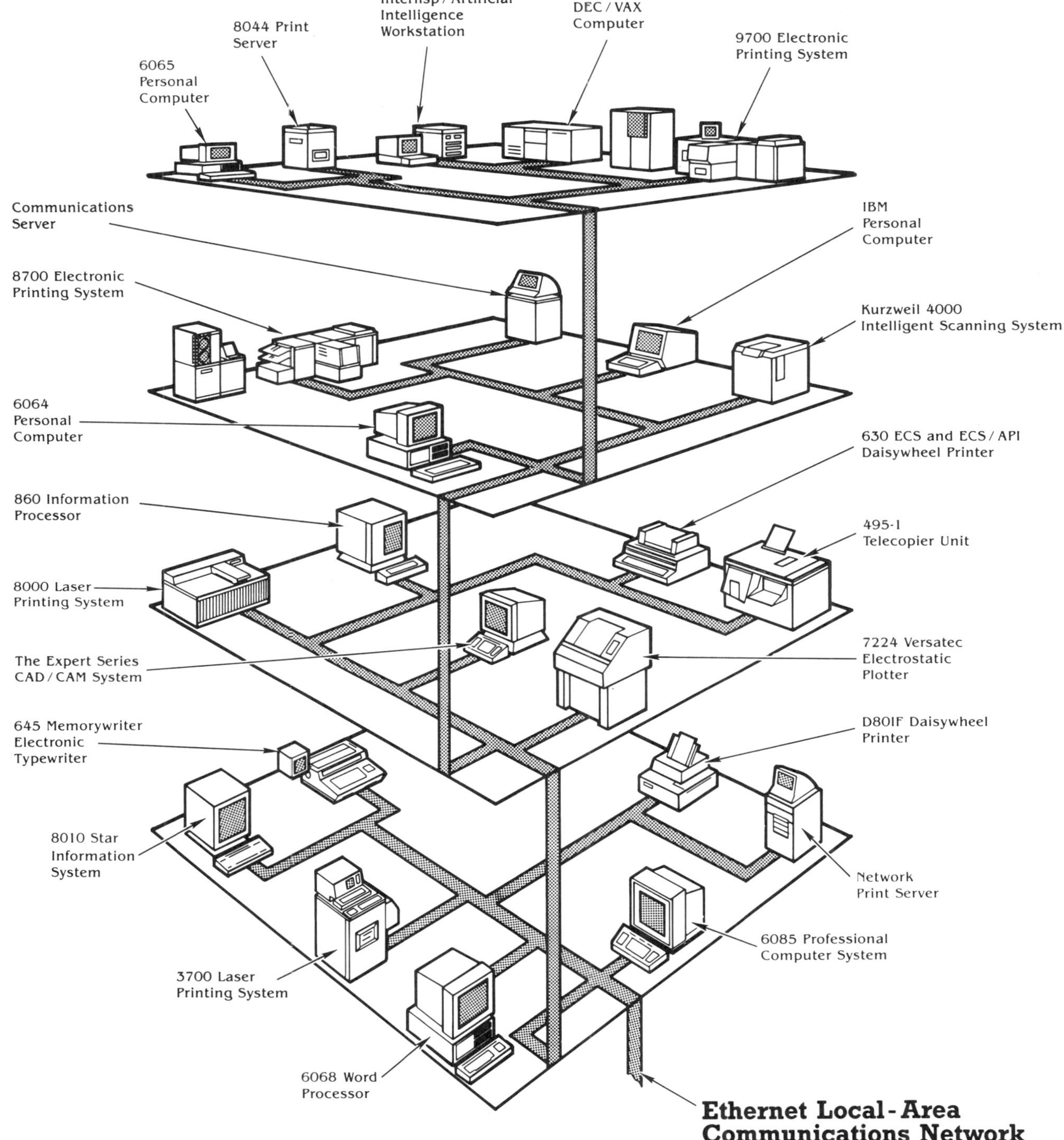

Figure 38

Courtesy Xerox Corporation

XEROX CORPORATION • XEROX COMMUNICATIONS 24 (XC 24)

Xerox Square
Rochester, NY 14644
(716)423-4828

David T. Kearns, President; Dan Minchen (PSC); Frank D. Steenburgh, Vice President, Information Systems Marketing (PSC)

Founded 1906; 103,500 employees

Branch Offices and Distributors:
Xerox Corporation, New York, NY (212)916-2300; Xerox Corporation, Arlington, VA (703)527-6400; Xerox Corporation, Atlanta, GA (404)255-5550; Xerox Corporation, Irvine, CA (714)660-0136; Xerox Corporation, Oakland, CA (415)430-3600

Xerox Communications 24 is a PC office network that can be implemented using thin coaxial cable (RG58) or standard Ethernet cabling. Network supports all Xerox printers used on 6060 workstations, as well as most printers with standard, parallel and serial interface. Network is compatible with IBM PC/XT/AT and their compatibles and all MS-DOS 3.1 software written for the IBM PC Network and Token-Ring Network. Service contracts, network installation, instruction on network operation, and network maintenance services available. First installed: 1986.

• XEROX COMMUNICATIONS 24 (XC 24) TECHNICAL CHARACTERISTICS

Transmission category: baseband

Transmission medium: baseband coaxial cable

Transmission speed: 10 Mbps maximum available for user connection; 10 Mbps burst

Topology: bus

Access method: CSMA/CD

Compatible operating systems: MS-DOS

Maximum number of workstations per node: 1

Maximum number of nodes: 900

Maximum distance between nodes: XC 24/RG 58, 1800 feet; XC 24/Thick cable Ethernet, 9000 feet

Network server: multivendor file server

Maximum number of file servers: 900

Site of network logic: terminal equipment

• STANDARDS/PROTOCOLS SUPPORTED

IEEE 802 standards: conforms to 802.3

ISO OSI Reference Model: conforms to layer 1 (802.3 and CSMA/CD) and layer 7 (file sharing, printer sharing, messaging, and support of DOS 3.1 applications)

XYPLEX INC. • XYPLEX SYSTEM

100 Domino Drive
Concord, MA 01742
(617)371-1400; telex 910-380-4463; FAX 371-0939

Paul Rosenbaum, President; Scott Wieder (PM); Paul Viau (MD); Jay Woodruff, Marketing Communications Manager (PR)

Founded 1981

Xyplex System is a hardware- and software-based distributed communications system that reduces terminal handling by VAX family computers. All terminal driver activities are handled by a front-end communications processor, freeing as much as 50 percent of VAX CPU cycles for computational tasks. Allows mainframes, minicomputers, PCs, dumb terminals, modems, and printers to be connected in an industrial, office, laboratory, or campus environment. Other compatible devices include the DEC VAX family, IBM PCs, and IBM 3270, as well as any asynchronous device. First installed: 1982. Number installed: 120. Average number of stations per installation: 200.

- ### XYPLEX SYSTEM TECHNICAL CHARACTERISTICS

Transmission category: baseband

Transmission mode: half duplex

Transmission medium: baseband coaxial cable, optical fiber, CATV, Ethernet

Transmission speed: 1 Mbps, linear coaxial cable; 10 Mbps, Ethernet cable

Topology: bus

Access method: CSMA/CD

Compatible operating systems: VMS

Gateways: Ethernet, HDLC

Maximum number of worksations per node: 8 per cluster controller

Means of host interconnection: host interface unit at VAX CPU

Site of network logic: resident in VMS operating system

- ### STANDARDS/PROTOCOLS SUPPORTED

Communications protocols: asynchronous and RS-232

IEEE 802 standards: conforms to 802.3

ISO OSI Reference Model: conforms to layers 1-7

ZENITH ELECTRONICS CORPORATION • Z-LAN 500

699 Wheeling Road
Mount Prospect, IL 60056
(312)699-2199; telex 254-396

Jerry Pearlman, President Greg Woodsum (PM); Bob Dranter (MD); Semir Sirazi (PSC); John Taylor (PR)

Z-LAN can accommodate four separate 500 Kpbs networks on a single 6 MHz channel, while allowing other data, video and voice services to co-exist on the same cable. Network connects terminals, printers, modems, PCs, minicomputers, mainframes, and all RS-232 devices. Target markets for Z-LAN include government agencies and military bases, large factories and other commercial and industrial customers, corporate and research enters, college and university campuses, and cable television system operators. Service contracts and instruction on network operation available. First installed: 1986.

• Z-LAN 500 TECHNICAL CHARACTERISTICS

Transmission category: broadband

Transmission mode: full duplex

Transmission medium: broadband coaxial cable

Transmission speed: 500 Kbps

Topology: bus

Access method: CSMA/CD

Gateways: SNA/SDLC, Ethernet, X.25 (available 12/86)

Maximum number of workstations per node: 16

Maximum number of nodes: unlimited

Maximum distance between nodes: 7 miles

Means of host interconnection: terminal ports

Network server: multivendor file server

Maximum number of file servers: unlimited

Network operation during backup: yes

Site of network logic: bus/network interface units

• STANDARDS/PROTOCOLS SUPPORTED

Communications protocols: asynchronous, RS-232, SNA/SDLC, bisynchronous and X.25 available 12/86

IEEE 802 standards: conforms to 802.3

ISO OSI Reference Model: conforms to layer 1 (CSMA/CD), layer 2 (Class 1), layer 4 (Class 4), layer 5 (proprietary), and layer 6

Chapter 2 — Manufacturers and Distributors

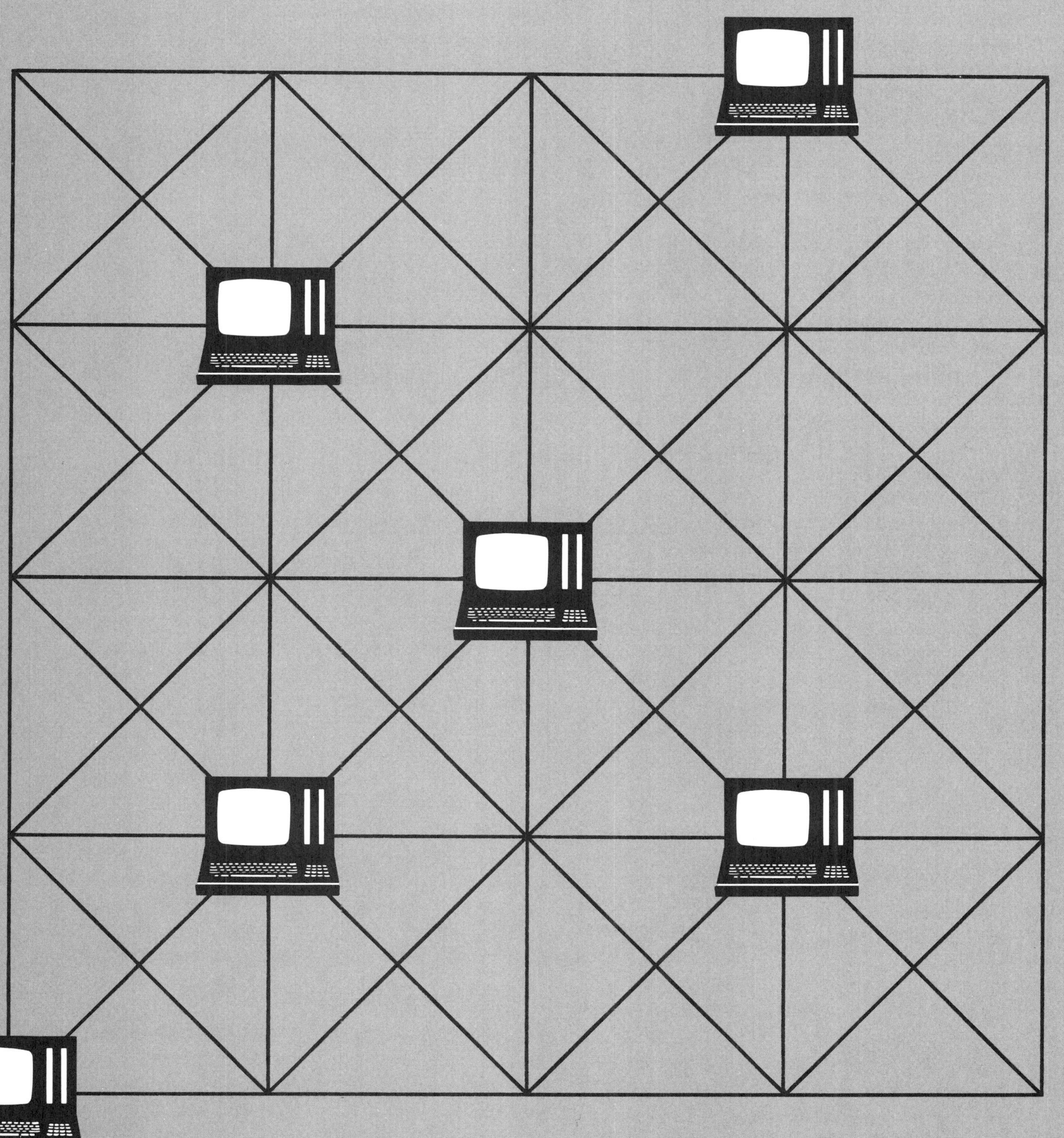

CHAPTER 2
MANUFACTURERS AND DISTRIBUTORS

This chapter lists manufacturers and distributors of local area networking hardware products.

Providers are indexed by product in the index that precedes the entries.

FUNCTION CODES

PM   Product Manager
MD   Marketing Director
PSC   Product Sales Contact
PA   Purchasing Agent

INDEX

ADAPTERS
Adacom Corporation
AMP Inc.
Amphenol Products
Apollo Computer Inc.
AST Research Inc.
Astra Communications Inc.
AT&T Information Systems
Avatar Technologies Inc.
Cabletron
Codenoll Technology Corporation
Commtex Inc.
Computer System Products
Contel Business Networks Inc.
Custom Cable Industries
Data General Corporation
Digital Equipment Corporation
EAC Corporation
Equinox Systems Inc.
Fibronics International Inc.
Fox Research Inc.
Genrad Inc.
Glasgal Communications Inc.
IDEAssociates Inc.
Infonet Inc.
International Business Machines—Information Systems Group
Lee Data Corporation
Mark Electronics Inc.
Marta Data Systems
MOD-TAP System
Mostek Corporation
NCR Corporation
Nevada Western
North Hills Electronics Inc.
Northern Wire & Cable
Panasonic Company
Patton Electronics Company
Sargent Cable Services
South Hills Electronics
Sunol Systems Inc.
Sytek Inc.
TCL Inc.
Texas Instruments—Data Systems Group
3Com Corporation
Transpac
Trellis Communications Corporation

Vertex Computer Cable & Products Inc.
Wang Laboratories Inc.
Waterloo Microsystems Inc.

AMPLIFIERS (REPEATERS)
Adacom Corporaton
Altos Computer Systems
American Photonics Inc.
Anixter Brothers Inc.
Astra Communications Inc.
AT&T Information Systems
Augat Inc.
Beal Communications
Cabletron
Canoga Data Systems
Chipcom Corporation
Codenoll Technology Corporation
Contel Business Networks Inc.
Digital Equipment Corporation
Excelan Inc.
Fox Research Inc.
General Instrument Corporation—Jerrold
  Distribution Systems Division
Genrad Inc.
Glasgal Communications Inc.
Hammer Cable Company
HCI
Infonet Inc.
International Bssiness Machines—Information
  Systems Group
Panasonic Company
Racal Milgo Systems Limited
Sargent Cable Services
TCL Inc.
Tellabs Inc.
Texas Instruments—Data Systems Group
Transpac
Trellis Communications Corporation
Ungermann-Bass Inc.
Wang Laboratories Inc.
Xyplex Inc.

BRIDGES
Allen-Bradley Company—Communications
  Division
Apollo Computer Inc.
Applitek Corporation
AT&T Information Systems
Banyan Systems

Bridge Communications Inc.
Communication Machinery Corporation
Concord Data Systems Inc.
Contel Business Networks Inc.
Corvus Systems Inc.
Digital Equipment Corporation
EAC Corporation
FiberCom Inc.
Fibronics International Inc.
Gateway Communications Inc.
Genrad Inc.
Glasgal Communications Inc.
Hammer Cable Company
HCI
Infonet Inc.
International Business Machines—Information
  Systems Group
KEE Inc.
Mark Electronics Inc.
Modular Computer Systems Inc. (Modcomp)
NCR Corporation
Novell Inc.
Panasonic Company
Sargent Cable Services
Sytek Inc.
Tangent Technologies
TeleVideo Systems Inc.
Tellabs Inc.
3Com Corporation
Transpac
Ungermann-Bass Inc.
Vitalink Communications
Wang Laboratories Inc.
Xyplex Inc.
Zenith Electronics Corporation—Communications
  Products Division

CABLE, BASEBAND COAXIAL
Advanced Computer Communications
AMP Inc.
Amphenol Products
Anixter Brothers Inc.
Avatar Technologies Inc.
Belden Electronic Wire & Cable
Berk-tek
BICC Data Networks Inc.
Cabletron
Capscan Cable Company
Comlink Inc.

Communication Machinery Corporation
Computer System Products
Contel Business Networks Inc.
Custom Cable Industries
Data Communications Systems Corporation
Glasgal Communications Inc.
HCI
Infonet Inc.
Lanlubber Systems Inc.
Lee Data Corporation
M/A-Com Network Cable Products
Martin Marietta Data Systems
MICOM-Interlan
MOD-TAP System
Montrose Products Company
National Electric Cable
Nestar Systems Inc.
Nevada Western
Northern Wire & Cable
Sargent Cable Services
South Hills Electronics
Teledyne Thermatics
3Com Corporation
Transpac
Verex Computer Cable & Products Inc.
Wang Laboratories Inc.
Waterloo Microsystems Inc.
The Wollongong Group
Xerox Corporation
Xyplex Inc.

CABLE, BROADBAND COAXIAL

AMP Inc.
Amphenol Products
Anixter Brothers Inc.
AST Research Inc.
Augat Inc.
Belden Electronic Wire & Cable
Berk-tek
Cabletron
Capscan Cable Company
Comlink Inc.
Communication Machinery Corporation
Computer System Products
Contel Business Networks Inc.
Custom Cable Industries
Data Communications Systems Corporation
General Instrument Corporation—Jerrold
  Distribution Systems Division

Glasgal Communications Inc.
HCI
Infonet Inc.
Lanlubber Systems Inc.
M/A-Com Network Cable Products
Martin Marietta Data Systems
MOD-TAP System
Montrose Products Company
National Electric Cable
Nevada Western
Northern Wire & Cable
Sargent Cable Services
South Hills Electronics
Teledyne Thermatics
Transpac
Vertex Computer Cable & Products Inc.
Wang Laboratories Inc.
The Wollongong Group
Xyplex Inc.

CABLE, DROP

AMP Inc.
Anixterrothers Inc.
Astra Communications Inc.
AT&T Information Systems
Belden Electronic Wire & Cable
Berk-tek
BICC Data Networks Inc.
Cabletron
Capscan Cable Company
Comlink Inc.
Computer System Products
Contel Business Networks Inc.
Custom Cable Industries
Data Communications Systems Corporation
Data General Corporation
Fox Research Inc.
General Instrument Corporation—Jerrold
  Distribution Systems Division
Infonet Inc.
Lanlubber Systems Inc.
M/A-Com Network Cable Products
MICOM-Interlan
MOD-TPP System
Montrose Products Company
National Electric Cable
Northern Wire & Cable
Sargent Cable Services
South Hills Electronics

Teledyne Thermatics
TeleVideo Systems Inc.
3Com Corporation
Transpac
Vertex Computer Cable & Products Inc.
Wang Laboratories Inc.

CABLE, FIBER OPTIC

AMP Inc.
Amphenol Products
Anixter Brothers Inc.
Apollo Computer Inc.
Astra Communications Inc.
AT&T Information Systems
Augat Inc.
Belden Electronic Wire & Cable
Berk-tek
BICC Data Networks Inc.
Cabletron
Canoga Data Systems
Canstar Communications
Comlink Inc.
Computer System Products
Contel Business Networks Inc.
Custom Cable Industries
Data Communications Systems Corporation
Dorran Photonics Inc.
FiberCom Inc.
Fibronics International Inc.
Gandalf Data Inc.
Glasgal Communications Inc.
HCI
Honeywell Inc.—Optoelectronics Division
Infonet Inc.
ITT/Valtec
Lanlubber Systems Inc.
Lee Data Corporation
National Electric Cable
NEC America
Raycom Systems Inc.
Sargent Cable Services
Siecor Corporatin—Electro-Optic Products
South Hills Electronics
Texas Instruments—Data Systems Group
Transpac
Trellis Communications Corporation
Vertex Computer Cable & Products Inc.
Wang Laboratories Inc.
Xyplex Inc.

CABLE, TRUNK

Anixter Brothers Inc.
Astra Communications Inc.
AT&T Information Systems
Belden Electronic Wire & Cable
Berk-tek
Cabletron
Capscan Cable Company
Comlink Inc.
Computer System Products
Contel Business Networks Inc.
Custom Cable Industries
General Instrument Corporation—Jerrold
    Distribution Systems Division
Infonet Inc.
Lanlubber Systems Inc.
Lee Data Corporation
M/A-Com Network Cable Products
Montrose Products Company
National Electric Cable
Northern Wire & Cable
Sargent Cable Services
South Hills Electronics
Teledyne Thermatics
TeleVideo Systems Inc.
3Com Corporation
Transpac
Vertex Computer Cable & Products Inc.
Wang Laboratories Inc.

CABLE, TWISTED WIRE PAIR

Adacom Corporation
Advanced Computer Communications
AMP Inc.
Amphenol Products
Anixter Broters Inc.
AST Research Inc.
Astra Communications Inc.
AT&T Information Systems
Avatar Technologies Inc.
Belden Electronic Wire & Cable
Berk-tek
Cabletron
Comlink Inc.
Computer System Products
Contel Business Networks Inc.
Corvus Systems Inc.
Custom Cable Industries
Data Communications Systems Corporation

Equinox Systems Inc.
Gandalf Data Inc.
Genrad Inc.
Glasgal Communications Inc.
HCI
Infonet Inc.
Intecom Inc.
Lanlubber Systems Inc.
Lee Data Corporation
M/A-Com Network Cable Products
OD-TAP System
Montrose Products Company
National Electric Cable
NCR Corporation
Nevada Western
Northern Wire & Cable
Sargent Cable Services
South Hills Electronics
Syntrex Inc.
Teledyne Thermatics
TeleVideo Systems Inc.
Transpac
Trellis Communications Corporation
Vertex Computer Cable & Products Inc.
Wang Laboratories Inc.

CONTROLLERS, CLUSTER
AST Research Inc.
Avatar Technologies Inc.
Banyan Systems
Bridge Communications Inc.
Codex Corporation
Commtex Inc.
Contel Business Networks Inc.
A.B. Dick Information Systems
Digital Products Inc.
EFData Corporation
Genrad Inc.
Infonet Inc.
International Business Machines—Information
    Systems Group
KEE Inc.
Lee Data Corporation
Mark Electronics Inc.
NBI Inc.
NCR Corporation
TeleVideo Systems Inc.
Tellabs Inc.
Texas Instruments—Data Systems Group

3Com Corporation
Transpac
Tri-Data
Ungermann-Bass Inc.
Wang Laboratories Inc.
Xyplex Inc.

CONTROLLERS, NETWORK INTERFACE
Advanced Computer Communications
Apollo Computer Inc.
Applitek Corporation
Asher Technologies Inc.
AST Research Inc.
Axis Inc.
Banyan Systems
Beal Communications
BICC Data Networks Inc.
Bridge Communications Inc.
Canoga Data Systems
Codenoll Technology Corporation
Codex Corporation
Commtex Inc.
Communication Machinery Corporation
Compucorp
Contel Business Networks Inc.
Corvus Systems Inc.
Data Communications Systems Corporation
Data General Corporation
Digital Equipment Corporation
EFData Corporation
FiberCom Inc.
Genrad Inc.
Glasgal Commucations Inc.
HCI
Infonet Inc.
Intecom Inc.
International Business Machines—Information
    Systems Group
Interphase Corporation
KEE Inc.
Lee Data Corporation
Martin Marietta Data Systems
MICOM-Interlan
Mostek Corporation
National Instruments
NCR Corporation
Network Development Corporation
Northern Wire & Cable
Proteon Inc.

Racal Milgo Systems Limited
Siemens Energy & Automation Inc.—
  Programmable Controls Division
Standard Microsystems Corporation
Sunol Systems Inc.
Sytek Inc.
Tellabs Inc.Texas Instruments—Data Systems
  Group
3Com Corporation
Transpac
Tri-Data
Ungermann-Bass Inc.
Vitalink Communications
Wang Laboratories Inc.
Western Digital Corporation
Xyplex Inc.

CONVERTERS, PROTOCOL

Adacom Corporation
Applitek Corporation
AST Research Inc.
Astrocom Corporation
AT&T Information Systems
Avatar Technologies Inc.
Banyan Systems
Beal Communications
Bridge Communications Inc.
Commtex Inc.
Contel Business Networks Inc.
Develcon Electronics Limited
Digital Equipment Corporation
Fibronics International Inc.
Gandalf Data Inc.
Genrad Inc.
Glasgal Communications Inc.
HCI
Honeywell Inc.—Optoelectronics Division
Infonet Inc.
Infotron Systems Corporation
Intecom Inc.
International Business Machines—Information
  Systems Group
Lee Data Corporation
Mostek Corporation
NCR Corporation
NEC America
Northern Wire & Cable
Novell Inc.
Patton Electronics Company

Sargent Cable Services
South Hills Electronics
Sytek Inc.
Tangent Technologies
Tellabs Inc.
Texas Instrument—Data Systems Group
Transpac
Tri-Data
Ungermann-Bass Inc.
Wang Laboratories Inc.
Xyplex Inc.

DIAGNOSTIC/TEST EQUIPMENT

ADC Telecommunications Inc.
Anixter Brothers Inc.
AT&T Information Systems
Banyan Systems
Bridge Communications Inc.
Cabletron
Codenoll Technology Corporation
Codex Corporation
Computer System Products
Contel Business Networks Inc.
Data Communications Systems Corporation
Digital Equipment Corporation
Fox Research Inc.
Gandalf Data Inc.
General Instrument Corporation—Jerrold
  Distribution Systems Division
Genrad Inc.
Glasgal Communications Inc.
Infonet Inc.
International Business Machines—Information
  Systems Group
Mark Electronics Inc.
MOD-TAP System
Modular Computer Systems Inc. (Modcomp)
National Instruments
Novell Inc.
Patton Electronics Company
Sargent Cable Services
Siecor Corporation—Electro-Optic Products
South Hills Electronics
Sunshine Electronics Inc.
Sytek Inc.
TCL Inc.
Test Equipment Corporation
Texas Instruments—Data Systems Group
Tranpac

Trellis Communications Corporation
Vertex Computer Cable & Products Inc.
Wang Laboratories Inc.
Wavetek Indiana Inc.
Xyplex Inc.

ENCRYPTION DEVICES
AST Research Inc.
Banyan Systems
Codenoll Technology Corporation
Contel Business Networks Inc.
Digital Equipment Corporation
EAC Corporation
Genrad Inc.
Glasgal Communications Inc.
Harris Corporation—Harris Semiconductor
Infonet Inc.
International Business Machines—Information
   Systems Group
NCR Corporation
Sunshine Electronics Inc.
Sytek Inc.
Transpac
Wang Laboratories Inc.

EXTENDERS
Adacom Corporation
Apollo Computer Inc.
AT&T Information Systems
Augat Inc.
Banyan Systems
Bridge Communications Inc.
Canoga Data Systems
Codenoll Technology Corporation
Contel Business Networks Inc.
Custom Cable Industries
Data Switch Corporation
Digital Equipment Corporation
Equinox Systems Inc.
FiberCom
General Instrument Corporation—Jerrold
   Distribution Systems Division
Genrad Inc.
Hammer Cable Company
Infonet Inc.
International Business Machines—Information
   Systems Group
National Instruments
Patton Electronics Company

Raycom Systems Inc.
Sargent Cable Services
Siecor Corporation—Electro-Optic Products
Sytek Inc.
TCL Inc.
Texas Instruments—Data Systems Group
Transpac
Trellis Communications Corporation
Vitalink Communications
Wang Laboratories Inc.
Xyplex Inc.

FILE SERVERS
ACS Telecom
Altos Computer Systems
Apollo Computer Inc.
Asher Technologies Inc.
AST Research Inc.
AT&T Information Systems
Banyan Systems
Codenoll Technology Corporation
Commtex Inc.
Communication Machinery Corporation
Compucorp
Contel Business Networks Inc.
Convergent Technologies
Corvus Systems Inc.
CYB Systems
Data General Corporation
Digital Equipment Corporation
FiberCom
Fox Research Inc.
Genrad Inc.
Glasgal Communications Inc.
Hammer Cable Company
HCI
Infonet Inc.
International Business Machines—Information
   Systems Group
Lee Data Corporation
Martin Marietta Data Systems
Modular Computer Systems Inc. (Modcomp)
NCR Corporation
Nestar Systems Inc.
Network Development Corporation
North Star Computers Inc.
Novell Inc.
Proteon Inc.
Seagate Technology

Sunol Systems Inc.
Sytek Inc.
TeleVideo Systems Inc.
Texas Instruments—Data Systems Group
3Com Corporation
Transpac
Ungermann-Bass Inc.
Wang Laboratories Inc.

GATEWAYS

Adacom Corporation
Altos Computer Systems
Apollo Computer Inc.
Applitek Corporation
Asher Technologies Inc.
AST Research Inc.
AT&T Information Systems
Avatar Technologies Inc.
Banyan Sytems
BICC Data Networks Inc.
Bridge Communications Inc.
Codex Corporation
Comdesign Inc.
Commtex Inc.
Communication Machinery Corporation
Compucorp
Contel Business Networks Inc.
Convergent Technologies
Corvus Systems Inc.
Data Communications Systems Corporation
Data General Corporation
Digital Equipment Corporation
Dorran Photonics Inc.
EFData Corporation
Equinox Systems Inc.
FiberCom
Fox Research Inc.
Gandalf Data Inc.
Gateway Communications Inc.
Genrad Inc.
Glasgal Communications Inc.
Hammer Cable Company
HCI
Infonet Inc.
Infotron Systems Corporation
Intecom Inc.
International Business Machines—Information
  Systems Group
KEE Inc.

Mark Electronics Inc.
Modular Computer Systems Inc. (Modcomp)
NCR Corporation
NEC America
Network Development Corporation
Proteon Inc.
Racal Milgo Systems Limited
Sargent Cable Services
Siemens Energy & Automation Inc.—
  Programmable Controls Division
Sunol Systems Inc.
Sytek Inc.
TeleVideo Systems Inc.
Tellabs Inc.
3Com Corporation
Tranpac
Tri-Data
TRW Inc.—Information Networks Division
Ungermann-Bass Inc.
Vitalink Communications
Wang Laboratories Inc.
Waterloo Microsystems Inc.
Xerox Corporation
Xyplex Inc.

INTERFACES, RS-232

ADC Telecommunications Inc.
Altos Computer Systems
American Laser Systems Inc.
AMP Inc.
Applitek Corporation
AST Research Inc.
AT&T Information Systems
Augat Inc.
Axis Inc.
Bridge Communications Inc.
Coastcom
Codenoll Technology Corporation
Codex Corporation
Comdesign Inc.
Commtex Inc.
Compucorp
Contel Business Networks Inc.
Convergent Technologies
Custom Cable Industries
CYB Systems
Data Communications Systems Corporation
Data General Corporation
Digital Equipment Corporation

EAC Corporation
EFData Corporation
FiberCom Inc.
Fibronics International Inc.
Fox Research Inc.
Gandalf Data Inc.
Gateway Communications Inc.
General Instrument Corporation—Jerrold
  Distribution Systems Division
Genrad Inc.
Glasgal Communications Inc.
HCI
Honeywell Inc.—Optoelectronics Division
Infonet Inc.
Infotron Systems Corporation
Intecom Inc.
KEE Inc.
Lee Data Corporation
MICOM-Interlan
Modular Computer Systems Inc. (Modcomp)
NCR Corporation
NEC America
Nevada Western
North Star Computers Inc.
Novell Inc.
Panasonic Company
Patton Electronics Company
Proteon Inc.
Racal Milgo Systems Limited
Raycom Systems Inc.
Sargent Cable Services
Siemens Energy & Automation Inc.—
  Programmable Controls Division
Sytek Inc.
Tellabs Inc.
Test Equipment Corporation
Texas Instruments—Data Systems Group
Transpac
Trellis Communications Corporation
Tri-Data
Ungermann-Bass Inc.
Vertex Computer Cable & Products Inc.
Vitalink Communications
Wang Laboratories Inc.
Waterloo Microsystems Inc.
The Wollongong Group
Xyplex Inc.

INTERFACES, RS-449
AMP Inc.

Applitek Corporation
AT&T Information Systems
Bridge Communications Inc.
Coastcom
Codenoll Technology Corporation
Commtex Inc.
Contel Business Networks Inc.
Custom Cable Industries
Data Communications Systems Corporation
Data Genera Corporation
Digital Equipment Corporation
EAC Corporation
EFData Corporation
FiberCom Inc.
Gandalf Data Inc.
Gateway Communications Inc.
Genrad Inc.
Glasgal Communications Inc.
Intecom Inc.
KEE Inc.
Modular Computer Systems Inc. (Modcomp)
NCR Corporation
Patton Electronics Company
Proteon Inc.
Raycom Systems Inc.
Sargent Cable Services
Test Equipment Corporation
Transpac
Trellis Communications Corporation
Ungermann-Bass Inc.
Vitalink Communications
Wang Laboratories Inc.
The Wollongong Group
Xyplex Inc.

INTERFACES, X.21
Codenoll Technology Corporation
Commtex Inc.
Contel Business Networks Inc.
Data Communications Systems Corporation
Data General Corporation
Digital Equipment Corporation
Gandalf Data Inc.
Genrad Inc.
Glasgal Communications Inc.
Intecom Inc.
Modular Computer Systems Inc. (Modcomp)
NCR Corporation
NEC America

Patton Electronics Company
Sargent Cable Services
Tellabs Inc.
Test Equipment Corporation
Transpac
Wang Laboratories Inc.

INTERFACES, X.25

Advaced Computer Communications
Altos Computer Systems
Apollo Computer Inc.
Applitek Corporation
Bridge Communications Inc.
Codenoll Technology Corporation
Codex Corporation
Commtex Inc.
Contel Business Networks Inc.
Convergent Technologies
Custom Cable Industries
Data Communications Systems Corporation
Data General Corporation
Digital Equipment Corporation
FiberCom Inc.
Gandalf Data Inc.
Gateway Communications Inc.
Genrad Inc.
Glasgal Communications Inc.
HCI
Infotron Systems Corporation
Intecom Inc.
KEE Inc.
Mark Electronics Inc.
Martin Marietta Data Systems
Modular Computer Systems Inc. (Modcomp)
Mostek Corporation
NCR Corporation
NEC America
Sargent Cable Services
Siemens Energy & Automation Inc.—
  Programmable Controls Division
Tellabs Inc.
Test Equipment Corporation
Transpac
Tri-Data
Ungermann-Bass Inc.
Vitalink Communications
Wang Laboratories Inc.
The Wollongong Group

NETWORK MANAGEMENT UNITS

Adacom Corporation
Apollo Computer Inc.
Applitek Corporation
Asher Tehnologies Inc.
AST Research Inc.
Avatar Technologies Inc.
Axis Inc.
Banyan Systems
BICC Data Networks Inc.
Bridge Communications Inc.
Canoga Data Systems
Coastcom
Codex Corporation
Communication Machinery Corporation
Contel Business Networks Inc.
Control Data Corporation
Corvus Systems Inc.
CYB Systems
Data Communications Systems Corporation
Data General Corporation
Data Switch Corporation
Digital Equipment Corporation
FiberCom Inc.
Gandalf Data Inc.
General Instrument Corporation—Jerrold
  Distribution Systems Division
Genrad Inc.
Glasgal Communications Inc.
Hammer Cable Company
HCI
Honeywell Information Systems Inc.
Infonet Inc.
Infotron Systems Corporation
International Business Machines—Information
  Systems Group
Martin Marietta Data Systems
Modular Computer Systems Inc. (Modcomp)
NCR Corporation
Network Development Corporation
Nevada Western
North Star Computers Inc.
Novell Inc.
Proteon Inc.
Racal Milgo Systems Limited
Sytek Inc.
TeleVideo Systems Inc.
Tellabs Inc.
Texas Instruments—Data Systems Group

Transpac
Trellis Communications Corporation
TRW Inc.—Information Networks Division
Ungermann-Bass Inc.
Vitalink Communications
Wang Laboratories Inc.
The Wollongong Group
Xyplex Inc.

TAPS/SPLITTERS

Adacom Corporation
AMP Inc.
Anixter Brothers Inc.
Applitek Corporation
Augat Inc.
Cabletron
Canstar Communications
Comlink Inc.
Computer System Products
Contel Business Networks Inc.
Data Communications Systems Corporation
Digital Equipment Corporation
Equinox Systems Inc.
Fibronics International Inc.
General Instrument Corporation—Jerrold
  Distribution Systems Division
Genrad Inc.
Glasgal Communications Inc.
HCI
Infonet Inc.
International Business Machines—Information
  Systems Group
NCR Corporation
North Hills Electronics Inc.
Panasonic Company
Sargent Cable Services
South Hills Electronics
Sytek Inc.
TeleVideo Systems Inc.
Texas Instruments—Data Systems Group
3Com Corporation
Transpac
Trellis Communications Corporation
Wang Laboratoies Inc.
Waterloo Microsystems Inc.

TERMINATORS

Adacom Corporation
Advanced Computer Communications

AMP Inc.
Amphenol Products
Anixter Brothers Inc.
Augat Inc.
Banyan Systems
Cabletron
Comlink Inc.
Computer System Products
Contel Business Networks Inc.
Data Communications Systems Corporation
Digital Equipment Corporation
General Instrument Corporation—Jerrold
  Distribution Systems Division
Genrad Inc.
Glasgal Communications Inc.
HCI
Infonet Inc.
International Business Machines—Information
  Systems Group
NCR Corporation
Northern Wire & Cable
Sargent Cable Services
South Hills Electronics
TCL Inc.
TeleVideo Systems Inc.
Tellabs Inc.
Texas Instruments—Data Systems Group
3Com Corporation
Transpac
Trellis Communications Corporation
Vertex Computer Cable & Products Inc.
Waterloo Microsystems Inc.
Xyplex Inc.

OTHER

ACS Telecom
Adacom Corporation
ADC Telecommunications Inc.
Advanced Computer Communications
Algo Inc.
Allen-Bradley Company—Communications
  Division
Alpha Systems Limited
American Laser Systems Inc.
American Photonics Inc.
AMP Inc.
Amphenol Products
Anixter Brothers Inc.
Apollo Computer Inc.

Applitek Corporation
Astrocom Corporation
AT&T Information Systems
AtLANta Technologies
Augat Inc.
Avatar Technologies Inc.
Axis Inc.
Cabletron
Canstar Communications
Chipcom Corporation
Coastcom
Codenoll Technology Corporation
Codex Corporation
Comdesign Inc.
Communication Machinery Corporation
Computer System Products
Computrol—A Division of Kidde Atomated
    Systems Inc.
Control Data Corporation
Corvus Systems Inc.
Coverguard Corporation
Data Communications Systems Corporation
Data Switch Corporation
Develcon Electronics Limited
Digital Microwave Corporation
Digital Products Inc.
Dorran Photonics Inc.
EFData Corporation
Equinox Systems Inc.
Excelan Inc.
Gandalf Data Inc.
Gateway Communications Inc.
General Instrument Corporation—Jerrold
    Distribution Systems Division
Hancock Electronics Corporation
Harris Corporation—Harris Semiconductr
Honeywell Inc.—Optoelectronics Division
Honeywell Information Systems Inc.
IDEAssociates Inc.
Infotron Systems Corporation

Intecom Inc.
Intel Corporation
ITT/Valtec
Lantel Corporation
LED Systems Inc.
Lightcom Inc.
MICOM-Interlan
MOD-TAP System
Molecular Computer
National Electric Cable
National Instruments
North Hills Electronics Inc.
Northern Wire & Cable
Panasonic Company
Patton Electronics Company
Sargent Cable Services
Seagate Technology
Seiscor Technologies Inc.
Siecor Corporation—Electro-Optic Products
Siemens Energy & Automation Inc.—
    Programmable Controls Division
The Software Link Inc.
South Hills Electronics
Sunol Systems Inc.
Sytek Inc.
Tangent Technologies
TCL Inc.
Tellabs Inc.
Test Equipment Corporation
Texas Instruments—Data Systems Group
Tiara Computer Systems Inc.
TRW Inc.—Information Networks Division
Vertex Computer Cable & Products Inc.
Vitalink Communications
VMX Inc.
Wang Laboratories Inc.
Xicom Technologies Corporation
Zenith Electronics Corpration—Communications
    Products Division

ACS TELECOM
25825 Eshelman Avenue
Lomita, CA 90717
(213)325-3055; telex 350-213

Todd Hays, Dale Hays
(PM)(MD)(PSC)

Founded 1981; 9 employees

File servers. Also distributes Fox Research's 10-Net local area network.

ADACOM CORPORATION
8871 Bond, P.O. Box 14745
Overland Park, KS 66214
(913)888-4999; (800)232-2662; telex
510-601-5185 ADACOMM UD;
FAX 913-888-7806

Moti Gura, President; Dan Cox, Director, Sales and Marketing (PM); Oscar Glottman, Vice President, Marketing (MD); Mike Holliger, Manager, Sales Support (PSC); Don Trotter, Chief Financial Officer (PA)

Founded 1985; 70 employees

Branch Offices and Distributors: Adacom Corporation, Staten Island, NY (718)983-0500; Adacom Corporation, Coppell, TX (214)462-1772; Adacom Corporation, Westlake Village, CA (818)707-0941; CSI Systems Inc., Lexington, MA (617)863-0525; Glasgal Communications, Northvale, NJ (201)768-8082

Adapters; repeaters; twisted wire cable; protocol converters; extenders; gateways; network management units; taps/splitters; terminators; multiplexers; and baluns. Product compatibility: 3270.

ADC TELECOMMUNICATIONS INC.
4900 West 78th Street
Minneapolis, MN 55435
(612)893-3081; telex 290-321;
TWX 910-576-2832; FAX 612-835-6800 ext. 315

Frederic R. Boswell, President and Chief Operating Officer; Craig Johnson, Vice President, Product Management (PM); Dennis Leese, Vice President, Sales and Marketing (MD)(PSC; Gary Crist (PA)

Founded 1935; 1800 employees

Diagnostic/test equipment; RS-232 interfaces; terminal blocks; data tech control equipment; cross-connect equipment; and jackfields.

ADVANCED COMPUTER COMMUNICATIONS
720 Santa Barbara Street
Santa Barbara, CA 93101
(805)963-9431

Roland Bryan, President; Mike Seto, Marketing Director (MD); Errol Forkner, Vice President, Sales and Marketing (PSC); Barbara Lynch (PA)

Founded 1975; 240 employees

Baseband coaxial and twisted wire pair cable; network interface controllers; terminators; X.25 interfaces; and connectors. Network compatibility: Ethernet.

ALGO INC.
9198 C-Red Branch Road
Columbia, MD 21045
(301)730-7442; telex 333405

George O'Mara, Vice President, Marketing (MD)(PSC)

Founded 1980; 10 employees

Switches and 6-, 8- and 24-port switching multiplexers.

ALLEN-BRADLEY COMPANY— COMMUNICATION DIVISION
555 Briarwood Circle
Ann Arbor, MI 48104
(313)668-2500

Dennis Gillespie, Division Vice President; Fred Gruhl, Director of Marketing (MD); Debbie Howe, Marketing Communications Supervisor (PSC)

Founded 1903; 150 employees

Bridges; interface cards; point-to-point modems; network interface bridges; remodulators; translators; modems; and broadband and baseband multiplexers. Vendor compatibility: IBM, Data General, Hewlett-Packard, and DEC.

ALPHA SYSTEMS LIMITED
205 West Wacker Drive
Chicago, IL 60606
(312)346-0707; telex 499-7627

Robert Sandsmark, Information Systems Analyst

Value-added reseller for NCR and Compucorp LAN products.

ALTOS COMPUTER SYSTEMS
2641 Orchard Parkway
San Jose, CA 95134
(408)946-6700; telex 184-815
ALTOS UT

Dave Jackson, President; Russ Aldrich, Communications Manager (PM); Jeff Bork, Director, Systems Marketing (MD)

Founded 1977; 700 employees

Amplifiers; file servers; gateways; and RS-232 and X.25 interfaces.

Standards/protocols supported: Ethernet and TCP/IP. Vendor compatibility: Excelan and CMC.

AMERICAN LASER SYSTEMS INC.

106 Fowler Road
Goleta, CA 93117
(805)967-0423; telex 494-1760 ALS

J. Parker, President; P. Hartloff, Project Engineer (PM); L. Shallenberger, Vice President, Marketing (MD)(PSC); D. Mann (PA)

Founded 1968; 11 employees

Branch Offices and Distributors:
Pacific Datacom Systems Inc., Long Beach, CA (213)494-2121; Scientific Systems, Bailey, CO (303)838-4615; Scientific Systems, Arlington, TX (817)467-3749; Statcom, Columbus OH (614)481-8303; New England Digital Distribution Inc., Gloucester, MA (617)927-8172

RS-232 interfaces; transmitters; and receivers. Manufactures optical infrared (atmospheric) transmission systems for the transmission of data/voice and video. These systems may be used in LANs to transmit signals from building to building.

AMERICAN PHOTONICS INC.

71 Commerce Drive
Brookfield, CT 06805
(203)775-8950; telex 821-353;

Jim Byrne, President; John Goehrke (PM)(MD); Catherine Koziatek (PSC)

Founded 1982; 40 employees

Transceivers, expanders; repeaters; modems; multiplexers; and couplers.

AMP INC.

P.O. Box 3608
Harrisburg, PA 17105
(717)564-0100; TWX 510-657-4110

Harold A. McInnes, President; W. Bennett Conner, Vice President, Marketing (MD)

Founded 1941; 22,800 employees

Branch Offices and Distributors:
AMP Inc., Cupertino, CA (408)255-3830; AMP Inc., Atlanta, GA (404)934-6363; AMP Inc., Framingham, MA (617)891-7500; AMP Inc., Witton-Salem, NC (919)725-8968; AMP Inc., Irving, TX (214)537-4490

Adapters; baseband coaxial, broadband coaxial, drop, fiber optic, and twisted wire pair cable; taps/splitters; terminators; RS-232 and RS-449 interfaces; coaxial and fiber optic connectors; and electronic and electrical connectors. Standards/protocols supported: IEEE 802.3, 802.4, 802.5, and 802.6; ANSI X3T9.5; ISDN; EIA 464; AT&T PDS system; IBM cabling system; MAP; TOP; MIL-1553; and MIL-1773. Interconnection devices designed for OEM, telecommunications, data communications, and premises wiring applications.

AMPHENOL PRODUCTS

4300 Commerce Court
Lisle, IL 60532
(312)983-3500; telex 190-215;
TWX 910-651-0219; FAX 3665

P.W. Arneson, President; D. Krob, Director, C&I Products (PM); D.M. Baker, Vice President, Marketing (MD); John Colwell, Product Manager (PSC)

Founded 1932; 8000 employees

Branch Offices and Distributors:
Amphenol Products, Oak Brook, IL (312)986-2330; Amphenol Products, Dallas, TX (214)343-8420; Amphenol Products, Carson, CA (213)532-3180; Amphenol Products, Hauppauge, NY (516)582-4466; Amphenol Products, Landover, MD (301)459-8484

Adapters; baseband coaxial, broadband coaxial, fiber optic, and twisted wire pair cable; terminators; fiber optic interfaces, connectors and cable assemblies; and electronic and electrical connectors.

ANIXTER BROTHERS INC.

4711 Golf Road
Skokie, IL 60076
(312)677-2600; telex 289-464;
FAX312-677-9480

John Pigott, President; Frank Mitchell, Mike Armstrong (PM)(PSC); Gordon Halverson, Vice President, Sales and Marketing, Broadband Products (MD); Ray Gensinger (PA)

Founded 1957; 2500 employees

Distributes amplifiers; baseband coaxial, broadband coaxial, drop, fiber optic, trunk, and twisted wire pair cable; diagnostic/test equipment; taps/splitters; terminators; power supplies; modulators; patch panels; cable assemblies; and tools. Vendor compatibility; IBM and Wang. Standards/protocols supported: Ethernet, MAP, TOP, and others. Authorized distributor of IBM Cabling System.

APOLLO COMPUTER INC.

330 Billerica Road
Chelmsford, MA 01824
(617)256-6600; TWX 710-343-6803;
FAX 617-250-0183

Dr. Thomas Vanderslice, President; Michael Gallup, Director of Product Marketing (PM); Edward Zander, Vice President, Marketing (MD); Angelo Guadagno, Vice President,

Sales (PSC); Richard Germani, Director of Purchasing (PA)

Founded 1980; 3400 employees

Adapters; bridges; fiber optic cable; network interface controllers; extenders; file servers; gateways; network management systems; X.25 interfaces; and computers. Vendor compatability: IBM and DEC. Other compatibility possible through source code alteration. Offers compatible Unix-based workstations and computing resources.

APPLITEK CORPORATION
107 Audubon Road
Wakefield, MA 01880
(617)246-4500; telex 510-600-1787;
  FAX 617-245-7340

Ashraf M. Dahod, President; Peter Gregory, Vice President, Sales, Marketing and Operations (PM); Gerald McDonald, Director of Marketing (MD); David Kurtzer, Product Marketing Manager (PSC); Susan Fennell, Materials Manager (PA)

Founded 1981; 80 employees

Branch Offices and Distributors:
Applitek Corporation, New York, NY (201)993-8361; Applitek Corporation, San Francisco, CA (415)651-4744; Los Angeles, CA (213)595-6212; Cambridge, MA (617)497-8268; Washington, DC (301)330-8700

Bridges; network interface controllers; protocol converters; gateways; network management units; taps; RS-232, RS-449 and X.25 interfaces; network interface units; and modems.

ASHER TECHNOLOGIES INC.
1009 Mansell Road
Roswell, GA 30076
(404)993-4590; FAX 404-642-1894

Wil Riner, President and Chief Executive Officer; Bruce Watson, Executive Vice President (MD); Robert Riner, Director of Sales (PSC); Margie Smith (PA)

Founded 1983; 40 employees

Network interface controllers; file servers; gateways; network management units; network boards; and interface cards. Network compatibility: Quadnet VI, Quadnet IX, ProNet, G/Net, and Novell NetWare.

AST RESEARCH INC.
2121 Alton Avenue
Irvine, CA 92714
(714)863-1333; telex 753-699
  ASTR UR; FAX (714)863-9478

Safi Qureshey, President; Mary Spaulding, Product Manager (PM); Rich Shapero (MD); Ron Blaisdel, Director of Sales (PSC)

Founded 1980; 850 employees

Adapters; broadband coaxial and twisted wire pair cable; cluster controllers; network interface controllers; protocol converters; encryption devices; file servers; gateways; network management units; and RS-232 interfaces. Product compatibility: NETBIOS.

ASTRA COMMUNICATIONS INC.
329 North Bernardo Avenue
Mountain View, CA 94043
(415)960-1100

Andrew K. Ludwick, President (PSC); Ronald V. Schmidt, Senior Vice President, Chief Technical Officer (PM); Susan E. Keck-Truman, Manager of Administration (MD); Robert Hernandez, Purchasing Manager (PA)

Founded 1985; 16 employees

Adapters and amplifiers. Products compatible with IBM wiring scheme. Network compatibility: Ethernet 802.3. Also distributes drop, fiber optic, trunk, and twisted wire pair cable. Manufacturers represented include Seicor.

ASTROCOM CORPORATION
120 West Plato Boulevard
St. Paul, MN 55107
(612)227-8651; telex 297-421

Sidney N. Jerson, President; John Sandberg, Vice President, Planning and Development (PM); Kent Johnson, Director, Marketing and Sales (MD); Stacey Jerson (PSC); Jerry Fingal (PA)

Founded 1968; 180 employees

Protocol converters; coaxial cable, statistical, and time division multiplexers; and modems.

AT&T INFORMATION SYSTEMS
1 Speedwell Avenue
Morristown, NJ 07960
(201)898-3278

Charles Marshall, Chairman of the Board; Robert Casale, President, Marketing and Sales (MD)(PSC); Frank Vigilante, President, Product Management and Development (PM)

Founded 1983; 100,000 employees

Adapters; amplifiers; bridges; drop, fiber optic, trunk, and twisted wire pair cable; protocol converters; diagnostic/test equipment; extenders; file servers; gateways; RS-232 and RS-449 interfaces; network interface units; network access units; and asynchronous line drivers. Standards/protocols supported: asynchronous, bisynchronous, SDLC, 802.3 10 Mpbs, and 802.3 1 Mbps. Network compatibility: Starlan.

ATLANTA TECHNOLOGIES

4501 Circle 75 Parkway, Suite C-
  3100
Atlanta, GA 30339
(404)984-9095

Robert Patrick, President
(PM)(MD)(PSC)(PA)

Founded 1985; 3 employees

Value-added reseller for Lantel, Allen-Bradley and Bridge Communications LAN products.

AUGAT INC.

710 Narragansett Park Drive
Pawtucket, RI 02861
(401)724-4400

Richard Prybyl, Group Vice President; Edward Knapp, Marketing Manager (MD)

300 employees

Amplifiers; broadband coaxial and fiber optic cable; extenders; taps/splitters; terminators; RS-232 interfaces; fiber optic modems; and coaxial and fiber optic connectors. Network compatibility: all broadband networks.

AVATAR TECHNOLOGIES INC.

99 South Street
Hopkinton, MA 01748
(617)435-6872; telex 710-390-0375;
  FAX 617-435-6872

John A. Carr, President; Michelle Leah Doyle, Vice President, LAN Development (PM); Neal Checkoway, Director of Marketing (MD); Richard Simpson, Vice President, Sales (PSC); Anita Lawler, Purchasing Manager (PA)

Founded 1981; 110 employees

Adapters; baseband coaxial and twisted wire pair cable; cluster con-

trollers; protocol converters; gateways; network management units; micro-to-mainframe links; connectors; and port concentrators.

AXIS INC.

7825 Engineer Road, Suite 208
San Diego, CA 92111
(619)560-7737

M.J. Prager, President; Barbara Paul (PM)(PA); Joe Monroe (MD)(PSC)

Founded 1974; 12 employees

Network interface controllers; network management units; RS-232 interfaces; and interface boards. Vendor compatibility: Hewlett-Packard.

BANYAN SYSTEMS

135 Flanders Road
Westboro, MA 01581
(617)366-6681

David Mahoney, President; Bob Martin, Product Marketing Manager (PM); Paul Bergeron, Vice President, Sales

Founded 1983; 80 employees

Bridges; cluster controllers; network interface controllers; protocol converters; diagnostic/test equipment; encryption devices; extenders; file servers; gateways; network management units; and terminators. Network compatibility: IBM PC Network and Token Ring Network, Proteon ProNET, Omninet, Ethernet, ARCnet, Net/One Broadband, and Starlan.

BEAL COMMUNICATIONS

9794 Forest Lane, Suite 246
Dallas, TX 75243
(214)340-2044

Robert C. Farrier, President; Brian Johnson, Vice President, Engineering (PM); Mike Miller, Vice President,

Marketing (MD); Kay George, Purchasing Manager (PA)

Founded 1984; 15 employees

Amplifiers; network interface controllers; and protocol converters.

BELDEN ELECTRONIC WIRE & CABLE

P.O. Box 1980
Richmond, IN 47375
(317)983-5200; TWX 810-345-1393

Roger Cornett, Vice-President; Ron Stier (MD)

Founded 1902; over 2000 employees

Baseband coaxial, broadband coaxial, drop, fiber optic, trunk, and twisted wire pair cable.

BERK-TEK

R.D. 1, Box 888
New Holland, PA 17557
(717)354-6200; TWX 510-651-0511

Joseph L. Boscov, President; Chet Klinke, Sales Director (PM)(PSC); Carl Bump, Marketing Director (MD); Allan Schoonover, Sales Director (PA)

Founded 1961; 350 employees

Branch Offices and Distributors: Wallace Electronics, Dallas, TX (214)340-0400; AmeriCable, Eden Prairie, MN (612)944-8880; Tec Electronics, New York, NY (212)944-1010; Graybar, Pittsburgh, PA (412)323-0600; Clifford, Bethel, VT (802)234-9921

Baseband coaxial, broadband coaxial, drop, fiber optic, trunk, and twisted wire pair cable. Vendor compatibility: Xerox, IBM and AT&T.

BICC DATA NETWORKS INC.

945 Concord Street
Framingham, MA 01701
(617)626-BICC; telex 948-477;
 FAX 617-879-0698

Arthur Cunningham, President; Joel Weinstein, Vice President, Sales and Marketing (MD)

Founded 1984; 100 employees

Branch Offices and Distributors:
 Cabletron, Gonic, NH (603)332-9400; Glasgal Communications, Northvale, NJ (201)768-8082; BICC Data Networks Inc., Mountain View, CA (415)965-9922

Baseband coaxial, drop, and fiber optic cable; network interface controllers; gateways; network management units. Network compatibility: all 802.3 network product types.

BRIDGE COMMUNICATIONS INC.

2081 Stierlin Road
Mountain View, CA 94043
(415)969-4400; telex 176-544; FAX
 415-940-1928

William N. Carrico, President; Oliver Lubliner, Product Manager (PM); Catherine S. Muther, Vice President, Marketing; Janak Pathak, National Sales Manager (PSC); Carole Silva, Purchasing Agent (PA)

Founded 1981; 245 employees

Branch Offices and Distributors:
 Bridge Communications Inc., Los Angeles, CA (213)312-9526; Bridge Communications Inc., New York, NY (12)986-0105; Bridge Communications Inc., Waltham, MA (617)890-6122; Bridge Communications Inc. McLean, VA (703)883-3790; Bridge Communications, Roswell, GA (404)641-8090

Bridges; cluster controllers; network interface controllers; protocol converters; diagnostic/test equipment; extenders; gateways; network management units; and RS-232, RS-449 and X.25 interfaces. Product compatibility: X.25 products, IBM SNA, Ethernet networks, Unix 4.2 hosts, and any RS-232 connection.

CABLETRON

P.O. Box 6257
Rochester, NH 03867
(603)332-9400

Robert Levine, President; Craig Benson, Director of Operations (PM); Jack Branowski, Marketing Manager (MD); Kenneth Levine, Director of Sales (PSC)

Founded 1983; 100 employees

Baseband coaxial, broadband coaxial, drop, fiber optic, trunk, and twisted wire pair cable; diagnostic/test equipment; taps; terminators; and cable assemblies. Also distributes adapters; amplifiers; transceivers; and receivers. Carries America Photonics product line.

CANOGA DATA SYSTEMS

6635 Independence Avenue
Canoga Park, CA 91303
(818)888-2003

Jack Buhn, President; Larry Totter, Vice President, Sales and Marketing (PM)(MD)(PSC)

Founded 1965; 115 employees

Amplifiers; fiber optic cable; network interface controllers; extenders; and network management units. Vendor compatibility: DEC.

CANSTAR COMMUNICATIONS

1240 Ellesmere Road
Scarborough, Ontario M1P 2X4
 CANADA
(416)293-9722; telex 065-25403;
 FAX 46-293-5756

D.C. Mitchell, General Manager

Founded 1977; 40 employees

Fiber optic cable; taps/splitters; cords; and couplers.

CAPSCAN CABLE COMPANY

P.O. Box 36
Adelphia, NJ 07710
(201)462-8700; (800)222-5388

Kevin M. Lynch, General Manager; Steven Wagner, Vice President, Sales (MD); Sheila Shultz, Customer Service Manager (PSC)

Founded 1981; 120 employees

Baseband coaxial, broadband coaxial, drop, and trunk cable.

CHIPCOM CORPORATION

193 Bear Hill Road
Waltham, MA 02154
(617)449-7666

Daniel Presser, President; Menachem Abraham, Vice President, Product Development (PM); Maureen Lawrence, Vice President, Marketing (MD); Alexandra Corson (PSC)

Founded 1983; 50 employees

Repeaters; modems; and frequency translators. Ethermodem products implement IEEE standard for 10 Mbps broadband Ethernet. Products are "plug compatible" and transparent to baseband equipment. Available on single or dual cable networks providing two or eight AUI ports.

Repeater cnnects a baseband Ethernet running on standard or thin coaxial cable to a broadband Ethernet network.

COASTCOM

2312 Stanwell Drive, P.O. Box 27068
Concord, CA 94527
(415)825-7500; TWX 910-481-5781; FAX 415-682-2015

Edgar M. Buttner, President; Greg Davis (PM); Richard D. Tallman, Vice President, Marketing (MD); Ruth Kavanaugh, Purchasing Supervisor (PA)

140 employees

Branch Offices and Distributors: Christopher M. Hegarty, East Regional Sales Manager, Farmingville, NY (516)732-2066; W. Larry Shaffer, Southeast Regional Sales Manager, Norcross, GA (404)266-4310; Edward Schowalter, Mid-Atlantic Regional Sales Manager, Summit, NJ (201)273-0093; Grady Gibson, Southwest Regional Sales Manager, Granbury, TX (817)573-4812; Dan Balfe, West Regional Sales Manager, Concord, CA (408)730-9666

Network management units; RS-232 and RS-449 interfaces; and multiplexers. System compatibility: ROLM PBX, Northern Telecom DMS 10 and AT&T ISN.

CODENOLL TECHNOLO CORPORATION

1086 North Broadway
Yonkers, NY 10701
(914)965-6300; telex 646-159; FAX 914-965-6300

Michael H. Coden, President; Edwin Sakaguchi, Vice President, Sales and Marketing (MD)(PSC); John Mulvey (PA)

Founded 1980; 70 employees

Adapters; amplifiers; network interface controllers; diagnostic/test equipment; encryption devices; extenders; file servers; RS-232, RS-449, X.21, and X.25 interfaces; and couplers. Vendor compatibility: Fibronics, Proteon, Ungermann-Bass, and Siecr.

CODEX CORPORATION

20 Cabot Boulevard
Mansfield, MA 02048
(617)364-2000

John Pugh, General Manager, LAN Business Unit; Ralph Rio, Senior Product Manager (PM); Dennis Hawley, Director, LAN Marketing (MD); John Dimitruk, Director, LAN Sales (PSC)

Founded 1984; 140 employees, LAN Division

Cluster controllers; network interface controllers; diagnostic/test equipment; gateways; network management units; and RS-232 and SNA interfaces. Standards/protocols supported: Ethernet and 802.3.

COMDESIGN INC.

751 South Kellogg Avenue
Goleta, CA 93117
(805)964-9852; TWX 910-334-1189; FAX 805-683-1758

Robert Dolan, President; Dave McMillen, LAN Product Manager (PM); Dwight Buck, Director, Network Sales (PSC)

Founded 1977; 140 employees

Gateways; RS-232 interfaces; and terminal servers. Vendor compatibility: DEC, Data General and Hewlett-Packard.

COMLINK INC.

116A West Broad Street
Falls Church, VA 22046
(703)237-9610

Michael S. Chambers, President

Founded 1983; 6 employees

Distributes baseband coaxial, broadband coaxial, drop, fiber optic, trunk, and twisted wire pair cable; taps/splitters; and terminators. Manufacturers represented include EAZY-Data Communications and Computer Accessories.

COMMTEX INC.

2411 Crofton Lane
Crofton, MD 21114
(301)721-3666; telex 752-065

Donald W. Parker, President; Dorothy C. Neiman, Product manager (PM); Alan Smith, Vice President, Sales (PSC); H. Scott Schaeffer, Purchasing Manager (PA)

Founded 1978; 65 employees

Branch Offices and Distributors: M/A-Com Information Systems, Rockville, MD (301)984-3636; Results Leasing, Reston, VA (703)478-0990; Shared Medical Systems, Malvern, PA (215)296-6300

Adapters; cluster controllers; network interface controllers; protocol converters; file servers; gateways; and RS-232, RS-449, X.21, and X.25 interfaces. Standards/protocols supported: SNA/SDLC, X.25 and ISDN.

COMMUNICATION MACHINERY CORPORATION

1421 State Street
Santa Barbara, CA 93101
(805)963-9471; TWX 910-334-3508; FAX 966-6547

Steve Holmgren, President; Steve Gibson (PM); Russell Sharer (MD); Dom Genovese (PSC); Theresa Aviani (PA)

Founded 1981; 75 employees

Bridges; baseband coaxial and broadband coaxial cable; network interface controllers; file servers; gateways; network management units; modems; frequency translators; and Ethernet front-end processor boards. Standards/protocols supported: Ethernet, TCP/IP, XNS, DDN, and X.25.

COMPUCORP
2211 Michigan Avenue
Santa Monica, CA 90404
(213)829-7453

Lee Davies, President; Bjorn Ahlen (PM); Leonard Winiecki (PA)

Founded 1969; 450 employees

Network interface controllers; file servers; gateways; and RS-232 interfaces. Vendor compatibility: Microsoft, IBM and Novell.

COMPUTER SYSTEM PRODUCTS
740 Washington Avenue North
Minneapolis, MN 55401
(612)338-0995; (800)422-2537;
   FAX 612-338-1512

Peter Lee, President; Tom Richardson (PM); Gary Doan (MD); Tim Anderson (PSC); Jo Miller (PA)

Founded 1980; 40 employees

Adapters; baseband coaxial, drop, fiber optic, and twisted wire pair cable; connectors; cable assemblies; patch panels; and baluns. Also distributes adapters; baseband coaxial, broadband coaxial, drop, fiber optic, trunk, and twisted wire pair cable; diagnostic/test equipment; taps/splitters;

and terminators. Represents various cable, connector, tool, and test equipment manufacturers.

COMPUTROL—A DIVISION KIDDE AUTOMATED SYSTEMS INC.
15 Ethan Allen Highway
Ridgefield, CT 06877-6297
(203)544-9371; telex 643-358

Chuck Brewer, Vice President, Sales and Marketing (MD); Morton G. Scheraga (PSC)

Modems and interfaces. Standards/protocols supported: IEEE 802.4 and MAP.

CONCORD DATA SYSTEMS INC.
397 Williams Street
Marlborough, MA 01752
(617)460-0808; telex 951-793; FAX
   617-480-0511

Bridges. Standards/protocols supported: MAP.

CONTEL BUSINESS NETWORKS INC.
4330 East-West Highway
Bethesda, MD 20814
(301)654-9120; FAX 301-654-6227

James Lakin, President; John Ambler, Vice President (PM)(PSC)(PA)

Founded 1960; 22,000 employees

Distributes adapters; amplifiers; bridges; baseband coaxial, broadband coaxial, drop, fiber optic, trunk, and twisted wire pair cable; cluster controllers; network interface controllers; protocol converters; diagnostic/test equipment; encryption devices; extenders; file servers; gateways, network management units; taps/splitters; terminators; and RS-232, RS-449, X.21, and X.25 interfaces. Manufacturers represented include 3Com, Bridge Communica-

tions, Concord Data Systems, Kee, DEC, and Northern Telecom. Contel is a telecommunications systems integrator, including voice and data systems.

CONTROL DATA CORPORATION
8100 34th Avenue South
Minneapolis, MN 55440
(612)931-3131

Robert M. Price, President; Bob Duncan (MD)

Founded 1957; 56,000 employees

Network management units and other LAN support hardware.

CONVERGENT TECHNOLOGIES
2700 North First Street, P.O. Box
   6685
San Jose, CA 95131
(408)434-2848; FAX 408-943-0564

Paul Ely, President; Thelma Bataille, Product Marketing Manager, Communications (PM); Dick Nisley, Director of Marketing, Network Divisions (MD); Dick Meise, Vice President, Sales

Founded 1980; 2500 employees

File servers; gateways; and RS-232 and X.25 interfaces. System compatibility: any Unix system running the TCP/IP protocols, such as DEC, Sun and Apollo.

CORVUS SYSTEMS INC.
2100 Corvus Drive
San Jose, CA 95124
(408)559-7000

James L. Sihl, President; Harry Blankenheim, Vice President, Finance; George McMurtry, General Manager, Distribution Division (MD); Bob Clark, Sales Manager, Distribution Division (PSC); S.R.

"Bob" Granger, General Manager, National Accounts Division (PA)

Founded 1979; 336 employees

Branch Offices and Distributors: Compac Microelectronics, Santa Clara, CA (408)720-0400; Softel Computer Products, Englewood, CA (213)412-1700; LAN East, Lawrence, MA (617)975-2000; Com Systems, Dallas, TX (214)637-0061; Compar, Eden Prairie, MN (612)944-8086.

Bridges; twisted wire pair cable; network interface controllers; file servers; gateways; network management units; and diskless workstations.

COVERGUARD CORPORATION

2037 Westfield Avenue
Scotch Plains, NJ 07076
(201)322-5222

Doris Stockel, President; Ted Weiner, Vice President, General Manager (PM); Sherry Weiner, National Sales Manager (MD); Patrick J. Murphy, Controller (PA)

Founded 1981; 22 employees

Protective covers for disaster prevention for all data processing equipment. Coverguard covers are featherweight nylon, waterproof, flame retardant, and anti-static custom covers for data processing equipment and tape libraries. Covers are free standing or in rows, and self-storing on the specific equipment each cover protects.

CUSTOM CABLE INDUSTRIES

3818 Bay Visvenue
Tampa, FL 33611
(800)237-4873

Richard N. Watson, President; George Henry (PM); Frank Luft (MD)(PSC); Richard Evans (PA)

Founded 1981; 50 employees

Adapters; baseband coaxial, broadband coaxial, drop, trunk, and twisted wire pair cable; extenders; and RS-232, RS-449 and X.25 interfaces. Also distributes fiber optic cable and RS-232, RS-449 and X.25 interfaces. Manufacturers represented include Stediwatt.

CYB SYSTEMS

2215 West Braker Avenue
Austin, TX 78758
(512)835-2266; telex 625-46700

Diana Goodrich, President; Gene Zimmer, Manufacturing Manager (PM); Gary G. Smith, Director of Marketing (MD)(PSC)

Founded 1982; 24 employees

File servers; network management units; and RS-232 interfaces. Standards/protocols supported: Ethernet, TCP/IP and NETBIOS. CYB produces network software and hardware systems which integrate DOS machines to a Unix system network. Network servers act as message centers, gateways and as virtual disk for networked personal computers.

DATA COMMUNICATIONS SYSTEMS CORPORATION

7206 South Hill Drive
Manassas, VA 22110
(703)361-2666

G. Dennis Murphy, President; M.J. Hoinski, Executive Vice President (MD)(PSC); J. Everett, Manager (PA)

Founded 1980; 22 employees

Twisted wire pair cable. Also distributes baseband coaxial, broadband coaxial, drop, and fiber optic cable; network interface controllers; diagnostic/test equipment; gateways; network management units;

taps/splitters; terminators; RS-232, RS-449, X.21, and X.25 interfaces; Codex 4020; and Teltone DOV. Manufacturers represented include Aydin, Codex, Teltone, Tellabs, LeeMah, Canoga Data, and Develcon. Vendor compatibility: Ethernet, Codex and Teltone.

DATA GENERAL CORPORATION

50 Maple Street
Milford, MA 01757
(617)478-4000

Edson deCastro, President; Paul R. Phaneuf, Marketing and Business Planning Director (PM)(MD); Gerry Cromwell, Sales Manager (PSC)

Founded 1967; 4000 emloyees

Adapters; drop cable; network interface controllers; file servers; gateways; network management units; and RS-232, RS-449, X.21, and X.25 interfaces.

DATA SWITCH CORPORATION

1 Enterprise Drive
Shelton, CT 06484
(203)926-1801; TWX 710-468-3210;
    FAX 203-929-6408

Robert Gilbertson, President; Russell Drew, Senior Vice President, Sales, Marketing and Service (PM)(PSC); Bo Linnell, Vice President, Marketing (MD); Robert Dennison, Purchasing Manager (PA)

Founded 1977; 300 employees

Extenders; network management units; matrix switching systems; configuration management systems; and channel extension systems using fiber optic technology. Vendor compatibility: IBM.

DEVELCON ELECTRONICS LIMITED

856 51st Street East
Saskatoon, Saskatchewan,
    CANADA S7K 5C7
(306)933-3300; telex 074-2686

Founded 1974

Branch Offices and Distributors: Develcon Electronics, Warminster, PA (215)443-5450; Develcon Electronics, Pleasanton, CA (415)847-2034

Procotol converters; limited-distance data sets; modems; switches; and statistical multiplexers.

A.B. DICK INFORMATION SYSTEMS

5700 West Touhy Avenue
Chicago, IL 60648
(312)763-1900

David Powell, Chief Executive Officer

Cluster controllers.

DIGITAL EQUIPMENT CORPORATION

146 Main Street
Maynard, MA 01754
(617)897-5111; telex 948-457;
    TWX 710-347-0212; FAX 617-493-8780

Kenneth H. Olsen, President; Peter Smith, Vice President, Product Applications Marketing (PM); John Shields, Vice President, Sales and Service, International (MD)(PSC); Ron Payne, Corporate Purchasing Manager (PA)

Founded 1957; 91,000 employees

Adapters; amplifiers; bridges; network interface controllers; protocol converters; diagnostic/test equipment; encryption devices; extenders; file servers; gateways; network man-

agement units; taps/splitters; terminators; and RS-232, RS-449, X.21, and X.25 interfaces.

DIGITAL MICROWAVE CORPORATION

2363 Calle del Mundo
Santa Clara, CA 95054
(408)727-5969; telex 759-597
    DIGMIC UD; FAX 408-748-9034

William E. Gibson, President; Mark Dwight (PM); Guido Soliz, Manager, Marketing/Sales Support (PSC); Douglas Alexander (PA)

Founded 1984

Microwave radio systems.

DIGITAL PRODUCTS INC.

108 Water Street
Watertown, MA 02172
(617)924-1680

Cornelius Peterson, President; William Pratt, Product Manager (PM); Marilyn Peterson, Marketing Communications (MD); Janis Harvey, Director of Sales (PSC); Walter Kopek, Purchasing Agent (A)

Founded 1974; 32 employees

Cluster controllers; network management; printer buffers; and matrix switches. Network compatibility: RS-232 asynchronous environments. Vendor compatibility: PC and peripheral manufacturers.

DORRAN PHOTONICS INC.

165 First Avenue, P.O. Box 304
Atlantic Highlands, NJ 07716
(201)291-8103

Jack Cook, President; Jack Ganis (PM)(MD); Peg Sharp (PSC); Jim McKee (PA)

Founded 1982; 270 employees

Branch Offices and Distributors: Dorran Photonics Inc., Danvers, MA (617)777-6592; Dorran Photonics Inc., Coopersburg, PA (215)282-1189; Dorran Photonics Inc., Atlanta, GA (404)399-5290; Dorran Photonics Inc., Evanston, IL (312)475-0858; Dorran Photonics Inc., Menlo Park, CA (415)322-2934

Fiber optic cable; gateways; and connectors. Offers the optical fiber portion of the IBM Token Ring Network. IBM-specified products are Dorran's Biconic Multimode Interconnection System on 100/140 microns fiber, featuring Hybrid Multimode Duplex Patch Cable with biconic to mini-biconic connectors which connect the Dorran systems to the IBM 8219 repeater.

EAC CORPORATION

4000 Cathedral Avenue NW,
    #253B
Washington, DC 20016
(202)555-1277

L. Ericcson, President; William T.R. Perry, Director of Marketing (MD); Sarah Ferguson, Director of National Accounts (PSC)

Founded 1985; 33 employees

Adapters; bridges; encryption devices; and RS-232 and RS-449 interfaces.

EFDATA CORPORATION

1233 North Stadem Drive
Tempe, AZ 85281
(602)968-0447

Robert C. Fitting, President; Steve Eymann (PM); Marla Evangelista (PA)

Founded 1984; 35 employees

Cluster controllers; network interface controllers; gateways; RS-232 and RS-449 interfaces; and modems.

EQUINOX SYSTEMS INC.

12041 Southwest 144th Street
Miami, FL 33186
(305)255-3500; telex 153-893

Bill Dambrackas, President; Doug Noble, Marketing Manager (PM); Robert Gintz, Director of Marketing (MD); Mike Vidal, Telemarketing (PSC); Rick Malinski, Purchasing Supervisor (PA)

Founded 1983; 125 employees

Branch Offices and Distributors:
Beta Distributors Inc., Englewood, CO (303)779-3604; Data Processing Sciences, Cincinnati, OH (513)961-0776; System Technology Associates, Houston, TX (713)440-8340; Teltone Corporation, Kirkland, WA (205)827-9626; W.C. Koepf Associates, Chagrin Falls, OH (216)247-5129

Adapters; twisted wire pair cable; extenders; gateways; taps/splitters; multiplexers; line boards; expansion units; distribution panels; data PBXs; line drivers; local multiplexers; and wiring accessories. Vendor compatibility: DEC, Hewlett-Packard, Prime, and Tandem. Manufactures data communications products for minicomputer and microcomputer users.

EXCELAN INC.

2180 Fortune Drive
San Jose, CA 95131
(408)434-2300; telex 176-610; FAX 408-434-2310

C. Richard Moore, President; Jay Weil, Director, Product Marketing (PM); Subhash Bal, Vice President, Marketing (MD); VG Gupta, Materials Director (PA)

Founded 1982; 125 employees

Repeaters; network analyzers; front-end processor boards; and transceivers.

FIBERCOM INC.

P.O. Box 11966
Roanoke, VA 24022-1966
(703)342-6700; telex 883-099; FAX 703-342-6700

Dr. Albert D. Bender, President; Jack Freeman, Vice President, Business Development (PM)(MD); Herb Hawthorne, Product Sales Manager (PSC); Rick Haynes, Purchasing Head (PA)

Founded 1982; 100 employees

Bridges; fiber optic cable; network interface controllers; extenders; file servers; gateways; network management units and RS-232, RS-449 and X.25 interfaces. Standards/protocols supported: IEEE 802.3 and Ethernet.

FIBRONICS INTERNATIONAL INC.

325 Stevens Street
Hyannis, MA 02601
(617)778-0700; telex 951-297; FAX 617-778-0821

Joseph Maayan, President; Ken Coons, Product Manager (PM); Hal Spurney, Sales and Marketing Manager, Network Products

Founded 1978; 450 employees

Branch Offices and Distributors:
Fibronics International Inc., Los Angeles, CA (213)470-3232; Fibronics International Inc., San Jose, CA (408)295-9011; Fibronics International Inc., Schaumburg, IL (312)885-0890; Fibronics International Inc., Gibsonia, PA (412)443-9210; Fibronics International Inc., Richardson, TX (214)437-2504

Adapters; bridges; fiber optic cable; protocol converters; taps/splitters; and RS-232 interfaces. Product compatibility: TCP/IP software.

FOX RESEARCH INC.

7016 Corporate Way
Dayton, OH 45459
(513)433-2238; telex 650-2-7-9125; FAX 513-233-5805

Don Roettele, President; Rick Rebo, Executive Vice President, Research and Development (PM); Greg Goodall, Executive Vice President, Sales and Marketing (MD); Dan Broussard, National Sales Manager (PSC); Gary Mercer (PA)

Founded 1983; 30 employees

Branch Offices and Distributors:
ACS Telecomp, Lomita, CA (213)325-3055; System Solutions, Evanston, IL (312)864-2283; AT&D, Austin, TX (512)478-5795; Vitronix, Westboro, MA (617)366-1144; Computeach, Washington, DC (202)861-2602

Adapters; amplifiers; drop cable; diagnostic/test equipment; file servers; gateways; and RS-232 interfaces. Vendor compatibility: IBM, Novell and Corvus.

GANDALF DATA INC.

1020 South Noel Avenue
Wheeling, IL 60090
(312)459-6630; TWX 910-651-4951

Alan Melkerson, President; Edward Milbury (PM); Howard Gunn (MD); Michael Salustri (PSC); Frank Connell (PA)

Founded 1970; over 1000 employees

Branch Offices and Distributors:
Gandalf Data Inc., Long Beach, CA (213)424-2258; Gandalf Data Inc., Atlanta, GA

(404)447-5425; Gandalf Data Inc., Boston MA (617)329-7630; Gandalf Data Inc., Dallas, TX (214)980-2690; Gandalf Data Inc., Washington, DC (301)421-1212

Fiber optic and twisted wire pair cable; protocol converters; diagnostic/test equipment; gateways; network management units; RS-232, RS-449, X.21, and X.25 interfaces; modems; and multiplexers. Manufactures data communications and networking products including data PBXs, modems, T1 multiplexers, data-over-voice networks and multiplexers, statistical multiplexers, networking software, and taxi dispatch systems.

GATEWAY COMMUNICATIONS INC.
16782 Red Hill Avenue
Irvine, CA 92714
(714)261-0762; telex 509462
 GATEWAY COM; FAX 714-261-6569

David McMaster, President; Larry Stephenson, Executive Vice President, Operations (PM); Mitchell E. Barrie, Marketing Coordinator (MD); Bert Ott, Natioaal Sales Manager (PSC)

Founded 1981; 30 employees

Bridges; gateways; RS-232, RS-449, and X.25 interfaces; and interface cards. Network compatibility: Novell NetWare and IBM PC Network.

GENERAL INSTRUMENT CORPORATION—JERROLD DISTRIBUTION SYSTEMS DIVISION
2200 Byberry Road
Hatboro, PA 19040
(215)674-4800; telex 627-87246;
 FAX 215-672-5130

William H. Lambert, Vice President and General Manager; James P. Duffy, Product Manager, LAN Products (PM); Geoffrey S. Roman, Vice President, Marketing and Sales (MD)

Amplifiers; broadband coaxial, drop and trunk cable; diagnostic/test equipment; extenders; network management units; taps/splitters; terminators; modems; and RS-232 interfaces. Offers line of broadband LAN products.

GENRAD INC.
300 Baker Avenue
Concord, MA 01742
(617)369-4400; telex 923-354;
 TWX 710-347-1051

William R. Thurston, President; Robert E. Anderson, Group Vice President (PM)(MD); Marshall Bates (PSC); Gil Wallace (PA)

Founded 1915; 2500 employees

Adapters; amplifiers; bridges; twisted wire pair cable; cluster controllers; network interface controllers; protocol converters; diagnostic/test equipment; encryption devices; extenders; file servers; gateways; network management units; taps/splitters; terminators; and RS-232, RS-449, X.21, and X.25 interfaces. Network compatibility: GE-Net and other manufacturing networks.

GLASGAL COMMUNICATIONS INC.
207 Washington Street
Northvale, NJ 07647
(201)768-8082; telex 710-991-8585;
 376-2911; FAX 201-768-2947

Ralph Glasgal, President; Al Merwede, Sales Manager; Gerry Burnett (MD)

Founded 1974; 50 employees

Distributes adapters; amplifiers; bridges; baseband coaxial, broadband coaxial, fiber optic, and twisted wire pair cable; network interface controllers; protocol converters; diagnostic/test equipment; encryption devices; file servers; gateways; network management units; taps/splitters; terminators; and RS-232, RS-449, X.21, and X.25 interfaces. Represents over 100 manufacturers.

HAMMER CABLE COMPANY
4707 Connecticut Avenue NW,
 #407
Washington, DC 20008
(202)555-3142; telex 701-654-9776

Eleanor O'Hammer, President; David K. Nail, Product Manager (PM); Tack O'Hammer, Vice President, Marketing and Sales (MD)(PSC); S. Driver, Office Manager (PA)

Founded 1981; 67 employees

Amplifiers; bridges; gateways; extenders; file servers; and network management units. Vendor compatibility: IBM, Xerox, Apple, and Wang.

HANCOCK ELECTRONICS CORPORATION
135 King Street, P.O. Box 557
Cohasset, MA 02025
(617)383-6610

Joyce Sturdy, President; David Sturdy (PM)(PA); Paula Dodrill (MD)

Founded 1985; 10 employees

Automation controllers, for use in process control, machine control, distributed control, factory automation, data acquisition and monitoring, and energy management.

HARRIS CORPORATION— HARRIS SEMICONDUCTOR

P.O. Box 883
Melbourne, FL 32902-0883
(305)729-4878; telx 808-949; TWX
510-959-6259; FAX 305-729-
5549

Jon Cornell, Executive Vice President; Armando Geday, Product Manager (PM); Bill Bahr, Director of Marketing (MD); Greg Steele, Manager, Marketing Communications (PSC)

Founded 1967 (Harris Semiconductor); 31,000 (Harris Corporation) employees

Encryption devices.

HCI

1850 Centennial Park Drive
Reston, VA 22091
(703)648-3900

Rodney Martin, President; Bill Bouie, Director of Telecommunications (PM); Michael Van Patten, Director of Marketing (MD); Hazel Edwards, Director of Business Development (PSC); Carol Beecherl, Office Manager (PA)

Founded 1985; 20 employees

Distributes amplifiers; bridges; baseband coaxial, broadband coaxial, fiber optic, and twisted wire pair cable; network interface controllers; protocol converters; file servers; gateways; network management units; taps/splitters; terminators; and RS-232 and X.25 interfaces. Manufacturers include Novell and Gateway Communications. Network compatibility: ARCnet, Ethernet and G/Net.

HONEYWELL INC.— OPTOELECTRONICS DIVISION

830 East Arapaho Road
Richardson, TX 75081
(214)234-4271; telex 730-890;
TWX 910-867-4757; FAX 214-
234-4271, ext. 417

Ed Spensor, President; John Buie (PM); Peter Orr (MD); Robert Procsal, Product Manager, Fiber Optic Link Products (PSC)

Founded 1885; 93,000 employees

Branch Offices and Distributors: Marshall Industries, Chatsworth, CA (818)442-4204; Lionex Corporation, Wilmington, MA (617)657-5170; Honeywell Optoelectronics, Englewood, CO (303)792-1390; Honeywell Optoelectronics, Bensenville, IL (312)860-3984; Honeywell Optoelectronics, Glastonbury, CT (203)659-4011

Fiber optic cable; protocol converters; RS-232 interfaces; modems; and multiplexers. Product compatibility: any RS-232 devices.

HONEYWELL INFORMATION SYSTEMS INC.

200 Smith Street, MS 486
Waltham, MA 02154
(617)895-6000

Steve Wales (PSC)

Network management units; communications servers; and gateway servers. Network compatibility: Ethernet.

IDEASSOCIATES INC.

35 Dunham Road
Billerica, MA 01821
(617)663-6878; telex 497-9780

Gautam Gupta, President; Nora Feldman Gildea, Director of Marketing (MD); James Bender, Vice President, Sales (PSC)

Founded 1982; over 100 employees

Adapters and modems.

INFONET INC.

10902 Wild Grape
San Antonio, TX 78230
(512)696-2590

Paul N. Criswell, President; L. James Beckman, Vice President, Marketing (MD)

Founded 1983; 12 employees

Distributes adapters; amplifiers; bridges; baseband coaxial, broadband coaxial, drop, fiber optic, trunk, and twisted wire pair cable; cluster controllers; network interface controllers; protocol converters; diagnostic/test equipment; encryption devices; extenders; file servers; gateways; network management units; taps/splitters; terminators; and RS-232 interfaces. Manufacturers represented include Novell.

INFOTRON SYSTEMS CORPORATION

Cherry Hill Industrial Center-9,
P.O. Box 5730
Cherry Hill, NJ 08003-1688
(609)424-9400; telex 710-940-1247;
FAX 609-424-6461

James C. Hahn, President; Bob Bauer (MD)

Founded 1968; 1000 employees

Protocol converters; gateways; network management units; RS-232 and X.25 interfaces; multiplexers; and switches. Products provide data switching, networking, network control, and LAN capabilities and can be used with twisted pair or fiber optic cabling.

INTECOM INC.
601 InteCom Drive
Allen, TX 75002
(214)727-941; telex 269-188; FAX
   (214)727-7142

Erik Ringkjob, President; Hal Denton, Director of Product Management (PM); Lynn Carey, Marketing Services (MD)(PSC)(PA)

Founded 1979; 1350 employees

Twisted wire pair cable; network interface controllers; protocol converters; gateways; RS-232, RS-449, X.21, and X.25 interfaces; and switches.

INTEL CORPORATION
3065 Bowers Avenue
Santa Clara, CA 95051
(408)987-8080

Coprocessors and controllers. Standards/protocols supported: IEEE 8023.

INTERNATIONAL BUSINESS MACHINES—INFORMATION SYSTEMS GROUP
1 Corporate Park, 900 King Street
Rye Brook, NY 10573
(914)397-7806

John Akers, President; Richard H. Goldberg, Group Director, Telecommunications Marketing (MD)

Adapters; amplifiers; bridges; cluster controllers; network interface controllers; protocol converters; diagnostic/test equipment; encryption devices; extenders; file servers; gateways; network management units; taps/splitters; and terminators.

INTERPHASE CORPORATION
2925 Merrell Road
Dallas, TX 75229
(214)350-9000

Michael E. Cope, President and Chief Executive Officer; Tom Thawley, Executive Vice President (PM); Tom Kent, Director of Marketing (MD); John L. Marshall, Director of Sales (PSC); Craig Scott, Vice President, Engineering (PA)

Founded 1974; 95 employees

Network interface controllers.

ITT/VALTEC
7635 Plantation Road
Roanoke, VA 24019
(703)563-0371; telex 829-458; FAX
   703-563-0371, ext. 59

George Ashmore, President and General Manager; Ken Taylor, Director, Business Development (MD); Marguerite G. Shapalis, Marketing Services Manager

Founded 1957; 900 employees

Fiber optic cable; LEDs; tubes and sensors; and star couplers.

KEE INC.
10727 Tucker Street
Beltsville, MD 20705
(301)595-4700; FAX 301-937-5205

Roderick Matheson, President; Joseph Greaney, Vice President, Engineering (PM); Patrick Kelly, Vice President, Sales and Marketing (MD); Daniel Brigati, Commercial LAN Representative (PSC); Thomas Blazek, Purchasing Manager (PA)

Founded 1968; 57 employees

Bridges; cluster controllers; network interface controllers; gateways; and RS-232, RS-449 and X.25 interfaces. Vendor compatibility: IBM; Xerox and DEC. Product compatibility: asynchronous, bisynchronous, synchronous, and Coax A devices.

LANLUBBER SYSTEMS INC.
9704 Kendale Road
Potomac, MD 20854
(301)555-7755

Eileen Duff, President; Terry Ellis, Vice President, Marketing (MD); O. Mayer, National Sales Manager (PSC); Carol Santman, Purchasing Agent (PA)

Founded 1979; 100 employees

Branch Offices and Distributors: Lanlubber Systems Inc., Memphis, TN (901)555-4666; Lanlubber Systems Inc., Washington, DC (202)555-6384

Distributes baseband coaxial, broadband coaxial, drop, fiber optic, trunk, and twisted wire pair cable.

LANTEL CORPORATION
3100 Northwoods Place
Norcross, GA 30071
(404)446-6000

H. Raymond Eckman, President; Dan McLemore, National Sales Manager (PM); Robert T. Hughes, Executive Vice President (MD); Stephen P. Healy, Sales Manager (PSC); Drew Daubenspeck, Director of Materials (PA)

Founded 1984; 40 employees

Broadband data modems; broadband voice modems and frequency translators. Vendor compatibility: Sytek, Ungermann-Bass, Allen-Bradley, IBM, and many private installations.

LED SYSTEMS INC.
1006 Apache Trail
Mechanicsburg, PA 17055
(717)697-2607

Dr. Jack Baird, Presiden (PA); Ralph Cleveland (PM)(MD)(PSC)

Founded 1980; 3 employees

Infrared optical links.

LEE DATA CORPORATION

7075 Flying Cloud Drive
Eden Prairie, MN 55344
(612)828-0500; TWX 910-576-1690;
  FAX 612-828-0723

Charles Askanas, President; John Roy, Vice President, Marketing (PM)(MD); Robert Pasquarella, Vice President, Sales (PSC); Dan Sherlock, Manager of Purchasing (PA)

Founded 1979; 1100 employees

Adapters; baseband coaxial, fiber optic, trunk, and twisted wire pair cable; cluster controllers; network interface controllers; protocol converters; file servers; and RS-232 interfaces. Vendor compatibility: IBM.

LIGHTCOM INC.

3853 Breakwater Avenue
Hayward, CA 94545
(415)786-1200

Dr. Staffan Fredricsson, President; John L. Armstrong, Product Marketing Manager (PM); Lionel Martin, Vice President, Marketing (MD); Michael Spies, Vice President, Sales (PSC); Ines Colombetti (PA)

Founded 1984; 25 employees

Fiber optic data multiplexers. Product compatibility: RS-232C, synchronous and asynchronous; and IBM 3270 Type A devices.

M/A-COM NETWORK CABLE PRODUCTS

P.O. Box 1729
Hickory, NC 28603
(704)324-2200; telex 802-166

Frank Drendel, President; Dale Sherrill (PM); Joe Teague, Vice President, Sales and Marketing (MD); Nita Hunsucker, Customer Service Manager (PSC)

Founded 1966; 850 employees

Baseband coaxial, broadband coaxial, drop, trunk, and twisted wire pair cable. Cable products include high temperature plenum cables, satellite communication cables, video broadcast cables, computer cables, and cables for military applications.

MARK ELECTRONICS INC.

10829D Amherst
Wheaton, MD 20902
(301)555-1342; telex 701-683-2977

Frank N. Furter, President; Joseph Blough, Vice President, Marketing (MD); Mallory Keaton, National Sales Manager (PSC)

Founded 1983; 35 employees

Adapters; bridges; cluster controllers; diagnostic/test equipment; gateways; and X.25 interfaces. Vendor compatibility: IBM, DEC, Apple, and Xerox. Standards/protocols supported: Ethernet.

MARTIN MARIETTA DATA SYSTEMS

P.O. Box 2392
Princeton, NJ 08540
(800)257-5171; telex 843-479

Patrick Zilvitis, President; Thomas Hoger, Vice President, Marketing and Operations (PM); Loren Hurwitz, Microcomputer Manager (MD); Lillian Greenhut (PSC); Scott Hagar (PA)

Founded 1980; 5400 employees

Distributes adapters; baseband coaxial and broadband coaxial cable; network interface controllers; file servers; network management units; and X.25 interfaces. Vendor compatibility: IBM, Gateway Communications and AT&T.

MICOM-INTERLAN

155 Swanson Road
Boxborough, MA 01719
(617)263-9929; (800)LAN TALK;
  telex 951-909; FAX (617)263-8655

Michael Barker, President; Bob Olsen, Director, Technology Products (MD); Jim Hertenstein, Director, End-User Marketing (MD); Jerry Wesel, Director, OEM Sales (PSC)

Founded 1981; 160 employees

Baseband coaxial and drop cable; network interface controllers; RS-32 interfaces; protocol processors; transceivers; and terminal servers. Manufactures Ethernet connections for DEC Unibus and Q-Bus systems, Intel Multibus-based systems, Data General minicomputers, and IBM personal computers and compatibles.

MOD-TAP SYSTEM

Ayer Road, P.O. Box 706
Harvard, MA 01451
(617)456-3500; telex 951-369
  MODTAP HAVD; FAX 617-772-2011

George Ekiert, President; Dave Bundy, General Manager; Paul Andres (MD)

Founded 1977; 100 employees

Branch Offices and Distributors:
  MOD-TAP System, Santa Rosa, CA (707)575-7296; MOD-TAP System, Studio City, CA (818)505-8074; MOD-TAP System, Lisle, IL (312)968-7030; MOD-TAP System, Hawthorne, NJ (201)427-3233; MOD-TAP System, Dallas, TX (214)742-8131

Adapters; baseband coaxial, broadband coaxial and drop cable; diagnostic/test equipment; switches; and connectors.

MODULAR COMPUTER SYSTEMS INC. (MODCOMP)

1650 West McNab Road
Fort Lauderdale, FL 33310
(305)974-1380; TWX 510-956-9414;
  FAX 55-977-1501

Gabriel Rosica, President; Jeanne Senatore, Senior Product Marketing Manager (PM)(MD)(PSC); Joe Ottaviano, Manager, Purchasing (PA)

Founded 1970; 850 employees

Branch Offices and Distributors: Modular Computer Systems Inc., Norcross, GA (404)662-8988; Modular Computer Systems Inc., Fort Lauderdale, FL (305)974-1380; Modular Computer Systems Inc., Houston, TX (713)333-3250; Modular Computer Systems Inc., Vienna, VA (703)442-8222; Modular Computer Systems Inc., San Jose, CA (408)947-7440

Bridges and RS-232, RS-449, X.21, and X.25 interfaces. Standards/protocols supported: X.25 and Ethernet. Also distributes diagnostic/test equipment; file servers; gateways; and network management units. Manufacturers represented: DCA.

MOLECULAR COMPUTER

1983 Concourse
San Jose, CA 95131
(408)434-9500; telex 499-0791;
  FAX 408-434-9531

Frank Zurcher, President; Bill Heil (PM); Corinne Moore (MD); Barry Dearborn (PSC)

Founded 1981; 150 employees

Branch Offices and Distributors: Crystal Computers, Lenexa, KS (913)541-1711; Cyber/Source, Southfield, MI (313)353-8660; Digital Solutions, Marietta, GA

(404)955-4488; Emeritus, Fresno, CA (209)251-3525; Innes Systems, New York, NY (212)679-6180

Expansion units; RS-422 interfaces; server-to-server kits.

MONTROSE PRODUCTS COMPANY

28 Sword Street, Auburn
  Industrial Park
Auburn, MA 01501
(617)791-3161; TWX 710-349-
  67500

George Levine, President; Marjorie R. Bacis (PM); Joseph G. Merkwaz, Vice President, Sales and Marketing (MD); Rene Morin (PSC); Robert Clemente (PA)

Founded 1942; 400 employees

Baseband coaxial, broadband coaxial, drop, trunk, and twisted wire pair cable. Network compatibility: Ethernet, IBM cabling system, WangNet, MAP, AppleTalk, Starlan, ARCnet, and special composites for intelligent building. LAN cables are designed to meet industry standards such as IEEE 802 and NEC 725-2 (b). The cables are suitable for use in information systems which require precise signal characteristics. Plenum and non-plenum network cables are available from stock. Customer composites available upon request.

MOSTEK CORPORATION

Communications Products
  Department, 1310 Electronics
  Drive
Carrollton, TX 75006
(214)466-6000; telex 730-643; FAX
  214-466-8024

Jim Fiebiger, President; Bill Cummings, Product Marketing Engineer (PM); Jim Garrett, Communications Products Marketing Manager (MD)

Founded 1969; 1400 employees

Branch Offices and Distributors: Mostek Corporation, Santa Clara, CA (408)287-5080; Mostek Corporation, Irvine, CA (714)250-0455; Mostek Corporation, Burlington, MA (617)273-3310; Mostek Corporation, Huntsville, AL (205)830-9036; Mostek Corporation, Marlton, NJ (609)596-9200

Adapters; network interface controllers; protocol converters; and X.25 interfaces. All products are exclusively integrated circuit devices.

NATIONAL ELECTRIC CABLE

1730 Elmhurst Road
Elk Grove Village, IL 60007
(312)593-8100; telex 280-546

Richard Sass, President; Don McGuire, Marketing Manager, General Manager (MD); Harry Reeb, Sales Manager (PSC); Marsh Wyatt, Purchasing Manager (PA)

Founded 1972; 110 employees

Baseband coaxial, broadband coaxial, drop, fiber optic, trunk, and twisted wire pair cable and cable assemblies. Also distributes coaxial baseband, coaxial broadband, drop, fiber optic, trunk, and twisted wire pair cable. Manufacturers represented include Belden and Montrose.

NATIONAL INSTRUMENTS

12109 Technology Boulevard
Austin, TX 78727-6204
(512)250-9119; telex 756-737 NAT
  INST AUS; FAX 512-250-0382

Dr. Jim Truchard, President; John Gardner (PM)(PA); Bill Harris (MD); Don Nadon, Vice President, Sales (PSC)

Founded 1976; 90 employees

Extenders; diagnostic/test equipment; converters; network interface controllers; and general purpose interface buses.

NBI INC.
3450 Mitchell Lane, P.O. Box 9001
Boulder, CO 80301
(303)938-2705; telex 216-159 NBI UR

Thomas S. Kavanagh, President; Greg Flynn (PM); Robert Reid, Vice President, Marketing (MD); David Scott, Vice President, Direct Sales (PSC); Rob Biegner, Purchasing Agent (PA)

Cluster controllers.

NCR CORPORATION
1700 South Patterson Boulevard
Dayton, OH 45479
(513)445-2380; telex 288-093

C.E. Exley Jr., President; Jon Meadows (PM); Jim Robinson (MD)

Founded 1884; 62,000 employees

Adapters; bridges; twisted wire pair cable; cluster controllers; network interface controllers; protocol converters; encryption devices; file servers; gateways; network management units; taps/splitters; terminators; and RS-232, RS-449, X.21, and X.25 interfaces. Vendor compatibility: DEC, Corvus Systems, Xerox, and Intel. Distributor for Ryan-McFarland Corporation.

NEC AMERICA
8 Old Sod Farm Road
Melville, NY 11747
(516)753-7000; telex 144-658; FAX 516-753-7420

T. Suzuki, President; M. Shinozaki, Vice President, Corporate Marketing (MD); D. Hoffman, Vice President

and Assistant General Manager (PSC)

Founded 1963; 1380 employees

Fiber optic cable; protocol converters; gateways; and RS-232, X.21 and X.25 interfaces. Vendor compatibility: Bridge Communications and Corvus Systems.

NESTAR SYSTEMS INC.
1345 Shorebird Way
Mountain View, CA 94043
(415)969-1777; telex 171-420 NESTAR; FAX 415-967-4258

Charles J. Hart, President; Craig Russell, Direcor of Product Planning (PM); Robert Oakley, Director of Marketing (DM); Ray Healy, Vice President, Marketing and Sales (PSC)

Founded 1978; 100 employees

Baseband coaxial cable and file servers. Vendor compatibility: IBM and compatibles.

NETWORK DEVELOPMENT CORPORATION
81 Great Valley Corporation
Malvern, PA 19355
(215)296-7420; telex 910-350-6937 DNANET

Alan Laffkas, President; George Palmer, Executive Vice President (PM); Bruce Quigley, Vice President, Marketing (MD); A. Tony Jacobs, National Sales Manager (PSC); Joanne Moore, Office Manager (PA)

Founded 1978; 15 employees

Network interface controllers; file servers; gateways; and network management units. Network compatibility: Device Network Architecture (DNA).

NEVADA WESTERN
930 West Maude Avenue
Sunnyvale, CA 94086
(408)737-1600; telex 750-111; FAX (408)737-8792

Rich Johnston, President; Ben Simon, Operations Manager (PM); Bo Conrad, Marketing Manager (MD); Dick Nelson, National Sales Manager (PSC); Dick Garrison, Purchasing Supervisor (PA)

Founded 1975; 100 employees

Adapters; baseband coaxial, broadband coaxial and twisted wire pair cable; network management units; and RS-232 interfaces.

NORTH HILLS ELECTRONICS INC.
1 Alexander Place
Glen Cove, NY 11542
(516)671-5700; telex 466-886; FAX (516)759-3327

Howard G. Anders, President; Herb Marx (PM)(MD); Joseph Dastaldo (PSC); Ray Castry (PA)

Founded 1953; 100 employees

Adapters; taps/splitters; baluns; and cable assemblies. Vendor compatibility: IBM, NBI, Wang, and ITT. Standards/protocols supported: IEEE 802.3.

NORTH STAR COMPUTERS INC.
14440 Catalina Street
San Leandro, CA 94577
(415)357-8500

Bruce MacKay, President; Frank Marra, Vice President, Sales (PM); Brad West, Director of Marketing Services (MD)

Founded 1976; 150 employees

Branch Offices and Distributors: Northern Lights, Berkeley, CA (415)527-4448; General Business Computers, Cherry Hill, NJ (609)424-6500; Microware Distributors, Redmond, WA (206)882-2037; CompuTime, St. Louis, MO (314)428-1428; Crystal Computers, Irving, TX (214)929-1300

File servers; network management units; and RS-232 interfaces. Network compatibility: Omninet, ARCnet and ProNET.

NORTHERN WIRE & CABLE

307 Robbins Drive, P.O. Box 1026
Troy, MI 48083
(313)589-0510; telex 313-589-2628

Robert Brzustewicz, President; Rodney A. Hoover, Director of Marketing and Advertising (MD); Dean Stanton, National Sales Manager (PSC); Paul Waleke, Purchasing Manager (PA)

Founded 1976; 227 employees

Distributes adapters; baseband coaxial, broadband coaxial, drop, trunk, and twisted wire pair cable; network interface controllers; protocol converters; and terminators. National distributor specializing in electrical and electronic wire and cable, electrical and electronic accessories and cable assemblies. Manufacturers represented include Belden, AMP, Columbia and Alpha.

NOVELL INC.

748 North 1340 West
Orem, UT 84057
(801)226-8238; TWX 910-971-4001;
 FAX 801-224-3034

Raymond J. Noorda, President; Jared Blaser, Director of Marketing Services (PM); Craig Burton, Vice President, Marketing (MD); Harry

Armstrong, Vice President, Sales (PSC); John Vance (PA)

Founded 1983; 376 employees

Bridges; protocol converters; diagnostic/test equipment; file servers; network management units; and RS-232 interfaces. Vendor compatibility: IBM.

PANASONIC COMPANY

One Panasonic Way
Secaucus, NJ 07094
(201)392-4466; FAX 201-348-7807

K. Saeki, President; Ren Franse (PM)(PSC); William Kopp (MD)

Founded 1953; 3100 employees

Branch Offices and Distributors: Panasonic Company, New York-Metro, Secaucus, NJ (210)348-7000; Panasonic Company, Baltimore, MD (301)761-1900; Panasonic Company, Chicago, IL (312)364-7900; Panasonic Company, Atlanta, GA (404)923-9700; Panasonic Company, Los Angeles, CA (714)895-7200

Adapters; amplifiers; bridges; taps/splitters; RS-232 interfaces; portable data terminals; integrated voice/data terminals; modem telephones; and modems. Network compatibility: any network with RS-232 termination.

PATTON ELECTRONICS COMPANY

11129 Arroyo Drive
Rockville, MD 20852
(301)493-9665; telex 650-280-2556
 MCI

Robert E. Patton, President (PM); Bruce E. Patton (MD); Burton A. Patton (PSC); Beverly J. Patton (PA)

Founded 1984; 15 employees

Adapters; protocol converters; diagnostic/test equipment; extenders; RS-232, RS-449 and X.21 interfaces; and data communication devices. Product compatibility: all RS-232 systems, IBM 3270, Type A devices, V.35, V.36, X.21, and others. Patton Electronics specializes in data communications devices including modems, switches, baluns, line drivers, and break-out boxes. Catalog available from above address.

PROTEON INC.

4 Tech Circle
Natick, MA 01760
(617)655-3340; telex 928-124; FAX 617-651-1612

Francis M. Scricco, President; John Shriver (PM); Tony Bolton (MD); Cynthia Ferrone (PSC)

Founded 1972

Branch Offices and Distributors: Proteon Inc., Elmford, NY (914)592-2122; Proteon Inc. Schaumburg, IL (312)303-1510; Proteon Inc., Norcross, GA (404)662-1510; Long Beach, CA (213)428-2241

Network interface controllers; file servers; gateways; network management units; and RS-232 and RS-449 interfaces. Network compatibility: IBM Token-Ring, Novell Advanced NetWare and Banyan VINES. Standards/protocols supported: IEEE 802.5. Products designed to support multivendor environments.

RACAL MILGO SYSTEMS LIMITED

1800 Corporate Boulevard Northwest, Suite 300
Boca Raton, FL 33431-7373
(305)997-9554; FAX 305-997-3052

Jeremy P.M. Thomas, Managing Director; David Bull, General Manager

(PM); Michael Harding, Director, Business Operations (MD)(PSC)

Founded 1969; 200 employees

Amplifiers; network interface controllers; gateways; network management units; and RS-232 devices.

RAYCOM SYSTEMS INC

6395 Gunpark Drive
Boulder, CO 80301
(303)530-1620; telex 704-100

Paul Adams, President; Masami Nakamori, Vice President, Engineering; Michael J. Levesque, Vice President, Marketing and Sales (PSC); Carletta Humphrey (PA)

Founded 1981; 28 employees

Fiber optic cable; extenders; and RS-232 and RS-449 interfaces. Designs and manufactures fiber optic local data communication products used to interconnect computers, terminals, printers, controllers, PBXs, digital microwave radios, multiplexers, and point-of-sale devices.

SARGENT CABLE SERVICES

2801 Liberty Avenue, P.O. Box 30
Pittsburgh, PA 15230
(412)394-7580; FAX 412-394-7426

Ralph D. Vryenhoek, President; Richard W. Suminski, General Manager (GM); James K. Scanlon, Operations Manager (MD); Jacqueline Fournier, Marketing Representative (PSC); Larry Comfort, Purchasing Manager (PA)

Founded 1982; 35 employees

Distributes adapters; amplifiers; bridges; baseband coaxial, broadband coaxial, drop, fiber optic, trunk, and twisted wire pair cable; protocol converters; diagnostic/test equipment; extenders; gateways; taps/splitters;

terminators; RS-232, RS-449, X.21, and X.25 interfaces; cable assemblies; and jumpers. Represents numerous fiber optic equipment and cable manufacturers.

SEAGATE TECHNOLOGY

920 Disc Drive
Scotts Valley, CA 95066-4544
(408)438-6550; telex 176455
  SEAGATE SCUL; FAX
  (408)438-0558

David T. Mitchell, President; Carter O'Brien, Director, Marketing (MD); John Fritch (PA)

Founded 1979; 8500 employees

Branch Offices and Distributors: Hamilton/Avnet, Englewood, CO (303)740-1000; Hamilton/Avnet, Norcross, GA (404)447-7507; Hamilton/Avnet, Woburn, MA (617)531-7430; Hamilton/Avnet, Hauppauge, NY (516)434-7421; Hamilton/Avnet, Houston, TX (713)240-7898

File servers and hard disk drives.

SEISCOR TECHNOLOGIES INC.

P.O. Box 470580
Tulsa, OK 74147
(918)252-1578; telex 796-091
  SEISCOR BKAW

Data-over-voice systems.

SIECOR CORPORATION— ELECTRO-OPTIC PRODUCTS

P.O. Box 13625
Research Triangle Park, NC 27709
(919)549-6571; telex 216-910

Fiber optic cable; diagnostic/test equipment; extenders; and cable assemblies.

SIEMENS ENERGY & AUTOMATION INC.— PROGRAMMABLE CONTROLS DIVISION

10 Technology Drive, Centennial Park
Peabody, MA 01960
(617)532-6720; telex 928-160; FAX
  617-532-6720, ext.144

Ray Leveille, Vice President and General Manager; R.L. Bailey, Vice President, Sles and Marketing (PM); Ken Appel, Manager, Marketing Communications (MD)

Founded 1984; over 100 employees

Branch Offices and Distributors: Siemens-Allis Automation Inc., Buffalo, NY (716)834-3817; Siemens-Allis Automation Inc., Houston, TX (713)681-5001; Siemens-Allis Automation Inc., Dallas, TX (214)247-4481; Siemens-Allis Automation Inc., Santa Ana, CA (714)979-6600; Siemens-Allis Automation Inc., Plymouth Meeting, PA (215)825-2120

Network interface controllers; gateways; RS-232 and X.25 interfaces; and programmable controllers. Vendor compatibility: IBM.

THE SOFTWARE LINK INC.

8601 Dunwoody Place, Suite 632
Atlanta, GA 30338
(404)998-0700; telex 449-6147
  SWLINK

Rod Roark, President and Director of Research and Development; Gary Robertson, Director of Sales and Marketing (MD); Don Johnson, Sales Manager (PSC)

Founded 1983; 70 employees

Multiported serial boards. Product compatibility: IBM PC.

SOUTH HILLS ELECTRONICS
760 Beechnut Drive
Pittsburgh, PA 15205
(412)921-9000; (800)245-6215

Bob Zubrycki, President; Richard Froebe (PM); Jim Edge (PSC); Joe Machione (PA)

Founded 1949; 35 employees

Adapters; baseband coaxial, broadband coaxial, drop, fiber optic, trunk, and twisted wire pair cable; protocol converters; diagnostic/test equipment; taps/splitters; terminators; connectors; switches; modems; couplers; baluns; and multiplexers. Also distributes adapters; baseband coaxial, broadband coaxial, drop, fiber optic, trunk, and twisted wire pair cable; protocol converters; taps/splitters; and terminators.

STANDARD MICROSYSTEMS CORPORATION
35 Marcus Boulevard
Hauppauge, NY 11788
(516)273-3100; TWX 510-227-8898

Paul Richman, President; John F. Tweedy, Vice President, Systems Products (PM); Jean-Pierre Chalmin, Vice President, Sales (PSC)

Network interface controllers. Compatible networks: ARCnet.

SUNOL SYSTEMS INC.
1177 Quarry Lane
Pleasanton, CA 94566
(415)484-3322

Dr. Robert McCullough, President (PM); Robert Morten (MD); Virginia Wurts (PSC); Jessie Velasquez (PA)

Founded 1983; 20 employees

Adapters; network interface controllers; file servers; gateways; disk serv-

ers; and SCSI disk drives. Offers capacities of 21 MB, 45 MB, 70 MB, 110 MB, and 160 MB drives. Vendor compatibility: IBM, AST Research, 3Com, Apple, Wang, Apricot, and Victor.

SUNSHINE ELECTRONICS INC.
4845 Willett Parkway
Chevy Chase, MD 20815
(301)555-9774

Sue Thomas Owe, President; David Baxter, Product Manager (PM); Henry Truman (PSC)

Founded 1977; 34 employees

Diagnostic/test equipment and encryption devices.

SYNTREX INC.
246 Industrial Way West
Eatontown, NJ 07724
(800)526-2829

Twisted wire pair cable.

SYTEK INC.
1225 Charleston Road
Mountain View, CA 94043
(415)966-7400; telex 276-572
   SYTEK UR

L. George Klaus, President; Suri Harish, Director of Product Marketing (PM); Joseph Seidler, Vice President, Product Marketing (MD); Jeff Wilbur, Headquarters System Engineer (PSC); Jeanne Blackmore, Purchasing Manager (PA)

Founded 1979; 500 employees

Branch Offices and Distributors: Sytek Inc., San Jose, CA (408)275-9860; Sytek Inc., Itasca, IL (312)250-0057; Sytek Inc., Bethesda, MD (301)530-5100

Adapters; bridges; network interface controllers; diagnostic/test equipment; encryption devices; extenders; gateways; network management units; splitters; RS-232 interfaces; switches; translators; and network servers. Also distributes protocol converters and file servers.

TANGENT TECHNOLOGIES
5720 Peachtree Parkway
Norcross, GA 30092
(404)662-0366

Roland Bates, President; Guy Mariande, Vice President, Marketing and Sales (PM)(MD); Steve Simpson, Sales Support Manager (PSC); Gayle McCauley (PA)

Founded 1984; 9 employees

Bridges; protocol converters; and Appletalk interfaces. Network compatibility: Appletalk.

TCL INC.
41829 Albrae Street
Fremont, CA 94538
(415)657-3800

Norm Erbacker, President; Michael Knefaty (PM)(MD)(PSC)(PA)

Founded 1976; 5200 employees

Adapters; amplifiers; diagnostic/test equipment; extenders; terminators; interfaces; and transceivers. Vendor compatibility: Xerox, DEC, Bridge Communications, Ungermann-Bass, and 3Com.

TELEDYNE THERMATICS
P.O. Box 909
Elm City, NC 27822
(919)236-4311; telex 579-441;
   TWX 510-929-1600

Roy Inscore, President; Bill Strickland, Quality Control/ Engineering Manager (PM); Tom McClave, Vice President, Marketing (MD); Frank

Brice, Vice President, Sales (PSC); Les Skinner, Purchasing Manager (PA)

Founded 1956; 400 employees

Branch Offices and Distributors: N.L. Pitch & Associates, Hauppauge, NY (516)234-7118; Warren Mount Company, Bethesda, MD (301)657-9333; Chenault & Associates, Dallas, TX (214)388-4796; Wilco Wire & Cable Company, San Jose, CA (408)926-8880; Southern States Wire, Atlanta, GA (404)455-4075

Baseband coaxial, broadband coaxial, drop, trunk, and twisted wire pair cable. Standards/protocols supported: Ethernet, IEEE 802.3, 802.4 and 802.5. Product compatibility: single and dual cable broadband; RS-232; RS-449; RS-422/423; IBM type 1 and 2; T1 systems; and several proprietary networks. Specializes in high-temperature (plenum) products.

TELEVIDEO SYSTEMS INC.

P.O. Box 3568
Sunnyvale, CA 94088-3568
(408)745-7760; TWX 474-5041
  TVISYS

Dr. K.P. Hwang, President; Ron Nakashima, Director, Systems Product Marketing (MD)

Founded 1976; 700 employees

Branch Offices and Distributors: TeleVideo Systems Inc., Newport Beach, CA (714)476-0244; TeleVideo Systems Inc., Norcross, GA (404)447-1231; Televideo Systems Inc., Woburn, MA (617)938-3282; Televideo Systems Inc., Syosset, NY (516)496-4777

Bridges; drop, trunk and twisted wire pair cable; cluster controllers; file

servers; gateways; network management units; taps/splitters; and terminators. Vendor compatibility: Novell.

TELLABS INC.

4951 Indiana Avenue
Lisle, IL 60532
(312)969-8800; TWX 910-695-3530;
  FAX 852-7346

Michael J. Birck, President; Brian Jackman, Vice President, Marketing (PM)(MD)(PSC); Art Bannon (PA)

Founded 1975; 1500 employees

Amplifiers; bridges; cluster controllers; network interface controllers; protocol converters; gateways; network management units; terminators; RS-232, X.21 and X.25 interfaces; and multiplexers. Product compatibility: RS-232 and RS-422 interfaces.

TEST EQUIPMENT CORPORATION

2232 Old Middlefield Way
Mountain View, CA 94043
(800)227-1995

John E. Fisher, President; Leon O'Dell, Marketing Director (MD); Bruce Bartley (PA)

54 employees

Distributes diagnostic/test equipment; fiber splicers; and RS-232, RS-449, X.21, and X.25 interfaces. Rentals, leases, purchases, and rent/purchase options on all telecommunications test equipment. Manufacturers include Anritsu, Hewlett-Packard, Tau-Tron, Phoenix Microsystems, and Venator Systems.

TEXAS INSTRUMENTS— DATA SYSTEMS GROUP

P.O. Box 2909
Austin, TX 78769
(214)995-2011

Jerry Junkins, President; Wendel Harrison, Marketing Manager, Computing Division (PM); Jerry Brown, Vice President, US Marketing and Sales (MD)

Founded 1930; 72,000 employees

Adapters; amplifiers; fiber optic cable; cluster controllers; network interface controllers; protocol converters; diagnostic/test equipment; extenders; file servers; network management units; taps/splitters; terminators; RS-232 interfaces; and chip sets. Vendor compatibility: IBM.

3COM CORPORATION

1365 Shorebird Way
Mountain View, CA 94041
(415)961-9602; telex 345-546; FAX
  415-961-9602

L. William Krause, President; John Marman, Vice President, Marketing and Sales (MD)(PSC); Joan Winklepeck (PA)

Founded 1979

Adapters; bridges; baseband coaxial, drop, and trunk cable; cluster controllers; network interface controllers; file servers; gateways; taps/splitters; and terminators. Vendor compatibility: Novell, Bridge Communications and IBM and IBM-compatibles. Standards/protocols supported: Ethernet and IEEE 802.3 and 802.5.

TIARA COMPUTER SYSTEMS INC.

2685 Marine Way
Mountain View, CA 94043
(415)965-1700; telex 499-6251;
  FAX 415-965-2677

Thomas G. Hong, President; William Y. Terrill, Director of Product Marketing (PM); Mike Paul, Vice President, Marketing and Sales

(MD); Robert Kong, Director of Manufacturing (PA)

Founded 1985; 35 employees

Starter kits; coaxial cable kits; hub chassis; and LAN cards. Network compatibility: TiaraLink.

TRANSPAC
5310B Derry Avenue
Agoura Hills, CA
(818)991-5204

Don Westerfeld, President; Ed Newhouse, Vice President, Engineering (PM); Percy Lipinski, Marketing Director (MD); Tony Voula, Project Manager (PSC); Bill Welch, Executive Vice President, Engineering (PA)

Founded 1957; 67 employees

Distributes adapters; amplifiers; bridges; baseband coaxial, broadband coaxial, drop, fiber optic, trunk, and twisted wire pair cable; cluster controllers; network interface controllers; protocol converters; diagnostic/test equipment; encryption devices; extenders; file servers; gateways; network management units; taps/splitters; terminators; and RS-232, RS-449, X.21, and X.25 interfaces. Manufacturers represented include Corvus, Artel, OFTI, and Optical Cable Corporation.

TRELLIS COMMUNICATIONS CORPORATION
5 Manor Parkway
Salem NH 03079
(603)898-3434; telex 628-611-94;
FAX 603-893-9326

Richard Cerny, President

Founded 1985; 6 employees

Distributes adapters; amplifiers; fiber optic and twisted wire pair cable; diagnostic/test equipment; extend-

ers; network management units; taps/splitters; terminators; and RS-232 and RS-449. Manufacturers represented AT&T Technologies, Dorran Photonics, Harvey Hubbel, and Plantronics.

TRI-DATA
505 East Middlefield Road
Mountain View, CA 94043
(415)969-3700

Piet Moolman, President; Tony Addario, Director, Customer Support (PM); Steve Mattioli, Vice President, Marketing (MD); Bob Fitzgibbons, Sales Manager (PSC)

Founded 1967; 70 employees

Cluster controllers; network interface controllers; protocol converters; gateways; and RS-232 and X.25 interfaces. Vendor compatibility: Datapoint and token-passing LAN manufacturers.

TRW INC.—INFORMATION NETWORKS DIVISION
23800 Hawthorne Boulevard
Torrance, CA 90505
(213)373-9161; FAX 21-375-5805

J. Edward Snyder, President; John Cahill, Manager, Marketing Planning (PM); Bronson Purdy Jr., Director of Marketing (MD)(PSC)

Founded 1985; 100 employees

Branch Offices and Distributors: TRW Information Networks Division, Chicago, IL (312)693-7730; TRW Information Networks Division, East Brunswick, NJ (201)238-1300; TRW Information Networks Division, Boston, MA (617)229-5809; TRW Information Networks Division, Arlington, VA (703)276-5100; Arc Associates, Westlake, OH (216)835-2055

Gateways; network management units; intelligent connector units; frequency translators; and interfaces.

UNGERMANN-BASS INC.
3900 Freedom Circle
Santa Clara, CA 95054
(408)496-0111

Ralph K. Ungermann, President; Cliff Rudolph, Vice President, Sales and Marketing (MD); Peter Kirschner, Director, Marketing Support (PSC)

Founded 1979; 700 employees

Branch Offices and Distributors: Ungermann-Bass Inc., Newport Beach, CA (714)955-1414; Ungermann-Bass Inc., Dallas, TX (214)385-7090; Ungermann-Bass Inc., Chicago, IL (312)882-6885; Ungermann-Bass Inc., St. Louis, MO (314)532-9366; Ungermann-Bass Inc., New York, NY (212)466-1763

Amplifiers; bridges; cluster controllers; network interface controllers; protocol converters; file servers; gateways; network management units; and RS-232, RS-449 and X.25 interfaces. Standards/protocols supported: IBM Token Ring, XNS, TCP/IP, DEC host, and OSI Reference Model.

VERTEX COMPUTER CABLE & PRODUCTS INC.
61 Executive Boulevard
Farmingdale, NY 11735
(516)293-9880

Eugene Markey, President; Pat Parelli, Vice President, Marketing (PM)(MD); Mike Scanzano, National Sales Manager (PSC); Bob Litwin, Purchasing Manager (PA)

Founded 1971; 175 employees

Branch Offices and Distributors: Vertex Computer Cable & Products Inc., Derby, CT (203)736-6511; Vertex Computer Cable & Products Inc., Hanover, MD (301)796-5000; Vertex Computer Cable & Prodcts Inc., Cleveland, OH (216)831-7140; Vertex Computer Cable & Products Inc., Torrance, CA (213)212-6066

Custom assemblies. Also distributes adapters; baseband coaxial, broadband coaxial, drop, fiber optic, trunk, and twisted wire pair cable; diagnostic/test equipment; terminators; RS-232 interfaces. Distributes IBM cabling system cables and accessories. Vendor compatibility: IBM and Wang.

VITALINK COMMUNICATIONS

1350 Charleston Road
Mountain View, CA 94043
(415)968-5465; telex 345-566
    VITALINT MNTV

George Archuleta, President; Mike Coker, Sales/Product Manager, Network Products (PM)(PSC); Paul Schaller, Vice President, Marketing and Sales (MD); Conna Condon, Contracts (PA)

Founded 1980; 175 employees

Bridges; network interface controllers; extenders; gateways; network management units; and RS-232, RS-449, X.25, 3270, HDLC, and SNA LAN interfaces. Standards/protocols supported: Ethernet and IEEE 802.3.

VMX INC.

17217 Waterview Parkway
Dallas, TX 75252
(214)907-3000

Dal Berry, President; Jim Hawkins, Vice President, Marketing and Sales (MD); Lee Dewey (PA)

Founded 1977; 300 employees

Manufactures Voice Message Exchange.

WANG LABORATORIES INC.

One Industrial Avenue
Lowell, MA 01851
(617)459-5000; telex 947-421;
    TWX 710-343-6769

Dr. An Wang, President; Stephen Young, WangNet Product Manager (PM)

Founded 1951; 30,000 employees

Branch Offices and Distributors: Wang Laboratories Inc., San Francisco, CA (415)956-7077; Wang Laboratories Inc., Chicago, IL (312)329-1530; Wang Laboratories Inc., Boston, MA (617)720-5700; Wang Laboratories Inc., New York, NY (212)599-3454; Wang Laboratories Inc., Rosslyn, VA (703)243-4700

Adapters; amplifiers; bridges; baseband coaxial, broadband coaxial, drop, fiber optic, trunk, and twisted wire pair cable; cluster controllers; network interface controllers; protocol converters; diagnostic/test equipment; encryption devices; extenders; file servers; gateways; network management units; taps/splitters; RS-232, RS-449, X.21, and X.25 interfaces, and computer systems. Standards/protocols supported: SNA and CCITT X.25.

WATERLOO MICROSYSTEMS INC.

175 Columbia Street West
Waterloo, Ontario, CANADA
    N2L 5Z5
(519)884-3141; telex 069-575-20

Dr. Michael Malcolm, President; Dave Bell, Manager, Dealer Marketing (MD); Bill Didur, Manager of Large Accounts (PSC)

Founded 1982; 28 employees

Branch Offices and Dstributors: Waterloo Microsystems Inc. Rosemont, IL (312)696-2110

Gateways and RS-232 interfaces. Also distributes adapters; baseband coaxial cable; taps/splitters; and terminators.

WAVETEK INDIANA INC.

5808 Churchman, P.O. Box 190
Beech Grove, IN 46107
(800)622-5515; (317)788-5965; telex
    864-2041 WAVTK UW; TWX
    810-341-3226

John Batten, President; Terry Bush, Product Manager (PM); Jack Webb, Sales Manager (PSC)

500 employees

Branch Offices and Distributors: A & M Communications, Minneapolis, MN (612)920-5213; CATV Services, Fremont, CA (415)651-4331; Cable Technology Associates, Syracuse, NY (315)422-9012; CWY Electronics, Lafayette, IN (317)448-1611; ComSE Sales, Lawrenceville, GA (404)963-7870

Diagnostic/test equipment. Offers sweep recovery systems, system analyzers, sweep generators, signal analysis meters, fully automated test systems for forward and return sweep alignment and verification, translator testing, and loop-loss tests. Also offers test equipment for cable fault location and leakage detection.

WESTERN DIGITAL CORPORATION

2445 McCabe Way
Irvine, CA 92714
(714)863-0102; TWX 910-595-1139

Roger Johnson, President; Jack Landau (PM); Mel Gable, Vice President, Engineering (MD); Steve Rodriguez (PSC)

Founded 1970; 3500 employees

Branch Offices and Distributors: Western Digital Corporation, Peabody, MA (617)535-5914; Western Digital Corporation, Boca Raton, FL (305)984-6900; Western Digital Corporation, Irvine, CA (714)851-1221; Western Digital Corporation, Bloomington, MN (612)835-1003; Western Digital Corporation, Mountain View, CA (415)941-0216

Token access controllers.

THE WOLLONGONG GROUP

P.O. Box 51860
Palo Alto, CA 94303
(415)962-7100; TWX 910-373-2085; FAX 415-969-5547

Herbert J. Martin, President; David J. Preston, Director, Product Marketing (PM); Carl W. Jack, Vice President, Marketing (MD)

Founded 1980; 90 employees

Baseband coaxial and broadband coaxial cable; network interface controllers; and RS-232, RS-449 and X.25 interfaces. Manufacturers represented include ACC. Network compatibility: DECnet and TCP/IP Defense Data Network.

XEROX CORPORATION

Xerox Square
Rochester, NY 14644
(716)423-4828

David T. Kearns, President; Dan Minchen (PSC)

Founded 1906; 103,500 employees

Baseband coaxial cable and gateways.

XICOM TECHNOLOGIES CORPORATION

1545 Carling Avenue, Suite 205
Ottawa, Ontario, CANADA K12 8P9
(613)728-909; telex 053-3303

John Taker, President; Bruce Ricketts (MD)(PSC)

Founded 1981; 21 employees

Network interface units. SBS-Micro-Node allows multiple IBM PCs and compatibles, connected to a LAN, to operate, through 3270 and 3770 emulation, on IBM SNA networks.

XYPLEX INC.

100 Domino Drive
Concord, MA 01742
(617)371-1400

Paul L. Rosenbaum, President; Paul Viau, Director of Marketing (PM) (MD); Robert Rosenbaum, Vice President, Marketing and Sales; Charlie Bastany, Purchasing Manager (PA)

Founded 1981; 50 employees

Amplifiers; bridges; baseband coaxial, broadband coaxial and fiber optic cable; cluster controllers; network interface controllers; protocol converters; diagnostic/test equipment; extenders; gateways; network management units; terminators; and RS-232 and RS-449 interfaces. Network compatibility: Ethernet.

ZENITH ELECTRONICS CORPORATION— COMMUNICATIONS PRODUCTS DIVISION

699 Wheeling Road
Mount Prospect, IL 60056
(312)699-2199; telex 254-396

Jerry Pearlman, President; Greg Woodsum (PM); Bob Dranter (MD); Semir Sirazi (PSC); John Taylor (PR)

Bridges; network interface units; and frequency translators. Network compatibility: Z-LAN 500.

Chapter 3 — Software

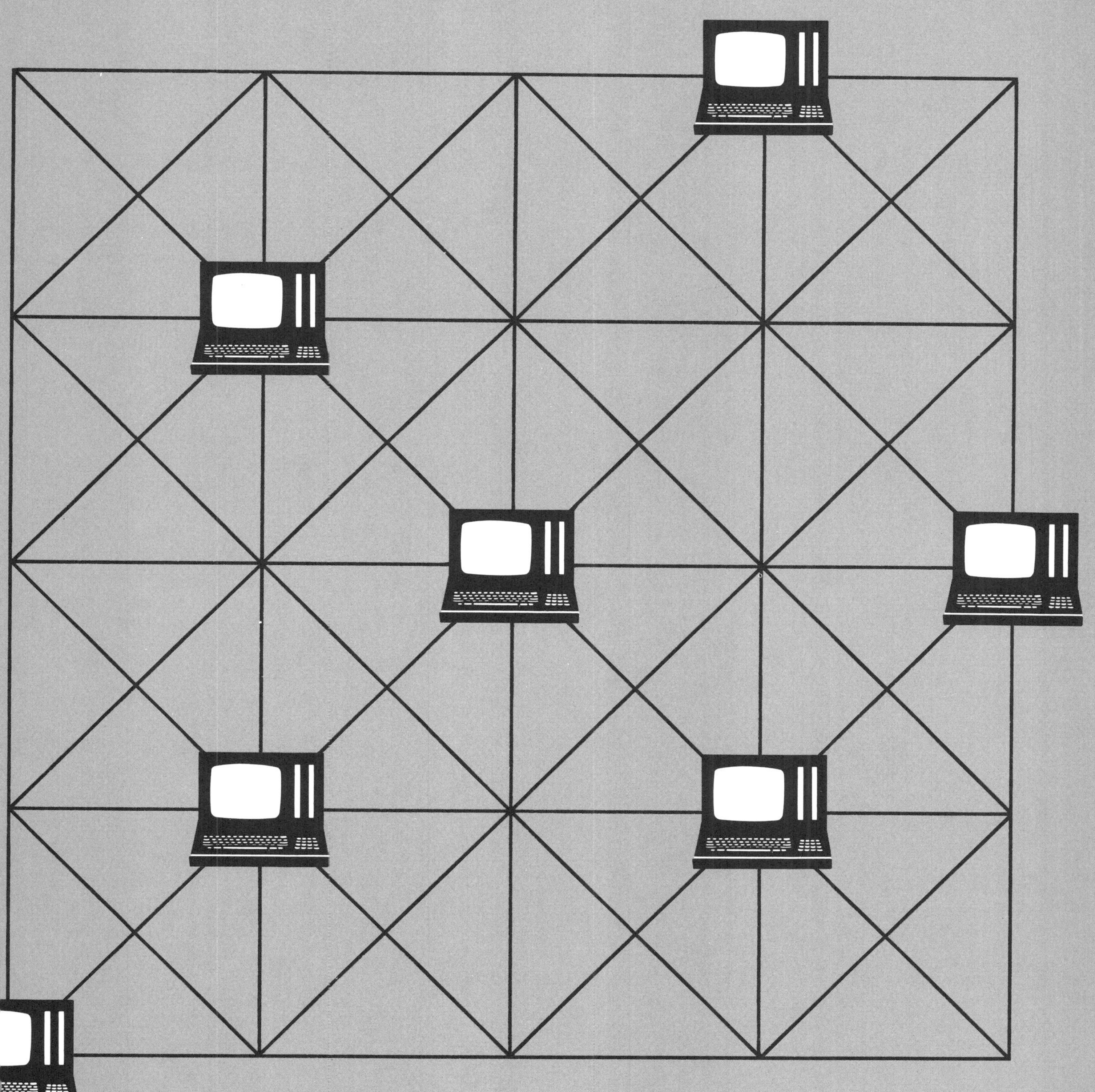

CHAPTER 3
SOFTWARE

This chapter lists suppliers of local area networking software. The name of a specific LAN software package and its description appear under the listing for the respective manufacturer.

Providers are indexed by software application in the index that precedes the entries.

FUNCTION CODES

PM Product Manager
MD Marketing Director
PSC Product Sales Contact

INDEX

BRIDGES AND GATEWAYS
AST Research Inc.
Fox Research Inc.
Standard Microsystems Corporation
3Com Corporation
Torus Systems Inc.
Ungermann-Bass Inc.

DATABASE MANAGEMENT
Apollo Computer Inc.
Basonje Systems
Data Access Corporation
Fox Research Inc.
Infonet Inc.
Innovative Software Inc.
Martin Marietta Data Systems—Information Technology Division
Microrim Inc.
Microstuf Inc.
NBI Inc.
Software Connections Inc.
Touch Communications Inc.
Wordtech Systems

ELECTRONIC MAIL
AST Research Inc.
AT&T Information Systems
Banyan Systems
Basonje Systems
Communication Machinery Corporation
Crowntek Communications Inc.
CYB Systems
A.B. Dick Information Systems
Gateway Cmmunications Inc.
Microstuf Inc.
North Star Computers Inc.
Software Connections Inc.
TeleVideo Systems Inc.
Texas Instruments—Data Systems Group
3Com Corporation
Torus Systems Inc.
2B Enterprises
Waterloo Microsystems Inc.
The Wollongong Group

FILE TRANSFER
Altos Computer Systems

AT&T Information Systems
Bridge Communications Inc.
Charles River Data Systems
Communication Machinery Corporation
Convergent Technologies
Crowntek Communications Inc.
CYB Systems
A.B. Dick Information Systems
Diversified Data Resources Inc. (DDRI)
Excelan Inc.
Fibronics International Inc.
Gateway Communications Inc.
Intel Corporation
MICOM-Interlan
Microstuf Inc.
Network Systems Corporation
Pathway Design Inc.
Prime Computer Inc.
Software Connections Inc.
Technology Concepts Inc.
3Com Corporation
Tiara Computer Systems Inc.
2B Enterprises
Waterloo Microsystems Inc.
The Wollongong Group

NETWORK OPERATING SYSTEMS

Apollo Computer Inc.
AT&T Information Systems
A.B. Dick Information Systems
Gateway Communications Inc.
International Business Machiness-Information
  Systems Group
Microsoft Corporation
Novell Inc.
Prime Computer Inc.
Proteon Inc.
The Software Link Inc.
Standard Microsystems Corporation
TeleVideo Systems Inc.
3Com Corporation
Tiara Computer Systems Inc.
Torus Systems Inc.
Ungermann-Bass Inc.
Waterloo Microsystems Inc.

PRINT SHARING

AST Research Inc.
AT&T Information Services

Banyan Systems
IDEAssociates Inc.
Novell Inc.
Server Technology Inc.
Texas Instruments—Data Systems Group
3Com Corporation
Torus Systems Inc.
Vianetix
Waterloo Microsystems Inc.

OTHER

Altos Computer Systems
Apollo Computer Inc.
AST Research Inc.
AT&T Information Systems
Banyan Systems
Basonje Systems
Bridge Communications Inc.
Charles River Data Systems
Communication Machinery Corporation
Convergent Technologies
Crowntek Communications Inc.
CYB Systems
Data Access Corporation
The Destek Group
A.B. Dick Information Systems
Diversified Data Resources Inc. (DDRI)
Excelan Inc.
Fibronics International Inc.
Fox Research Inc.
Gandalf Data Inc.
Gateway Communications Inc.
Gould Inc.—Industrial Automation Systems
  Division
Hayes Microcomputer Products Inc.
International Business Machines—Information
  Systems Group
IDEAssociates Inc.
Infonet Inc.
Innovative Software Inc.
Intel Corporation
Martin Marietta Data Systems—Information
  Technology Division
MICOM-Interlan
Microrim Inc.
Microsoft Corporation
Microstuf Inc.
NBI Inc.
Network Research Corporation

Network Systems Corporation
North America MICA Inc.
North Star Computers Inc.
Novell Inc.
Pathway Design Inc.
Prime Computer Inc.
Proteon Inc.
Ryan-McFarland Corporation
Server Technology Inc.
Simborg Systems Corporation
Software Connections Inc.
The Software Link Inc.
Standard Microsystems Corporation
Sunol Systems Inc.
Sytek Inc.

Tangent Technologies
Technology Concepts Inc.
TeleVideo Systems Inc.
Texas Instruments—Data Systems Group
3Com Corporation
Tiara Computer Systems Inc.
Torus Systems Inc.
Touch Communications Inc.
2B Enterprises
Ungermann-Bass Inc.
Vianetix
Waterloo Microsystems Inc.
The Wollongong Group
Wordtech Systems

ALTOS COMPUTER SYSTEMS

2641 Orchard Parkway
San Jose, CA 95134
(408)946-6700; telex 184-815
ALTOS UT

Dave Jackson, President; Russ Aldrich, Communications Manager (PM); Jeff Bork, Director, Systems Marketing (MD)

Founded 1977; 700 employees

•**Worknet/PC Path.** File services, peripheral support, gateway access, transparent processing across network. Software updates available. Compatible operating systems: Unix, Xenix and MS-DOS • Network standards/protocols supported: RS-422 and CSMA/CA • Year introduced: 1983 • Number installed: 2000.

•**Async.** Xenix- and Unix-based communications program that enables an Altos computer to exchange data or files with another Altos computer, or with any other system that supports either Xmodem or asynchronous communications. Can also be used to access public data networks such as Telenet, Tymnet and Uninet, and databases such as The Source and Compuserve. Software updates available. Compatible operating systems: Xenix and Unix.

•**PC Plex.** Links IBM PCs or compatibles to databases on the Altos systems either through WorkNet II/PC Path II or remotely through a simple asynchronous connection. Software updates available. Compatible operating systems: PC-DOS, MS-DOS 2.0 and above • Memory requirements: 320K.

•**3270 SNA/SDLC Emulator.** Allows Altos system to emulate a remote IBM 3274-51C control unit. Up to 16 terminal and printers can share a single synchronous SDLC connection to the remote mainframe. Gives users interactive access to remote mainframe databases and applications such as Time Sharing Option, Information Management System and Customer Information Control Systems. Software updates available.

•**3270 Cluster Emulator (Bisynchronous).** Allows Altos system to emulate the functions of an IBM 3274 or 3276 control unit. Gives users interactive access to remote mainframe databases and applications. Can be used from terminals and printers connected directly to Altos systems or connected via WorkNet II. Software updates available.

•**3780 Plus Emulator.** Makes a standard ASCII terminal act like an IBM 2780 or 3780 RJE terminal. Users can exchange files and messages with remote mainframes or minicomputers that support the 2780/3780 protocol. Can be used from a terminal connected directly to an Altos system or connected via WorkNet II.

APOLLO COMPUTER INC.

330 Billerica Road
Chelmsford, MA 01824
(617)256-6600; TWX 710-343-6803;
FAX 617-250-0183

Thomas Vanderslice, President; Michael Gallup, Product Marketing Director (PM); Edward Zander, Vice President, Marketing (MD); Angelo Guadagno, Vice President, North American Sales (PSC)

Founded 1980; 3400 employees

•**Distributed Data Management (D3M).** Database management package. Full-function, Codasyl-compliant database manager. Includes relational query language and formatting package.

•**DPSS/MAIL.** Allows users to perform routine office chores and scientific and engineering functions from the same workstation.

•**DOMAIN/IX.** Apollo's twin port of Unix Berkeley 4.2 System V Release 2. Allows users to run applications in either Unix standard, or both simultaneously, from a single workstation. Compatible networks: Domain.

•**Aegis.** Operating system. Provides multiwindow, multitasking environment and distributed data access system. Integrates data on each workstation into a single-system image. Compatible networks: Domain.

AST RESEARCH INC.

2121 Alton Avenue
Irvine, CA 92714
(714)863-1333; telex 753-699
ASTR UR; FAX 714-863-9478

Safi Qureshey, President; Mark Stieglitz, Director of LAN Products (PM)(MD); Ron Blaisdell, Director of Sales (PSC)

1000 employees

•**AST-NETBIOS Option.** Software emulation of IBM's NETBIOS interface compatible with all AST local area networks. Allows support of peripheral devices and resource sharing. Compatible operating systems: DOS 3.1 or higher • Memory requirements: 64K.

•**KNIGHT Data Security Manager.** Complete data security package for system management and security including electronic mail and usage auditing. System ensures that PC data files remain secure, correct and protected from accidental or unauthorized use, modification or deletion. Compatible operating systems: DOS 2.0, 2.1, 3.0, and 3.1 • Memory requirements: 128K.

•**AST-SNA/BSC Gateway.** Provides communications from AST, IBM or other fully NETBIOS compatible LAN to IBM mainframe computer. Allows 31 PCs and PC-attached printers, connected to a designated, non-dedicated "Gateway" PC, to simultaneously communicate with a host computer.

AT&T INFORMATION SYSTEMS

1 Speedwell Avenue
Morristown, NJ 07960
(201)898-3278

Charles Marshall, Chairman of the Board; Robert Casale, President, Marketing and Sales (MD)(PSC); Frank Vigilante, President, Product Management and Development (PM)

Founded 1983; 100,000 employees

•**PC 6300 Network Program.** Allows workers using different applications to share file and print services through the Starlan network as if they were all part of one larger system. Provides resource sharing among AT&T PC 6300, and IBM PC, XT, AT, and compatibles. Compatible operating systems: MS-DOS 3.1 • Compatible networks: Starlan.

•**Unix Network Program.** Gives AT&T Unix PC users access to electronic mail and file and resource sharing features. Enables Unix System workstations to communicate at 1 Mbps. Available in 2 versions: Unix PC Network Program and 3B2 Network Program. Compatible operating systems: Unix System V.

•**Unix Server Program.** Allows AT&T Unix PCs or AT&T 3B2 Computers to provide file and print sharing services to an MS-DOS environment. Supports record and file locking. Available in 2 versions:

Unix PC Server Program and 3B2 Server Program. Compatible operating systems: Unix System V.

BANYAN SYSTEMS

135 Flanders Road
Westboro, MA 01581
(617)366-6681

David Mahoney, President; Bob Martin (PM); Cyril Spratt (MD); Paul Bergeron, Vice President, Sales (PSC)

Founded 1983; 80 employees

•**VINES.** Provides file sharing, print sharing, network mail, post-terminal emulation, post-file transfer and access, IBM SNA backup and recovery, global naming system, system security, and multiserver networking. Software updates available. Compatible operating systems: any MS-DOS 2.0-3.1 • Compatible networks: Ethernet, IBM PC Network and Token-Ring, Proteon ProNET, Ungermann-Bass Net/One. • Memory requirements: 100K • Year introduced: 1983.

BASONJE SYSTEMS

138 Huron Street
Toronto, Ontario, CANADA M5T 2B2
(416)598-7992; telex 069-63548
  KAMPORT; FAX 416-593-7660

Allan Wong, President; James Kan (MD)

Founded 1982

•**Trans-Net Mail.** Electronic mail system. Enables memos and documents to be transmitted throughout the network.

•**Trans-Net Monitor.** Provides central control, monitoring and broadcasting screen to other workstations.

•**Trans-Net DMS.** Data management system to support single-user business application software under DOS to run on multi-user and multitasking environment.

•**Trans-Net Spool.** A powerful printer spooler package to direct printout of files from any network station into a high-speed buffer before queueing to the printer for output.

•**Trans-Net Disk.** Physically partitions hard disk into various volumes, allowing shared access by users at various priority levels.

BRIDGE COMMUNICATIONS INC.

2081 Stierlin Road
Mountain View, CA 94043
(415)969-4400; telex 176-544; FAX
  415-940-1928

William N. Carrico, President; Oliver Lubliner, Product Manager (PM); Catherine S. Muther, Vice President, Marketing (MD); Janak Pathak, National Sales Manager (PSC)

Founded 1981; 245 employees

Branch Offices and Distributors:
  Bridge Communications Inc., Houston, TX (713)872-8450; Bridge Communications Inc., New York, NY (212)986-0105; Bridge Communications Inc., Waltham, MA (617)890-6122; Bridge Communications Inc., McLean, VA (703)883-3790; Bridge Communications Inc., Roswell, GA (404)641-8090

•**SW/1-A/BSC/SDLC.** Software for CS/1 communications server. Similar software is also available for the CS/100 and CS/200 communications servers. Compatible with all Bridge Communications network products. Software updates available. Network standards/protocols supported: Xerox Network Systems (XNS) • Fees: $150 one-time fee.

•**SW/1-T.** Software for CS/1 communications server. Software updates available. Compatible operating systems: Unix • Network standards/protocols supported: TCP/IP • Fees: $250 one-time fee.

•**SW/1-X.25.** Software for CS/1-X.25 communications server. Software updates available. Network standards/protocols supported: X.25 between CS/1-X.25 and host • Fees: $2000 one-time fee.

•**SW/1-SNA 3270 and SW/1-SNA 3270-T.** Software packages for CS/1-SNA communications server. Provides access to IBM SNA hosts. Software updates available. Network standards/protocols supported: SNA, XNS and TCP/IP • Fees: $1000 one-time fee.

•**SW/1-SPMUX.** Software for CS/1 communications server. Provides access to Sperry host computers. Software updates available. Network standards/protocols supported: XNS • Fees: $1000 one-time fee.

•**Etherterm.** Allow IBM Ps and PC-compatibles to communicate with hosts and other network resources on an Ethernet LAN. Provides terminal emulation and file transfer capabilities. Compatible with all Bridge Communications network products. Software updates available. Compatible networks: Ethernet, X.25 public data networks and 3270 SNA systems • Network standards/protocols supported: Ethernet and XNS • Memory requirements: 384K • Fees: $300 to $1500 one-time fee; $300 to $1500 maintenance fee • Year introduced: 1985.

CHARLES RIVER DATA SYSTEMS
983 Concord Street
Framingham, MA 01701
(617)626-1000; telex 681-7373

Richard Shapiro, President; Ken Osowski, Manager, Product Marketing (PM); Tom Doyle, Director of Marketing (MD); Dan Capone, Vice President, Marketing and Sales

Founded 1973; 160 employees

Network software is integrated into the operating system kernel for maximum efficiency. Software updates available.

•**UniverseNet.** Distributed file system, remote execution, virtual terminal. Compatible operating systems: Unos • Network standards/protocols supported: ISO, MAP and TOP • Memory requirements: 250K • Fees: $1500 one-time fee • Year introduced: 1984 • Number installed: 15.

•**UN/TCP-IP.** FTP, Telnet, rsh, and rlogin. Compatible operating systems: Unos • Network standards/protocols supported: TCP/IP • Memory requirements: 10K • Year introduced: 1986 • Number installed: 4.

COMMUNICATION MACHINERY CORPORATION
1421 State Street
Santa Barbara, CA 93101
(805)963-9471; TWX 910-334-3508

Steve Holmgreen, President; Steve Gibson, Product Manager (PM)(PSC); Russ Sharer, Director of Marketing (MD)

Founded 1981; 50 employees

Branch Offices and Distributors: Communication Machinery Corporation, Framingham, MA (617)879-0953

•**TCP/IP.** Upper level protocol providing a full military specification implementation of Transmission Control Protocol and Internet Protocol with file transfer, virtual terminal, utilities, run time library, and electronic mail. Special programs include rcp, rsh and rlggin. Software updates available. Compatible operating systems: Unix 4.2 and V.2 and VMS • Compatible networks: Ethernet 1.0 and 2.0 and IEEE 802.5 networks • Network standards/protocols supported: TCP/IP • Memory requirements: 128K-512K • Fees: $1000 one-time fee • Year introduced: 1984 • Number installed: 4000.

•**XNS.** File transfer, virtual terminal and electronic mail. Software updates available. Compatible operating systems: Unix 4.2 and V.2 • Compatible networks: Ethernet 1.0 and 2.0 and IEEE 802.5 networks • Memory requirements: 128K-512K • Fees: $1200 one-time fee.

CONVERGENT TECHNOLOGIES
2700 North First Street, P.O. Box 6685
San Jose, CA 95131
(408)434-2848; FAX 408-943-0564

Paul Ely, President; Thelma Bataille, Product Marketing Manager, Communications (PM); Dick Nisley, Director of Marketing, Network Divisions (MD); Dick Meise, Vice President, Sales (PSC)

Founded 1980; 2500 employees

•**TCP/IP.** Network software for Ethernet-based LANs. Allows CTIX-based systems to commnicate with each other, and with non-Convergent systems supporting the TCP/IP protocols. Provides file transfer, remote logon, network status, and network management. Compatible operating systems: CTIX.

CROWNTEK COMMUNICATIONS INC.

3000 Steeles Avenue East
Markham, Ontario, CANADA
   L3R-4T9
(416)493-0800

D. Wood, President; P. Grys (PM);
R. Percy, Marketing Manager,
Prod/Net (MD); A. Marsell, Prod-
uct Sales Manager (PSC)

•**Micro Prod/Net.** Icons, windows, multitasking, mouse support,
electronic mail, document transfer,
file transfer, and host distribution to
other devices (LANs, PC, TSO,
JES). Software updates available.
Compatible operating systems: Port
and DOS 2.0-3.1 • Compatible networks: Arcnet, Davong and IBM
Cluster and Token Ring • Memory
requirements: up to 300K, depending
on options • Fees: $1300-$1800 one-
time fee (Canadian prices) per workstation; $350 annual maintenance fee
after first year • Year introduced:
1985 • Number installed: 22.

CYB SYSTEMS

2215 West Braker Avenue
Austin, TX 78758
(512)835-2266; telex 625-46700

Diana Goodrich, President; Gene
Zimmer, Manufacturing Manager
(PM); Gary G. Smith, Director of
Marketing (MD)(PSC)

Founded 1982; 24 employees

•**UNITE.** Networking software
featuring virtual file system, environment switching, IBM mainframe
SNA communications, electronic
mail, print spooling, electronic bulletin board, file transfers, and smart
terminal environment. Compatible
operating systems: Unix.

DATA ACCESS CORPORATION

8525 Southwest 129th Terrace
Miami, FL 33156
(305)238-0012; telex 469-021

Cory B. Casanave, Vice President,
Software Development (PM);
Charles L. Casanave III, Vice Presi-
dent, Sales and Marketing (MD); Les
Gay, Sales Manager (PSC)

Founded 1976; 33 employees

Branch Offices and Distributors:
   Cache Data Products, St. Louis,
   MO (314)962-1015; C.O.M.
   Systems, Dallas, TX (214)637-
   0061; General Software, North-
   ridge, CA (818)349-7758; Soft-
   ware Control International,
   Washington, DC (202)337-2600;
   Stark Asociates, Medfield, MA
   (617)359-4621

•**Dataflex.** Data management
system. Allows a multi-user environment complete read/write access to
all database records at all times while
maintaining data integrity. Requires
no user interaction with network operating system. Software updates
available. Compatible operating systems: PC-DOS, MS-DOS, CP/M,
Novell NetWare, and TurboDOS •
Memory requirements: 256K • Fees:
$1250 one-time fee • Year intro-
duced: 1981 o Number installed:
over 38,000.

THE DESTEK GROUP

830 East Evelyn
Sunnyvale, CA 94086
(408)737-7211

T.P. McReynolds, President

Founded 1981

Software meets industry software
standards for popular operating systems and IBM NETBIOS. Software
updates available.

•**desNet BIOS.** Compatibility
software making desNet products
compatible with industry standards
for IBM NETBIOS. Compatible operating systems: MS-DOS, PC-DOS

1.1 and higher • Compatible networks: Destek desNet • Network
standards/protocols supported:
CSMA/CD, Ethernet and IBM Token Ring • Memory requirements:
40K • Fees: $100 one-time fee • Year
introduced: 1986.

•**Turbo desNet.** Driver for TurboDOS network. Compatible operating systems: TurboDOS 1.1 and
higher • Compatible networks: Destek desNet o Network stan-
dards/protocols supported:
CSMA/CD, Ethernet and IBM Token Ring • Memory requirements:
8K • Fees: $100 one-time fee • Year
introduced: 1985.

•**desNet 86.** Driver for concurrent CP/M 86 running on S-100,
IBM PC and multibus computers.
Compatible operating systems: con-
curent CP/M 86 • Compatible networks: Destek desNet • Network
standards/protocols supported:
CSMA/CD, Ethernet and IBM Token Ring • Memory requirements:
8K • Fees: $100 one-time fee • Year
introduced: 1986.

A.B. DICK INFORMATION SYSTEMS

5700 West Touhy Avenue
Chicago, IL 60648
(312)763-1900

•**CTOS.** Real-time, message-
based multitasking operating system
for the A.B. Dick Knowledge Worker Series. Can be expanded by means
of Knowledge-Net which allows
LAN communications capabilities.
Supports CTIX, MS-DOS and
CP/M-86 guest operating systems.

•**Knowledge-Net.** Distributed
environment for inter-cluster communication on A.B. Dick Knowledge
Worker workstations, via local or inter-office networks. Supports a wide
variety of communications media including leased and circuit-switched

support and X.25 packet-switched networks. Provides network access for CTOS, MS-DOS and CP/M-86 applications. Compatible operating systems: CTOS. Memory requirements: 170K.

•**KWS-Mail.** Decentralized mail system consisting of several A.B. Dick Knowledge Worker Series clusters capable of operating as a mail system. Message management through file system which emulates file folder office environment. Transmits documents, graphs, spreadsheets, and programs. Compatible operating systems: CTOS • Memory requirements: 162K-200K for master or cluster users.

DIVERSIFIED DATA RESOURCES INC. (DDRI)
25 Mitchell Boulevard, Suite 7
San Rafael, CA 94903
(415)499-8870; telex 910-380-2875

George Faucher, President; Dave Gortner (PM)(MD)(PSC)

Founded 1981; 15 employees

•**RCOM.** General purpose PC communication program for transferring data between IBM PCs or to the IBM mainframe via a HYDRA controller. Software updates available. Compatible operating systems: PC-DOS and MS-DOS • Compatible networks: IBM PC Network and Token Ring Network, Ungermann-Bass Net/One. Memory requirements: 96K • Fees: $69.95 one-time fee per PC; $3000 host • Year introduced: 1983 • Number installed: over 5000.

EXCELAN INC.
2180 Forne Drive
San Jose, CA 95131
(408)434-2300; telex 176-610; FAX 408-434-2310

C. Richard Moore, President; Jay Weil, Director, Product Marketing (PM); Subhash Bal, Vice President, Marketing (MD)

Founded 1982; 125 employees

•**EXOS 8010 Series.** Allows IBM PC AT to communicate as a peer with DEC VAXs, PDPs and supermicros over Ethernet. Includes standard FTP and Telnet applications as well as rcp, rsh and rlogin. Compatible operating systems: Unix, Xenix and VMS • Network standards/protocols supported: TCP/IP.

•**EXOS 8030 Series.** Designed for DEC's PDP/11 series of minicomputers. Includes standard FTP and Telnet applications. Compatible operating systems: RSX-11, M, M+ • Network standards/protocols supported: TCP/IP.

•**EXOS 8040 Series.** Designed for VAX and MicroVAX computers. Compatible operating systems: VMS • Network standards/protocols supported: TCP/IP.

•**EXOS 8050 Series.** Provides PC-to-host communications over an Ethernet network for IBM PC, XT, AT, and compatibles. Compatible operating systems: PC DOS • Network standards/protocols supported: TCP/IP, NETBIOS.

FIBRONICS INTERNATIONAL INC.
325 Stevens Street
Hyannis, MA 02601
(617)778-0700; telex 951-297; FAX 617-778-0821

Joseph Maayan, President; Ken Coons, Product Manager (PM); Hal Spurney, Sales and Marketing Manager, Network Products (PSC)

Founded 1978; 450 employees

•**KNET TCP/VM Network Software.** Allows application-to-application communication between IBM mainframe and workstations over Ethernet. Also permits mainframe connections over binary synchronous lines and channel-to-channel adapters. Provides Telnet and FTP services. Compatible operating systems: Unix 4.2 • Network standards/protocols supported: TCP/IP, XNS, OSI.

•**KNET XNS/VM Network Software.** Allows IBM mainframe to function as a peer on an Ethernet network. Network standards/protocols supported: XNS, OSI.

•**KNET TCP/PC Network Software.** Allows IBM PC, XT, AT, and compatibles to participate on an Ethernet LAN as a peer with other network hosts. PC emulates an full-screen 3270 terminal. Provides Telnet and TFTP services. Compatible operating systmes: PC-DOS 2.0, 2.1 or 3.0 • Network standards/protocols supported: TCP/IP.

•**KNET TCP/MVS Network Software.** Allows IBM/MVS mainframe to attach to Ethernet to communicate with IBM and non-IBM workstations and computers. Provides TELNET and FTP services. Compatible operating systems: UNIX 4.2 • Network standards/protocols supported: TCP/IP, XNS and OSI.

FOX RESEARCH INC.
7016 Corporate Way
Dayton, Ohio 45459
(513)433-2238; (800)358-1010; telex 650-207-9125; FAX 513-233-5805

Leo Kessler, President; Greg Goodall (MD); Dan Broussard (PSC)

Founded 1983; 40 employees

Branch Offices and Distributors:
    ACS Telecomp, Lomita, CA

(213)325-3055; System Solutions, Evanston, IL (312)864-2283; AT&D, Austin, TX (512)478-5795; Vitronix, Westboro, MA (617)366-1144; Computeach, Washington, DC (202)861-2602

•10-NET RS-232 Gateway. Allows the use of the 10-NET user-to-user communications feature (CHAT) across the RS-232 link. Data file sharing with all network security and concurrency control functioning. Allows use of all standard 10-NET utilities (calendar, mail, news, spooling, remote job submission) between 10-NET LANs. Compatible operating systems: DOS 2.x, 3.x • Compatible networks: 10-NET • Memory requirements: 40K RAM

•10-BASE. Relational database management system. Flexible database design and retrieval ability. Unlimited file access within DOS limitations. DOS xtended record locking calls. Compatible operating systems: DOS 3.1 or higher for multi-user version • Compatible networks: 10-NET • Memory requirements: 256K; 320K for multi-user version • Fees: $495 one-time fee; $895 for multi-user version

•10-NET RS-232 PC Remote. Enables IBM PC, XT, AT, or compatible in a remote location to become part of a 10-NET LAN. Allows use of all standard 10-NET utilities (calendar, mail, news, spooling, remote job submission). Compatible operating systems: DOS 2.x, 3.xo Compatible networks: 10-NET • Memory requirements: 40K RAM

GANDALF DATA INC.
1020 South Noel Avenue
Wheeling, IL 60090
(312)459-6630; TWX 910-651-4951

Alan Melkerson, President; Edward Milbury (PM); Howard Gunn (MD); Michael Salustri (PSC)

Founded 1970; over 1000 employees

Branch Offices and Distributors: Gandalf Data Inc., Long Beach, CA (213)424-2258; Gandalf Data Inc., Atlanta, GA (404)447-5425; Gandalf Data Inc., Boston, MA (617)329-7630; Gandalf Data Inc., Dallas, TX (214)98-2690; Gandalf Data Inc., Washington, DC (301)421-1212

•NetScan 2000. Enables Gandalf data network to be completely monitored from a central workstation. Software collects data from the network via monitoring points, scans the data for alarm conditions and enters the data into a daily history file. Will maintain the network status and report failure alarms or any system degradation. Compatible operating systems: Venix System V 2.0 or higher • Memory requirements: 256K RAM • Compatible hardware: Gadalf PACX 2000 and IBM PC XT

•Link 2000. Combines with Gandalf's PACX 2000 to form the hub of a flexible PC network. Allows PC-to-PC and PC-to-mainframe communications. Runs on IBM PC/XT/AT. Compatible operating systems: MS-DOS and PC-DOS. Memory requirements: 128K.

GATEWAY COMMUNICATIONS INC.
16782 Redhill Avenue
Irvine, CA 92714
(714)261-0762; telex 509-462 GATEWAY COM; FAX 714-261-6569

David S. McMaster, President; Larry Stephenson, Executive Vice President, Operations (PM); MitchelEE. Barrie, Marketing Coordinator (MD); Bert Ott, National Sales Manager (PSC)

Founded 1981; 30 employees

Software developed for Gateway's G/Net local area network. Software updates available.

•Netware/G. Full-featured file server operating system. Includes electronic mail and disk optimization. Supports up to 50 users on one file server. Compatible operating systems: DOS 2.1-3.0 • Compatible networks: Gateway Communications G/Net • Network standards/protocols supported: Novell • Fees: $1595 one-time fee • Year introduced: 1983.

•Advanced Netware/G. Full-featured file server operating system includes electronic mail and disk optimization. Supports up to 100 users on up to eight file servers. Compatible operating systems: DOS 2.1-3.1 • Compatible networks: Gateway Communications G/Net • Network standards/protocols supported: Novell and NETBIOS • Fees: $1695 one-time fee • Year introduced: 1985.

•G/NETBIOS. Network operating environment for G/NET. Provides instant access to all appliciions software developed for IBM/s PC Network Program operating system. Also allows G/NET to run Microsoft's MS-Net network operating system.

•G/SNA. Provides PC access to IBM Systems Network Architecture networks using the SDLC transmission method. Provides wide range of SNA communications applications, including PC-to-mainframe, LAN-to-mainframe, PC-to-LAN, and PC-to-PC links. Network standards/protocols supported: IBM 3270 and 3770 RJE.

•G/Carbon Copy. Remote-control communications program fo IBM PCs, XTs, AT, and compatibles. Permits one PC to control and monitor the activities of a remotely-located PC. Includes complete file transfer capabilities. Can be used as a PC-to-PC or PC-to-LAN link.

GOULD INC.—INDUSTRIAL AUTOMATION SYSTEMS DIVISION

P.O. Box 3083
Andover, MA 01810
(617)475-4700; telex 470-2780;
    FAX 617-443-0078

Michael S. Bernath, President; Bruce MacAloney, Product Marketing Manager (PM); Robert A. Contino, President and General Manager, Industrial Automation Systems Division (MD)(PSC)

Founded 1969; 1500 employees

Branch Offices and Distributors: Commonwealth Controls, Richmond, VA (804)271-7700; Commonwealth Controls, Hanover, MD (301)796-5960

•**MAP.** Software updates available. Compatible networks: MAP-compatible networks • Network standards/protocols supported: MAP Protocol Suites • Year introduced: 1985 • Number installed: 10.

HAYES MICROCOMPUTER PRODUCTS INC.

P.O. Box 105203
Atlanta, GA 30348
(404)449-8791; telex 703-500
    HAYES USA; FAX 404-41-
    1213

Dennis C. Hayes, President; Garry Betty, Vice President, Sales (PSC)

Founded 1978; 600 employees

•**Smartcom II for the PC Network.** Provides modem and port sharing capabilities and through support of terminal emulation. Transparent user interface. Compatible op-

erating systems: DOS 3.10 or higher • Network standards/protocols supported: Hayes Verification, Xmodem, Stop/Start, or Send Lines • Memory requirements: 512K on each computer o Year introduced: 1986.

IDEASSOCIATES INC.

29 Dunham Road
Billerica, MA 01821
(617)663-6878; telex 497-9780

Gautam Gupta, President; Nora Feldman Gildea, Director of Marketing (MD); James Bender, Vice President, Sales (PSC)

Founded 1982; over 100 employees

•**IDEAshare.** Resource sharing package which links up to four ATs, PCs, XTs, Portables, and JCjrs. Enables users to share hard disks, printers and data in a business or home environment. Fees: $595.

INFONET INC.

10902 Wild Grape
San Antonio, TX 78230
(512)696-2590

Paul N. Criswel, President; L. James Beckman, Vice President, Marketing (MD)

Founded 1983; 12 employees

•**MCS/Monitor and Control System.** Controls user access to system software and databases. Provides network access and utilization statistics. Enables queuing of jobs to be performed by network ports. Compatible operating systems: NetWare • Compatible networks: NETBIOS compatible networks • Fees: $895 LAN 4 terminal server; $395 four terminal LAN additions.

INNOVATIVE SOFTWARE INC.

9875 Widmer Road
Lenexa, KS 66215
(913)492-3800; (800)GET-SMAR;
    telex 209-542; FAX 913-492-
    2965

Michael J. Brown, President; Douglas Edwards (PM); Ronald Ferguson (MD); Paul Donohue (PSC)

Founded 1979; 100 employees

Branch Offices and Distributors: Innovative Software, Inc., New York, NY (212)594-1188; Innovative Software Inc., Washington, DC (301)345-0655; Innovative Software Inc., Atlanta, GA (404)256-4166; Innovative Software, Chicago, IL (312)692-5640; Innovative Software, San Francisco, CA (415)397-0251

•**The Smart Software System, LAN Multi-user Version.** Integrated database management, spreadsheet, graphics, word processing, spell checking, telecommunications, time manager, programming language, mulitlevel password protection, file and record locking. Disk-based database manager. Software updates available. Compatible operating systems: DOS 3.1 and Novell NetWare • Compatible networks: IBM PC Network, 3Com 3+, AT&T Starlan, and other DOS 3.1 call compatibles • Memory requirements: 320K • Fees: $795 one-time fee includes 3 workstations; additional access at $595 each • Year introduced: 1985.

•**The Smart Database Manager, LAN Multi-user Version.** Database manager, telecommunications, programming language, time manager, multilevel password protection, and record locking. Disk-based database. Software updates available. Compatible operating systems: DOS 3.1 and Novell NetWare • Compatible networks: IBM PC Network, 3Com 3+, AT&T Starlan, and others • Memory requirements: 320K • Fees: $995 one-time fee includes 3 workstations; additional access at $295 each • Year introduced: 1985.

•The Smart Spreadsheet with Graphics, LAN Multi-user Version. Spreadsheet, graphics, telecommunications, time manager, programming language, multilevel password protection, and file locking. Software updates available. Compatible operating systems: DOS 3.1 and Novell NetWare • Compatible networks: IBM PC Network, 3Com 3+, AT&T Starlan, and others • Memory requirements: 320K • Fees: $995 one-time fee includes 3 workstations; additional access at $295 each • Year introduced: 1985.

•The Smart Word Processor. Word processing, spell checking, telecommunications, time manager, programming language, multilevel password protection, and file locking. Software updates available. Compatible operating systems: DOS 3.1 and Novell NetWare • Compatible networks: IBM PC Network, 3Com 3+, AT&T Starlan, and others • Memory requirements: 320K • Fees: $795 one-time fee includes 3 workstations; additional access at $235 each • Year introduced: 1986.

INTEL CORPORATION

3065 Bowers Avenue
Santa Clara, CA 95051
(408)987-8080; telex 346-372;
   TWX 910-338-0026

Branch Offices and Distributors:
   Intel Corporation, San Diego, CA (619)452-5880; Intel Corporation, Denver, CO (303)321-8086; Intel Corporation, Hauppauge, NY (516)231-3300; Intel Corporation, Richmond, VA (804)282-5668; Intel Corporation, Dallas, TX (214)241-8087

•Xenix Networking Software. Provides transparent file access between iRMX, Xenix and MS-DOS systems across a LAN. Users can use local file systems commands to read, write, open, and close files residing at remote systems. Implements upper layer protocols user by Microsoft Networks. Compatible operating systems: Xenix 3.0. Standards/protocols supported: ISO OSI layers 5-7.

•iRMX Networking Software. Network file access software providing transparent file access between iRMX and XENIX and iRMX and MS-DOS systems across a LAN. Users can use local file systems commands to read, write, open,aand close files residing at remote iRMX, MS-DOS, PC-DOS, and Xenix systems: Compatible operating systems: iRMX 86 • Standards/protocols supported: ISO OSI layers 5-7.

•iNA 960. General purpose LAN software package implementing the class 4 services of the ISO transport specification. Features include comprehensive network management services, guaranteed message integrity, multiple connection capability, virtual circuit services, and datagram service. Compatible operating systems: iRMX 86.

INTERNATIONAL BUSINESS MACHINES—INFORMATION SYSTEMS GROUP

900 King Street
Rye Brook, NY 10573

John Akers, President and Chief Executive Officer; Richard H. Goldberg, Group Director of Telecommunications Marketing (MD)

•Advanced Program-to-Program Communications for the IBM PC (APPC/PC). Application program interface for creating programs with program-to-program capabilities. Enables distributed transaction processing. Software updates available. Compatible operating systems: DOS 3.1 and 3.2 • Network standards/protocols supported: SNA LU 6.2 • Memory requirements: SDLC link only, 185K; Token Ring only, 195K; SDLC and Token Ring, 208K; additional 7K required for adapter handler program • Fees: $150 one-time fee.

•IBM Token Ring NETBIOS Program. Allows programs written using the NETBIOS interface to operate on the Token Ring Network. Software updates available. Compatible operating systems: DOS 3.1 and 3.2 • Memory requirements: 46K; additional 7K required for adapter handler program • Fee: $35 one-time fee.

•IBM Token Ring Network/IBM PC Network Interconnect Program. Allows exchange of information between PC's on two PC Networks. Also allows interconnection of a Token Ring Network and a PC Network. Software updates available. Compatible operating systems: DOS 3.2 • Memory requirements: Dedicated PC XT or AT, 256K • Fees: $495 one-time fee.

•PC LAN Program, Version 1. Provides network operating system extensions on the IBM PC Network and the Token Ring. Replaces the PC Network program. Software updates available. Compatible operating systems: DOS 3.1 and 3.2 • Memory requirements: Redirector, 30K; server, 186K • Fees: $125 one-time fee.

•IBM PC 3270 Emulation Program, Version 3. Allows 3270 emulation on a PC over communication lines, through a terminal controller or over the Token Ring Network to a 370 host. Software updates available. Compatible operating systems: DOS 3.2 for direct attachment to 3725 over the Token Ring • Memory requirements: 161K to 200K, depending on usage as gateway • Fees: $475 one-time fee.

MARTIN MARIETTA DATA SYSTEMS—INFORMATION TECHNOLOGY DIVISION
P.O. Box 2392
Princeton, NJ 08540
(800)257-5171; telex 843-479

Donald R. Shaw, General Manager, Information Technology; Loren Hurwitz, Director of Operations (PM)

Founded 1969; 5400 employees

Branch Offices and Distributors: Martin Marietta Data Systems, Atlanta, GA (404)261-0641; Martin Marietta Data Systems, Boston, MA (617)357-9424; Martin Marietta Data Systems, Houston, TX (713)850-8697; Martin Marietta Data Systems (212)819-0313; Martin Marietta Data Systems, Philadelphia, PA (215)963-0225

•**ShareIT (KeepIT PLUS).** Multi-user database management system. Offers shared access with full protection of record and file locks. COGENT Database Machine board functions as independent file server. No need for dedicated workstation as a file server. Software updates available. Compatible operating systems: PC-DOS 1.1 or 2.0 • Compatible networks: IBM PC Network • Memory requirements: 192K • Fees: one-time fee dependent on number of units; $850 minimum • Year introduced: 1985 • Number installed: 21.

MICOM-INTERLAN
155 Swanson Road
Boxborough, MA 01719
(617)263-9929; (800)LAN TALK; telex 951-909; FAX 617-263-8655

Michael Barker, President; Barbara Finer, Product Manager (PM); Bob Olsen, Director, Technical Product Marketing (MD); Jerry Wesel, Director, OEM Sales (PSC)

Founded 1981; 160 employees

XNS/ITP and TCP/IP protocols run on MICOM-Interlan's NP-Series protocol processors to offload host CPU. Software updates available.

•**TCP/IP for VAX/VMS.** Allows open systems communications between VMS, MicroVMS and Unix operating systems. Department of Defense Telnet and FTP applications software included. Compatible operating systems: DEC VMS and MicroVMS • Compatible networks: Ethernet and IEEE 802.3 • Network standards/protocols supported: TCP/IP • Memory requirements: 256K • Year introduced: 1986.

•**TCP/IP for 4.2BSD and 4.3BSD.** Allows 4BSD to be run on board intelligent NP100 protocol processor. Contains 4.2 software utilities, C-callable socket library, FTP, Telnet, and r-utilities. Compatible operating systems: 4.2BSD and 4.3BSD • Compatible networks: Ethernet and IEEE 802.3 • Memory requirements: 256K • Year introduced: 1986.

•**XNS Protocols for NP and NI Services.** Complete implementation of XNS/ITP protocols for high-performance Ethernet applications. Package includes board-resident operating system (NCX), device driver and management utilities. Copatible operating systems: VAX/VMS, RSX-11M/M+, Unix Systems V, and MS-DOS • Compatible networks: Ethernet and IEEE 802.3 • Network standards/protocols supported: XNS/ITP • Memory requirements: 256K • Year introduced: 1983.

•**TCP/IP for Unix System V.** Allows open systems communications between UNIX System V and other systems over Ethernet networks. Compatible operating systems: Unix System V • Compatible networks: Ethernet and IEEE 802.3 • Network standards/protocols supported: TCP/IP • Memory requrrements: 256K • Year introduced: 1986.

MICRORIM INC.
3380 146th Place Southeast
Bellevue, WA 98007
(206)641-6619

Founded 1981

•**R:Base 5000 Multi-user.** Relational database management system. Allows multiple users to share databases. Users can concurrently load and modify data, and also display and print information. Password security to restrict access at table or database level. Compatible operating systems: PC-DOS 3.1 • Compatible networks: IBM PC Network and 100% compatible networks • memory requirements: 640K server

MICROSOFT CORPORATION
10700 Northrup Way, P.O. Box 97200
Bellevue, WA 98009
(206)882-8080; telex 328-945

Jon Shirley, President; Steve Ballmer, Vice President, Marketing (MD)

Founded 1974; 550 employees

•**MS-Net.** Provides networking features as an extension to the DOS operating system. MS-DOS 3.1 and 3.2 have been modified to operate the MS-Net network. Compatible operating systems: MS-DOS 3.1 and 3.2 • Compatible networks: IBM PC Network, AT&T Starlan, 3Com 3+, Ungermann-Bass Net/One • Network standards/protocols supported:

SMB protocol • Memory requirements: 256K per server; 128K per workstation o Year introduced: 1984.

MICROSTUF INC.
1000 Holcomb Woods Parkway, Suite 440
Roswell, GA 30076
(404)998-3998

Les Freed, President; Owen Greeson, Vice President, Marketing and Sales; Janice Walker, Sales Administration (PSC)

41 employees

Branch Offices and Distributors: Microstuf Inc., Sunnyvale, CA (408)733-4397; Kenfil Software, Reseda, CA (818)342-2507; Softcell, Inglewood, CA (213)412-1700; First Software, Lawrence, MA (617)689-0077; Ingram Software, Buffalo, NY (716)874-1874

•**Crosstalk XVI for IBM PC Network.** File transfers through modem, or PC-to-PC within network (file server not necessary for this application). Terminal emulation, automate portions of calls with script files. Allows sharing of resources. Software updates available. Compatible operating systems: PC-DOS • Fees: $600 one-time fee • Year introduced: 1986.

•**Crosstalk XVI.** File transfers. Terminal emulation, automate portions of calls with script files, automatic dial and answer. Software updates available. Compatible operating systems: DOS • Fees: $195 one-time fee • Number installed: 300,000.

•**Remote.** Allows remote operation of a PC and its software. Electronic mail system. Crosstalk and Xmodem file transfers. Software updates available. Compatible operating systems: PC-DOS • Compatible

networks: IBM PC Network • Fees: $195 one-time fee.

•**Transporter.** Automated unattended file transfers. Software updates available. Compatible operating systems: PC-DOS • Fees: $295 one-time fee.

•**Infoscope.** Dynamic information management system. Allows manipulation and rapid, extensive sorts of database information. Software updates available. Compatible operating systems: PC-DOS • Fees: $79 one-time fee.

NBI INC.
3450 Mitchell Lane, P.O. Box 9001
Boulder, CO 80301
(303)938-2705; telex 216-159 NBI UR

Thomas S. Kavanagh, President; Greg Flynn (PM); Robert Reid, Vice President, Marketing (MD); David Scott, Vice President, Direct Sales (PSC)

•**TEAM-UP.** Multi-user relational database management system providing concurrent access by multiple users. IBM PC compatible. Allows up to 32 users access to same file. Security measures embedded throughout system with multiple levels available for each user, file, record, field, and function. Compatible operating systems: MS-DOS.

NETWORK RESEARCH CORPORATION
2380 North Rose Avenue
Oxnard, CA 93030
(805)485-2700; telex 297-579

Wayne Martson, President; James Hunter, Vice President, Marketing and Sales (MD); Kathy Graham, Director of Sales (PSC)

Founded 1982; 35 employees

Branch Offices and Distributors: Advanced Data Marketing, Parker, CO (303)841-4903; Remtek Inc., Dallas, TX (214)387-2855; W.C. Koepf Associates Inc., Chagrin Falls, OH (216)247-5129; C.E. Network Systems Inc., Foxboro, MA (617)543-7200; Burland Associates Inc., (602)894-5564

•**Fusion.** Portable networking software fr use in heterogeneous computing environments. Software updates available. Compatible operating systems: MS-DOS, Unix and VMS (DEC) • Compatible networks: Ethernet (3Com, CMC, Interlan, Excelan, and DEC) and Proteon Pro-NET • Network standards/protocols supported: TCP/IP and XNS • Memory requirements: PC, 128K; VAX/VMS 300K • Fees: $350-12,000 one-time fee; maintenance fee 10% of purchase price per year • Year introduced: 1984 o Number installed: over 7000.

NETWORK SYSTEMS CORPORATION
7600 Boone Avenue North
Minneapolis, MN 55428
(612)424-4888; telex 201-678; FAX 612-424-2853

Lyle Altman, President; Mahlon Moore, Vice President, Marketing (MD); Robert Klein (PSC)

Founded 1976; 900 employees

Branch Offices and Distributors: Network Systems Corporation, Los Angeles, CA (213)216-7009; Network Systems Corporation, Denver, CO (303)779-6996; Network Systems Corporation, Vienna, VA (703)281-0455; Network Systems Corporation, Paramus, NJ (201)368-8024; Network Systems Corporation, Dall, TX (214)578-1554

•**Network Executive (Netex).** Software product family that provides a universal access method for computer systems which are interconnected by a HYPERchannel network. Facilitates file transfer, job transfer and transaction processing in either a single or multivendor environment and on a real-time demand basis.

•**Bulk File Transfer (BFX).** Allows users of Netex communications software to move large quantities of sequential file data between similar or dissimilar types of processors on a HYPERchannel network. Allows file transfer between computers and operating systems of mixed manufacture.

•**Interactive File Transfer (IFX).** Allows access to and manipulation of files on a remote computer from a host computer. Both computers must be equipped with Netex and IFX.

NORTH AMERICA MICA INC.

5230 Carroll Canyon Road, #110
San Diego, CA 92121
(619)458-1327

E.A. Vanderpool, President; A.J. Arpad Tota, Sales Manager (PM); Ann Kalitzke, Marketing Manager (MD); Sharyn Keyse (PSC)

Founded 1980

•**TEAMPLAN.** PMS-II file control manager for use with LANs and multi-user systems. Allows 2 to 26 users to run PMS-II simultaneously. Software updates available. Compatible operating systems: MS-DOS, PC-DOS and CP/M 86 • Memory requirements: 128K RAM • Fees: One-time fee dependent on number of users • Year introduced: 1985 • Number installed: 27.

NORTH STAR COMPUTERS INC.

14440 Catalina Street
San Leandro, CA 94536
(415)357-8500; telex 910-366-7001;
　FAX 415-895-1309

Bruce MacKay, President; Frank Marra, Vice President, Sales (PM)

Founded 1976; 150 employees

•**North Star NetWare.** Full implementation of the industry standard Novell NetWare operating system especially optimized for North Star use. High-performance file server, system security and electronic mail system. Compatible operating systems: DOS 3.1.

•**North Star DOS.** Supports 3Com semaphore system, allowing system to run true multi-user software written to 3Com standard. Also supports MS-DOS and PC-DOS Version 2.11. Fixed disk partitioned into personal, public and shared areas. Print spooling, electronic mail and high-performance tape-backup utilities.

NOVELL INC.

748 North 1340 West
Orem, UT 84057
(801)226-8238; TWX 910-971-4001;
　FAX 801-224-3034

Raymond J. Noorda, President; Jared Blaser, Director of Marketing Services (PM); Craig Burton, Vice President, Marketing (MD); Harry Armstrong, Vice President, Sales (PSC)

Founded 1983; 376 employees

Novell NetWare Systems are categorizedby server type: NetWare/68, NetWare/86 and NetWare/286. The NetWare Operating System is then divided into two different categories: Advanced NetWare and System Fault Tolerant NetWare. NetWare Systems available in four different network hardware configurations: S-Net, ProNET, ARCnet, and G-Net.

•**Advanced NetWare/68.** Supports multiple file servers on a single network. Twenty-four active workstations per server. Dedicated server; five shared printers. Supports internetworking with Advanced NetWare/86 and SFT NetWare Systems through NetWare Bridges. Compatible operating systems: PC-DOS and MS-DOS 2.0, 2.1, 3.0, and 3.1

•**Advanced NetWare/86.** Supports multiple file servers on a single network. Fifty active workstations per server. Dedicated or non-dedicated file server; three shared printers. Supports internetworking with SFT NetWare servers through NetWare Bridges. Compatible operating systems: PC-DOS and MS-DOS 2.0, 2.1, 3.0, and 3.1

•**Advanced NetWare/286.** One hundred twenty-eight active workstations per server. Dedicated file server only. Three shared printers; 252 MB volume sizes. Compatible operating systems: PC-DOS and MS-DOS 2.0, 2.1, 3.0, and 3.1.

•**System Fault Tolerant NetWare/286.** Offers fault resiliency to system or component failure. Dedicated file server; three shared printers. One hundred twenty-eight active workstations per server. Internetworking with Advanced NetWare and other SFT NetWare servers supported through NetWare Bridges.

PATHWAY DESIGN INC.

1 Apple Hill, P.O. 8179
Natick, MA 01760
(617)237-7722

Robert Broggi, President; Mark Mackaman (PM); Vic Forgetta (MD); Mike Ingham (PSC)

Founded 1983; 60 employees

Branch Offices and Distributors: Cache Data Products, St. Louis, MO (314)962-1015; Com Systems, Dallas, TX (214)637-0061; Comtec Inc., Roanoke, VA (703)981-0326; Costa Distributing West, South San Francisco, CA (415)952-6113; Microserve Technologies, Needham, MA (617)449-6468

•**NetPATH SNA 3270.** Allows IBM PCs on a LAN to access an IBM host through a single PC running the package. NetPATH emulates a 3274/76 cluster controller and attached devices in an SNA/SDLC environment. Includes bundled file transfer package. Software updates available. Compatible operating systems: Novell NetWare • Compatible networks: Any network supported by Novell NetWare • Memory requirements: 256K • Fees: $2,595 one-time fee for 8 sessions; $3,595 fee for 16 sessions; $4,595 fee for 32 sessions • Year introduced: 1985.

PRIME COMPUTER INC.
Prime Park
Natick, MA 01760
(617)655-8000; telex 174-170

Joe M. Henson, President and Chief Executive Officer; Wendy Wheeler, Vice President, Systems Marketing (MD)

Founded 1972; 8115 employees

Branch Offices and Distributors: Prime Computer Inc., Parsippany, NJ (201)993-8400; Prime Computer Inc., Oak Brook Terrace, IL (312)953-9250; Prime Computer Inc., Woodland Hills, CA (818)992-8633

•**Primenet.** Distributed networking facility that provides complete local and remote network communication services fr all Prime systems. In LAN configurations, allows Prime computers to be attached via a high-bandwidth, multipoint ring arrangement to other Prime systems. File transfer and packet network interface available at an additional cost. Software updates available. Compatible operating systems: PRIMOS o Compatible networks: any Prime 50 Series system • Fees: $7500 one-time fee; $60 monthly maintenance fee.

•**Primelink.** Fully functional interconnect package that links a variety of personal computers to corporate databases, enabling users to retrieve, analyze and manipulate data. Supports Performer PC option, IBM-PC, IBM-PC XT, IBM-PC AT, and other IBM-compatible PC systems. File transfer and virtual disk capabilities.

•**Primix.** Operating system based on Unix System V. Provides standard Unix user environment and portability of Unix-based applications. Allows the Primos operating system and Unix to operate simultaneously. Operates with Primenet networking software and transparent remote files.

•**Primos.** Multipurpose, multiprogramming operating system. Fully compatible across all Prime 50 Series systems. Supports Primenet networking software.

PROTEON INC.
4 Tech Circle
Natick, MA 01760
(617)655-3340; telex 928-124; FAX 617-651-1612

Fran Scricco, President; John Shriver (PM); Tony Bolton (MD); Pat Lally (PSC)

Founded 1972; 250 employees

•**NetWare/P.** NetWare operating system allowing IBM PCs, XTs, ATs and compatibles to share one or multiple file servers, each with as much as 252 MB of disk storage. Each file server on the network can support 54 PCs. Memory requirements: 256K file server; 128K PC.

•**Advanced NetWare/P.** Expands NetWare capabilities to embrace multiple file servers coexisting on a potentially heterogeneous internetwork. Workstation may simultaneously use files from multiple file servers, allowing data integration across logical and/or physical boundaries.

RYAN-MCFARLAND CORPORATION
609 Deep Valley Drive
Rolling Hills Estates, CA 90274
(213)541-4828; telex 294-253; FAX 213-377-5062

Donald R. Ryan, President; Mike Saccomano, Director, Product Marketing (PM); Charles Runge, Vice President, Marketing (MD); David McFarland, Vice President, Sales (PSC)

Founded 1971

•**RM/COBOL.** ANSI standard compiler. Designed for serious small system computing. Software updates available. Compatible operating systems: DOS, Xenix, Unix, CP/M, CP/M 86 and RM/COS • Compatible networks: IBM PC Network, 3Com and Novell • Network standards/protocols supported: IBM Token Ring and NETBIOS • Memory requirements: 64K • Fees: $950 one-time fee, DOS; $1250 one-time fee, network • Year introduced: 1976 o Number installed: 400,000.

•**RM/COBOL-8X.** Advanced ANSI standard compiler with 1985

Cobol features and IBM VS COBOL extensions. Fast compilation and application execution. Software updates available. Compatible operating systems: DOS • Compatible networks: IBM PC Network, 3Com and Novell • Network standards/protocols supported: IBM Token Ring and NET-BIOS • Memory requirements: 192K • Fees: $1250 one-time fee, DOS; $1500 one-time fee, network DOS • Year introduced: 1985.

•**RM/InfoExpress.** Add-on to RM/COBOL-8X. Maximizes Cobol IO speed. Can allow multi-user applications to execute an average of 6 times faster on a DOS network with five users with no source or object code changes. Software updates available. Compatible operating systems: DOS 3.1 or higher • Compatible networks: IBM PC Network, 3Com and Novell • Network standards/protocols supported: IBM Token Ring and NETBIOS • Memory requirements: 384K, server; 256K, client • Fees: $595 one-time fee • Year introduced: 1986.

SERVER TECHNOLOGY INC.
1095 East Duane Street, Suite 107
Sunnyvale, CA 94086
(408)738-8377

Carrel Ewing, President; Jay Williams (PM)

Founded 1984; 10 employees

•**Easy LAN.** Network software allowing PC users to share printer and disk peripherals. Optional passwords and disk directory access restrictions. Runs on all IBM PC models and compatibles. Software updates available. Compatible operating systems: MS-DOS and PC-DOS • Network standards/protocols supported: RS-232 and IBM NETBIOS • Memory requirements: 20K • Year introduced: 1985 • Number installed: 10,000.

SIMBORG SYSTEMS CORPORATION
21 Tamal Vista Boulevard
Corte Madera, CA 94925
(415)927-1122

Dr. Donald Simborg, President; Wes Rishel, Technical Director (PM); Jeffrey J. Werner, Vice President, Marketing and Sales (MD)(PSC)

Founded 1984; 12 employees

•**Stat LAN.** For use in hospitals and other healthcar environments. Integrates systems at the application level. Supports ISO Reference Model to layer 7. Software updates available. Compatible with all major operating systems. Compatible networks: Ethernet and Ungermann-Bass Net/One • Fees: variable with the size of system and hospital • Year introduced: 1985.

SOFTWARE CONNECTIONS INC.
1435 Koll Circle, Suite 112
San Jose, CA 95112-4610
(408)293-3400

Buck Gee, President; Gary Kwok, Director of Marketing (PM)(MD); Pamela Flournoy, National Sales Manager (PSC)

Founded 1981; 20 employees

Branch Offices and Distributors: Computerland, Columbia, SC (803)736-3900; Atlantic Computers, Waltham, MA (617)893-0040; Entre Computer Center, Austin, TX (512)451-0223; Businessland, Oakland, CA (415)839-4687; Businessland, Sunnyvale, CA (408)735-7711

Database, electronic mail and software tools written specifically for networks. Over 25 supported networks include those from IBM, Novell, 3Com, Nestar, Orchid, Corvus,

Ungermann-Bass, TeleVideo, Standard Microsystems, Proteon, and AST.

•**Datastore:LAN.** Menu-driven relational database management system for non-programmers. Built-in custom report writer and application generator; automatic record-locking; file-locking option for exclusive use; password security (encrypted); check sums; audit trails; and data privacy through field masking. Compatible operating systems: DOS 1.1-3.1 • Compatible networks: IBM PC Network and Token Ring Network, Novell NetWare, Corvus Omninet, Nestar PLAN Series, 3Com EtherSeries and 3 Plus, Orchid PCnet, AST PCnet II, and TeleVideo Personal Mini • Network standards/protocols supported: Semaphore calls and DOS 3.1 compatible operating systems • Memory requirements: 237K of available memory plus network operating system and DOS • Fees: $1195 one-time fee; $295 annual maintenance fee includes free updates and unlimited phone support • Year introduced: 1983 • Number installed: over 5000.

•**LAN:Datacore.** Relational database development tool for higher-level langage programmers. Provides a library of DOS subroutines callable from Pascal, C and Basic. Network features include automatic record-locking, file-locking option for exclusive use, encrypted passwords, and check sums. Compatible operating systems: DOS 1.1-3.1 • Compatible networks: IBM PC Network and Token-Ring Network, Novell NetWare, Corvus Omninet, Nestar PLAN Series, 3Com EtherSeries and 3 Plus, Orchid PCnet, AST PCnet II, Televideo Personal Mini, and Fox 10Net • Network standards/protocols supported: Semaphore calls and DOS 3.1 compatible operating systems • Memory requirements: 91K plus application, network operating system and DOS • Fees: $995 one-time fee; $500 maintenance fee per 5 hours of development support • Year introduced: 1983.

•**LAN:Mail Monitor.** Store-and-forward electronic mail system for local area network users. Allows transmission of letters and file enclosures to other LAN users or over phone lines to users at remote sites. Features include certified and absentee mail delivery; built-in letter editor; edit-and-forward routing system; automatic date and time stamping; distribution lists/alias names; automatic dial-and-answer; and mailbox passwords. Compatible operating systems: DOS 1.1-3.1 • Compatible networks: IBM PC Network and Token Ring Network, Novell NetWare, Corvus Omninet, Nestar PLAN Series, 3Com EtherSeries and 3 Plus, Orchid PCnet, AST PCnet II, and TeleVideo Personal Mini • Network standards/protocols supported: Semaphore calls and DOS 3.1 compatible calls • Memory requirements: 256K on user rstations • Fees: $995 one-time fee; $295 annual maintenance fee includes free updates and unlimited phone support • Year introduced: 1982.

THE SOFTWARE LINK INC.
8601 Dunwoody Place, Suite 632
Atlanta, GA 30338
(404)998-0700; telex 449-6147
SWLINK

Rod Roark, President and Director of Research and Development; Gary Robertson, Director of Sales and Marketing (MD); Don Johnson, Sales Manager (PSC)

Founded 1983; 70 employees

•**Multilink Advanced.** Software-based multi-user system that partitions RAM into nine segments which can be assigned to a specific ASCII terminal or task. Can be used with Software Link's LANLink to creat a multiuser LAN with up to 73 workstations. Software updates available. Compatible operating systems: MS-DOS and PC-DOS • Network standards/protocols supported: NETBIOS • Memory requirements: 128K • Fees: $495 one-time fee • Year introduced: 1983 • Number installed: over 30,000.

•**LANLink.** Software-driven LAN which allows users to connect as many as eight satellite microcomputers to one non-dedicated server. Provides record-locking and file-locking. Software updates available. Compatible operating systems: MS-DOS and PC-DOS • Network standards/protocols supported: NETBIOS • Memory requirements: 60K for server; 40K for each satellite microcomputer • Fees: $495 one-time fee o Year introduced: 1985 • Number installed: 10,000.

•**NetProfit.** Multi-user accounting system written in Business Basic Extended (BBx), which allows as many as 30 users simultaneous access to accounting files. Software updates available. Compatible operating systems: PC-DOS and BBx • Network standards/protocols supported: proprietary • Memory requirements: 256K • Fees: $795/module • Year introduced: 1986 • Number installed: 100.

STANDARD MICROSYSTEMS CORPORATION
35 Marcus Boulevard
Hauppauge, NY 11788
(516)273-3100; TWX 510-227-8898

Paul Richman, President; John F. Tweedy, Vice President, Systems Products (PM); Jean-Pierre Chalmin, Vice President, Sales (PSC)

•**Advanced NetWare.** Operating system for SMC's ARCnet network. Supplies bridge between workstations on the system and the ARCnet token-passing protocol hardware. Can connect network of up to 255 nodes. Compatible operating systems: MS-DOS, PC-DOS • Memory requirements: 256K RAM.

•**ViaNet.** Distributed LAN software system linking two or more PCs. Supplies bridge between existing operating system and Arcnet token-passing protocol and hardware. Compatible operating systems: MS-DOS, PC-DOS 2.0 -3.1 • Memory requirements: 256K RAM.

SUNOL SYSTEMS INC.
1177 Quarry Lane
Pleasanton, CA 94566
(415)484-3322; telex 703-175

Robert McCullough, President (PM); Robert Morten (MD); Virginia Wurts (PSC)

Founded 1983; 20 employees

•**Sun*Plus.** Multi-user networking software product. Supports IBM PCs and compatibles, Apricot, Victor, and DEC Rainbow. Compatible operating systems: MS-DOS • Fees: $295 one-time fee.

SYTEK INC.
1225 Charleston Road
Mountain View, CA 94043
(415)966-7400; telex 276-572

L. George Klaus, President; Suri Harish, Director of Product Marketing (PM); Joseph Seidler, Vice President, Product Marketing (MD); Jeff Wilbur, Headquarters System Engineer (PSC)

Founded 1979; 500 employees

Branch Offices and Distributors:
Sytek Inc., San Jose, CA (408)275-9860; Sytek Inc., Itasca, IL (312)250-0057; Sytek

Inc., Bethesda, MD (301)530-5100

•**2540 Asynchronous Loader Software.** Operating program for the System 2000. Utilizes LocalNet architectue to provide services between asynchronous devices. Features include access security, call routing and concurrent access to multiple resources.

TANGENT TECHNOLOGIES

5720 Peachtree Parkway
Norcross, GA 30092
(404)662-0366

Roland Bates, President; Guy Mariande, Vice President, Marketing and Sales (PM)(MD); Steve Simpson, Sales Support Manager (PSC)

Founded 1984; 9 employees

•**Laser Script.** Converts any text or ASCII file into postscript. Software updates available. Compatible networks: AppeTalk • Memory requirements: 30K • Fees: $650 one-time fee • Year introduced: 1985 • Number installed: over 1000.

TECHNOLOGY CONCEPTS INC.

40 Tall Pine Drive
Sudbury, MA 01776
(617)443-7311; telex 517-682

Stuart Wecker, President; Mitch Kramer (PM)(MD)(PSC)

Founded 1981; 49 employees

•**CommUnity-DOS.** Allows a PC to participate in a DECnet network as an end node. Provided are program-to-program interface, virtual terminal and remote file access. Software updates available. Compatible operating systems: MS-DOS • Compatible networks: DECnet • Network standards/protocols sup-

ported: Digital Network Architecture • Memory requirements: 50K plus Excelan Communications Controller (128K) • Fees: $1395 one-time fee for hardware and software; $150 annual maintenance fee • Year introduced: 1986.

TELEVIDEO SYSTEMS INC.

P.O. Box 3568
Sunnyvale, CA 94088-3568
(408)745-7760; TWX 474-5041
  TVISYS

Dr. K.P. Hwang, President; Ron Nakashima, Director, Systems Product Marketing (MD)

Founded 1976; 700 employees

Branch Offices and Distributors:
  TeleVideo Systems Inc., Newport Beach, CA (714)476-0244; TeleVideo Systems Inc., Norcross, GA (404)447-1231; TeleVideo Systems Inc., Woburn, MA (617)938-3282; TeleVideo Systems Inc., Syosset, NY (516)496-4777

•**PM/Netware.** Network operating system. Software updates available. Compatible operating systems: Novell Advanced NetWare 2.0 • Compatible networks: Novell networks • Network standards/protocols supported: Novell NetWare, RS-422 • Memory requirements: 512K; 1024K recommended o Fees: one-time fee included with server • Year introduced: 1984 • Number installed: over 4000.

•**PM/Mail Monitor.** Electronic mail. Remote users supported. Software updates available. Compatible operating systems: Novell Advanced NetWare 2.0 • Compatible networks: all Novell networks • Memory requirements: 256K • Fees: $795 one-time fee, local; $795 remote upgrade • Year introduced: 1985 • Number installed: over 200.

TEXAS INSTRUMENTS— DATA SYSTEMS GROUP

P.O. Box 809063
Dallas, TX 75380-9063
(214)995-2011; telex 73-324; TWX 910-867-4702

Jerry R. Junkins, President; Walden C. Rhines (PM); Jerome L. Brown, Vice President, Marketing (MD)

Founded 1930; 77,872 employees

•**EtherShare.** Allows TI professional computer clients in a network to share a network server's fixed disk space, thus providing faster access, greater capacity and increased reliability. Compatible operating system: MS-DOS 2.1 • Memory requirements: 256K.

•**EtherVoice.** Facilitates message-sending by allowing user to record a voice message and/or attach it to a text message, and then allowing EtherMail to "mail" the message to a receiver's "mail box" for storage. Operates in conjunction with Ether-Mail.

•**EtherPrint.** Supports serial and parallel printers, allowing a number of network clients to share printer resources and eliminating the need for a dedicated printer for each PC. Data transmitted over the network transparent to normal program operations. Compatible operating systems: MS-DOS 2.1 • Memory requirements: 256K.

•**EtherMail.** Electronic mail system. Messages can be addressed to an individual or distribution list. Allows up to 26 attachments to each message. Mail can be read from all clients on the network. Compatible operating systems: MS-DOS. Memory requirements: 192K.

3COM CORPORATION

1365 Shorebird Way
Mountain View, CA 94041
(415)961-9602; telex 345-546; FAX
    415-961-9602

L. William Krause, President; John
Marman, Vice President, Marketing
and Sales (MD)(PSC)

Founded 1979

•**3+Share.** Distributed PC network operating system. Provides file
service, print service, and naming
service. Network stan-
dards/protocols supported: NET-
BIOS • Year introduced: 1985.

•**3+Route.** Interlinks 2 or
more 3+ networks using asynchronous public telephone lines or dedicated high-speed links. Compatible
operating systems: 3+Share, MS-
DOS 3.1 • Year introduced: 1985.

•**3+Remote.** Gives remote PCs
full network access over public links.
Compatible operating systes:
3+Share, MS-DOS 3.1 • Year introduced: 1985.

•**3+Mail.** Permits store-and-
forward electronic mail on a single
network or other networks joined by
3+Route. Compatible operating systems: 3+Share, MS-DOS 3.1 • Year
introduced: 1985.

•**3+Menues.** Provides users
with menus and windows for access
to network resources. Compatible
operating systems: 3+Share, MS-
DOS 3.1 • Year introduced: 1985.

•**3+3270.** Allows networked
PCs to emulate IBM 3278/79 terminals for communication with IBM
mainframes. Compatible operating
systems: 3+Share, MS-DOS 3.1 •
Year introduced: 1985.

•**3+Path.** Allows migration
from EtherSeries to 3+ networks.
Compatible operating systems: MS-
DOS 3.1 • Year introduced: 1985.

TIARA COMPUTER SYSTEMS INC.

2685 Marine Way
Mountain View, CA 94043
(415)965-1700; telex 499-6251;
    FAX 415-965-2677

Thomas G. Hong, President; Wil-
liam Y. Terrill, Director of Product
Marketing (PM); Mike Paul, Vice
President, Marketing and Sales
(MD)

Founded 1985; 35 employees

•**TiaraLink LanWare.** For IBM
PC, XT, AT, and compatible computers. Allows sharing of data files
and shared volumes in network operation. Multitasking feature allows
host operating systems to run while
the network server is active. Compatible operating systems: IBM DOS
version 2.0, 2.1, 3.0, or 3.1 • Memory
requirements: 256K server; 192K
RAM for other PCs. Fees: $500 one-
time fee.

•**Tiara Multi-OS.** DOS version
software for the IBM PC, XT, AT,
and compatible computers. Includes
file transport utility, cache memory,
DMA operation, password protection, network ready disk installation
and install program for IBM PC
DOS version 2.0 and 3.0. Compatible
operating systems: IBM DOS version
2.0 and 3.0 • Memory requirements:
128K RAM.

TORUS SYSTEMS INC.

495 Seaport Court
Redwood City, CA 94063
(415)363-2418; (800)872-5335

Tim Sutton, President; Keri Long
(PM); Mitchell Martin, Vice President, Marketing & Sales (MD)

Founded 1984; 5 employees

•**Tapestry.** LAN operating environment. Features include full
BM/PC, AT and XT support, fixed
disk and printer sharing, applications
and communications management,
electronic mail, telephone directory,
file management, and online help.
Compatible operating systems: PC-
DOS 2.0, 2.1 or 3.0 • Compatible
networks: IBM Token Ring and PC
Network, any NETBIOS compatible
LAN and 3Com Ethernet • Memory
requirements: 256K user memory;
320K per server station • Fees: $295
per workstation pack; $495 per net-
work manager pack • Year introduced: 1985.

•**Remote Network Link.** Provides Tapestry users remote access to
their Tapestry network using ordinary phone lines and a PC equipped
with a modem. Memory requirements: 320K • Fees: $295 • Year in-
troduced: 1986.

•**Remote Access Gateway.** Con-
figures a Tapestry network so that it
may support users of the Remote
Network Link. Allows any number
of workstations to act as undedicated
Remote Gateway servers. Memory
requirements: 320K • Fees: $250 •
Year introduced: 1986.

•**Torus 3270 SNA Gateway.**
Provides up to 32 Tapestry users
concurrent access to an IBM mainframe computer. Enables a Tapestry
workstation to emulate a 3274 cluster controller, with 3278 screen emulation. Fees: $5495, 8-port; $5995,
16-port; $7495, 32-port • Year intro-
duced: 1986.

•**Cacher.** Disk caching program
that increases the performance of
Tapestry LANs by a factor of between two and four. Reduces the
time taken to read data from file
servers, mail servers and software li-

brary servers. Compatible with and transparent to all normal PC-DOS applications software. Fees: $99 • Year introduced: 1986.

•**Advanced Gateway Support.** Provides VT100 emulation for use via the standard Tapestry asynchronous gateway, thus allowing user access to DEC computers, or others which support VT100, via single port, PC-hosted gateways over direct or dial-up connections. Fees: $795 • Year introduced: 1986.

TOUCH COMMUNICATIONS INC.

10 Victor Square, Suite 150
Scotts Valley, CA 95066
(408)438-4800

Charlie Bass, President and Chief Executive Officer; Ken Klos, Director of Marketing (PM)(MD); Gary Gysin, Manager, OEM Sales (PSC)

Founded 1985; 18 employees

•**Touch Communications Services.** Extensive network management facilities. Extension of local applications across the network. Orientation toward user applications. Software updates available. Compatible operating systems: VAX, VMS, MS-DOS, Unix V • Compatible networks: 802.3 Ethernet, 802.4 and 802.5 Token Ring • Network standards/protocols supported: OSI Reference Model layers 3-7 • Memory requirements: 512K • Year introduced: 1986.

2B ENTERPRISES

1252 Columbia Road NW
Washington, DC 20009
(202)234-2117; telex 158-225-361

W.A. Spencer, President; B.C. Oppermann (MD)

Founded 1986; 2 employees

•**MIST+.** Application language for wide area networking and network-to-network file transfer. Software updates available. Compatible operating systems: PC-DOS 2.1 and above • Compatible network vendors: 3Com, Fox Research and Orchid Technology • Network standards/protocols supported: Xmodem • Memory requirements: 256K • Fees: $495 one-time fee • Year introduced: 1983 • Number installed: 1000.

•**Conexus.** Electronic mail and conferencing for up to 900 private accounts. Unlimited topic-specific conferences and keyword-accessible bulletin boards. Software updates available. Compatible operating systems: PC-DOS 2.1 and above • Compatible network vendors: 3Com, Fox Research and Orchid Technology • Network standards/protocols supported: Xmodem • Memory requirements: 256K • Fees: $624 one-time fee • Year introduced: 1984 • Number installed: 1000.

UNGERMANN-BASS INC.

3900 Freedom Circle
Santa Clara, CA 95052
(408)496-0111

Ralph K. Ungermann, President; Cliff Rudolph, Vice President, Marketing (MD); Peter Kirschner, Director, Marketing Support (PSC)

Founded 1979; 700 employees

Branch Offices and Distributors: Ungermann-Bass Inc., Newport Beach, CA (714)955-1414; Ungermann-Bass Inc., Dallas, TX (214)385-7090; Ungermann-Bass Inc., Chicago, IL (312)882-6885; Ungermann-Bass Inc., St. Louis, MO (314)532-9366; Ungermann-Bass Inc., New York, NY (212)466-1763

•**Net/One Operating System.** Operates in conjunction with Net/One hardware. Software updates available. Compatible networks: IBM Token Ring • Network standards/protocols supported: XNS, TCP/IP and OSI Reference Model • Year introduced: 1980 • Number installed: over 1000.

•**X.25 Gateway.** Software updates available. Compatible operating systems: Net/One • Network standards/protocols supported: X.25 • Year introduced: 1983 • Number installed: over 100.

•**Net/One 3270 Personal Connection.** High-performance local connection to the IBM mainframe from the IBM PC or compatible, allowing PC to become a universal workstation. Transparent to mainframe application and to PCs on network. Allows PC to connect concurrently to multiple mainframe applications, file and print servers, and minicomputers. Compatible operating systems: PC-DOS 2.0, 2.1, 3.0, and 3.1.

VIANETIX

2900 Center Green Court South
Boulder, CO 80301
(303)440-0700

C.H. Buffington, President; A.C. McDowell, Director of Marketing (MD); G.M. Holtwick, Vice President, Marketing (MD); J. Igoe, Vice President, Sales (PSC)

Founded 1984; 40 employees

•**ViaNet.** Fully distributed LAN software system. Requires no dedicated server and allows all disks, peripherals and data files to be shared in the network. Supports a variety of topologies including bus, ring and star. Compatible operating systems: MS-DOS, Unix and Xenix • Compatible networks: Ethernet, ARCnet, Omninet, Starlan, and IBM Token Ring • Network standards/protocols supported: IEEE

802.3-802.5 and DOS 3.1 locking calls • Year introduced: 1984.

WATERLOO MICROSYSTEMS INC.
175 Columbia Street West
Waterloo, Ontario, N2L 5Z5
  CANADA
(519)884-3141; telex 069-575-20

Dr. Michael Malcolm, President; Dave Bell, Manager, Dealer Marketing (MD); Bill Didur, Manager of Large Accounts (PSC)

Founded 1982; 28 employees

Branch Offices and Distributors: Waterloo Microsystems Inc., Rosemont, IL (312)696-2110

•**Port.** Network operating system. Integrates sophisticated networking with a simple multi-tasking interface while allowing PC-DOS to run as a "guest" operating system. Multiple file, print and communication services and software downloading services can be distributed throughout the network. Mouse-driven, icon-based user interface, on-line help facility, automatic spooling, and electronic mail. Provides up to 640K for DOS and its applications. Virtual RAM Card available for increased cppabilities. Compatible operating systems: DOS 2.0, 2.1, 3.0, and 3.1 • Fees: $1695 plus $695 per workstation.

THE WOLLONGONG GROUP
P.O. Box 51860
Palo Alto, CA 94303
(415)962-7100; TWX 910-373-2085;
  FAX 415-969-5547

Herbert Martin, President; David J. Preston, Director, Product Marketing (PM); Carl W. Jack, Vice President, Marketing (MD)

Founded 1980; 90 employees

•**WIN/VX.** Login to remote computers, file transfer and electronic mail. Software updates available. Compatible operating sytems: VMS • Compatible networks: DECnet and all TCP/IP networks • Network standards/protocols supported: TCP/IP • Memory requirements: 100K • Fees: $15,000 one-time fee; $3000 maintenance fee • Year introduced: 1982 • Number installed: over 500.

•**WIN/SVX.** Login to remote computers, file transfer and electronic mail. Software updates available. Compatible operating systems: System V Unix • Compatible networks: DECnet • Network standards/protocols supported: TCP/IP • Memory requirements: 150K • Fees: $15,000 one-time fee; $3000 maintenance fee • Year introduced: 1985 • Number installed: 25.

•**WIN/VX (DDN).** Login to remote computers, file transfer and electronic mail. Connection via an IMP to the DDN. Software updates available. Compatible operating systems: VAX-VMS • Compatible networks: DECnet and Defense Data Network • Network standards/protocols supported: TCP/IP • Memory requirements: 150K • Fees: $25,000 one-time fee; $3000

maintenance fee • Year introduced: 1984 • Number installed: 50.

•**WIN/PC.** Remote login, file transfer and electronic mail. Software updates available. Compatible operating systems: MS/PC DOS 2.0, 2.1 or 3.0 • Network standards/protocols supported: TCP/IP • Memory requirements: 128K or 256K • Fees: $800 one-time fee; $200 maintenance fee • Year introduced: 1985 • Number installed: 30.

WORDTECH SYSTEMS
21 Altarinde Road, P.O. Box 1747
Orinda, CA 94563
(415)254-0900; telex 503-599

David Miller, President; Michael Gardner, Director of Development (PM); Bart Van Voorhis, Vice President (MD); Geri Trovato, Account Executive (PSC)

Founded 1983; 40 employees

•**DB 3 Compiler.** Full compatibility with dBase. Includes debugger. Software updates available. Compatible operating systems: 3Com 3+, DOS 3.1 • Compatible networks: Novell, IBM PC Network. Network standards/protocols supported: DOS 3.1 • Memory requirements: 256K • Fees: $750 one-time fee; $100 maintenance contract available after 1 year • Year introduced: 1985 • Number installed: over 10,000.

Chapter 4 — Business and Technical Services

CHAPTER 4
BUSINESS AND TECHNICAL SERVICES

Listed in this chapter are business and marketing consultants, market research firms, professional groups, software and technical consultants, network design and installation firms, and other providers of LAN-related services.

Firms are listed by category in the index that precedes the entries.

FUNCTION CODES

MD   Marketing Director
PR   Public Relations Contact

INDEX

ASSOCIATIONS/PROFESSIONAL GROUPS
Association for Media-Based Continuing
   Education for Engineers Inc. (AMCEE)
Data Processing Management Association
IEEE Computer Society
Manufacturing Automation Protocol &
   Technical and Office Protocol
Users Group of SME
Office Automation Society International (OASI)

BUSINESS AND MARKETING CONSULTING
AAC Associates Inc.
Arlen Communications Inc.
Benton, Schneider & Associates
Booz, Allen & Hamilton Inc.
The Herbert Boyer Company
CIMI Corporation
Communications Center
Communications Networks Inc.
Datamation
The Diebold Group
The DMW Group
Hyatt Research Corporation
International Management Services Inc.
Kalba Bowen Associates Inc.
Lante Corporation
Link Resources Inc.
Arthur D. Little Inc.
Logica Inc.
Management Information Corporation
The Market Information Center Inc.
J.H. Morgan Consultants
Network Planning Corporation
Network Strategies Inc.
Michael L. Rothberg Associates
Ship Star Associates Inc.
Strategic Market Trends Inc.
Wohl Associates
Zatyko Associates

HARDWARE EVALUATION AND SELECTION
AAC Associates Inc.
Allied Data Communications Group Inc.
AtLANta Technologies
Benton, Schneider & Associates
Booz, Allen & Hamilton Inc.
CIMI Corporation

Communication Control Corporation
Communications Network Architects Inc.
The Comsul Group
The Consultant Group
Datamation
The DMW Group
FiberLAN Inc.—A BellSouth-Siecor Company
Hyatt Research Corporation
Infonet Inc.
International Management Services Inc.
Lante Corporation
Arthur D. Little Inc.
Logica Inc.
Mangement Information Corporation
J.H. Morgan Consultants
Network Planning Corporation
Network Strategies Group
Network Strategies Inc.
Michael L. Rothberg Associates
Sargent Cable Services
Systems Oriented
Telecommunication Resources
Trellis Communications Corporation
Wohl Associates
Zatyko Associates

MARKET RESEARCH AND ANALYSIS
AAC Associates Inc.
Arlen Communications Inc.
Benton, Schneider & Associates
Sanford C. Bernstein & Company Inc.
Booz, Allen & Hamilton Inc.
The Herbert Boyer Company
CIMI Corporation
Communications Center
Communications Network Architects Inc.
The Consultant Group
The Diebold Group
The DMW Group
Forrester Research Inc.
Frost & Sullivan Inc.
Hyatt Research Corporation
International Data Corporation
International Management Services Inc.
International Resource Development Inc.
Kalba Bowen Associates Inc.
Lante Corporation
Link Resources Inc.
Logica Inc.

Management Information Corporation
The Market Information Center Inc.
Network Planning Corporaoon
Network Strategies Inc.
Newton-Evans Research Company Inc.
Michael L. Rothberg Associates
Strategic Market Trends Inc.
Wohl Associates
Zatyko Associates

NETWORK DESIGN
AAC Associates Inc.
Allied Data Communications Group Inc.
American Communications Company
AtLANta Technologies
Axis Inc.
Benton, Schneider & Associates
Booz, Allen & Hamilton Inc.
Cabletron
CIMI Corporation
Codenoll Technology Corporation
Communication Control Corporation
Communications Network Architects Inc.
The Comsul Group
The Consultant Group
The Diebold Group
The DMW Group
Durable Systems Engineering Corporation
FiberLAN Inc.—A BellSouth-Siecor Company
General Instrument Corporation—Jerrold
  Distribution Systems Division
Honeywell Network Design Center
Infonet Inc.
International Management Services Inc.
Interphase Corporation
KEE Inc.
Lante Corporation
Logica Inc.
J.H. Morgan Consultants
Network Planning Corporation
Network Strategies Group
Network Strategies Inc.
Michael L. Rothberg Associates
Sargent Cable Services
Ship Star Associates Inc.
Systems Oriented
Technology Concepts Inc.
Tele-Engineering Corporation
Telecommunication Resources

Trellis Communications Corporation
W and J Partnership
Wohl Associates
Zatyko Associates

NETWORK EVALUATION AND SELECTION
AAC Associates Inc.
Allied Data Communications Group Inc.
AtLANta Technologies
Benton, Schneider & Associates
Booz, Allen & Hamilton Inc.
CIMI Corporation
Communication Control Corporation
Communications Center
Communications Network Architects Inc.
The Comsul Group
The Consultant Group
The DMW Group
Durable Systems Engineering Corporation
FiberLAN Inc.—A Bell-South Siecor Company
Hyatt Research Corporation
Infonet Inc.
International Management Services Inc.
KEE Inc.
Lante Corporation
Logica Inc.
Management Information Corporation
J.H. Morgan Consultants
Network Planning Corporation
Network Strategies Group
Network Strategies Inc.
Michael L. Rothberg Associates
Sargent Cable Services
Ship Star Associate Inc.
Systems Oriented
Technology Concepts Inc.
Telecommunication Resources
Trellis Communications Corporation
Wohl Associates
Zatyko Associates

NETWORK INSTALLATION
AAC Associates Inc.
Allied Data Communications Group Inc.
American Communications Company
Cabletron
Codenoll Technology Corporation
Comlink Inc.
Communications Network Architects Inc.

The Comsul Group
The Consultant Group
FiberLAN Inc.—A BellSouth-Siecor Company
Infonet Inc.
KEE Inc.
Lante Corporation
Logica Inc.
J.H. Morgan Consultants
Network Strategies Inc.
Michael L. Rothberg Associates
Sargent Cable Services
Systems Oriented
Technology Concepts Inc.
Tele-Engineering Corporation
Telecommunication Resources
Trellis Communications Corporation

SEMINARS/TRAINING
AAC Associates Inc.
Allied Data Communications Group Inc.
Association for Media-Based Continuing
    Education for Engineers Inc. (AMCEE)
Booz, Allen & Hamilton Inc.
Business Communications Review
Center for Advanced Professional Education
Codenol Technology Corporation
The Consultant Group
Data Processing Management Association
Datamation
Delphi Inc.
The DMW Group
Dorran Photonics Inc.
FiberLAN Inc.—A BellSouth-Siecor Company
Frost & Sullivan Inc.
IEEE Computer Society
Infonet Inc.
International Data Corporation
International Management Services Inc.
Lante Corporation
J.H. Morgan Consultants
Network Strategies Group
Network Strategies Inc.
Office Automation Society International (OASI)
Ship Star Associates Inc.
Siecor Corporation
Systems Technology Forum Inc.
Technology Concepts Inc.
Technology Transfer Institute
Telecommunication Resources

Trellis Communications Corporation
W and J Partnership
Wohl Associates
Xerox Network Systems Institute
Zatyko Associates

SOFTWARE CONSULTING
AAC Associates Inc.
AtLANta Technologies
Booz, Allen & Hamilton Inc.
CIMI Corporation
The Consultant Group
The DMW Group
Durable Systems Engineering Corporation
Infonet Inc.
International Management Services Inc.
Lante Corporation
Arhur D. Little Inc.
Logica Inc.
Management Information Corporation
Network Strategies Group
Network Strategies Inc.
Michael L. Rothberg Associates
Ship Star Associates Inc.
Telecommunication Resources
Wohl Associates

TECHNICAL CONSULTING
AAC Associates Inc.
Allied Data Communications Group Inc.
AtLANta Technologies
Axis Inc.
Benton, Schneider & Associates
Booz, Allen & Hamilton Inc.
CIMI Corporation
Codenoll Technology Corporation
Communication Control Corporation
Communications Center
Communications Network Architects Inc.
The Comsul Group
The Consultant Group
Delphi Inc.
The Diebold Group
The DMW Group
Durable Systems Engineering Corporation
FiberLAN Inc.—A BellSouth-Siecor Corporation
Honeywell Network Design Center
Hyatt Research Corporation
Infonet Inc.

International Management Services Inc.
Interphase Corporation
Kalba Bowen Associates Inc.
Lante Corporation
Arthur D. Little Inc.
Logica Inc.
Management Information Corporation
J.H. Morgan Consultants
Network Stratggies Group
Network Strategies Inc.
Office Automation Society International (OASI)
Michael L. Rothberg Associates
Sargent Cable Services
Ship Star Associates Inc.
Systems Oriented
Technology Concepts Inc.
Technology Transfer Institute
Tele-Engineering Corporation
Telecommunication Resources
Trellis Communications Corporation
W and J Partnership
Xerox Network Systems Institute
Zatyko Associates

OTHER
Arlen Communications Inc.
Sanford C. Bernstein & Company Inc.
The Herbert Boyer Company
Cabltron
CIMI Corporation
Communications Network Architects Inc.
The Consultant Group
ETL Testing Laboratories Inc.
FiberLAN Inc.—A BellSouth-Siecor Company
Frost & Sullivan Inc.
IEEE Computer Society
Arthur D. Little Inc.
J.H. Morgan Consultants
Network Planning Corporation
Phillips Publishing Inc.
Sargent Cable Services
Siecor Corporation
Strategic Market Trends Inc.
Systems Oriented
Telecommunication Resources
Wohl Associates
Xerox Network Systems Institute

AAC ASSOCIATES INC.

8470 Tyco Road, Suite C
Vienna, VA 22180
(703)448-8666; telex 379-2777

Tony Carlson, President; John Dieudonne (PR)

Founded 1983; 40 employees

Provides business and marketing consulting, hardware evaluation and selection, market research and analysis, network design, network evaluation and selection, network installation, seminars/training, and software and technical consulting services. Primary markets include educational and financial institutions, Fortune 1000 companies and the Department of Defense.

ALLIED DATA COMMUNICATIONS GROUP INC.

5375 Oakbrook Parkway
Norcross, GA 30093
(404)923-4866; FAX 404-923-4833

J. Randell Hales, President; Donald A. Pisarcik, Vice President, Sales and Marketing (MD)(PR)

Founded 1978; 150 employees

Engineering contractor. Provides hardware evaluation and selection, network design, network evaluation and selection, and network installation services. Installation capabilities include aerial, underground/duct systems and intrabuilding distribution. Also provides technical consulting and offers seminars on broadband local area network-network planning, design and implementation and RF maintenance training. Primary markets include data communications firms, educational and financial institutions, Fortune 1000 companies, government, and hospitals.

AMERICAN COMMUNICATIONS COMPANY

7535 Little River Turnpike
Annandale, VA 22003
(703)941-6510, (800)336-4564

H.T. Curran, President; Joseph D. Ford, Director of Business Development (MD)

Founded 1975; 150 employees

A division of American Systems Corporation, ACC specializes in the design and installation of cable systems to support local area networks and office automation systems. Technologies supported include baseband, broadband and fiber optics. Markets to data communications firms, educational and financial institutions, Fortune 1000 companies, government, hospitals, system integrators, and LAN vendors.

ARLEN COMMUNICATIONS INC.

7315 Wisconsin Avenue, Suite 600E
Bethesda, MD 20814
(301)656-7940; telex 499-6981

Gary H. Arlen, President; Patti Fischer (PR)

Founded 1980; 3 employees

Research and consulting firm specializing in marketing, strategic alliance, LAN development, and financial services. Primary markets include data communications firms, network developers and telephone companies.

ASSOCIATION FOR MEDIA-BASED CONTINUING EDUCATION FOR ENGINEERS INC. (AMCEE)

500 Tech Parkway, Suite 200A
Atlanta, GA 30313
(404)894-332

Linda DeGrand, Executive Director; Gail Reid, Associate Director (PR)

Founded 1978; 33 member institutions

A consortium of 33 educational institutions with engineering programs that markets videotaped courses for engineers for continuing non-credit education. Course topics include LAN technology, implementation and management.

ATLANTA TECHNOLOGIES

4501 Circle 75 Parkway, Suite C-3100
Atlanta, GA 30339
(404)984-9095

Robert Patrick, President (MD)(PR)

Systems integrators. Services include hardware evaluation and selection, network design, network evaluation and selection, and software and technical consulting. Primary markets include educational institutions, government, hospitals, and manufacturing.

AXIS INC.

7825 Engineer Road, Suite 208
San Diego, CA 92111
(619)560-7737

M.J. Prager, President; Joe Monroe (MD)

Founded 1974; 12 employees

Network design and technical consulting. Clients include aerospace, chemical, electronics, computer, and process industries and government.

BENTON, SCHNEIDER & ASSOCIATES

2021 Spring Road, Suite 409
Oak Brook, IL 60521
(312)357-3131

William Benton, President; Carl Axelson (MD)(PR)

Founded 1971; 15 employees

Provides business and marketing consulting, hardware evaluation and selection, market research and analysis, network design, network evaluation and selection, and technical consulting services. Primary markets include data communications firms, educational and financial institutions, Fortune 1000 companies, and government.

SANFORD C. BERNSTEIN & COMPANY INC.

767 5th Avenue
New York, NY 10153
(212)486-8512

L. Sanders, President; Dawn Moore (MD)

Founded 1968; 250 employees

Investment research and analysis firm.

BOOZ, ALLEN & HAMILTON INC.

4330 East-West Highway
Bethesda, MD 20814
(301)951-2200; telex 710-824-0552

R. Michael McCullough, President and Chief Executive Officer; Skip Gunther, Telecommunications Practice (MD)

Founded 1914; 2700 employees

Services include business and marketing consulting, hardware evaluation and selection, market research and analysis, network design, network evaluation and selection, seminars/training, and software and technical consulting. Markets domestically and internationally to data communications firms, educational and financial institutions, Fortune 1000 companies, government, and hospitals.

THE HERBERT BOYER COMPANY

14 East 77th Street
New York, NY 10021
(212)744-7558

Herbert Boyer, President; William F. Parsons, Vice President (MD)

Founded 1970; 10 employees

Engineering, marketing, and investment consulting firm. Specializes in performance evaluation, acquisitions, market research, product planning, executive/technical search, general management, organizational studies, asset management, turnaround situations, and capital formation. Primary markets include data communications firms and Fortune 1000 companies.

BUSINESS COMMUNICATIONS REVIEW

950 York Road
Hinsdale, IL 60521
(312)986-1432

Jerry Goldstone, President; Paul Wagner, Director of Marketing (MD)(PR)

Founded 1971; 11 employees

Conducts telecommunications seminars.

CABLETRON

P.O. Box 6257
Rochester, MN 03867
(603)332-9400

Robert Levine, President; Jack Branowski, Marketing Manager (MD)

Founded 1983; 100 employees

Offers network design and installation services and network troubleshooting tests.

CENTER FOR ADVANCED PROFESSIONAL EDUCATION

1820 East Garry Street, Suite 110
Santa Ana,, CA 92705
(714)261-0240; telex 650-285-6353

Herb Stern, President; Barbara Stern, Marketing Director (MD)(PR)

Founded 1982; 10 employees

Offers "Implementing Local Area Networks" seminar, designed for network planners and network managers within Fortune 1000 companies.

CIMI CORPORATION

520 Haddon Avenue
Haddonfield, NJ 08033
(609)354-1088

Thomas L. Nolle, President

Founded 1982; 6 employees

Professional reviewer of LAN products for major publishers. Specializes in IBM PC Network, Token Ring Network and compatible products. Experienced in IBM LU 6.2 APPC/PC products. Other services include business consulting, hardware evaluation and selection, market research and analysis, network design, software and technical consulting, and special software development. Primary markets include data communications firms, financial institutions, Fortune 1000 companies, and hospitals.

CODENOLL TECHNOLOGY CORPORATION

1086 North Broadway
Yonkers, NY 10701
(914)965-6300; telex 646-159-131;
    FAX 914-965-6300

Michael H. Coden, President; Edwin M. Sakaguchi, Vice President, Marketing (MD); Ernest Raasch, Senior Vice President, Operations (PR)

Founded 1980; 70 employees

Provides network design and installation, seminars/training and technical consulting services. Primary markets include data communications firms, educational and financial institutions, Fortune 1000 companies, government, hospitals, military, telephony, and process control.

COMLINK INC.

116A West Broad Street
Falls Church, VA 22046
(70)237-9610

Michael S. Chambers, President

Founded 1983; 6 employees

Data cable installation, including fiber optic cable.

COMMUNICATION CONTROL CORPORATION

106 Hobart Street
Hackensack, NJ 07601
(201)488-1825

Arthur J. Bedder Jr., President

Founded 1976; 6 employees

Provides hardware evaluation and selection, design and network evaluation and selection services for educational and financial institutions, Fortune 1000 companies and hospitals.

COMMUNICATIONS CENTER

2723 Green Valley Road
Clarksburg, MD 20871
(301)428-9000; telex 904-109;
    TWX 440-687; FAX 301-865-5577

Walter L. Morgan, President; Peggy Petronchak, Research Specialist (PR)

Founded 1980

Provides business and marketing consulting, market research and

analysis, network evaluation and selection, and technical consulting services for financial institutions and Fortune 1000 companies.

COMMUNICATIONS NETWORK ARCHITECTS INC.

P.O. Box 32063
Washington, DC 20007
(202)775-8000

Francis X. Dzubeck, President; Kathryn A. Dzubeck, Vice President (MD)(PR)

Founded 1973; 12 employees

Plans, designs and implements large multi-premises metropolitan area networks which interconnect LANs. Also provides strategic planning and specialized assistance to vendors in developing product line approaches to LAN environments. Primary markets include data communications firms, educational and financial institutions, Fortune 1000 companies, and government.

THE COMSUL GROUP

353 Sacramento Street, Suite 80
San Francisco, CA 94111
(415)989-6700; telex 415-788-1108

Peter Valentine, President; Colette McMullen (MD)(PR)

Founded 1967; 40 employees

Provides hardware evaluation and selection, network design, network evaluation and selection, network installation, and technical consulting services to educational and financial institutions, Fortune 1000 companies, hospitals, and law firms.

THE CONSULTANT GROUP

3531-35 North Martens Street
Franklin Park, IL 60131
(312)678-3434; FAX 678-8588

Jay Rich, President; William Kline (MD); James Lichter (PR)

Founded 1949; 400 employees

Services include hardware evaluation and selection, market research and analysis, network design, network evaluation and selection, network installation, seminars/training, software and technical consulting, and implementation consulting. Primary markets include educational and financial institutions and Fortune 1000 companies.

DATA PROCESSING MANAGEMENT ASSOCIATION

505 Busse Highway
Park Ridge, IL 60068
312)825-8124

John Venator, Executive Director; Scott S. Gottlieb, Marketing Manager (MD); Bill Zalud, Director of Communications (PR)

Founded 1951; over 35,000 members

Association comprised of all levels of management personnel actively pursuing a career in information processing. Offers 53 courses providing managerial training in motivation, communication and human resource development.

DATAMATION

10 Mulholland Drive
Hasbrouck Heights, NJ 07604
(212)732-3824

Jerome Raymond, President (PR); Morton J. Raymond (MD)

Founded 1963; 25 employees

Conducts business and marketing consulting, hardware evaluation and selection and seminars/training for data communications firms, financial institutions and government.

DELPHI INC.

20 Passaic Avenue
Pompton Lakes, NJ 07442
(201)839-5770

Gary Audin, President; Carolyn Park, Manager (PR)

Founded 1978; 15 employees

Provides technical consulting for financial institutions and Fortune 1000 companies. Also sponsors seminars, including "Local Networks—LANs, PBXs and PCs" and "Transmission Technologies—Optical Fibers, Coax and Wire."

THE DIEBOLD GROUP

475 Park Avenue South
New York, NY 10016
(212)684-4700; telex 427-395

John Diebold, Chairman of the Board; Theodore Freiser, President (MD); Susan Landstreet, Assistant Vice President (PR)

Founded 1954; 300 employees

Business and marketing consulting, market research and analysis, network design, and technical consulting. Clients include educational and financial institutions, Fortune 1000 companies, government, and hospitals.

THE DMW GROUP

2020 Hogback Group
Ann Arbor, MI 48104
(313)971-5234; telex 810-223-2412

Dr. Dixon Doll, President and Chief Executive Officer; Gerald Mayfield, President, Consulting Division; Joseph Cacopardo (PR)

Founded 1971; 55 employees

Services include business and marketing consulting, hardware evaluation and selection, market research and analysis, network design, network evaluation and selection, seminars/training, and software and technical consulting. Primary markets include educational and financial insti-

tutions, Fortune 1000 companies, government, hospitals, and banking communications.

DORRAN PHOTONICS INC.

165 First Avenue, P.O. Box 304
Atlantic Highlands, NJ 07716
(201)291-8103

Offers two-day optical fiber termination course for IBM token-ring networks. Provides training for the designer/installer planning to implement the optical portion of the IBM Token Ring.

DURABLE SYSTEMS ENGINEERING CORPORATION

5603 Glenwood Road
Bethesda, MD 20817
(301)555-3677

Buff Tarkenton, President; Jeff Davis, Director of Marketing (MD); Franklin Coopers, Director of Corporation Communications (PR)

Founded 1980; 22 employees

Services include network design, network evaluation and selection, and software and technical consulting. Primary markets include data communications firms, educational and financial institutions, and government.

ETL TESTING LABORATORIES INC.

Route 11, Industrial Prrk, P.O.
  Box 2040
Cortland, NY 13045
(607)753-6711; TWX 510-252-0792

Fulvio Bertini, Marketing Manager (MD)

Offers network cable certification program. Under the program, sample reels of cable selected periodically and randomly from participants' production lines or stock are inspected

and tested by ETL as to their conformity to specified IBM standards. Manufacturers meeting the specified standards may carry the ETL mark on products.

FIBERLAN INC.—A BELLSOUTH-SIECOR COMPANY

P.O. Box 127
Research Triangle Park, NC
  27709
(919)549-6551; telex 216-910; FAX
  919-541-9034

F. Ray McDevitt, President; Nanita Vendrillo, Marketing Manager (MD)(PR)

Founded 1982; 60 employees

A joint venture between BellSouth and Siecor, FiberLAN provides hardware evaluation and selection, network design, network evaluation and selection, network installation and post-installation support, system integration, technical consulting, and seminars/training. Primary markets include educational and financial institutions, Fortune 1000 companies, local and state government, hospitals, interconnects, airlines, consultants, utilities, and other common carriers.

FORRESTER RESEARCH INC.

Harvard Square, P.O. Box 1091
Cambridge, MA 02238
(617)497-7090

George F. Colony, President

Market research and analysis firm. Primary markets include data communications firms and Fortune 1000 companies.

FROST & SULLIVAN INC.

106 Fulton Street
New York, NY 10038
(212)233-1080; telex 235-986

Daniel M. Sullivan, President; Robert A. Sanzo, Vice President, Marketing (MD); Terry McGuire, Director of Public Relations (PR)

Founded 1961; 200 employees

Conducts market research and analysis, seminars/training and political risk conferences for Fortune 1000 companies. Marketing research studies include "LANs in the Factory" and "LAN."

GENERAL INSTRUMENT CORPORATION—JERROLD DISTRIBUTION SYSTEMS DIVISION

2200 Byberry Road
Hatboro, PA 19040
(215)674-4800

William H. Lambert, Vice President and General Manager; Geoffrey S. Roman, Vice President, Marketing and Sales (MD)

Provides network design services for educational institutions, government, hospitals, and manufacturers.

HONEYWELL NETWORK DESIGN CENTER

200 Smith Street, MS 486
Waltham, MA 02154

Network design and technical consultation covering such topics as LAN configurations, voice and data integration, interfaces to SNA systems, and capacity planning.

HYATT RESEARCH CORPORATION

P.O. Box 662
Andover, MA 01810
(617)475-04

Eric H. Killorin, President

Founded 1983; 5 employees

Provides business and marketing consulting, hardware evaluation and selection, market research and analy-

sis, network evaluation and selection, and technical consulting services to data communications firms. Published reports include "Executive's Guide to PC Networks" and "IBM Token Ring."

IEEE COMPUTER SOCIETY

1730 Massachusetts Avenue NW
Washington, DC 20036
(202)371-0101; telex 710-825-0437
IEEE COMPSO

Dr. T.M. Elliott, Executive Director; C.G. Stockton, Director, Computer Society Press

Founded 1951; 90,000 members

Association of engineers and computer scientists. Activities include seminars/training, technical conferences and standards development. Published the IEEE 802 Standard on local area networks.

INFONET INC.

10902 Wild Grape
San Antonio, TX 78230
(512)696-2590

Paul N. Criswell, President; L. James Beckman, Vice President, Marketing (MD); Geri Criswell, Vice President (PR)

Founded 1983; 12 emploees

Hardware evaluation and selection; network design; network evaluation and selection; network installation; seminars/training; and software and technical consulting. Clients include data communications firms, financial institutions, and government.

INTERNATIONAL DATA CORPORATION

5 Speen Street
Framingham, MA 01701
(617)872-8200; telex 951-168

Peter Rowell, President; Nina Ricci (MD)

Founded 1964; over 300 employees

Branch offices: McLean, VA (703)893-0833; Palo Alto, CA (415)424-8844; Atlanta, GA (404)394-0758; Des Plaines, IL (312)827-5740; Paramus, NJ (201)967-1350.

Offers market research and analysis and seminars/training to data communications firms, Fortune 1000 companies and government.

INTERNATIONAL MANAGEMENT SERVICES INC.

2 Frederick Street
Framingham, MA 01701-8399
(617)879-5955; telex 755-916

Raymond P. Wenig, President; Ronald N. Nickles, Director of Marketing (MD); Terry D. Pardoe, Vice President, Services (PR)

Founded 1973; 28 employees

Provides business and marketing consulting; hardware evaluation and selection; market research and analysis; network design; network evaluation and selection; software consulting; and technical consulting services. Primary markets include data communications firms, financial institutions, Fortune 1000 companies, government, and manufacturing. Also sponsors LAN seminars worldwide, including "Introduction to LANs"; "Planning and Implementing LANs"; "Manufacturing LANs"; and "MAP, TOP, and Other Protocols."

INTERNATIONAL RESOURCE DEVELOPMENT INC.

6 Prowitt Street
Norwalk, CT 06855
(203)866-7800; telex 643-452

Kenneth G. Bosomworth, President; Joann K. Niedzwiecki (MD); Suzanne Bores (PR)

Founded 1971; 25 employees

Conducts market research and analysis for data communications firms, financial institutions and Fortune 1000 companies.

INTERPHASE CORPORATION
2925 Merrell Road
Dallas, TX 75229
(214)350-9000

Michael E. Cope, President and Chief Executive Officer; Tom Thawley, Director of Marketing (MD)

Network design and technical consulting.

KALBA BOWEN ASSOCIATES INC.
12 Arrow Street
Cambridge, MA 02138
(617)661-2624; telex 951-861

Kas Kalba, President; Tom Lucke, Director of Consulting Services (MD); Pat Kalba, Vice President, Administration (PR)

Founded 1973; 15 employees

Services include business and marketing consulting, market research and analysis and technical consulting. Markets to data communications firms, financial institutions, Fortune 1000 companies, and government.

KEE INC.
10727 Tucker Street
Beltsville, MD 20705
(301)595-4700; FAX 301-937-5205

Roderick Matheson, President; Patrick Kelly, Vice President, Marketing and Sales (MD); Kathleen Janson, Marketing Communications Manager (PR)

Founded 1968; 57 employees

Offers network design, evaluation, selection, and installation services to data communications firms, educational and financial institutions, Fortune 1000 companies, government, and hospitals.

LANTE CORPORATION
100 South Wacker, Suite 1110
Chicago, IL 60606
(312)236-5100

Mark Tedde, President (MD); Fred Haught (PR)

Founded 1984; 20 employees

Provides business and marketing consulting, hardware evaluation and selection, market research and analysis, network design, network evaluation and selection, network installation, seminars/training, and software and technical consulting. Training courses designed for LAN administrators include internetworking topics. Clientele includes educational and financialinstitutions, Fortune 1000 companies, government, hospitals, and legal and service organizations.

LINK RESOURCES INC.
215 Park Avenue South
New York, NY 10003
(212)473-5600; telex 429-328

Hanies Gassner, President; Mark Winther, Program Director, New Communications Services (MD); Laura Burland (PR)

Founded 1976; 30 employees

A subsidiary of International Data Corporation, Link Resources Inc. is a market research and consulting firm for the electronic services industry. In-depth analyses focus on electronic information, telecommunications services, videotex, personal and educational computing, consumer electronics, telecommuting, optical media, and entertainment software. Primary clients include data communications firms, financial institutions, Fortune 1000 companies, and publishers.

ARTHUR D. LITTLE INC.
Acorn Park
Cambridge, MA 02140
(617)864-5770; telex 921-436;
    TWX 710-320-0820

John F. Magee, President; Alma Triner, Vice President, Public Relations (PR)

Founded 1886; 2609 employees

Provides technical assistance and management consulting. Services include needs assessment, development of long-range plans and hardware and software specification. Assists communications users with strategic planning of telecommunications systems, including voice, data and video networks.

LOGICA INC.
666 Third Avenue
New York, NY 10017
(212)599-0828; telex 238-539-
    LOGUR

Steve Stevenson, President; Bob Braudy (MD); Victoria Hall (PR)

Founded 1970; 150 employees

Services include business and marketing consulting, hardware evaluation and selection, market research and analysis, network design, network evaluation and selection, network installation, and software and technical consulting. Clientele includes data communications firms, educational and financial institutions, Fortune 1000 companies, local and state government, and hospitals.

MANAGEMENT INFORMATION CORPORATION
401 East Route 70
Cherry Hill, NJ 08034
(609)428-1020

Lawrence Feidelman, President; Jim Brisbane, Vice President, Marketing and Sales (MD)

Founded 1971; 19 employees

Services include business and marketing consulting, hardware evaluation and selection, market research and analysis, network evaluation and selection, and software and technical consulting. Markets to data communications firms, educational and financial institutions, Fortune 1000 companies, government, and hospitals.

MANUFACTURING AUTOMATION PROTOCOL & TECHNICAL AND OFFICE PROTOCOL USERS GROUP OF SME

One SME Driee, P.O. Box 930
Dearborn, MI 48121
(313)271-1500; telex 297-742 SME
   UR; FAX 313-271-2861

Mark Anthony Shaw, Administrator

Founded 1985

Industry group dedicated to educating users and encouraging industry-wide adoption of standards-based communications technology. Objectives include generating a standard set of communication specifications using current industry standards, user-driven MAP and TOP specifications, and accepted industry operating practices.

THE MARKET INFORMATION CENTER INC.

Marlborough Executive Park, 65
   Boston Post Road West
Marlborough, MA 01752
(617)460-0880

Harold Henry, President; Barry S. Gilbert, Executive Vice President (MD)(PR)

Founded 1983; 6 employees

Market research and consulting firm specializing in the communications industry. Primary clients are data communications firms.

J.H. MORGAN CONSULTANTS

Post House Road
Morristown, NJ 07960
(201)766-0969

J.H. Morgan, President (MD)(PR)

Founded 1976; 2 employees

Business and marketing consulting, hardware evaluation and selection, network design, network evaluation and selection, network installation, seminars/training, technical consulting, and strategic planning. Clients include data communications firms, educational and financial institutions, Fortune 1000 companies, government, health care institutions, and transportation and utilities companies.

NETWORK PLANNING CORPORATION

2705 Newlands Avenue
Belmont, CA 94002
(415)592-2270

Dieter Lohr, President; Bruce McDonald Vice President (MD)

Founded 1979; 5 employees

Plans and designs universal wiring systems for high-rise buildings and building complexes. Also provides business and marketing consulting, hardware evaluation and selection, market research and analysis, network design, and network evaluation and selection services for Fortune 1000 companies, government and hospitals.

NETWORK STRATEGIES GROUP

1435 Koll Circle
San Jose, CA 95112
(408)293-3765

Gail R. James, Managing Consultant

Founded 1986; 10 employees

Management consulting firm specializing in hardware evaluation and selection, network design, network evaluation and selection, training for LAN administrators, and software and technical consulting. Primary markets include Fortune 1000 companies and government agencies.

NETWORK STRATEGIES INC.

10201 Lee Highway
Fairfax, VA 22030
(703)352-9700

Charles Joyce, President; Richard Deal, Marketing Director (MD)(PR)

Founded 1981; 100 employees

Services include business ad marketing consulting, hardware evaluation and selection, market research and analysis, network design, network evaluation and selection, network installation, seminars/training, and software and technical consulting. Primary markets are data communications firms, educational and financial institutions, Fortune 1000 companies, government, hospitals, and law firms.

NEWTON-EVANS RESEARCH COMPANY INC.

10176 Baltimore National Pike,
   Suite 204, Bethany Center
Ellicott City, MD 21043
(301)465-731

Charles W. Newton, President; Karen Dargis, Marketing Services Manager (MD); Jeanne Small, Information Program Manager (PR)

Founded 1978; 8 employees

Market research and analysis for data communications firms, financial institutions and Fortune 1000 companies. Published reports track the usage trends of data communications in a variety of industries.

OFFICE AUTOMATION SOCIETY INTERNATIONAL (OASI)

15269 Mimosa Trail, Suite B
Dumfries, VA 22026
(703)690-3880

Paul D. Oyer, President;ackie Potts (MD); Sue Pickard (PR)

Founded 1982; 2500 members

Professional group which provides technical consulting and seminars on voice/data communications and local area networks to data communications firms, educational institutions and government. Offers the Certified Office Automation Professional designation.

PHILLIPS PUBLISHING INC.

7811 Montrose Road
Potomac, MD 20854
(301)340-2100; FAX 301-424-4297

Thomas L. Phillips, Publisher; David Durham, Vice President, Director of Marketing; Ellen O. Hamm, Vice President, Director of Publications, Conferences and Executive Programs; John Farley, Vice President and Executive Editor.

Publishes professional newsletters, including *Data Channels, Outlook on IBM, Outlook on AT&T, Fiber Optics News, Military Fiber Optics News, Telephone News, Digital Bypass Report,* and others, covering all areas of telecommunications. Produces related trade directories, industry studies and loose-leaf services, such as *The Satellite Directory, Telecommunications Regulatory Monitor, DTS Survey, Interconnect Industry Survey,* and *Phillips Publishing's 1987 Telephone Industry Directory and Sourcebook.*

MICHAEL L. ROTHBERG ASSOCIATES

27 Heather Drive
Somerset, NJ 08873-2847
(201)247-0377

Michael Rothberg, President (PR); Judy Morgenstern (MD)

Founded 1980; 6 employees

Specializes in the design, development and implementation of local and wide-area computer networks for both commercial and government clients. Also provides market research and planning programs for communications products suppliers.

SARGENT CABLE SERVICES

28th and Liberty Avenue, P.O. Box 30
Pittsburgh, PA 15230
(412)394-7580; FAX 412-394-7426

Richard W. Suminski, General Manager; James K. Scanlon, Operations Manager (MD); Jackie Fournier, Marketing Representative (PR)

Founded 1982; 35 employees

Provides services in the field of fiber optic design, installation and repair. Has performed work for several power companies including Virginia Power & Electric, all branches of the military, IBM, DEC, Wang, Burroughs, and GE. Communications applications include baseband and broadband data networks, telecommunications, process control, CAD, CAM, and video. Other services include consulting, equipment procurement, quality control, splicing, terminating, and system maintenance.

SHIP STAR ASSOCIATES INC.

36 Woodhill Drive
Newark, DE 19711
(302)738-7782

Robert S. Crowder, President

Business and marketing consulting, network design, network evaluation and selection, seminars/training, and software and technical consulting. Specializes in education and consulting covering MAP, TOP and OSI. Seminar topics include "MAP Network Design and Performance" and "MAP, TOP & OSI Technology". Clients include data communications firms and Fortune 1000 companies.

SIECOR CORPORATION

48 Siecor Park
Hickory, NC 28603-0489
704-327-5000

Joseph Hicks, General Manager, Data Communications Products

Offers a variety of field engineering services, including troubleshooting and testing. Also offers training courses on fiber optic cable installation, splicing and troubleshooting.

STRATEGIC MARKET TRENDS INC.

14 Page Terrace
Stoughton, MA 02072
(617)341-2200

Charles R. Robbins, President

Founded 1984; 7 employees

Business and marketing consulting, market research and analysis and business and product planning. Primarily markets to data communications firms.

SYSTEMS ORIENTED

261 Cleveland Avenue
Highland Park, NJ 08904
(201)246-4010; (800)556-0038

Jeffrey S. Deckman, President; Allen Pillar, Director of Operations

Founded 1981; 100 employees

Contracting firm specializing in design, construction, engineering, and service/maintenance of broadband and baseband LANs. Specific services include material management and distribution, underground construction, pavement excavation, internal building wiring, aerial construction, splicing, and outlet and modem installation. Services the East Coast and Midwest.

SYSTEMS TECHNOLOGY FORUM INC.

10201 Lee Highway, Suite 150
Fairfax, VA 22030
(703)591-3666, (800)336-7409

Richard L. Deal, President; Heidi Chorosinski, Director of Administrative Operations (MD)(PR)

Founded 1980; 5 employees, 23 instructors

Conducts LAN seminars for data communications firms, financial institutions, Fortune 1000 companies, and government. Topics include network design, operations and management, protocols and standards, SNA, and PBXs.

TECHNOLOGY CONCEPTS INC.

40 Tall Pine Drive
Sudbury, MA 01776
(617)443-7311; telex 517-682

Stuart Wecker, President; Gigi Wang, Director of Marketing (MD)

Founded 1981; 55 employees

Services include network design, network evaluation and selection, network installation, seminars/training, and technical consulting. Specializes in consulting services for college and university network communications and on-site seminars for the telecommunications industry.

TECHNOLOGY TRANSFER INSTITUTE

741 Tenth Street
Santa Monica, CA 90402
(213)394-8305

Dr. Leonard Kleinrock, President; Randolph Burns (MD)(PR)

Founded 1976; 10 employees

Services include a comprehensive curriculum of seminars, a speakers bureau and expert consulting on complex problems in information technology.

TELECOMMUNICATION RESOURCES

14 Page Terrace
Stoughton, MA 02072
(617)341-2219

Gregory R. Cipriano, Senior Partner

Founded 1984; 11 employees

Services include hardware evaluation and selection, network design, network evaluation and selection, network installation, seminars/training, software and technical consulting, and acceptance testing. Markets to educational and financial institutions, Fortune 1000 companies and hospitals.

TELE-ENGINEERING CORPORATION

3 Speen Street, Suite 230
Framingham, MA 01701
(617)877-6494; FAX 617-788-0324

E.O. Tunmann, President; Vior Colantonio (MD); Gary Cooper (PR)

Founded 1973; 70 employees

Services include technical consulting and design, engineering and installation of broadband coaxial, fiber optic and microwave LANs. Clients include data communications firms,

educational and financial institutions, Fortune 1000 companies government, hospitals, and regional Bell operating companies.

TRELLIS COMMUNICATIONS CORPORATION

5 Manor Parkway
Salem, NH 03079
(603)898-3434; telex 628-611-94;
  FAX 603-893-9326

Richard A. Cerny, President

Founded 1985; 6 employees

Conducts hardware evaluation and selection, network design, network evaluation and selection, network installation, seminars/training, and technical consulting. Emphasis is on fiber optics communications.

W AND J PARTNERSHIP

17211 Quail Court
Morgan Hill, CA 95037
(408)779-1714; telex 517-889
  WJPARTNERSHIP; TWX 910-380-9559

William A. Morgan, Managing Partner

Founded 1982; 10 employees

Systems design and engineering; seminars/training; and technical consulting. Engineering projects have included artificial intelligence, fiber optics transmission systems, PBX and CO switch design, and broadband, baseband, fiber optic and twisted wire pair local area networks. Clients include data communications firms, Fortune 1000 companies and government.

WOHL ASSOCIATES

555 City Line Avenue, Suite 240
Bala Cynwyd, PA 19004
(215)669-4842

Amy D. Wohl, President; May Giacalone, Marketing Director (MD)

Founded 1984; 8 employees

Provides bssiness and marketing consulting, hardware evaluation and selection, market research and analysis, network design, network evaluation and installation, seminars/training, software consulting, and office automation consulting services to data communications firms and Fortune 1000 companies. Sponsors The Wohl/Kutnick Office Systems/Networks Dialogue Conference.

XEROX NETWORK SYSTEMS INSTITUTE

Xerox Corporation, Office Systems
  Division, 2100 Geng Road
Palo Alto, CA 94303

Provides support to non-Xerox implementors of Xerox Network System (XNS) architecture. Offers seminars and workshops for programmers, as well as consulting services to clients of the institute. Based upon request from clients, Xerox will develop and make available various implementation aids.

ZATYKO ASSOCIATES

P.O. Box 1800
Tustin, CA 92680
(714)838-8294; TWX 650-258-5727

Daniel C. Zatyko, President; Alice W. Lahtela, Marketing Manager (MD)(PR)

Founded 1979; 20 employees

Provides business and marketing consulting, hardware evaluation and selection, market research and analysis, network design, network evaluation and selection, training, and technical consulting services. Markets to data communications firms, educational institutions, Fortune 1000 companies, and government.

Chapter 5 — Local Area Network Standards

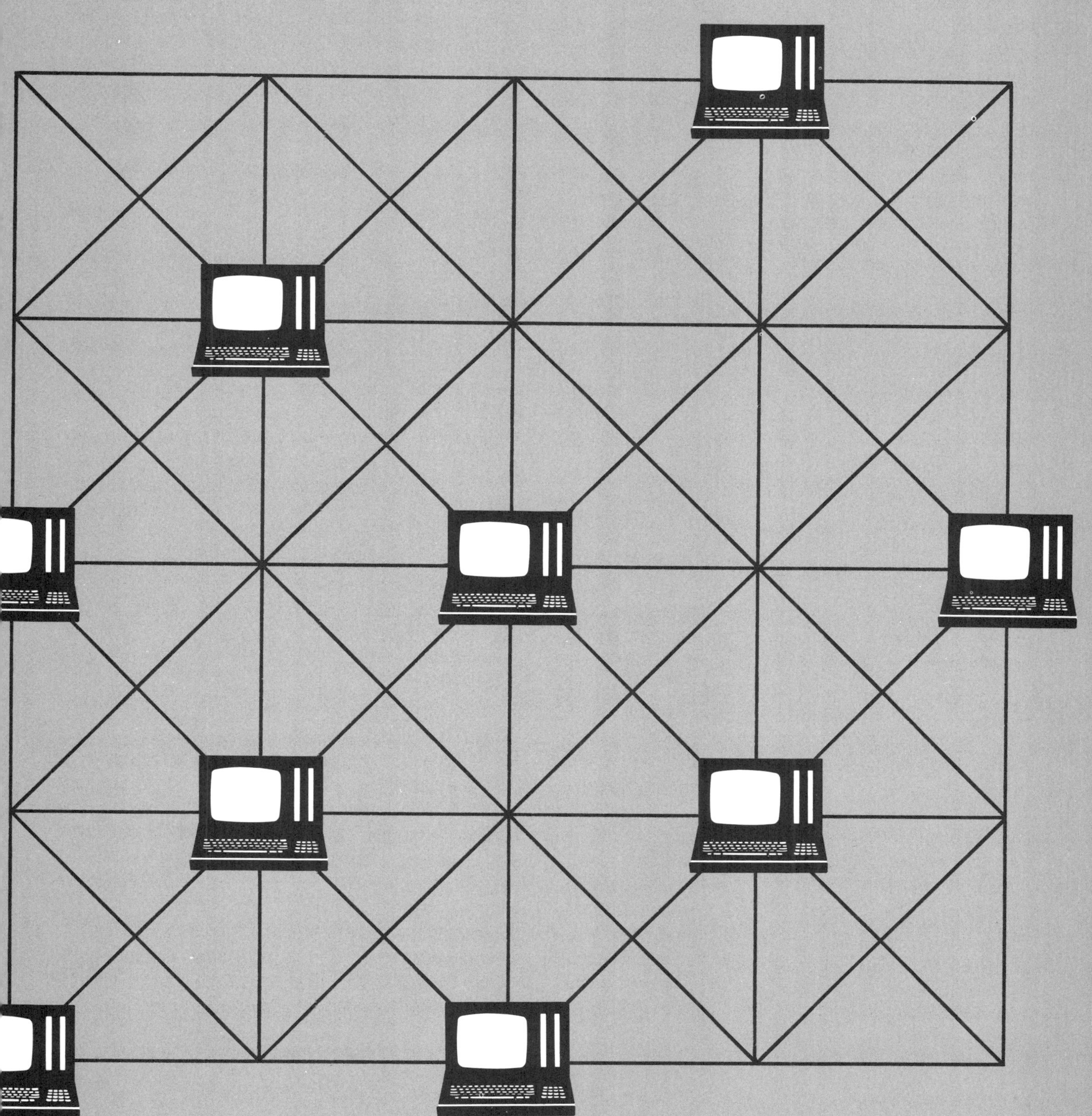

This chapter provides general descriptions of several LAN standards, including the IEEE 802 Project, Ethernet, the ISO OSI Reference Model, the Manufacturing Automation Protocol (MAP), IBM Systems Network Architecture (SNA), Transmission Control Protocol/Internet Protocol (TCP/IP), Token Ring, Technical and Office Protocols (TOP), and Xerox Network Systems Architecture (XNS).

Listings are also provided for national and international organizations active in LAN standardization.

Table 1

STANDARDS AND PROTOCOLS

	ISO REFERENCE MODEL	ISO STANDARDS	TCP/IP
LAYER 7	Application	ISO Virtual Terminal Protocol File Transfer, Access and Management	
LAYER 6	Presentation	ISO Presentation	Telnet/File Transfer Protocol
LAYER 5	Session	ISO Session	
LAYER 4	Transport	ISO Transport	Transmission Control Protocol
LAYER 3	Network	ISO Network	Internetwork Protocol
LAYER 2	Data link	IEEE 802.2	Ethernet
LAYER 1	Physical	IEEE 802.3, 4, 5	Ethernet

XNS	TOP V1.0	MAP V2.1
erpress, Interscript, Mail Format, ster Encoding Standard nting, Filing, Mail Transport, Inbasket, d Gateway Access Protocols aringhouse Authentication, and Time Protocols; nt Standards, Character Code Standard	ISO FTAM (DP) 8571 File Transfer Protocol	ISO TRAM (DP) 8571 File Transfer Protocol, Manufacturing Messaging Format Standard (MMFS), and Common Application Service Elements (CASE)
urier — Message Stream, Object Stream, ck Stream	NULL (ASCII and Binary Encoding)	
urier — Bulk Data Transfer Protocol	ISO Session (IS) 8327 Basic Combined Subset and Session Kernel, Full Duplex	
ho Protocol, Sequenced Packet Protocol, or Protocol, cket Exchange Protocol, uting Information Protocol	ISO Transport (IS) 8073 Class 4	
ernetwork Datagram Protocol	ISO Internet (DIS) 8473 Connectionless and for X.25 — Subnetwork Dependent Convergence Protocol (SNDCP)	
ernet	ISO Logical Link Control (DIS) 8802/2 (IEEE 802.2) Type 1, Class 1	
thernet	ISO CSMA/CS (DIS) 8802/3 (IEEE 802.3) CSMA/CD Medium Access Control 10Base5	ISO Token Passing Bus (DIS) 8802/4 (IEEE 802.4) Token Passing Bus Medium Access Control

LOCAL AREA NETWORK STANDARDS

Michael L. Rothberg

Local area networking! There seems to be no end to the multitude of products being thrust upon the market, or to the proliferation of published material that is available on the subject. Local networks are becoming the heart of computer communications today, and will remain so for the foreseeable future. Since the advent of the microprocessor, no single technology has had such significant impact upon the world of computer and workstation communications. Needless to say, the divestiture of the world's most extensive telephone system and the growth of cable television technology have contributed to the development and acceptance of local area networks. The adoption of standards and the entry into the market by such giants as IBM have placed local area networks in a more credible and acceptable light than at any time since the introduction of the original Experimental Ethernet at the Xerox Palo Alto Research Center (PARC).

Legitimacy aside for a moment, there still remains a tremendous amount of work to be done in the realm of internetworking and higher layer protocols before local area networks can take their rightful place among computer network architectures. Developments are continuing at such a frenetic pace, however, that the gap between conception and publication of new material inevitably causes some degree of immediate obsolescence. For this reason, and our natural inclination to look ahead, I have taken the liberty to speculate on the possible outcome of certain standards development strategies. Where applicable, I have been most careful to identify these ideas as "speculative." On the other hand, new products and developments are continuing to turn these speculative ideas into reality.

One of the more challenging tasks in discussing local area networking standards is to present a perspective of local area networks in which they are treated as integral parts of the global distributed computer internetwork. This is becoming easier to do as higher layer standards and implementations continue to evolve. However, one should realize that existing standards, particularly IEEE 802, primarily address the unique LAN requirements of mechanisms for arbitrating and managing access to the physical channel. The issues concerning interconnection of remote local area network segments are being resolved rapidly, and will undoubtedly be influenced by developing interfaces to de facto architectural standards such as IBM's System Network Architecture (SNA) as well as the development of protocol suites such as the General Motors Manufacturing Automation Protocol (MAP) and the Boeing Company's Technical and Office Protocol (TOP).

HISTORY OF LAN STANDARDS FROM ETHERNET TO IEEE 802

During the Neanderthal period preceding the development of Ethernet a number of promisingly successful attempts were made tying host computers and their workstations together within moderate geographic areas using local area network architectures. Some early examples of these implementations were the University of Hawaii's ALOHA network, MITRE Corporation's MITRIX, Bell Laboratories' SPIDER, and the University of California at Irvine's Distributed Computing System (DCS). All of these networks shared common objectives with Ethernet satisfying them to varying degress.

Despite these activities, it wasn't until 1976, when Metcalf and Boggs[1] introduced the Experimental

---

Michael L. Rothberg is president of Michael L. Rothberg Associates, a consulting firm specializing in the design, development and implementation of local and wide area computer networks for government and commercial clients.

[1]Metcalfe, Robert M. and Boggs, David R. *Ethernet: Distributed Packet Switching for Local Computer Networks, Communications of the ACM,* July 1976, Volume 19, Number 7.

Ethernet at Xerox PARC, that the first commercial local area networking product become a reality.

As the Experimental Ethernet evolved into a product, Xerox, Digital Equipment Corporation (DEC) and Intel published the first Ethernet Specification, Version 1.0, September 30, 1980. This rapidly became a de facto standard for local area networks. Version 2.0 of the Ethernet Specification was introduced in November 1982, but was subsequently withdrawn. At the present time there are tens of thousands of licensed Ethernets and Ethernet compatible networks installed and in operation. It is for this reason that, when the IEEE was chartered with Project 802 to develop local area networking standards, they prioritized the adoption of a functionally equivalent standard. One should exercise caution in assuming compatibility between Ethernet and the IEEE standard since there are a number of minor, but still incompatible, differences between them.

Although Ethernet provided a great deal of functionality, other competing proprietary architectures were also highly functional within the realm of their specific product spectrum. In fact, some of these yielded higher levels of deterministic performance. It was important to the many different vendors of computer equipment that a standard architecture be adopted which in the best case reflected and leveraged their own product interests, while at worst, did not exclude them from the potentially lucrative markets nor require enormous redevelopment efforts. As a result, the IEEE 802 committee adopted several different implementations as separate standards. It was recognized that each of these different approaches yielded a series of advantages and disadvantages for different application environments.

OVERVIEW OF THE IEEE 802 LOCAL AND METROPOLITAN AREA NETWORK STANDARDS

The IEEE standards reflect a number of different implementations that generally accommodate inter-computer communications over serial channels at less than 20 megabits per second. Implementations at greater speeds will be addressed by standards to be developed in the future. The following are the current standardization efforts of the IEEE 802 committee:

802.1—Architecture and Internetworking Guidelines. Not a standard but rather an introduction to the IEEE 802 architecture;

802.2—Logical Link Control—Those data link control functions that are common to all standard LAN implementations and form a common sublayer where different implementations converge;

802.3—A baseband bus utilizing Carrier Sense Multiple Access with Collision Detection (CSMA/CD);

802.4—A broadband bus employing a token-passing access method on a logical ring;

802.5—A baseband ring employing a token-passing access method;

802.6—A Metropolitan Area Network (MAN) covering a larger geographic area potentially usefl in connecting equipment on large university and office campuses.

The IEEE 802 standards can be viewed as a protocol suite that occupies the lower layers of an open system architecture. In this sense, then, it is completely compatible with the International Organization for Standardization's Open System Interconnection Reference Model (ISO/OSI).

EMERGING LOCAL AREA NETWORK STANDARD ARCHITECTURES

The adoption of the IEEE 802 standards, as well as the ISO Open Systems Interconnection reference model, have created some trepidations among users as well as feelings of comfort. Recognizing that the "nice" thing about standards was the variety of options from which one could choose, users also began to worry about the issues of compatibility between different standard implementations. As a result, General Motors developed an architecture called the Manufacturing Automation Protocol (GM-MAP). The interesting point here is that, for the first time in standards development, a large user has developed a suite of standard protocols and has told the vendor community that it would only procure products that complied with this architecture. In order to assure that the architecture would garner support from other large users, GM used only standard protocols and implementations. The support has been overwhelming on the user front, and vendors are rapidly developing products to meet this new set of requirements.

Because of the requirements for deterministic network access and performance, and the special cabling requirements of manufacturing environments, GM adopted the IEEE 802.4 broadband token passing bus architecture for its implementation of MAP.

Other user-developed standard protocol suites are also developing. The Boeing Company has developed the Technical and Office Protocol (TOP) which has also been receiving widespread support. Where the GM-MAP architecture is intended for factory communications, Boeing TOP is designed for office communications. As such, the Manufacturing Message Format Standard/EIA RS-1393A does not appear in the TOP suite, and the IEEE 802.4 Token Bus of MAP has been replaced with IEEE 802.3 Carrier Sense Multiple Access with Collision Detection bus. In all other respects, the TOP and MAP architectures are identical.

FUTURE OF LAN STANDARDS

Standards development is not a static activity. In fact, as technology improves, one can expect to see new developments in the standards arena. Some of the developments we are likely to see in the near future include:

> *Broadband CSMA/CD*—A working group of the IEEE 802 committee has developed a draft standard for broadband bus implementations of CSMA/CD.

> *Optical Fiber CSMA/CD*—Optical fiber will enhance the bandwidth and performance characteristics of CSMA/CD architectures and are likely to become an important alternative for LANs in the very near futre.

> *Optical Fiber Token-Passing Ring*—The American National Standards Institute (ANSI) has developed a proposed standard for a 100 Mbps token ring on optical fibers. This proposed standard entitled X3T9 Fiber Distributed Data Interface (FDDI) will likely be adopted in the near future and will provide enormous increases in the functionality and performance of token rings.

One of the more pressing issues concerning LAN standards revolves around the need for an enrichment of the higher layer protocols and standards. Although GM-MAP and Boeing TOP are certainly the correct focus for the moment, additional services and protocols will be required. Until then, one can correctly view LANs as railroad tracks with few if any trains to run on them. Considering how LAN standards map against OSI, these same issues become applicable to wide area networks as well. The ball is in the vendors' court. The near future should yield some promising developments.

ETHERNET

Ethernet is the local area communication network developed by Xerox, Digital Equipment Corporation and Intel Corporation. Its specifications determine the kind of transmission medium, electrical signaling levels and the data link or transmission protocols.

The Ethernet transmission protocols are independent of the medium. Products supporting these protocols may communicate with each other using fiber optics, twisted pairs of wires or even radio broadcasting into the "ether." With passage of the IEEE 802.3 standard, Ethernet is now aninternationally accepted communication standard. There are some minor differences between the version of Ethernet that Xerox has been using for several years and that adopted recently by the IEEE 802 Committee and ISO. Now that this standard has been accepted, Xerox is migrating its products to the official 802.3 version of Ethernet, a process that started in 1985 with the incorporation of standard 802.3 transceivers and controllers into the product line.

ETHERNET ARCHITECTURE

The major division in the Ethernet architecture is between the physical layer and the data link layer, corresponding to the lowest two layers in the ISO model. The interface between the higher network client layer and the data link layer includes facilities for transmitting and receiving frames, and provides status information. The interface between the data link and the physical layer includes signals for framing (carrier sense, transmit initiation) and contention resolution (collision detect), facility for receiving and transmitting serial bitstreams, and a wait function for timing.

PHYSICAL LAYER

This layer performs all the functions needed to transmit and receive data at the physical level while supporting the data link layer interface. The Ethernet specification describes the 10 Mbps baseband coaxial system. Other physical layers have also been specified for broadband channels, fiber optic channels and twisted pair wires. All these diverse physical media work with the same Ethernet data link protocol.

The figure below shows the five fields in an Ethernet data link layer frame: the source and destination address; the type field (called "length" in IEEE 802.3 standard); a data field containing the transmitted data; and the frame check sequence field, containing a cyclic redundancy check (CRC) value to detect transmission errors. The total length of the Ethernet frames can be 64 to 1518 bytes long. The Ethernet source and destination addresses are 48 bits long, thus uniquely identifying over 281 trillion network devices. The 48-bit host number space is large enough to ensure uniqueness and provides adequate room for growth at little extra cost.

DATA LINK LAYER

The data link layer itself is divided into two sublayers. The data encapsulation sublayer performs the framing, addressing and error detection functions. The link management layer performs the channel allocation and contention resolution functions. The general Ethernet approach uses a shared communications channel managed with CSMA/CD.

Taken together, the physical and data link portions of Ethernet provide the foundation for a comprehensive, sophisticated local area network capability useful in a wide variety of applications and environments.

Source: Xerox Corporation

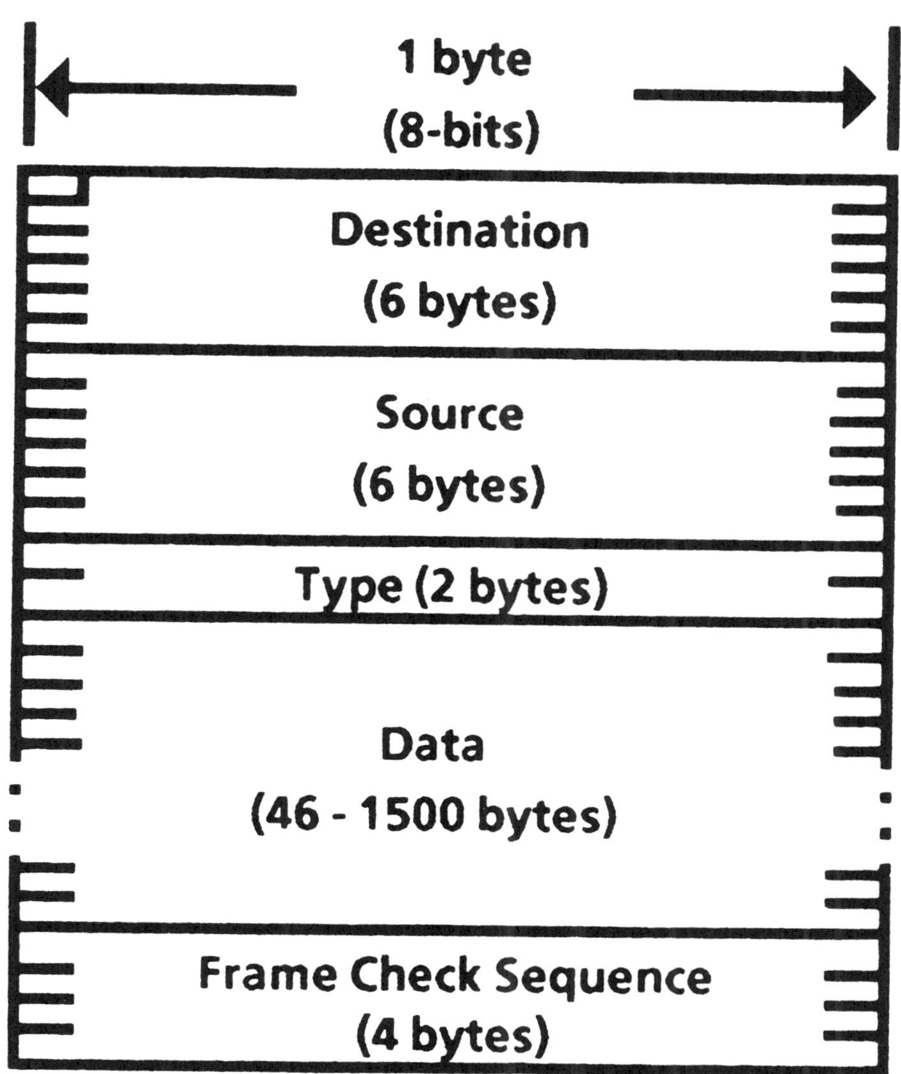

Ethernet frame

Figure 39

ISO OPEN SYSTEM INTERCONNECTION REFERENCE MODEL

Robert S. Crowder

The International Organization for Standardization (ISO), with support in the United States from American National Standards Institute (ANSI), Computer and Business Equipment Manufacturers Association (CBEMA), and the National Bureau of Standards (NBS), began work in the mid-1970s on a series of communication standards which are now known as Open System Interconnection (OSI) standards.

OSI REFERENCE MODEL

The ISO communication standards effort began by formulating a model which standards committees could use to divide and coordinate the work of specifying a complete open communications architecture. Use of this model has enabled concurrent standards and protocol development activities relating to all aspects of open communication. Without the OSI model, coordinated standards could not have been developed in a useful time frame. Unfortunately, some communication practitioners attribute almost mystical powers to the division of functionality specified by the OSI model. The fallacy of this view is easily seen from the extensions that are now being added to the model and from the awkward structure of the topmost or Application layer. It almost seems that the addition of layers 8 and 9 will be required to restore the crisp architectural distinctions envisaged by the model's authors.

Because of the universal acceptance of the OSI model, modern communication standards and architectures are typically viewed against the 7-layer perspective of the OSI model. It should be noted that the OSI mmodel is intended as a frame of reference for describing a communications architecture, not as a specification for partitioning communications functions within real systems.

OSI LAYERS

Within the context of local area networks, the functionality of the layers of the OSI model can be defined as:

1. Physical—performs electrical signaling between stations (nodes) on a single LAN, i.e., delivers a bit stream between communicating stations on the LAN. In the context of a broadband LAN, which shares a single cable between many logical services by use of frequency division multiplexing, this function includes the head end (frequency converting element) and the modem at each station. Also specifies connections between each station and the transmission medium (which is not included in the OSI model).

2. Data link—transfers frames across a single LAN, including: resolution of contention for use of the shared transmission medium; delimiting and selecting frames addressed to this station; detection of noise via a frame check sequence; and any error correction or retries performed within the LAN.

The resolution of contention is known within IEEE 802 as Medium Access Control. The major techniques specified by the IEEE 802 committee are a contention-based system (CSMA/CD) and two controlled access mechanisms—token bus and token ring.

3. Network—routes and relays packets between OSI End Systems across an arbitrary set of subnetworks while maintaining the Quality of Service

Robert S. Crowder is president of Ship Star Associates Inc., a Newark, DE, consulting firm specializing in MAP, TOP and OSI networking standards.

(QOS) appropriate to this communication. A globally unique node address is used by the Network layer.

4. Transport—provides end-to-end data delivery across the possibly extended network between communicating OSI End Systems. The data transfer service provided by the Transport layer, using the services of the Network, Data Link, and Physical layers, constitutes the communications aspects of OSI.

5. Session—supports an orderly dialog between application programs including Two Way Simultaneous (TWS) and Two Way Alternate (TWA) dialog structures. Provides a check-pointing and resynchronizing capability.

6. Presentation—negotiates contexts and formats for the exchange of data (i.e., the scheme for representing graphical models and coordinate data). Transforms data from the local system representation into the agreed upon context and format for interchange via OSI.

7. Appliation—the Application layer consists of three major categories of protocols:

• Common Application Services (CASE)—the "sublayer" forms associations between other OSI application protocols or between user programs that use OSI services for the purpose of exchanging information (as opposed to data). Switches between presentation contexts (i.e., between Files and Terminal activities) and provides for concurrent atomic

actions at the distributed locations such as multinational funds transfer). The information transfer service provided by CASE, using the services of the Presentation and Session layers, constitutes the generic interworking aspects of OSI.

• Specific Application Services (SASE)—this general category of application protocols provides generic services for a specific class of interactions. Some of the best known of these protocols are: File Transfer, Access and Management (FTAM); Virtual Terminal Protocol (VTP); Job Transfer and Manipulation (JTM), related to Remote Job Entry; and Message Handling Systems (MHS), a generic electronic mail service developed by the CCITT.

• Management—protocols to coordinate the management of OSI networks in conjunction with management capabilities embedded within each of the OSI layer protocols.

• Directories—provides the information necessary to access a user program or capability at an arbitrary location within the global OSI network.

The summary of the MAP 2.1 application layer given just above indicates the potential desirability of recasting the OSI model to include additional layers.

It should also be noted that the description of the Data Link and Physical layers given above is specific to local area networks and is not included in the current OSI model which was developed with an orientation to telephony systems.

MANUFACTURING AUTOMATION PROTOCOL (MAP)

Robert S. Crowder

The International Organization for Standardization (ISO), with support in the U.S. from American National Standards Institute (ANSI), Computer and Business Equipment Manufacturers Association (BEMA), and the National Bureau of Standards (NBS), began work in the mid 1970s on a series of communication standards which are now known as Open System Interconnection (OSI) standards. At the same time the International Electrotechnical Commission (IEC), with support in the U.S. from Instrument Society of America (ISA), began work on the PROWAY standard for Industrial & Process Data Highways. In 1980 the Institute of Electrical and Electronic Engineers (IEEE) formed the Project 802 committee which began work on Local Area Network (IEEE) standards. These standards became the basis for MAP.

In the early 1980's, General Motors realized that their United States operations were not competitive with those of the Japanese auto manufacturers. GM adopted a strategy of automating their plants to allow them to compete with the Japanese. They realized that they would require multivendor factory automation solutions and that this could be accomplished only on the basis of a widely supported nonproprietary factory communication standard. This economic reality, which was felt first by GM and is now becoming widely accepted, led GM to create MAP (Manufacturing Automation Protocol).

GM selected OSI standards as the basis for MAP because of the worldwide acceptance these standards are coming to enjoy. This support for international standards will guarantee that MAP achieves the broadly based constituency that is necessary for any effective standard. Computer and control vendors have also enthusiastically supported the OSI basis of MAP because this will allow them access to a much broader and larger market than is available to any proprietary or U.S.-based solution. Further, large users, both within the U.S. and throughout the developed world, have realized that they can also benefit from an OSI-based nonproprietary communication solution.

Selection of international communication standards has another significant advantage, as they represent over 1000 man years of effort by many of the leading communications specialists in the world. With this wealth of information available, choosing another basis for MAP would be impractical and irresponsible!

WHAT IS MAP?

The OSI model divides communication functionality into 7 conceptual layers. While standards at the lower layers are rapidly maturing, there is much work to be done at the upper layers and in the management of networks. In addition, several standards have been adopted for layers 1, 2 and 3. Each of these standards is intended to fill a particular marketplace need. However, it is not always clear which technologies are best suited to a particular environment, such as manufacturing automation. The MAP specification is a selection of currently available standard protocols that are most appropriate for manufacturing automation, combined with a series of interim GM specifications covering topics for which no standards exist. GM and the MAP Users Group, a committee of the Society of Manufacturing Engineers, have made a commitment to replace these GM "specials" with international standards as soon as the standards become available. Thus, the ultimate goal of MAP, and in fact the aspect of MAP which has enabled it to gain such broad support, is a commitment to a full suite of international standards which support an Open Sys-

Robert S. Crowder is president of Ship Star Associates Inc., a Newark, DE, consulting firm specializing in MAP, TOP and OSI networking standards.

tem Interconnection Environment within the arena of factory automation.

In the remainder of this article we will note the evolution of MAP from a GM document to a public MAP Users Group document, which provides significantly enhanced functionality, and the emergence of TOP (Technical & Office Protocol) which will specify a compatible suite of OSI protocols that are appropriate to the technical and office environment. TOP joins MAP and the banking community in defining a set of protocols appropriate to their application and environment. Within the next few years we will undoubtedly see additional user interest groups which select a protocol suite best suited to their needs.

BENEFITS OF MAP

MAP is serving as the basis for rapid evolution of nonproprietary international, factory floor communications. It supports the application of multivendor automation systems. Both vendors and users of MAP-based products will benefit.

It has been estimated that within the automobile industry automated factories, made possible by MAP, will lead to savings of up to $2000 per car, along with significant improvements in quality and reductions in the lead time for introduction of new models of up to two years.

At the same time, vendors are seeing that their ability to compete in factory automation markets as large as $40 billion per year may depend on their products' compliance with MAP.

EVOLUTION OF MAP AND TOP

In the early 1980s the GM Broadband Task Force began work on a communication specification for factory automation. GM soon realized that a proprietary specification would never achieve universal support, and wisely adopted IEEE 802 and ISO standards as the basis for MAP. The heavy installed base of broadband within GM, as well as the background of the individuals involved, led to a natural emphasis on broadband cable sharing tech-

nology underlying a backbone local area network that traversed the entire plant and provided flexible communication between any nodes within the factory. This emphasis is reflected in the GM MAP 1.0, 2.0 and 2.1 specifications. GM's MAP 2.1 was issued in March of 1985 and is the current GM specification.

During 1984 the MAP Users Group was formed as an organization of interested users and vendors to bring a broad base of support to MAP. Concerns within this group over the exclusive broadband-backbone nature of MAP quickly surfaced. These concerns were expressed by both users and vendors, particularly within the continuous process industries and in Europe. Many users and vendors also expressed concern over the lack of a streamlined communication architecture that supported the fast response times needed for control, and promised support for low cost devices such as programmable controllers and even individual sensors. The PRO-WAY-LAN standard developed by the ISA SP72 committee and endorsed by the IEC as PROWAY-C offered a solution to both of these concerns.

In June 1985, the MAP Users Group issued a public MAP specification which summarizes the standards specified by GM MAP 2.1 (the MAP Backbone architecture) and extended the specifications to include a MAP Cell architecture. This article will discuss both the Backbone and Cell architecture specified in the public MAP document.

At the same time, an effort to support OSI standards for technical and office applications was being spearheaded by Boeing Computer Services. This effort made its first public appearance at the National Computer Conference in July 1984 that saw MAP unveiled. Organizational efforts for a publicly-based TOP Users Group within SME are now complete and we can anticipate a TOP specification which makes appropriate protocol selections at the lowest and highest layers of OSI while retaining compatibility with MAP whenever possible.

Thus we see within the MAP/TOP effort a growing recognition of a reality which this author has stressed. Namely, that a total corporate communications solution must address a wide variety of business applications and their supporting communication requirements, and that each of these applications will require its own coordinated suite of communications protocols. These protocol suites will differ primarily at the lowest and highest layers of the OSI architecture.

Consideration of the OSI model indicates that a prolification of protocols will be required at the Presentation and Application layers to service the diverse requirements of personal, business and industrial users. At the same time the varied topologies of offices, factories, metropolitan, national or worldwide communications dictate the need for diverse Physical and Data Link protocols. Unfortunately, prior to the emergence of MAP, this diversity had diluted the efforts of vendors and the focus of users on the essential unity of OSI.

MAP provided a clear selection of protocols at all levels of the OSI structure (known as the protocol suite or stack) that is appropriate to an economically significant marketplace. Thus GM, MAP and the MAP Users Group provide a focus for vendors and users in implementing and applying an initial suite OSI protocol.

The public MAP specification of the MAP Users Group defines two architectures:

- MAP Backbone Architecture (also specified by GM's MAP 2.1)

- MAP Cell Architecture.

The MAP Backbone architecture supports MAP End Systems which implement the MAP suite of OSI protocols (6/7)layers and can communicate with all other MAP End Systems either on the same plant or at remote sites via the internetwork protocol. It is GM's intention that all but the simplest factory devices support the protocol suite selected for MAP End Systems to simplify network management. However, there are users and vendors that question this requirement.

The MAP Cell architecture includes nodes that support the MAP End System protocol suite as well as a reduced protocol suite based on the confirmed Data Link service provided by PROWAY. The

PROWAY suite provides the realtime responsiveness required for control application. These nodes are known as MAP/PROWAY nodes. This architecture also supports PROWAY systems that implement only the reduced protocol suite and are expected to provide economical and efficient connection of low cost devices, such as micro programmable controllers and smart sensors, to the MAP network.

MAP specifies two systems (Bridges and Routers) which can be used to interconnect parts of a plant-wide MAP subnetwork, and one device (a Gateway) for connecting MAP systems to non-OSI networks. MAP Bridges use an algorithm operating over a common Data Link protocol to join LAN segments.

The Protocol suite specified for MAP End Systems is:

- Physical

  - IEEE 802.4 Broadband 10-Mbps data rate, 2-channel, midsplit format preferred (MAP 2.1);

  - IEEE 802.4 Phase Coherent Carrier Band 5-Mbps data rate, per modifications by the IEEE 802.4 B committee, in July 1985, using the media specified by ISA S72.01-1985. This specification was developed as the result of extensive testing at Eastman Kodak using factory noise data supplied by Inland Steel and Ford. Adoption by the IEEE 802.4 and ISA SP72 committees is expected in 1986-87.

- Data link

  - Media access—IEEE 802.4 Token Bus, 48-bit addresses, no options required.

  - Link control—IEEE 802.2 Type 1 Connectionless service.

- Network

ISO DIS 8473 Connectionless Network Service (CLNS) ISO DAD1/8028. Within one subnetwork inactive (null) implementation; to nodes on another subnetwork use subset specified by MAP 2.1, Chapter 3 and NBS/OSI Implementors Workshop.

•Addresses—IOS DAD2/8208 as specified by MAP 2.1-Appendix 4.

• Transport

ISO IS 8072/8073 Class 4 Connection Oriented Transport Service (COTS) with implementation restrictions specified by MAP 2.1, Chapter 3, Class 4 is require for operation over the CLNS.

• Session

ISO IS 8326/27 Kernel subset with restrictions specified by MAP 2.1-Chapter 3. The Kernel subset provides TWS functionality and graceful termination of Transport Connections.

• Presentation

Null.

• Application

•Case ISO DP 8649/50: MAP 2.1 subset of CASE Kernel as specified by MAP 2.1-Appendix 7. The MAP CASE subset provides associations and pass thru of Session Kernel services.

•FTAM—ISO DP 8571-Phase 1 Implementation as specified by MAP 2.1-Chapter 3 and NBS/OSI Implementors Workshop, Phase 1 FTAM provides access to complete files, but not to individual records, and supports limited file attributes.

•MMFS—MAP 2.1-Appendix 6: Manufacturing Messaging Format Standard—A specification for encoding messages and limited file transfers to manufacturing nodes such as numerical control systems, programmable controllers, and robots.

•Network Management—Layer 3-7—MAP 2.1-Chapter 4A. An initial specification for network montoring and traffic analysis based on current ISO drafts. Layer 1-2—Proprietary to LAN vendor (MAP 2.1). IEEE 802.1—Systems Management (Public MAP).

•Directories—MAP 2.1 Directory Appendix: A specification based on current ISO drafts.

As can easily be appreciated, a great deal of effort is being expended on the current MAP 2.1 specification.

The OSI Implementors Workshop, sponsored by the NBS, which has played a key role in setting priorities for OSI implementations of MAP and TOP, is defining an enhanced Phase 2 FTAM specification that includes use of the CASE and Presentation protocols, provides access to individual records and supports an expanded set of file attributes and management actions.

The GM MAP Task Force, which includes participants from GM and MAP vendors and users, is developing specifications for a Connection-Oriented Network Service (CONS) based on ISO standards for use of the X.25 Packet Level Protocol (PLP), and expansions of the Network Management and Directory Services specifications.

Finally, the Electronic Industries Association (EIA) 1393 committee, in conjunction with the GM Task Force, is developing an ISO-based standard for a Manufacturing Messaging Service (MMS) to be known as RS511. This standard will replace MMFS in the 1986/87 time frame. Unfortunately, conversion to RS511 will affect codes produced by both users and vendors, and thus creative interim strategies for using MMFS are in order.

The ISA and IEC are cooperating with the EIA 1393 committee to extend the RS511 standard, which will be submitted to ISO, to cover process control applications.

The additional protocol suites specified by MAP are: oBridges Protocol Suite: the Physical layer protocol is the MAP End System; the Data Link protocol is the MAP End System (TOP will allow Bridges to CSMA/CD and probably to Token Ring in this layer); oRouter Protocol Suite: Physical lyer protocol is MAP End System and CCITT V.11; Data Link is MAP End System and HDLC-LAPB; network is MAP End System plus convergence to X.25 PLP and Routing per MAP 2.1, Chapter 3 and NBS/OSI Implementators Workshop Agreement.

The reduced PROWAY protocol suite is: Physical layer protocol is the MAP End System; Data Link layer Media Access protocol is IEEE 802.4 Token Bus with Immediate Response Priority and Active Station List Options specified by ISA S72.01; Data Link layer Link Cottrol protocol is ISA S72.01 Send Data with Acknowledge and Request Data with Reply services (Revisions to IEEE 802.2 Type 3 proposal are expected to make these services a subset of Type 3); Network layer is null; Transport layer is null or a multiplexing protocol; Session layer is null; Presentation layer protocol is anticipated to be ANS.1; Application layer protocol for Messaging is anticipated to be RS 511; Directory is anticipated to be a subset of MAP Directory.

In a real sense, MAP is an idea whose time has come. It capitalizes on a decade of work by the standards community of the world. In the opinion of this author there is no question that MAP will succeed in its goals of focusing development effort on OSI and related standards, and accelerating the pace at which the resulting open communication architecture becomes widely accepted.

With the recent spate of MAP product announcements and growing worldwide user support for MAP, it appears that theiighest hurdle remaining for the propononets of MAP will be the education of the broader community of users and vendors in the the benefits of MAP.

SNA (SYSTEMS NEWORK ARCHITECTURE)

SNA is the description of the rules that enable IBM's customers to transmit and receive information through their computer networks.

SNA was designed as a set of rules for a networking system that would evolve and grow as new products and technologies appeared and as network user requirements changed. As part of that evolutionary growth, SNA has been enhanced several times since 1974, and it has contributed to the explosive growth of distributed data processing, office automation and large data networks.

Source: IBM Corporation

SNA is a specification governing the design of IBM products that are to communicate with one another in a network. It is called an architecture because it specifies the operating relationships of those products as part of a system.

In 1974, SNA supported single-host networks. Today, multiple SNA networks may be tied together, allowing open interconnection of both IBM and non-IBM networks and products.

To date, users around the world are using SNA in more than 20,000 host computers.

TCP/IP

The development of the Transmission Control Protocol/Internet Protocol (TCP/IP) began in the early 1970s when the Department of Defense Advanced Research Projects Agency (DARPA) offered grants to several organizations, including Stanford University and the University of California at Berkeley, which used TCP/IP for developing Unix-based systems. As a result of this research, the Defense Department adopted TCP/IP as its standard communication protocol, mandatory in many federal government and defense-related networks.

TECHNICAL SPECIFICATIONS

The layers of the TCP/IP protocol set are IP, TCP, User Datagram Protocol (UDP), Telnet Protocol, and File Transfer Protocol (FTP). Most implementations of TCP/IP also include ARP and the Internet Control Message Protocol (ICMP).

IP, which corresponds to layer three, or the connectionless-mode network layer, of the OSI model, provides datagram service across a network or internetwork. Layer three addresses messages and routes them across a network, provides functions and procedures to exchange data between two systems independent of routing and switching considerations, and furnishes service independent of the transfer technology.

TCP corresponds to OSI layer four, the connection-oriented transport protocol. Layer four sequences messages into a transaction, controls data transfer with an end-to-end service and optimizes the use of available network service. UDP, another OSI layer-four protocol, is used for remote network-management and name-service-access applications. Name-service-access allows users to assign a name, such as "VAX," to a physical, or numeric, address.

The Telnet Protocol corresponds roughly to OSI layers five and six—the Session and Presentation layers—of the OSI model. Layer five establishes communicatins, or sessions, that manage and synchronize data exchange between entities and provide mechanisms to structure the communication. These mechanisms also map user-oriented session addresses to network-oriented transport addresses. The TCP/IP application protocol for interfacing to terminals, Telnet supports virtual circuits between terminals and host computers.

FTP, which corresponds roughly to OSI layers six and seven—Presentation and Application—allows file transfer between dissimilar machines or operating systems. Layer six determines data forms and data representation, and layer seven performs applications and provides semantics specific to application programs and functions. Such applications include electronic mail and filing.

ARP, which is required for use with Ethernet, maps IP addresses to Ethernet addresses, and ICMP includes a set of functions for network-layer management and control.

Users in the Unix environment have adopted two other simple protocols that are not Defense Department standards: rlogin and rcopy. Users sometimes employ rlogin as an alternative to Telnet for remotely logging into one Unix system from a terminal attached to another UNIX system. However, rlogin does not include all Telnet features, such as parameter negotiation. The other non-standard protocol, rcopy, is used to move files between Unix hosts.

These layers are fully compatible across all TCP/IP implementations. This means that Ethernet/IEEE 802.3-compatible devices running TCP/IP not only can coexist on the same cable, sharing the physical medium, but also can communicate with each other across that medium. Outside the LAN arena, users can find a comparable level of compatibility only in such mainframe protocols as IBM's Systems Network Architecture.

Source: *Mini-Micro Systems*

TOKEN RING

The ring topology with token-access control, while difficult to implement, offers advantages of flexibility and reliability over CSMA/CD networks.

In CSMA/CD networks, if 2 workstations or nodes on the network attempt to transmit at the same time, there is a "collision" on the network and both nodes wait and retransmit at different intervals. On this type of network, all the nodes in use are contending for time on the network although, unless the network is very heavily used, the actual amount of time spent "waiting" is not noticeable to the users.

On the token ring, data flows unidirectionally around the ring, with access to the network controlled by the token. The control scheme for regulating data flow in a ring topology is generally based on the idea that permission to use the communications link is passed sequentially from node to node around the ring. With the token access control scheme, the token circulates on the ring, giving each node in turn an opportunity to transmit data when it receives the token.

A node having data to transmit can seize the token, change the status to "frame" and begin transmitting data. The node that initiates a data transfer must remove that data from the ring and issue a token upon receiving the data, allowing other nodes an opportunity to transmit. A logical peer-to-peer communication link exists in which any node can send data to any other node.

As exemplified by the IBM Token-Ring Network, the network intelligence is implemented in the network adapters, which reside in each device attached to the network and which also provide all the network management and diagnostic capabilities.

In addition to the basic access control functions, one ring interface adapter on each ring acts as an active token monitor to perform error recovery if normal token behavior is disrupted. Other ring adapters on the ring act as passive monitors and are prepared to take over the functions of the active monitor should it be removed from the ring. The ring interface adapter also regenerates the encoded electrical signals, thus extending the reach of the network.

Source: *Outlook on IBM*

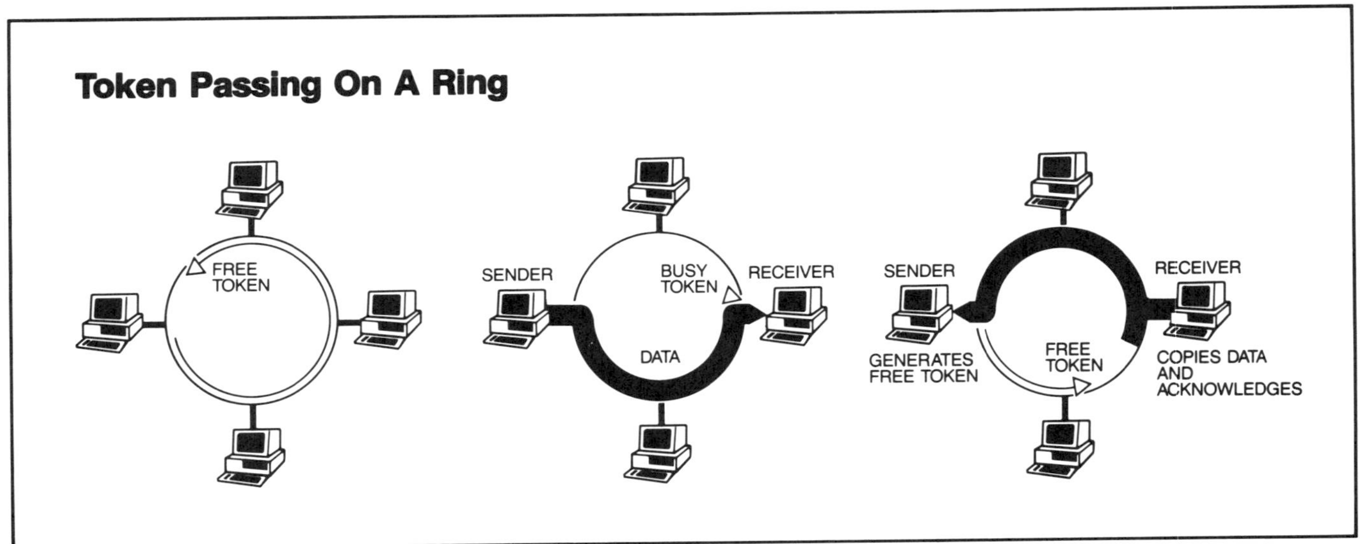

Figure 40

Courtesy IBM Corporation

TOP

TOP (Technical and Office Protocols) is a specification built on national and international standards used to specify functional networks for distributed information processing in technical and business office environments.

HISTORY

The Boeing Company realized the need for networking standards in the late 1970s. Work was begun to develop an architecture for future networks in the company in 1976. The architecture would provide a framework for network planners and designers to use in their work. The initial architecture statements provided standards for data communications between the company's mainframes, minis and micros. The long-term direction stated by the architecture was to use the ISO Open System Interconnection model and protocols; migrate all proprietary networks to OSI networks; and, most recently adopt MAP as a standard for factory floor communications.

GOAL

The goal and intent of TOP is to establish a specification for data communications and information exchange in multi-vendor technical and office networks. TOP is designed to provide a general, nonproprietary solution to the multi-vendor networking problem and to hasten the development and acceptance of international standards and conforming products.

Source: The Boeing Company

TOP OSI LAYER ARCHITECTURE

TOP network architecture, like its Manufacturing Automation Protocol (MAP) counterpart, is based on the ISO Open System Interconnection Model for data communication networks.

TOP and MAP area intended to use the same base suite of protocols. These common protocols of the initial TOP Specification are:

- Layer 7—ISO File Transfer, Access and Management

- Layer 5—ISO Session

- Layer 4—ISO Transport

- Layer 3—ISO Connectionless Internet

- Layer 2—IEEE 802.2 Logical Link Control (LLC)

The only areas in whih TOP and MAP initally differ are:

- Layer 7—Manufacturing Messaging Format Standard (MMFS) (Not required by TOP at this time)

- Layer 7—Common Application Service Elements (CASE) (Not defined for TOP at this time)

- Layer 7—Network management and directory services (Not defined for TOP at this time)

- Layer 1—IEEE 802.3 CSMA/CD Media Access Control (MAC)

The commonality of the implementation of TOP and MAP allows interconnection between TOP and MAP networks.

XEROX NETWORK SYSTEMS ARCHITECTURE (XNS)

The principles underlying Xerox Network Systems Architecture are:

- To distribute computing elements throughout an organization according to need without centralized computer control;

- To provide fast communication links for the users and providers of information;

- To implement national and international standards to allow easy interconnection of XNS systems with other networks and systems built on other architectures.

XNS LAYERS

The XNS architecture groups some the the ISO model functions into fewer layers for convenience. Each XNS layer corresponds functionally to the ISO layers. Even when the functions are grouped, as in the case of Ethernet, a separation is maintained between the physical and data link layers to allow different physical media to be used with the same Ethernet data link protocol. The XNS architecture is particularly open-ended in respect to multiple transmission protocols corresponding to different types of communication services, and to multiple application protocols corresponding to different functions performed within the architectural boundaries.

As in the ISO model, the XNS bottom layer provides for physical transmission interfaces. The functions provided by the XNS architecture rise in hierarchical order—through communication control (Internet) and remote procedures (Courier)—to the application layer. Although the lower layers are important, the full functional richness of XNS is revealed by an examination of the application layer. This layer provides a great variety of important office and computing functions to XNS users.

PHYSICAL INTERFACES

At the lowest layer, Ethernet provides its own unique physical interface. It is unlike traditional data communication physical interfaces (RS-232C, RS-449, X.21), which, strictly speaking, are part of XNS by adoption rather than by special design.

DATA LINK PROTOCOLS

At the next lowest layer, the CCITT X.25 Virtual Circuit Protocol is part of XNS by adoption. It is used as part of XNS utilization of packet-switching data networks.

INTERNET TRANSPORT PROTOCOLS

Internet is shown as a set of protocols corresponding to ISO Model layers 3 and 4. The word "internet" is also used to refer to the set of all interconnected Ethernets in different locations, a relationship implemented by these protocols.

COURIER

XNS implements the session and presentation layers in Courier, the XNS protocol for remote procedure calls [requests].

APPLICATION PROTOCOLS

At the application layer (ISO Model layer 7) the Application Support Environment provides support resources called on by users and/or the application protocols shown immediately above. These protocols—mailing, printing, filing, and gateway access—are implemented in hardware/software to provide the XNS application services.

Source: Xerox Corporation

DOCUMENT FORMATS

Within the application layer, the standards for the format or language for the encoding of document form or content are labeled with italic type. In many respects, the utility of XNS depends as much on the innovative approach to document descriptions as it does on the actual protocols. The document encoding techniques referred to in the illustration—particularly Interscript and Interpress—make it possible for XNS documents to be edited, printed or communicated anywhere on the system. Other encoding standards are the Character Code Standard for representing text in many languages, and the Raster Encoding Standard for representing compressed and uncompressed bitmap images.

INTEGRATION AND COMPATIBILITY

The internal structure of XNS enables effective integration between individual hardware and software elements within XNS-compatible products. Techniques are also provided within XNS for bi-directional protocol and format conversion, permitting other systems to achieve integration with XNS.

STANDARDS GROUPS

THE AMERICAN NATIONAL STANDARDS INSTITUTE

1430 Broadway
New York, NY 10018
(212)354-3300

The American National Standards Institute is a privately funded, nonprofit organization founded in 1918 by five professional/technical societies and three federal government agencies to coordinate the development of voluntary standards in the United States and to approve standards as national consensus standards.

ANSI is the U.S. dues-paying member of the International Organization for Standardization (ISO) and the International Electrotechnical Commission (IEC). The institute is currently responsible for the secretariats of 83 ISO and 31 IEC technical committees and subcommittees.

In addition to these international responsibilities, ANSI provides interface with and advice to departments and agencies of the U.S. government at all levels on standards-related issues, coordinates and harmonizes private sector standards activity and encourages due process in domestic standards development.

COMPUTER AND BUSINESS EQUIPMENT MANUFACTURERS ASSOCIATION (CBEMA)

311 1st Street NW
Washington, DC 20001
(201)737-8888

CBEMA serves as the secretariat for ANSI's X3 Committee on Information Processing Systems, providing administrative support for the committee and housing the semi-autonomous group in its offices. X3's technical subcommittees and task groups assess the need for and develop standards for information processing and data communications systems. Upon reaching a consensus, the committee submits a proposed standard to ANSI for approval.

X3 reviews existing standards at five-year intervals, at which time it reaffirms, revises or withdraws them.

THE INSTITUTE OF ELECTRICAL AND ELECTRONICS ENGINEERS INC.

345 East 47th Street
New York, NY 10017-2394
(212)705-7900

The Institute of Electrical and Electronics Engineers Inc. is the world's largest professional engineering society. Founded in 1884, its purposes are directed toward the advancement of the theory and practice of electrical engineering, electronics, computer engineering, and computer sciences and the allied branches of engineering and the related arts and sciences. In addition, the IEEE strives for the advancement of the standing of the members of the professions it serves.

In 1980, the IEEE 802 Project was initiated to further the development of local area networking standards. The resultingstandards deal with the physical and data link layers as defined by the International Organization for Standardization (ISO) Open System Interconnection Reference Model. Three of the standards have been approved by the ANSI as American National Standards and are currently classified as drafts for International Standards by the ISO.

INTERNATIONAL ELECTROTECHNICAL COMMISSION (IEC)

1 rue de Varembe
1211 Geneva 20
Switzerland
(022)34-01-50

IEC attempts to facilitate and coordinate the unification of international electrotechnical standards. The commission serves as the electrical division of the International Organization for Standardization (ISO).

THE INTERNATIONAL ORGANIZATION FOR STANDARDIZATION

1 rue de Varembe
Geneva, Switzerland
(022)34-12-40 The International Organization for Standardization was founded in 1946 "to promote the development of standardization and related activities in the world with a view to facilitating international exchange of goods and services and to developing cooperation in the sphere of intellectual, scientific, technological and economic activity." (Article 2, ISO Constitution)

As the largest international organization for industrial and technical collaboration, the ISO membership comprises the national standards bodies of 90 countries including the U.S. representative, the American National Standards Institute. According to its constitution, the ISO may:

• take action to facilitate the coordination and unification of national standards;

• develop and issue International Standards and take action for their worldwide implementation;

• arrange for exchange of information regarding work of its member bodies and of its technical committees;

• cooperate with other international organizations interested in related matters, particularly by undertaking at their request studies relating to standardization projects.

The ISO structure includes 163 technical committees, each engaged in the preparation and review of International Standards in a specific technical field. Work on local area networks is in progress in two subcommittees of technical committee ISO/TC 97, Information processing systems—SC 6: Telecommunications and information exchange between systems, and SC 21: Information retrieval, transfer and management for Open System Interconnection (OSI).

So far, no International Standards for local area networking have been published, but the following drafts are being prepared ISO/TC 97 for eventual publication as International Standards, subject to approval by the ISO Council:

• DP 8802/1   Local area networks, Part 1: General introduction

• DIS 8802/2   Information processing systems, local area networks, Part 2: Logical link control

• DIS 8802/3   Information processing systems, local area networks, Part 3: Carrier sense multiple access with collision detection

• DIS 8802/4   Information processing systems, lcal area networks, Part 4: Token-passing bus access method and physical layer specifications

• DP 8802/5   Information processing systems, local area networks, Part 5: Token-ring access method and physical layer specification

• DP 8802/6   Information processing systems, local area networks, Part 6: Slotted ring access method and physical layer specification.

NATIONAL BUREAU OF STANDARDS (NBS)

Gaithersburg, MD 20899
(301)921-1000

The National Bureau of Standards set U.S. measurement standards. The bureau's overall goal is to strengthen and advance domestic science and technology and facilitate their effective application for public benefit.

The bureau, in effect, has a dual role in the field of computer science and data networking, providing standards both for the federal procurement program, in the form of Federal Information Processing Standards, and for the private sector by encouraging the development and acceptance of voluntary standards in the economy at large. In both cases, the National Bureau of Standards maintains an active program of research, publications and seminars.

NATIONAL COMMITTEE OF THE UNITED STATES ORGANIZATION FOR THE INTERNATIONAL TELEGRAPH AND TELEPHONE CONSULTATIVE COMMITTEE (CCITT)

Office of International Communications Policy
Department of State

Washington, DC 20520
(202)632-1007

The committee, composed of representatives from both the public and private sectors, is responsible for U.S. participation in the activities of the CCITT.

Glossary

A

access method—In a data processing system, any of the techniques available to the user for moving data between main storage and an input/output device or channel. The techniques are usually part of the operating system.

ACK—See acknowledge character.

acknowledge character (ACK)—1. A transmission control character transmitted by a station as an affirmative response to the station with which the connection has been made 2. A transmission control character transmitted by a receiver as an affirmative response to a sender. An acknowledge character also may be used as an accuracy control character.

active line—A communication line that is available for transmission of data.

A/D—Analog to digital signal conversion.

address—1. A coded representation of the origin or destination of data. 2. Symbolic reference to the memory location used for data storage.

Advanced Communications Function—A set of IBM program built on SNA concepts to allow resource sharing and to distribute network control through an SNA network.

ALOHA—An experimental data communications network, developed at the University of Hawaii, that uses radio communications channels as the means of transmitting data packets.

alphanumeric character set—A character set that contains both letters and digits and may include control characters, special characters and the space character.

AM—See amplitude modulation.

American Natonal Standards Institute (ANSI)—The coordinating organization for voluntary standards in the United States.

American Standard Code for Information Interchange (ASCII)—The standard code, using a coded character set consisting of 7-bit coded characters (8-bits including parity check), used for information interchange among data processing systems, data communications systems and associated equipment. The ASCII set consists of control characters and graphic characters.

amplifier—A device that increases the power of an electrical signal.

amplitude modulation (AM)—A way of modifying a sine wave carrier signal to convey information by modifying the amplitude in accordance with the information.

analog—1. Pertaining to representation by means of continuously variable physical quantities. 2. Compare with digital.

analog transmission—Transmission of a continuously variable signal as opposed to a digital signal.

ANSI—See American National Standards Institute.

application layer—The top layer of the Open System Interconnection (OSI) Reference Model. This is where the user's work is done. When a person is using a terminal, the person performs all the functions of the application layer.

Arpanet—A project of the (U.S. Department of Defense) Advanced Research Projects Agency (ARPA), which developed many of the concepts of packet switching. Arpanet is the progenitor of most public data networks, except Tymnet, which was contemporary.

ASCII—See American Standard Code for Information Interchange.

asynchronous data transmission—A mode of data transmission wherein the occurrence of each character is not related to a fixed time frame of reference, but in which the bits of each character are transmitted synchronously. See start-stop transmission; compare with synchronous transmission.

automatic answering—A facility whereby the terminal installation which is called automatically responds to the incoming call, thereby establishing a data circuit.

B

backend network—A local area network that connects computers' I/O subsystems to shared storage devices. Also may be used for high data rate inter-computer data transfer. Compare with front-end network.

band—The frequency spectrum between two defined limits, especially those delimiting a channel.

bandwidth—1. The difference, expressed in hertz, between the two limiting frequencies of a band. 2. The information capacity of a channel.

baseband—With reference to a LAN, the system whereby digitally encoded information is directly connected to the transmission medium without being modulated. Compare with broadband.

baud—A unit of modulation rate; a unit of signaling speed. One baud corresponds to a rate of one unit-time interval per second. The speed in bauds is equal to the number of times the line condition changes per second. Thus, the signaling speed in bauds is equal to the number of discrete conditions or signaling events per second. Usually a code element or character occurs in the given unit time interval. If the duration of the unit interval is 20 milliseconds, then the modulation rate is 50 bauds.

BCD—See binary-coded decimal notation.

BEL—See bell character.

bell character (BEL)—A control character that is used when there is a need to call for human attention and to activate the alarm or other attention devices.

binary-coded decimal notation (BCD)—A binary-coded notation in which each of the decimal digits is represented by a binary numeral; e.g., in binary-coded decimal notation that uses the weights 8-4-2-1, the number "twenty-three" is represented by 0010 0011 (compare its representation with 1011 in the pure binary number system).

binary digit—See bit.

binary exponential backoff—An algorithm used by LANs to reschedule transmissions after a collision. Delay between successive attempts is, on the average, twice the previous delay.

bisync (BSC)—A family of IBM character-oriented binary synchronous communications protocols.

bit—Contraction of binary digit, the smallest unit of information in the binary number system. Made up of the digits 0 or 1.

bit stream—A binary signal without regard to grouping by character.

bit transfer rate—The number of bits transferred per unit of time, usually expressed in bits per second (bps).

BIU—See bus interface unit.

bridge—A LAN active device that permits a communication between logically or physically separate networks. See also gateway.

broadband—A LAN frequency-division multiplexing scheme which commonly employs CATV technology to provide digital and analog signals (e.g., video) on the same distribution medium. Compare with baseband.

broadcast transmission—Message transmission which may be read by a large number of destinations rather than just one.

BSC—See bisync.

buffer—1. A routine or storage used to compensate for a difference in flow rate of data, or time of occurrence of events, when transferring data from one device to another. 2. An isolating circuit used to prevent a driven circuit from influencing the driving circuit. 3. To allocate and schedule the user of buffers.

burst—In data communications, a sequence of signals counted as one unit in accordance with some specific criterion or measure.

bus—One or more conductors used for transmitting signals or power. In a LAN, a bus usually is in a broadcast transmission mode.

bus interface unit (BIU)—The data-circuit terminating equipment which provides access to a LAN. It may also provide packet assembly/disassembly functions.

bus topology—A network structure in which all stations are connected to a linear cable serving as the transmission medium.

byte—A binary string operated as a unit. The byte usually is shorter than a computer word and often is used to represent a character. Byte is used colloquially to refer to eight bits.

C

cable—One or more conductors within a protective sheath. See also coaxial cable, twisted pair cable.

call—In data communications, the action performed by the calling party, the operations necessary in making a call or the effective use made of a connection between two stations.

carriage return character (CR)—A format effect that causes the print or display position to move to the first position on the same line.

carrier—A continuous frequency capable of being modulated by an information carrying signal.

carrier sense multiple access (CSMA)—A contention algorithm for a bus LAN whereby a station wishing to transmit determines first whether another transmission is in progress by sensing if a carrier is present. Collision detection also is emloyed commonly. Compare with multilevel multiple access, token passing.

carrier system—A means of obtaining a number of channels over a single path by modulating each channel on a different carrier frequency and demodulating at the receiving point to restore the signals to their original form.

cathode ray tube (CRT)—An electronic device that can be used to display graphic images and which is commonly used in data processing. See also video display terminal.

CATV—Cable television (previously community antenna television) technology, commonly employed by broadband LANs for signal distribution.

CBMS—see computer-based message system.

CBX—Computer PBX. See digital PBX.

CCITT (Consultative Committee on International Telegraph and Telephone)—A component division of the International Telecommunications Union (ITU) that attempts to establish international telecommunications standards by issuing recommendations which express, as closely as possible, an international consensus.

central office (CO)—Telephone company location connected to customer by a trunk circuit.

central processing unit (CPU)—The "brain" of a omputer, containing the computer's logic, switching and control capability.

channel—1. A path along which signals can be sent. 2. The portion of a storage medium accessible to a given reading or writing station, e.g., track, band. 3. In information theory, the part of a communications system that connects the message source with the message sink. 4. In data communications, a means of one-way transmission. 5. Compare with data circuit.

character—1. Any letter, digit, diacritic, punctuation mark, or special mark used to represent data in printed matter. 2. The combination of bits used to represent printing or non-printing characters. 3. See also byte.

character fill—1. To insert, as often as necessary, into a storage medium the representation of a specified character that does not itself convey data but may delete unwanted data. 2. See also zerofill.

character printer—1. A device that prints a single character at a tme; e.g., a typewriter. 2. Compare with line printer.

character set—1. A finite set of different characters upon which agreement has been reached and that is considered complete for some purpose. 2. See also alphanumeric character set.

chip—A small piece of semiconductor such as silicon, typically .25 inches square, on which an integrated circuit is fabricated.

circuit—See data circuit.

circuit switching—A method of communications whereby an electrical connection between calling and called stations is established on demand for exclusive use of the circuit until the connection is released. See also message switching, packet switching, store-and-forward.

clock—A precisely-timed repetitive signal used to synchronize events, such as digital logic transmission.

CO—See central office.

coaxial cable—A cable consisting of one conductor (usually a small copper tube or wire) surrounded by a shield made of separate, electrically insulated wire.

code—1. A set of unambiguous symbols and rules specifying the way in which data may be represented. 2. In data communications, a system of rules and conventions according to which the signals representing data can be formed, transmitted, received, and processed.

code conversion—The process of translating from one code to another, e.g., EBCDIC to ASCII.

code extension character—1. Any control character used to indicate that one or more of the succeeding coded representations are to be interpreted according to a different code or according to a different coded character set. 2. See also escape character.

code transparent—Pertaining to the capability of transmitting characters regardless of their binary codes, e.g., no distinction is made between control characters and information characters.

Codec: 1—Coder-decoder (analog-to-digital and digital-to-analog converter). Used to convert analog signals, such as speech, for digital transmision.

collision—A simultaneous transmission of data by two or more nodes of a packet communications network, especially a LAN, resulting in destruction of that data.

collision detection—Determination that two stations have transmitted simultaneously by comparing transmitted and received signals in a station which is transmitting.

communications computer—A computer that acts as the interface between another computer or terminal and a network, or a computer controlling data flow in a network. See also concentrator, front end computer.

communications controller—See communications computer, front-end computer.

communications hardware—Electronic or electro-mechanical devices employed for transmission, switching and termination of communications signals. Includes data terminals, modems, acoustic, couplers, PBX equipment, store-and-forward message switching computers, etc.

communications link—See data link.

communications network—A complex of data communications equipment, data links and channels that connect one or more data processing systems.

communications protocol—A strict procedure or interchange convention required to initiate and maintain communications over a communications channel.

compandor—A combination of a compressor at one point in a communications path for reducing the volume range of signals, followed by an expandor at another point for restoring the original volume range. Usually used to improve signal-to-noise ratio in the path.

computer-based message system (CBMS)—A computer communications system wherein character-encoded messages can be accepted from one user's terminal, stored in the memory of a computer system connected to a telecommunications network, transmitted to one or more computers on the network (if necessary) servicing the intended recipient(s) and then delivered to the recipient's terminal(s) on demand.

computer-based office system—An aggregation of automated components, one or more of which contains a processor, that function together for the accomplishment of one or more office work activities.

computer network—A collection of computers connected by a data communications network.

concentration—The function of routing information from a number of communications links into a smaller number of higher capacity links and providing the reverse flow from fewer to more links. A device which performs this function usually is called a concentrator. Unlike the multiplexer, the concentrator is a programmable device.

concentrator—A communications device that provides communications capability between many low-speed, usually asynchronous channels and one or more high-speed, usually synchronous channels. Generally, different speeds, codes and protocols can be accommodated on the low-speed side. The low-speed channels usually operate in contention requiring buffering. The concentrator may have the capability to be polled by a computer and, in turn, poll terminals.

connect time—The length of time during which a terminal is interacting with a computer.

Consultative Committee on International Telegraph and Telephone—See CCITT.

contention—1. A condition arising when two or more data stations attempt to transmit at the same time over a shared channel, or in either-way communications when two data stations attempt to transmit at the same time. 2. Unregulated bidding for a line by multiple users.

control character—1. A character whose occurrence in a particular context initiates, modifies or stops a control operation. A control character may be recorded for use in a subsequent action. A control character is not a graphic character, but may have a graphic representation in some circumstances. 2. See also acknowledge character, bell character, code extension character, format effector, information, transmission control character.

conversational mode—1. A mode of operation of a computer system in which a sequence of alternating entries between a user and the system takes place in a manner similar to a dialogue between two persons. 2. Synonymous with interactive mode.

CPU—See central processing unit.

CR—See carriage return character.

CRC—See cyclic redundancy check character.

CRT—See cathode ray tube.

CSMA—See carrier sense multiple access.

cursor—A movable, visible mark used to indicate a position on a display space.

cyclic redundancy check character (CRC)—A character used in a modified cyclic code for error detection and correction.

D

D/A—Digital to analog signal conversion.

data—1. A representation of facts, concepts or instruction in a formalized manner suitable for communications, interpretation or processing by manual or automatic means. 2. Any representation such as characters or analog quantities to which meaning is or might be assigned. 3. Compare with information.

data circuit—1. In data communications, a means of two-way transmission comprising associated transmit and receive channels. 2. Synonymous with circuit. 3. Compare with channel.

data circuit-terminating equipment (DCE)—The functional unit of a data station that establishes, maintains and releases a connection, and provides those functions necessary for any code or signal conversion between the data terminal equipment and the data transmission line.

data communications—The transmission and reception of data.

data communications network—An integrated combination of various communications facilities (channels and communications services), data circuit-terminating equipment (multiplexers, modems, etc) and data terminal equipment (teleprinters, CRTs, RJEs, etc.) necessary for

the transmission of data between various data input/output points and the host processor.

data concentrator—In data transmission, equipment that permits a common transmission medium to serve more message sources than there are channels currently available within the transmission medium.

data conversion—The changing of data from one form of representation to another, according to specified rules, while preserving the meaning of the data.

data element—The basic unit in information processing and exchange. The data element is the fundamental building block from which all records, files and data bases are structured.

datalink—1. The physical means of connecting one location to another for the purpose of transmitting and receiving data. 2. Synonymous with communications link.

data multiplexing—See multiplexing.

data network—The assembly of functional units that establish data circuits among data terminal equipment. See also data communications network.

data signaling rate—1. In data communications, the data transmission capacity of a set of channels. The data signaling rate is expressed in bauds. 2.CCompare with data transfer rate.

data terminal equipment (DTE)—The equipment that serves as a message source or a message sink and provides for the communication control function; subscriber equipment.

data transfer rate—1. The average number of bits, characters or blocks per unit of time passing between corresponding equipment in a data transmission system. It is expressed in terms of bits, characters or blocks per second, minute or hour. 2. Compare with data signaling rate.

data transmission—The conveying of data from one place for reception elsewhere by signals transmitted over a data circuit.

datagram—A user facility in a packet network in which individual packets are accepted by the network from source terminals and are delivered independently to the destination identified in its address field. The order of delivery bears no fixed relationship to the order of entry into the network.

DCE—See data circuit-terminating equipment.

DECnet—The Digital Equipment Corporation's (DEC) program product implementing distributed processing functions on DEC computers.

dedicated channel—A specific communications channel that has been reserved, committed or set aside for a specific use, application or system.

dedicated circuit—A communications ciruit that has been reserved, committed or allocated for a specific use, application or system.

dedicated connection—1. A mode of operating a data link in which a permanent circuit i established; that is, without the use of the switching facilities of, for example, a public switched network. 2. Compare with switched connection.

demodulation—The process of separating the information signal from the carrier signal.

diameter—The distance between the outermost points on a network.

digital—1. Pertaining to the utilization of discrete integral numbers in a given base to represent all the quantities that occur in a problem or a calculation. It is possible to express in digital form all information stored, transferred or processed by a dual-state condition; e.g., on-off, open-closed and true-false. 2. Compare with analog.

digital interface unit (DIU)—The equipment that permits data terminal equipment to connect to a public data network. Many of its functions are similar to those of a modem.

digital PBX (DPBX)—A PBX (see private branch exchange) designed to switch digital signals. Telephones used with a DPBX must digitize the voice signals. Computers and terminals can communicate directly through the DPBX, which functions as a point-to-point local area network. See also CBX.

directory—1. A table that provides a mapping of logical addresses (names of sharable objects) to physical addresses (object locations at the processor). 2. A list of network subscribers; names, addresses and other information.

distributed network—A network in which all node pairs are connected, either directly or through redundant paths through intermediate nodes.

distributed processing—1. A decentralized alternative to the large-scale computer installation whereby data processing services are provided to multiple users via the direct installation of communicating computers at various user locations. 2. A technique for implementing one logically related set of information processing functions within multiple geographically or logically separated physical devices.

DIU—See digital interface unit.

domain—The geographic scope of a network.

DPBX—See digital PBX.

DTE—See data terminal equipment.

duplex transmission—1. Data transmission over a circuit capable of transmitting in both directions at the same time. 2. Synonymous with full duplex transmission.

E

EBCDIC—See Extended Binary-Coded Decimal Interchange Code.

echo check—A method of checking the accuracy of data transmission in which the received data are returned to the sending end for comparison with the original data.

effective data transfer rate—The average number of bits, characters or blocks per unit of time transferred from a message source and accepted as valid by a message sink. It is expressed in bits, characters or blocks per second, minute or hour.

EIA—See Electronic Industries Association.

Electronic Industries Association (EIA)—A U.S. manufacturers' group which, as one of its functions, sets some interface standards.

electronic mail—A paperless method of storing messages and communicating over a computer system.

encryption—The conversion of plain text into an unintelligible form from which the original meaning can be recovered.

end user—The source and/or destination of information sent through the data communications system.

endpoint—The logical or physical entity at the end of a branch of a network. Endpoints include application processes, terminals and people at terminals.

error burst—In data communications, a sequence of signals containing one or more errors but counted only as one unit in accordance with some specific criterion or measure. An example of a criterion is that if three consecutive correct bits follow an erroneous bit, then an error burst is terminated.

error control—The part of a protocol controlling the detection, and possibly the correction, of errors.

error correcting code—A code in which each acceptable expression conforms to specific rules of construction that also define one or more equivalent unacceptable expressions, so that if certain errors occur in an acceptable expression the result will be one of its equivalents and thus the error can be corrected.

error detecting code—A code in which each expression conforms to specific rules of construction, so that if certain errors occur in an expression the resulting expression will not conform to the rules of construction and thus the presence of the errors is detected.

ESC—See escape character.

escape character (ESC)—A code extension character used, in some cases with one or more succeeding characters, to indicate by some convention or agreement that the coded representations following the character or group of characters are to be interpreted according to a different code or character code set.

Ether—The medium over which classical physicists believed radio waves traveled. It is from this reference that Ethernet derives its name.

Ethernet—1. In a local computer network, a branching broadcast communications system for carrying digital data packets among locally distributed computing stations. 2. A low-level, baseband, local-area data communications network developed by Xerox and supported by DEC and Intel, among others.

Extended Binary-Coded Decimal Interchange Code (EBCDIC)—A set of 256 characters, each represented by eight bits. Used extensively by IBM.

F

FDM—Frequency-division multiplexing. See multiplexing.

FE—See format effector.

Federal Information Processing Standards (FIPS)—ADP standards issued by the National Bureau of Standards; mandatory for federal agencies.

FF—See form feed character.

fiber optics—The technology for guidance of optical power, including rays and wave guide modes of electromagnetic waves along conductors of electromagnetic waves in the visible and near-visible region of the frequency spectrum, specifically when the optical energy is guided to another location through thin transparent strands. An alternative medium for data communications.

file—A collection of logically related records, usually of the same type. A named increment of storage or an unstructured or user-structured form of data storage.

file server—A storage subsystem shared by multiple workstations on a LAN.

file transfer protocol (FTP)—An application layer protocol for transferring files among hosts connected to a computer network. Transfer among heterogeneous operating systems usually supports only stream unstructured character data.

FIPS—See Federal Information Processing Standards.

firmware—1. Software stored in a fixed way, usually in read-only memory. 2. A consolidation of hardware and software.

flag—1. An indicator used for identification, e.g., a word mark. 2. A character that signals the occurrence of some condition, such as the end of a word. 3. In bit-oriented protocols, an indicator used to identify the start of a frame.

flow control—The procedure for controlling the rate of packet transfer between two specific points in a data network; for example, between a CTE and a data switching exchange.

FM—See frequency modulation.

form feed character (FF)—A format effector that causes the print or display position to move to the next predetermined first line on the next form, the next page or the equivalent.

format effector (FE)—1. Any control character used to control the positioning of printed, displayed or recorded data. 2. See also carriage return character, form feed character, line feed character.

four-wire circuit—1. A two-way communications circuit using two paths, arranged such that signals may be transmitted in one direction only on one path and in the other direction on the other path. The transmission cable may or may not employ four wires, for the same ground wire may serve both directions. 2. Compare with two-wire circuit.

frame—In bit-oriented protocols, the vehicle for every command, each response and all information that is transmitted. Each frame begins and ends with a flag.

frequency-division multiplexing (FDM)—See multiplexing.

frequency modulation (FM)—A method of modifying a sine wave signal to carry information by modifying the frequency according to the information being transmitted.

frequency translation—Changing the carrier frequency. Used in a LAN to differentiate inbound and outbound signals. See also midsplit, sub-slit.

front-end computer—A communications computer associated with a host computer. It may perform line control, message handling, code conversion, error control, and applications functions such as control and operation of special purpose terminals. See also communications computer.

front-end network—A network, often a LAN, connected to a front-end computer or a computer's communications ports.

FTP—See file transfer protocol.

full duplex transmission—See duplex transmision.

fully connected network—A network system in which every node in the network is directly connected to every other node.

G

gateway—A node common to two or more networks through which data flows from network to network. The gateway may reformat the data as necessary and also may participate in error and flow control protocols. Used to connect LANs employing different protocols and to connect LANs to public data networks. See also port.

H

half-duplex transmission—Data transmission over a circuit capable of transmitting in either direction, one direction at a time.

handshaking—Exchange of predetermined signals when a connection is established between two data set devices.

HDLC—See High-Level Data Link Control.

headend—The point in a LAN where the inbound signals are transferred into outbound signals. The headend may be passive or contain an amplifier or frequency translation equipment.

hertz—A unit of signal frequency equal one to cycle per second. Abbreviated Hz.

High-Level Data Link Control (HDLC)—The protocol defined by ISO in 1976 for bit-oriented, frame-delimited data communications.

hit—A transient disturbance to a communications medium.

host computer—1. A computer attached to a network providing primarily services such as computation, database access or special programs or programming languages. 2. An information processor which provides supporting services and/or guidance to users and/or satellite processors, terminals and other subsidiary devices. A host processor generally is assumed to be self-sufficient and to require no supervision from other processors. 3. Compare with communications computer.

hybrid local network—1. A local network into which two or more types of local networks are integrated. 2. A local network engaging two or more components representing different applications or different vendors.

I

I/O—See input/output.

identifier—A character or group of characters used to identify or name an item of data and possibly to indicate certain properties of that data.

idle character—A transmission control character used to maintain synchronization between data terminal devices.

idle time—Time during which a functional unit is not operated.

IEEE—Institute of Electrical and Electronics Engineers.

IEEE Project 802—An IEEE standards development project concerned with LANs.

IMP (interface message processor)—In Arpanet, the communications computer through which hosts connect to the data communications network.

information—1. The meaning individuals assign to data by means of the known conventions used in their representation. 2. Compare with data.

information bits—In telecommunications, those bits generated by the data source and not used for error control or other control purposes by the data transmission system.

information network—Geographically dispersed resource centers, including information processors and terminals, which are interconnected using data communications facilities.

information separator—Any control character used to delimit like units of data in a hierarchical arrangement. The name of the separator does not necessarily indicate the units of data that it separates.

information transfer—The capability to transport information electronically (e.g., document image mail, character-encoded mail and speech mail) between specifed individuals.

infrared—The frequency range that falls above that of microwave and below the red end of the visible spectrum.

input—Information entered into a machine, usually prior to processing.

input/output (I/O)—The machine or device used to insert information, data or instructions into a computing system or the medium or device used to transfer information or data, usually processed data, from a computing system to the 'outside' world. Input/output also can refer to the act of entering or retrieving information.

inquiry station—A user terminal primarily for the interrogation of a data processing system.

Integrated Services Digital Network (ISDN)—An integrated digital network in which the same digital switches and digital paths are used to establish connections for different services; for example, telephony, data, etc.

intelligent terminals—A terminal which contains an integral microprocessor with some logical capability.

interactive mode—See conversational mode.

interface—1. A shared boundary defined by common physical interconnection characteristics, signal characteristics and meanings of interchanged signals. 2. A device or equipment making interoperation of two systems possible; for example, a hardware component or common storage register. 3. A shared logical boundary between two software components.

interface message processor—See IMP.

International Organization for Standardization (ISO)—An association of the standards organizations of the member nations.

Internet Protocol (IP)—A protocol developed by the U.S. Department of Defense to support data communications among networks.

internetworking—The connection of two or more networks, allowing communication among devices across multiple networks.

IP—See Internet Protocol.

ISDN—See Integrated Services Digital Network.

ISO—See International Organization for Standardization.

L

LAN—See local area network.

LAP—See Link Access Protocol.

LAP-B—See Link Access Protocol-Balanced.

LF—See line feed character.

line—The portion of a data circuit external to the data circuit-terminating equipment (DCE) that connects it to an exchange, other DCEs or connects two exchanges.

line feed character (LF)—A format effector that causes the print or display to move to the corresponding position on the next line.

line printer—A high-speed device that prints a complete line of characters almost simultaneously. Compare with character printer.

line switching—See circuit switching.

link—The interconnection of two nodes in a network. A link may consist of a data communications circuit or a direct channel (cable) connection.

Link Access Protocol (LAP)—An unbalanced subset of HDLC specified in X.25, which requires that the communications line have a single control point.

Link Access Protocol-Balanced (LAP-B)—An alternative to LAP in X.5 which specifies that the communications link does not have a single controller so that either connected station may control the state of the link.

Listen Before Talk—See carrier sense multiple access (CSMA).

Listen While Talk—Carrier sense multiple access with collision detection (CSMA/CD).

local—In data communications, pertaining to devices that are attached to a controlling unit by cables, rather than by data links.

local area network (LAN)—A communications system whose dimensions typically are less than five kilometers. Transmissions within a local area network generally are digital, carrying data among stations at rates usually above one megabit per second.

logical channel—In packet mode operation, a means of two-way simultaneous transmission across a data link, comprising associated send and receive channels. loop—In data communications, an electrical path connecting a station and a channel.

loopback test—A test in which signals are looped from a test center through a data set or loopback switch and back to the test center for measurement.

M

Manchester Encoding—A means by which separate data and clock signals can be combined into a single, self-synchronizing data stream. Each bit cell contains a midpoint transaction. The first half is the complement of the bit value; the second half is the true bit value. Used by Ethernet and other LANs.

message—A collection of data to be moved as a logical entity within an information network.

message interchange format—A standard format definition that permits messages to be exchanged between separate automated systems.

message processing—The act or function of dealing with incoming messages (e.g., reading, deleting, filing, forwarding, replying).

message processing directives—A command sequence entered by an operator to control message processing operations.

message switching—1. The process of routing messages by receiving, storing and forwarding complete messages within a data network. 2. Computer controlled transfer of messages from a terminal to other terminals.

metropolitan area network—An extended LAN serving a city.

microwave—Electromagnetic waves sufficiently short to fall below the infrared frequency range.

midsplit—Frequency translation that divides the band into two equal parts.

MLMA—See multilevel multiple access.

modem—A device that modulates and demodulates signals transmitted over data communications facilities, providing an interface between a terminal or a processor and the data communications facilities.

modulation—1. The process by which some characteristics of one wave are varied in accordance with another wave or signal. This technique is used in data sets and modems to make business machine signals compatible with communications facilities. 2. Compare with demodulation.

multidrop—A communications system configuration using a single channel or line to serve two or more terminals. This type of configuration normally requires some protocol control mechanism, addressing each terminal with a unique identification. See also contention, multipoint connection, polling.

multilevel multiple access (MLMA)—A reservation scheme for LAN transmission.

multiplexing—1. The division of a transmission facility into two or more channels either by splitting the frequency band transmitted by the channel into narrower bands, each of which is used to constitute a distinct channel (frequency-division multiplexing), or by allotting this common channel to several different information channels, one at a time (time-division multiplexing). 2. The support on a single physical link of two or more logical links. A device which performs this function is usually called a multiplexer. Unlike a concentrator, a multiplexer is not programmable.

multipoint connection—1. A connection established among three or more data stations. The connection may include switching facilities. 2. See also multidrop, point-to-point connection.

N

NCP—See network control program.

network—See data network.

network architecture—A formalized definition of the structures, interaction and protocols of a computer network.

network control program (NCP)—1. The program providing an interface between a host computer and a data communications network. 2. In Arpanet, the NCP originally was implemented as a major modification to the host operating system. Subsequently, some NCPs were implemented in a front-end computer. 3. In IBM's Systems Network Architecture (SNA), the network-specific program residing in the front end.

network interface unit (NIU)—A collective term defining all the circuitry used to interface a terminal to a network.

network processor—A computer devoted to the control of data communications facilities, performing functions such as routing, switching, concentration, line/terminal control, and host interfaces.

NIU—See network interface unit.

node—1. A well-defined volume of space. Two nodes have no points in common. 2. An endpoint of any branch of a network, or a junction common to two or more branches of a network. 3. In a data network, a point where one or more functional units interconnect data transmission lines. 4. Distributed system nodes include information processors, network processors, terminal controllers, and terminals.

noise—Any unwanted interference or random disturbance that negatively affects the clarity of transmission over a communications system.

O

OEM—See original equipment manufacturer.

office automation—A concept of automation in an office environment using systems that transform ideas into written communications via the interaction of people, procedures and equipment (e.g., data processing, word processing, telecommunications).

open architecture—A network structure in which network hardware and software are based on industry standards, thus allowing for multi-vendor compatibility.

Open System Interconnection (OSI) Reference Model—A seven-layer model developed by the International Organization for Standardization as a framework for building computer networks supporting distributed processing.

original equipment manufacturer (OEM)—A manufacturer who buys equipment from other suppliers and integrates it into a single system for resale. Note that the correct meaning of this term is contrary to the meaning one would infer logically.

OSI—See Open System Interconnection Reference Model.

out-of-band signaling—1. A method of signaling that uses a frequency outside of that normally used for voice transmission. 2. A control signal independent of the data transmission.

output—Information retrieved from a machine, usually after some processing.

P

PABX—Private automatic branch exchange. See private branch exchange.

packet—A group of binary digits, including data and call control signals, switched as a composite whole. The data, all control signals and possible error control information, are arranged in a specific format.

packet assembler/disassembler (PAD)—A communications computer defined by the CCITT as the interface between asynchronous terminals and a packet switching network. A PAD is one way of implementing a virtual terminal protocol. See also X.29.

packet switching—1. A mode of data transmission in which messages are broken into smaller increments called packets, each of which is routed independently to the destination. 2. The process of routing and transferring data by means of addressed packets, whereby a channel is occupied during the transmission of the packet only; the channel is then available for the transfer of other packets. 3. See also circuit switching.

packet switching network—A data communications network employing packet switching. It can be a local area network or a wide area network. See also public data network.

PAD—See packet assembler/disassembler.

parallel transmission—1. In data communications, the simultaneous transmission of a certain number of signal elements constituting the same telegraph or data signal. For example, use of a code according to which each signal is characterized by a combination of three out of twelve frequencies transmitted simultaneously over the channel. 2. Compare with serial transmission.

parity check—A redundancy check for error detection that tests whether the number of either of the binary characters, e.g., one or zero, on an array is odd or even, according to a given convention.

password—Character string used to identify a (remote) computer user. Passwords may be required for access to various system resources.

path—In a data network, a route between any two nodes.

PBX—See private branch exchange.

PCM—See pulse code modulation.

peer protocol—In a layered architecture, a protocol for interaction between corresponding layers. See also Open System Interconnection Reference Model, protocol, network architecture.

phase modulation—A way to make a sine wave carry information by changing its phase in accordance with the information. To avoid ambiguity, bits are signaled by changes in phase.

point-to-point connection—1. In data communications, a connection established between only two datasstations for data transmission. The connection may include switching facilities. 2. See also multipoint connection.

polling—1. Interrogation of devices to avoid contention, determine operational status or determine readiness to send or receive data. 2. In data communications, the process of inviting data stations to transmit, one at a time.

port—1. A functional unit of a node through which data can enter or leave a data network. 2. In data communications, that part of a data processor dedicated to a single data channel for the purpose of receiving data from or transmitting data to one or more external, remote devices. 3. An access point for data entry or exit.

print server—A shared spooled printer in a LAN.

private branch exchange (PBX)—A telephone switching device serving a specific customer. The PBX often is located on customer premises and may be customer owned. See also digital PBX.

protocol—The set of rules governing the format and relative timing of information exchange. See also communications protocol.

public data network—A network established and operated for the specific purpose of providing data transmission services to the public. See also data communications network.

pulse code modulation (PCM)—Representation of an analog signal, such as speech, by sampling at a regular rate and converting each sample to a binary number.

Q

query—1. In data communications, the process by which a master station asks a slave station to identify itself and to give its status. 2. In interactive systems, an operation at a terminal that elicits a response from the system.

queue—A line or list formed by items in a system waiting for service; for example, tasks to be performed or messages to be transmitted in a message switching system.

R

recovery procedure—In data communications, a process whereby a specified data terminal installation attempts to resolve conflicting or erroneous condtions arising during the transfer of data.

redundancy check—A check for errors using extra (redundant) data systematically inserted for that purpose.

redundancy check character—A check character that is derived from a record and appended to the record. See also cyclic redundancy check character.

remote access—Pertaining to communications with a data processing facility through a data link.

remote job entry (RJE)—Submission of jobs through an input unit that has access to a computer through a data link.

remote station—Data terminal equipment for communicating with a data processing system through a data link.

repeater—A device used to extend the length and topology of a physical channel, particularly a LAN cable, up to the maximum allowable end-to-end channel propagation limit. See also bridge, compare with gateway.

resource—An information-system component (hardware or software) which can serve a user requirement. Resources inclue processing time, storage devices, databases, and language compilers.

resource sharing—Allocating the processing load of an enterprise to the available processing facilities when multiple facilities exist.

response time—The elapsed time between the end of an inquiry or demand on a data processing system and the beginning of the response; e.g., the length of time between the end of an inquiry and the display of the first character of the response at a user terminal.

ring network—1 A distributed system in which the information processors are connected via a circular arrangement of data communications facilities. 2. A LAN in which data flow is unidirectional among stations ordered sequentially.

RJE—See remote job entry.

routing—The function of selecting the appropriate path(s) for the movement of data within a network, ensuring that all data are directed to the appropriate destination(s).

RS-232—A Recommended Standard (RS) produd by the Electronic Industries Association (EIA) for connecting data terminal equipment (DTE) to data circuit-terminating equipment (DCE). The ISO equivalent is known an V.24.

S

SDLC—See Synchronous Data Link Control.

serial transmission—1. In data communications, transmission at successive intervals of signal elements constituting the same telegraph or data signal. The sequential elements may be transmitted with or without interruption, provided that they are not transmitted simultaneously. For example, telegraph transmission by a time-divided channel. 2. Compare with parallel transmission.

session—1. The period of time during which a user of a terminal can communicate with an interactive system; usually, the elapsed time from when a terminal user logs on the system until he logs off. 2. The period of time during which programs or devices can communicate with each other.

sharable object—An object or resource that can be referenced and accsssed by users at multiple modes; for example, print servers and file servers.

signal—Waves propagated along a transmission channel which convey some meaning to a receiving unit.

simplex transmission—Data transmission over a circuit capable of transmitting in one preassigned direction only.

site—A physical location for the housing of information system equipment.

slotted ring—A LAN architecture in which a constant number of fixed-length slots (packets) circulate continuously around the ring. A full/empty indicator within the slot header indicates when a station may place information into the slot.

SNA—See Systems Network Architecture.

SP—See space character.

space character (SP)—A character usually represented by a blank site in a series of graphics. The space character, though not a control character, has a function equivalent to that of a format effector that causes the print or display position to move one position forward without producing the printing or display of any graphic. Similarly, the space character may have a function equivalent to that of an information separator.

special character—A graphic character in a character set that is not a letter, not a digit and not a space character.

splitter—A device used to connect branches of broadband coaxial cable on a network without altering network impedance.

star network—1. A computer network in which each peripheral network node is connected only to the computer or computers at a single central facility. 2. A configuration in which remote terminals and/or processors are connected radially to a central processing location.

start-stop transmission—Asynchronous transmission such that a group of signals representing a character is preceded by a start element and is followed by a stop element.

station—The location of data terminal equipment on a network which may be the source or destination of information.

store-and-forward—A method of passing a message along a series of nodes. Each node stores a message on receipt for subsequent retransmission to the succeeding node.

sub-split—Headend frequency translation equipment that divides the band into uneven parts.

switched connection—1. A mode of operating a data link in which a circuit or channel is established to switch facilities, as in a public switched network. 2. Compare with dedicated connection.

switching center—A location that terminates multiple circuits, and is capable of interconnecting circuits or transferring traffic between circuits.

Synchronous Data Link Control (SDLC)—IBM's bit-oriented data communications protocol. Similar to the unbalanced normal class of the High-Level Data Link Control protocol.

synchronous transmission—Data transmission in which the occurrence of each signal representing a bit is related to a fixed time frame. Compare with asynchronous data transmission.

Systems Network Architecture (SNA)—IBM's network architecture for computer networks of their products. Introduced in 1974.

T

table—1. An array of data, each item of which may be unambiguously identified by means of one or more arguments. 2. A collection of data in which each item is uniquely identified by a label, its position relative to the other items or by some other means.

TAC—Terminal access controller. An Arpanet packet assembler/disassembler.

tap—A device used to insert or remove transmitted signals from twisted wire pair or coaxial cable.

TCP—See Transmission Control Protocol.

TDM—See time division multiplexing. See multiplexing.

telecommunications access method—A system program providing control and transmission of messages between applications program and terminals.

teleconferencing—Simultaneous processing of data messages of several participants communicating over a network.

teleprocessing—Data processing by means of a combination of computer data terminal equipment and data communications facilities.

teletex—An international telecommunications service enabling subscribers to exchange character-encoded text on an automatic memory-to-memory basis via public networks (similar to the telex service, but at higher rates with enhanced subscriber terminals).

teletext—Generic term for a class of one-way data distribution systems in which a terminal (typically a specially modified television receiver) copies frames under the user's control from a continuous stream. Compare with videotex.

terminal—1. A device, such as a teletypewriter or a keyboard/CRT device, which embodies a set of human/system interface functions. 2. A point in a system or communications network at which data can either enter or leave.

terminal controller—A hardwired or intelligent (programmable) device which provides detailed control for one or more terminal devices.

terminal network—See front-end nework.

terminator—An electrical resistance at the end of a cable which absorbs a transmitted signal.

throughput—A measure of the amount of work performed by a computer system over a given period of time; e.g., jobs per day.

time division multiplexing (TDM)—See multiplexing.

TIP—The Arpanet terminal interface processor. The TIP combines the functions of an IMP and a packet assembler/disassembler. Became obsolete in 1982.

token—A special message used in LANs to grant permission for a station to transmit. In a ring network the token circulates continuously; in a bus it must be addressed.

token passing—A noncontention network access allocation method in which a terminal can transmit only when it has acquired the network's circulating token.

topology—Description of the physical connections of a specific network's nodes.

transceiver—1. A device used for sending data over the network and receiving data from the network. 2. Coupling device linking a user device to network coaxial cable.

transfer time—The time interval between the time data transfer starts and is completed.

transmission control character—Any control character used to control or facilitate transmission of data between data terminal equipment.

Transmission Control Protocol (TCP)—An Arpanet protocol for establishing a communications link between two processors. Often coupled with the Internet Protocol.

transmission medium—The physical structure employed by a network for carrying information, e.g., coaxial cable, twisted wire pair, optical fiber.

transparent—In data communications, the ability to transmit arbitrary information, including control characters, which will be received as data.

tree topology—A network structure in which all stations are connected to a branching cable serving as the transmission medium.

trunk—The circuits connecting a private branch exchange (PBX) to the telephone company's central office.

turnaround time—1. The elapsed time between submission of a job and the return of complete results. 2. In data communications, the actual time required to receive a response after a message is transmitted from sender to receiver, or vice versa, using duplex transmission.

turnkey—Pertaining to a design and/or installation in which the user receives a complete running system ready to be used.

twisted pair cable—A type of interconnection cable consisting of pairs of wires twisted together.

two-wire circuit—1. A metallic circuit formed by two conductors insulated from each other. It is possible to use the two conductors as a one-way transmission, half-duplex or duplex path. 2. Compare with four-wire circuit.

U

user-friendly—An imprecise design philosophy which states that systems should be created to be understood easily by the user. Unnecessary confusing jargon and technology are avoided.

Attributes include adaptability, command completing and error correction.

V

value-added network (VAN)—A network in which some signal processing is added by the network to a transmission prior to its reception at a destination point.

VAN—See value-added network.

video display terminal—A cathode ray tube (CRT) or gas plasma display screen terminal that permits the viewing of keyed or stored text for operator manipulation.

videotex—Generic term for a class of two-way, interactive data distribution systems with output typically handled as in teletext systems and input typically accepted through the telephone or public data network. Compare with teletext.

viewdata—Narrowband videotex service, using the telephone system or similar networks to distribute data under the user's control at relatively slow speeds (not over 2400 bps).

virtual—Conceptual or appearing to exist, rather than actually existing (e.g., virtual memory in computer systems).

virtual circuit—A communications path established by computerized switching. The virtual circuit exists only while it is carrying data. No exclusive use reservation of resources exists.

V.nn—The V.nn series of the CCITT standards relate to the connection of digital equipment to the analog public telephone network.

voice-grade channel—A channel suitable for transmission of speech, digital or analog data or facsimile, generally with a frequency range of about 300 to 3000 cycles per second.

V.24—The CCITT equivalent of RS-232.

W

wide area network—A data communications network designed to serve an area of hundreds or thousands of miles. Compare with local area network.

workstation—A terminal station, perhaps connected to a LAN, providing some local processing capability and storage as well as access to other workstations and shared resources.

X

X.nn—The X.nn series of the CCITT standards relate to the connection of digital equipment to a public data network which employs digital signaling.

X.3—The CCITT standard defining the packet assembler/disassembler (PAD).

X.21—The CCITT standard defining the interface between packet-type data terminal equipment and a digital interface unit.

X.25—The CCITT standard defining the interface between packet-type data terminal equipment and a public data network.

X.29—The CCITT standard for exchange of control information between a packet assembler/disassembler and a host.

Z

zerofill—To character fill with the representation of the character zero.

Appendix

Table 2

LAN FORECAST WORLDWIDE
1983–1990

PC Networks	1983	1984		1985		1986	
	IB	Shipments	IB	Shipments	IB	Shipments	IB
Number of networks	15,500	17,700	33,200	26,550	59,750	37,970	97,7
Avg. PCs per network	6.0	6.5	7.0	7.0	7.5	7.5	
No. of connected PCs	93,000	115,050	232,400	185,850	448,125	284,775	781,7
Avg. price per PC conn.	625	595	595	475	475	380	3
Value of PC connect.	58,125,000	82,943,000	138,278,000	102,469,375	212,859,375	126,781,300	297,068,8
Add-on PC connect.		24,350		29,875		48,860	
# of connected PCs	93,000	139,400	232,400	215,725	448,125	333,635	781,7
Total PCs	5,040,000	3,859,000	8,870,000	4,586,000	13,355,000	5,595,000	18,790,0
Percent of total PCs	1.85	3.61	2.62	4.70	3.36	5.96	

Terminal/Systems Nets	1983	1984		1985		1986	
	IB	Shipments	IB	Shipments	IB	Shipments	IB
No. of networks	9,597	5,203	14,800	6,765	21,565	8,525	30,
Avg. nodes per network	4.0	4.0	4.0	4.3	4.2	4.7	
# of nodes	38,388	20,812	59,200	29,090	90,573	40,068	132,
Avg. wrkstns. per node	8.0	8.5	9.0	9.0	9.5	9.6	
# of connect. wrkstns.	307,104	176,902	532,800	261,806	860,444	384,648	1,376,
Avg. price per wrkstn. con.	1,200	800	800	635	635	550	
Value wrkstn. connect.	368,524,800	180,556,800	426,240,000	208,053,623	546,381,623	284,061,195	757,305,
Add-on wrkstn. connect.		48,794		65,838		131,827	
# of connect. wrkstns.	307,104	225,696	532,800	327,644	860,444	516,475	1,376,
Total wrkstns.	16,791,667	7,443,167	23,578,333	8,879,333	31,521,667	10,661,667	40,820,
Percent of total wrkstns.	1.83	3.03	2.26	3.69	2.73	4.84	

Subtotal	1983	1984		1985		1986	
	IB	Shipments	IB	Shipments	IB	Shipments	IB
No. of networks	25,097	22,903	48,000	33,315	81,315	46,495	127,
Avg. wrkstns. per net	15.9	15.9	15.9	16.3	16.1	18.3	
# of connect. wrkstns.	400,104	365,096	765,200	543,369	1,308,569	850,110	2,158,
Avg. price per connect. wrkstn.	1,066	722	738	571	580	483	
Value wrkstn. connect.	426,649,800	263,499,800	564,518,000	310,522,998	759,240,998	410,842,495	1,054,373,
# of connect. wrkstns.	400,104	365,096	765,200	543,369	1,308,569	850,110	2,158,
Total wrkstns.	16,791,677	7,443,167	23,578,333	8,879,333	31,521,667	10,661,667	40,820,
Percent of total wrkstns.	2.38	4.91	3.25	6.12	4.15	7.97	

| 1987 | | 1988 | | 1989 | | 1990 | | ACG% | |
ents	IB	Shipments	IB	Shipments	IB	Shipments	IB	Ships.	IB
,155	150,875	71,755	222,630	93,285	315,915	121,270	437.185	37.82	53.67
8.0	8.5	8.5	9.0	9.0	9.5	9.5	10.0	6.53	6.12
,240	1,282,438	609,918	2,003,670	839,565	3,001,193	1,152,065	4,371,850	46.81	63.08
300	300	240	240	200	200	160	160	-19.66	-19.66
,250	384,731,250	173,095,800	480,880,800	199,504,500	600,238,500	219,305,200	699,496,000	17.59	31.02
438		111,315		157,958		218,593		44.16	
,678	1,282,438	721,233	2,003,670	997,523	3,001,193	1,370,658	4,371,850		
,000	25,163,000	7,855,000	32,441,000	9,113,000	40,222,000	10,497,000	46,169,000	18.15	32.58
7.49	5.10	9.18	6.18	10.95	7.46	13.06	9.08	23.88	23.01

| 1987 | | 1988 | | 1989 | | 1990 | | ACG% | |
ents	IB	Shipments	IB	Shipments	IB	Shipments	IB	Ships.	IB
400	40,490	12,480	52,970	14,725	67,695	17,080	84,775	21.91	33.76
5.2	5.0	5.6	5.4	6.0	5.8	6.4	6.2	8.15	7.58
080	202,450	69,888	286,038	88,350	392,631	109,312	525,605	31.84	43.90
10.0	10.6	10.5	11.1	11.2	11.5	11.7	12.0	5.47	4.91
800	2,145,970	733,824	3,175,022	989,520	4,515,257	1,278,950	6,307,260	39.06	50.97
485	485	430	430	380	380	345	345	-13.08	-13.08
026	1,040,765,450	442,492,274	1,365,259,374	509,289,186	1,715,797,470	618,241,208	2,176,004,700	22.77	31.22
252		295,228		350,715		513,053		48.01	
052	2,145,970	1,029,052	3,175,022	1,340,235	4,515,257	1,792,004	6,307,260		50.97
667	51,588,000	14,645,000	63,796,000	16,803,000	77,087,000	19,097,000	91,102,333	17.00	25.27
6.11	4.16	7.03	4.98	7.98	5.86	9.38	6.92	20.72	20.52

| 1987 | | 1988 | | 1989 | | 1990 | | ACG% | |
ents	IB	Shipments	IB	Shipments	IB	Shipments	IB	Ships.	IB
555	191,365	84,235	275,600	108,010	383,610	138,350	521,960	34.95	48.84
20.0	17.9	20.8	18.8	21.6	19.6	22.9	20.5	6.19	4.25
729	3,428,408	1,750,284	5,178,692	2,337,757	7,516,449	3,162,661	10,679,110	43.31	55.16
412	416	352	356	303	308	265	269	-15.39	-15.46
276	1,425,526,700	615,588,074	1,846,140,174	708,793,686	2,316,035,970	837,546,408	2,875,500,700	21.26	31.17
729	3,428,408	1,750,284	5,178,692	2,337,757	7,516,449	3,162,661	10,679,110	43.31	55.16
667	51,588,000	14,645,000	63,796,000	16,803,000	77,087,000	19,097,000	91,102,333	17.00	25.27
10.09	6.65	11.95	8.12	13.91	9.75	16.56	11.72	22.48	23.87

Courtesy International Data Corporation

Table 2 Notes

1. The forecast assumes strong growth in PC LAN implementations as users take advantage of low-entry LAN technology to consolidate PC resources into manageable work groups around functional or common application areas. The availability of LAN-based multiuser software will also contribute to increased volumes of PC LAN implementations. The terminal/systems network forecast considers the consolidation of multiple PC LANs into more corporatewide entities. Most terminal systems LANs shipped represent an increasing percentage of intermediate systems installed base, as vendors of such systems strive to provide both logical and physical peer-to-peer connectability over the term of the forecast.

2. LAN workstation connections shipped are determined on the basis of a percentage of total workstations shipped and installed as forecasted by IDC.

3. In determining the total workstations connected to LANs over the period of the forecast, a formula which estimated the number of PCs to be used in standalone mode, based on projected shipped/installed standalone software sales, was used. In addition, terminal emulation board use, remote modem access, and PBX workstation connection estimates were calculated in relation to the estimated number of LAN workstation connections.

4. Add-on workstation/PC connections represent those connections shipped to installed networks as users add to existing LAN facilities. Number of connected workstations/PCs represents those connections shipped as part of new LAN facilities implemented in a given year. Number of connected workstations/PCs represents the sum of new network connections and add-on connections.

Table 3

LOCAL AREA NETWORKS
MARKET SIZE PROJECTIONS
NETWORKS SHIPPED AND INSTALLED WORLDWIDE
1984–1990

	1984 Actual		1990 Projected		ACG %	
Market Segment	#	$(M)	#	$(M)	#	$
Networks Shipped:						
PC LANs	17,700	82.9	121,270	219.3	37.8	17.6
Terminal/System LANs	5,203	180.5	17,080	618.2	21.9	22.7
TOTALS	22,903	263.4	138,350	837.5	34.9	21.2
Networks Installed:						
PC LANs	33,200	138.3	437,185	699.5	53.7	31.0
Terminal/Systems LANs	14,800	426.2	84,775	2,176.0	33.8	31.2
TOTALS	48,000	564.5	521,960	2,875.5	48.8	31.2

$ACG = (FV/PV)(1/\# \text{ yrs.}) - 1$

Courtesy International Data Corporation

Table 4

MARKET GROWTH RATE: NETWORKS
SHIPPED WORLDWIDE, 1984–1990

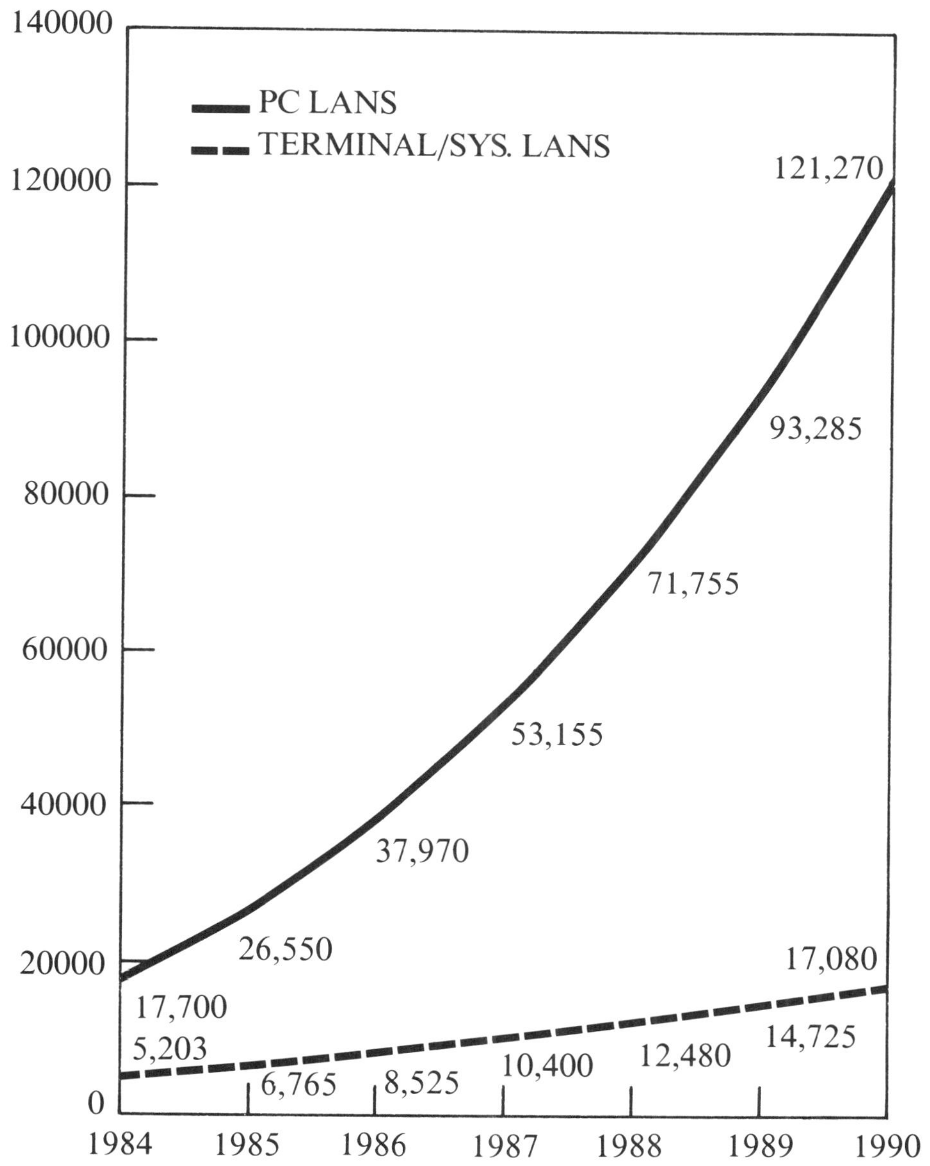

Courtesy International Data Corporation

Table 5

MARKET GROWTH RATES: SHIPMENTS
NUMBER OF WORKSTATION CONNECTIONS
(000)

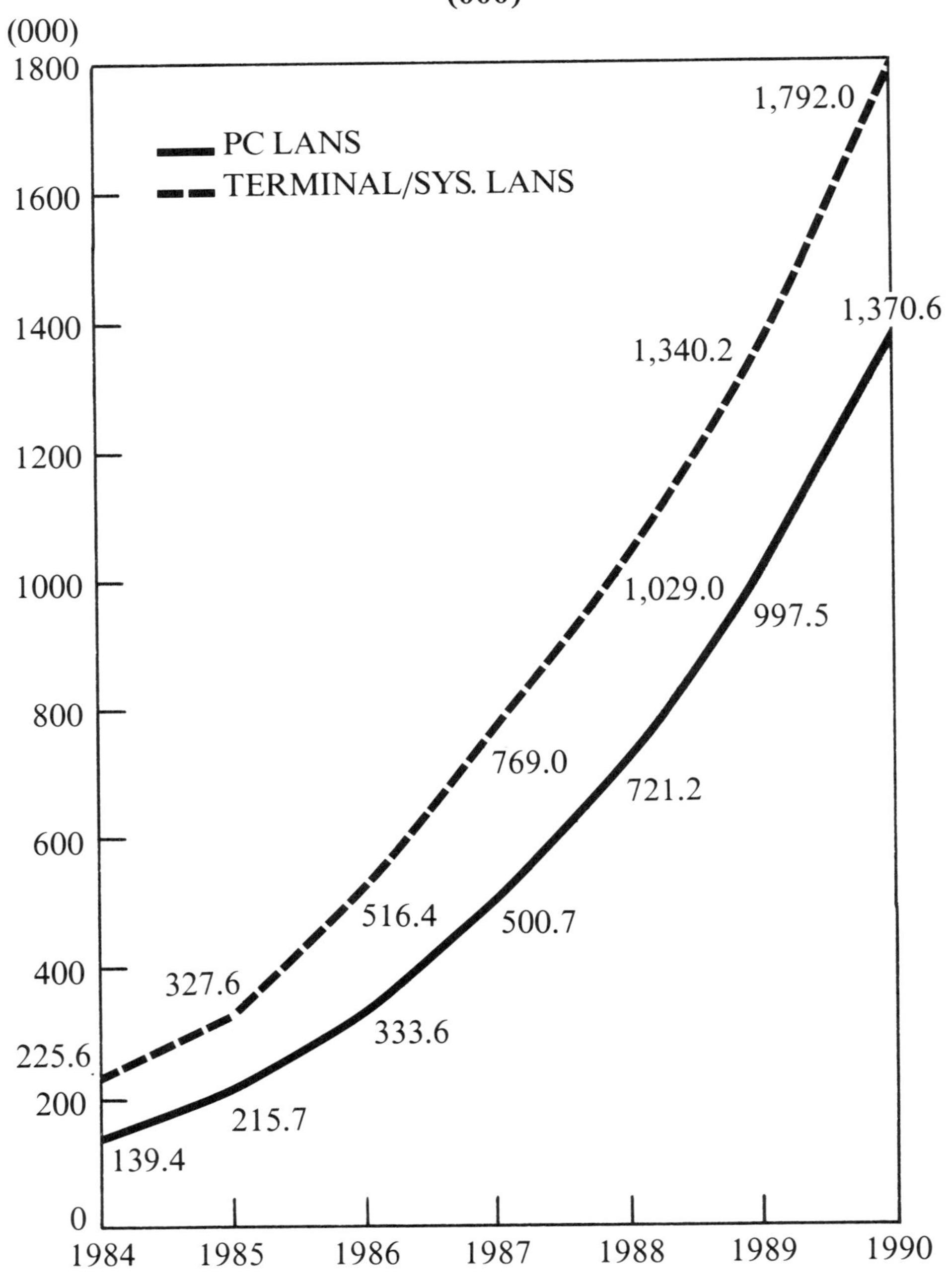

COPYRIGHT 1985 INTERNATIONAL DATA CORP.

Courtesy International Data Corporation

Table 6

MARKET GROWTH RATES: SHIPMENTS
AVERAGE PRICE PER WORKSTATION CONNECTION

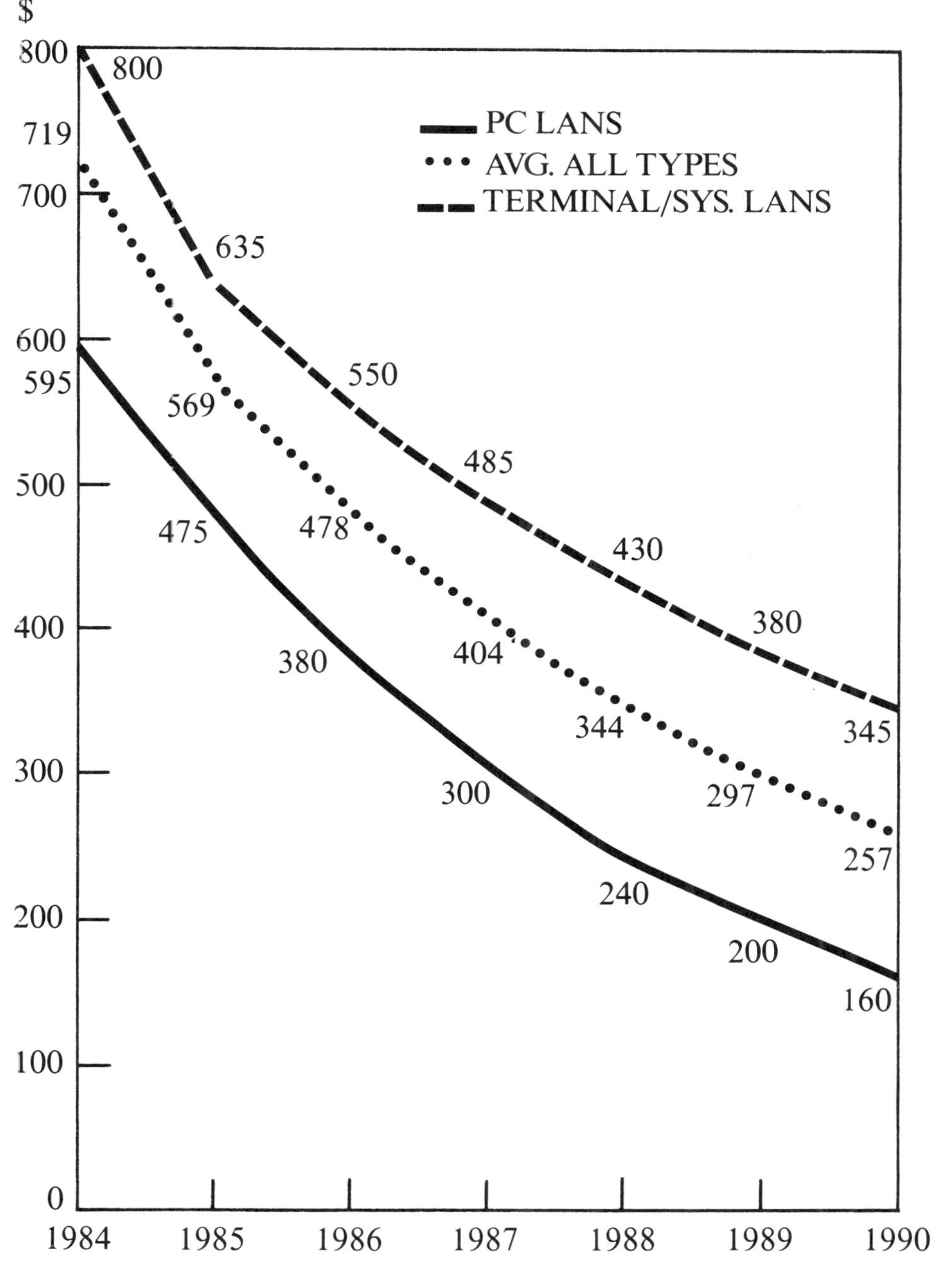

COPYRIGHT 1985 INTERNATIONAL DATA CORP.

Courtesy International Data Corporation

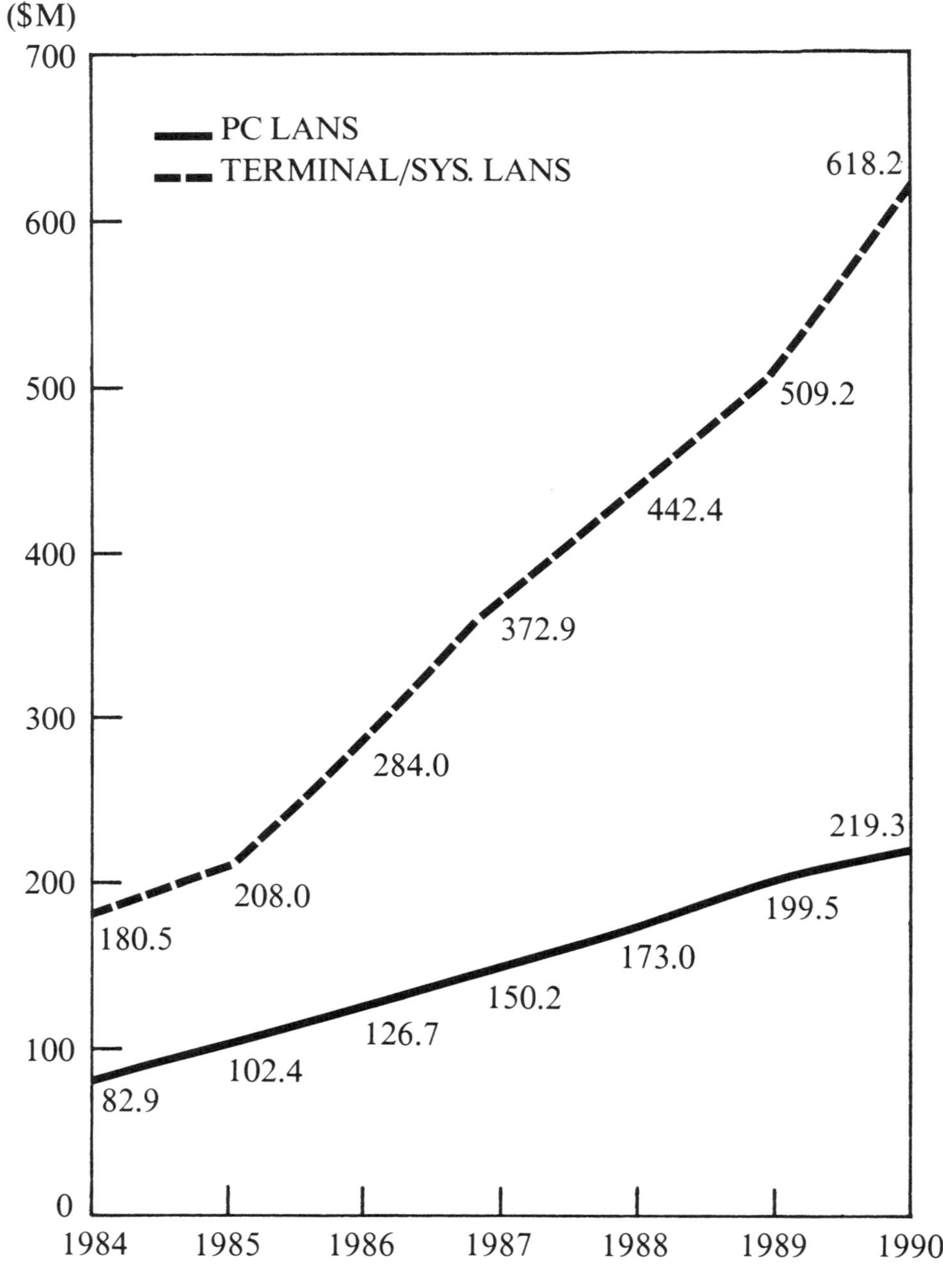

Table 7

**MARKET GROWTH RATES: SHIPMENTS
DOLLAR VALUE OF NETWORK CONNECTIONS
($M)**

COPYRIGHT 1985 INTERNATIONAL DATA CORP.

Courtesy International Data Corporation

Table 8

MARKET GROWTH RATES: LANS INSTALLED WORLDWIDE, 1983–1989

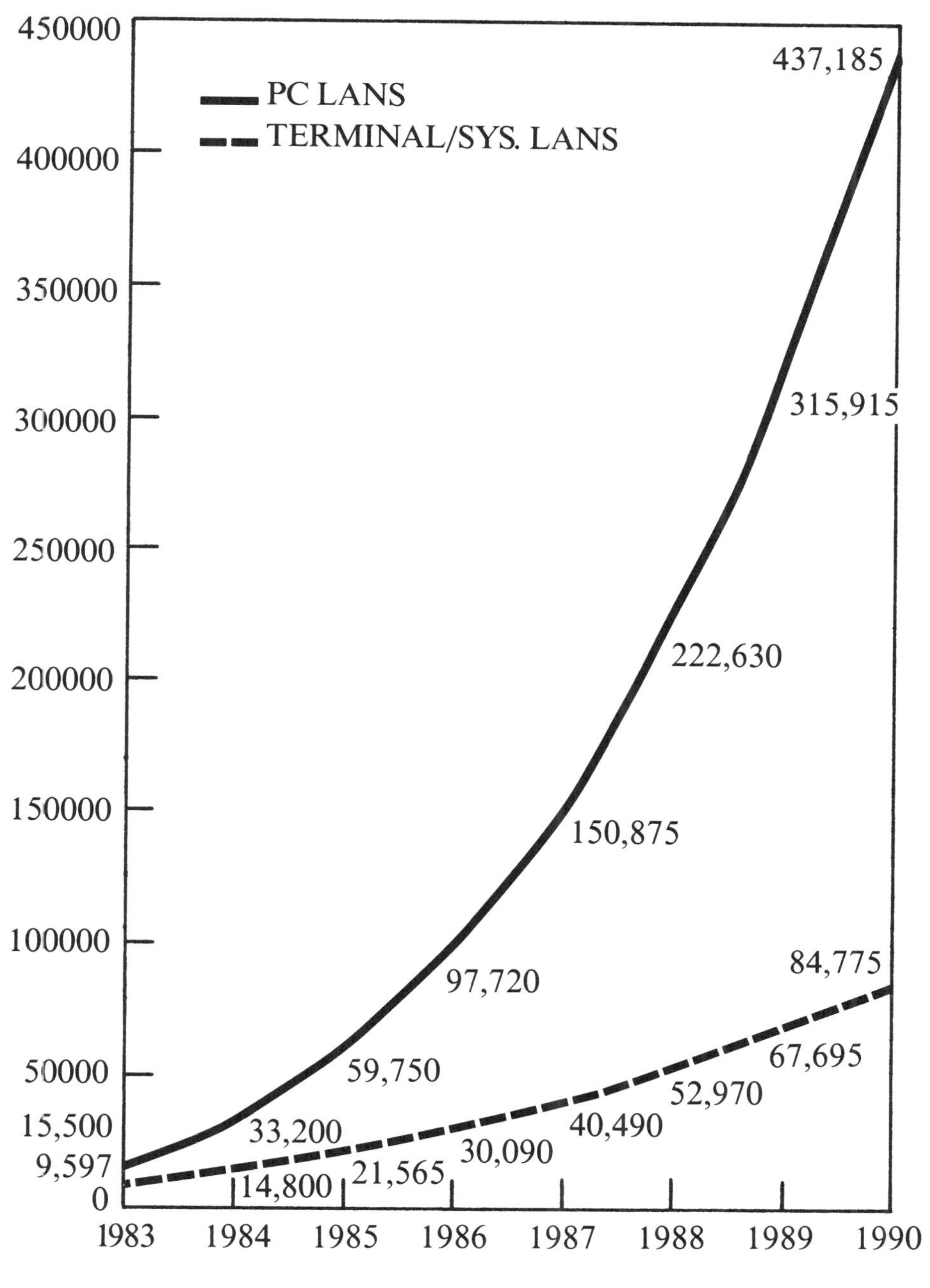

COPYRIGHT 1985 INTERNATIONAL DATA CORP.

Courtesy International Data Corporation

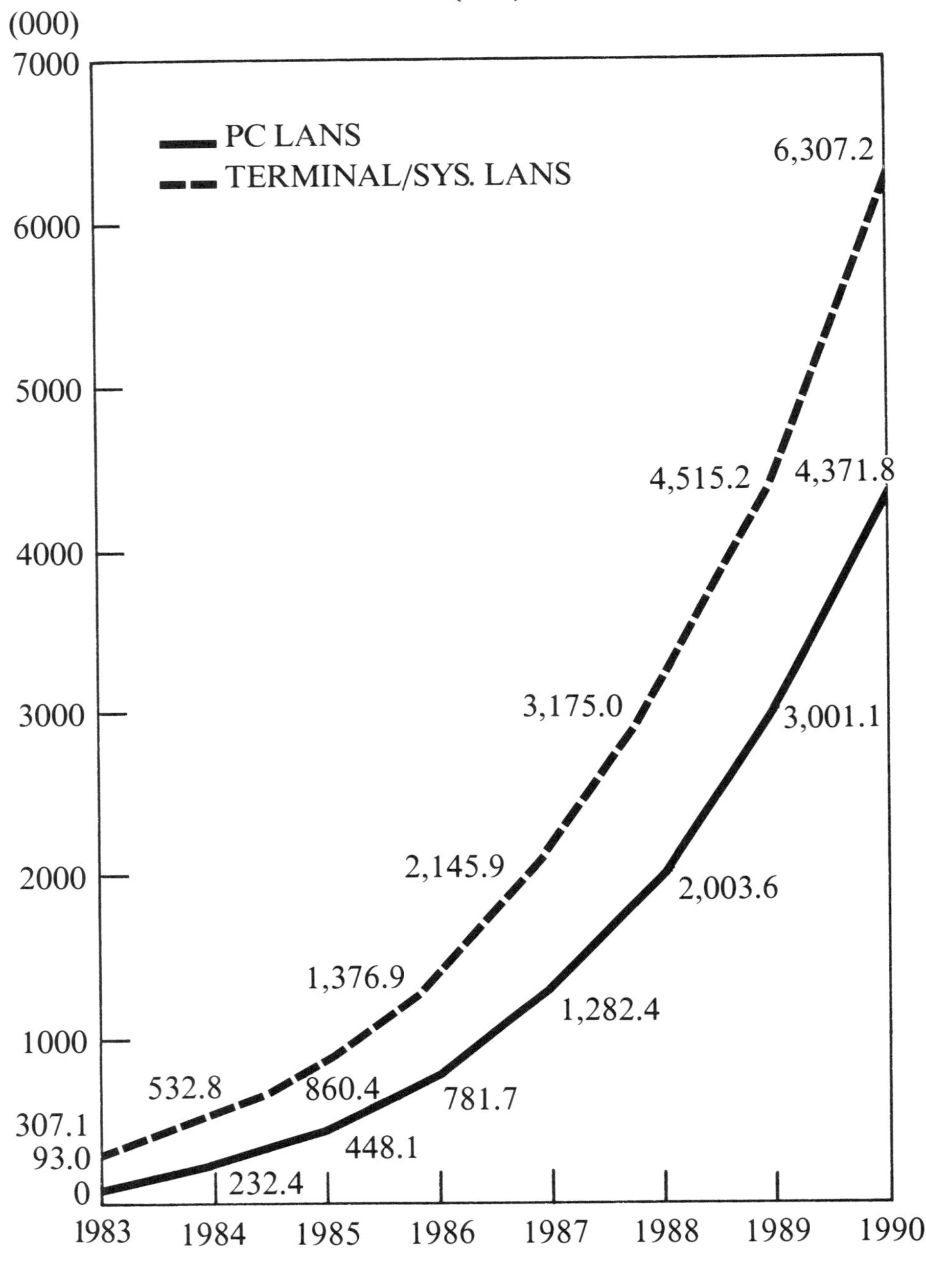

Courtesy International Data Corporation

Table 10

MARKET GROWTH RATES: NETWORKS INSTALLED
DOLLAR VALUE OF NETWORK CONNECTIONS
($M)

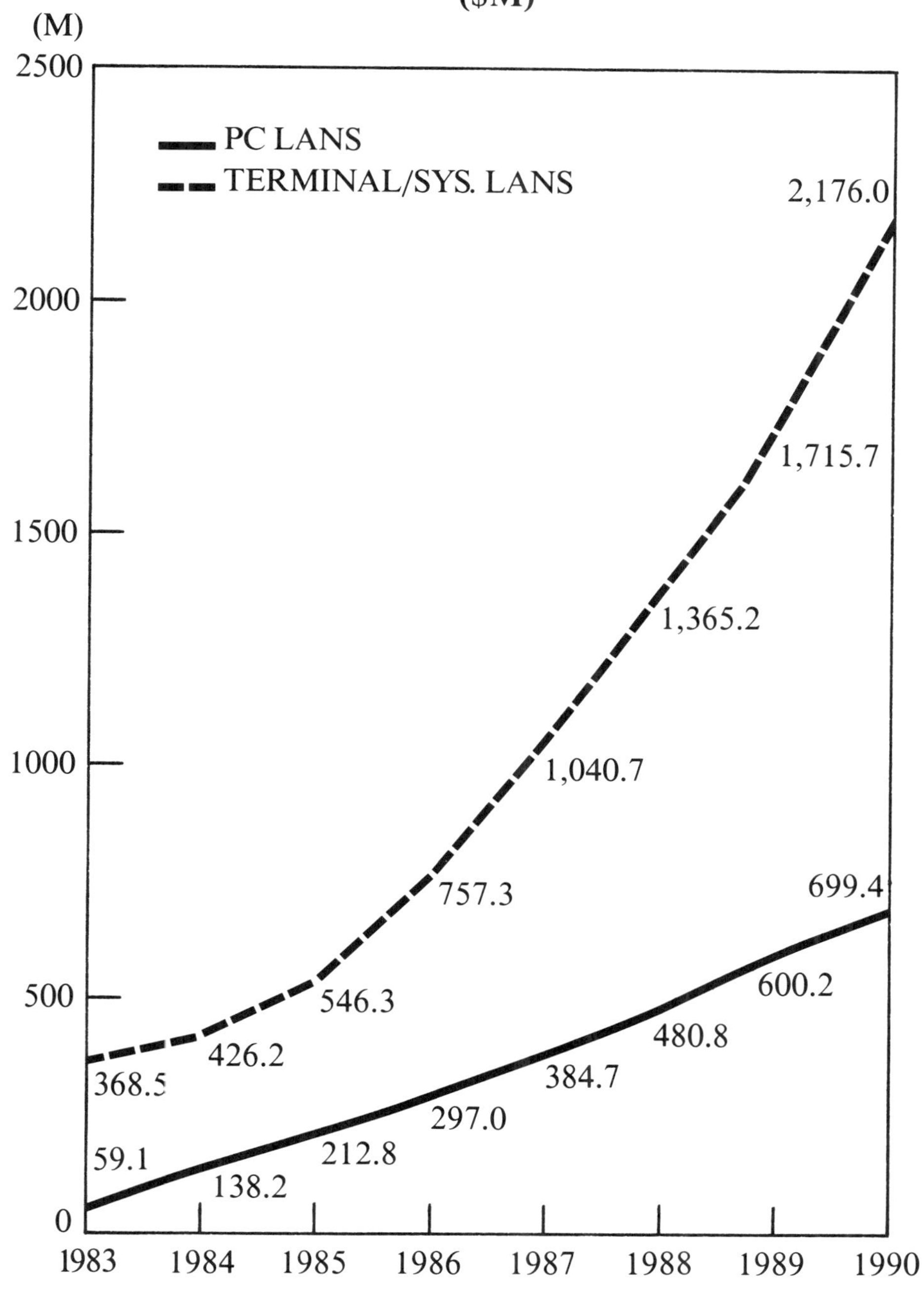

COPYRIGHT 1985 INTERNATIONAL DATA CORP.

Courtesy International Data Corporation

Table 11

**MARKET GROWTH: INSTALLED LAN
WORKSTATION CONNECTIONS***

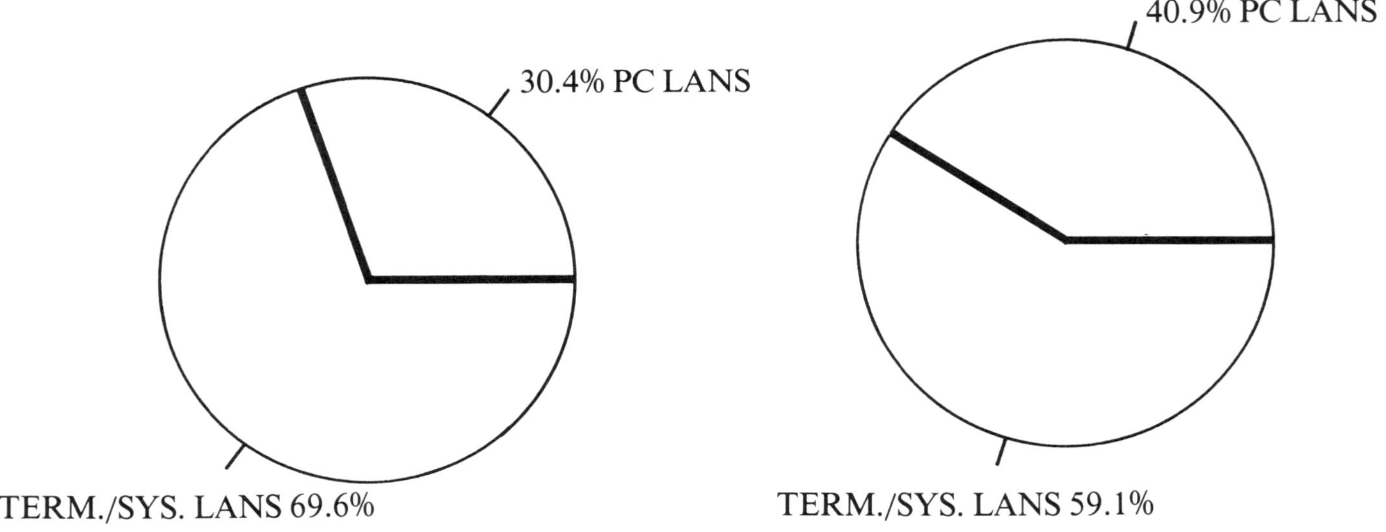

*Workstation refers to CRT-type terminals and business/scientific personal computers.

Courtesy International Data Corporation

Table 12

MARKET GROWTH: DOLLAR VALUE OF
INSTALLED LAN WORKSTATION CONNECTIONS*

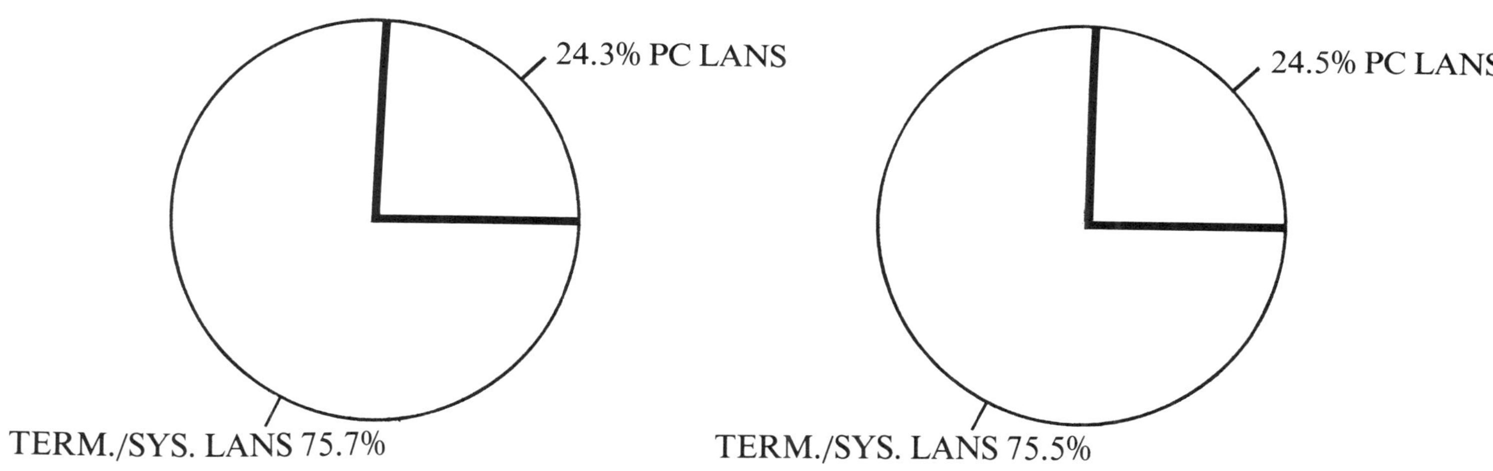

*Workstation refers to CRT-type terminals and business/scientific personal computers.

Courtesy International Data Corporation

Table 13

LAN* WORKSTATION CONNECTIONS AS A PERCENT
OF TOTAL WORKSTATION** INSTALLED WORLDWIDE

WORKSTATION UNITS

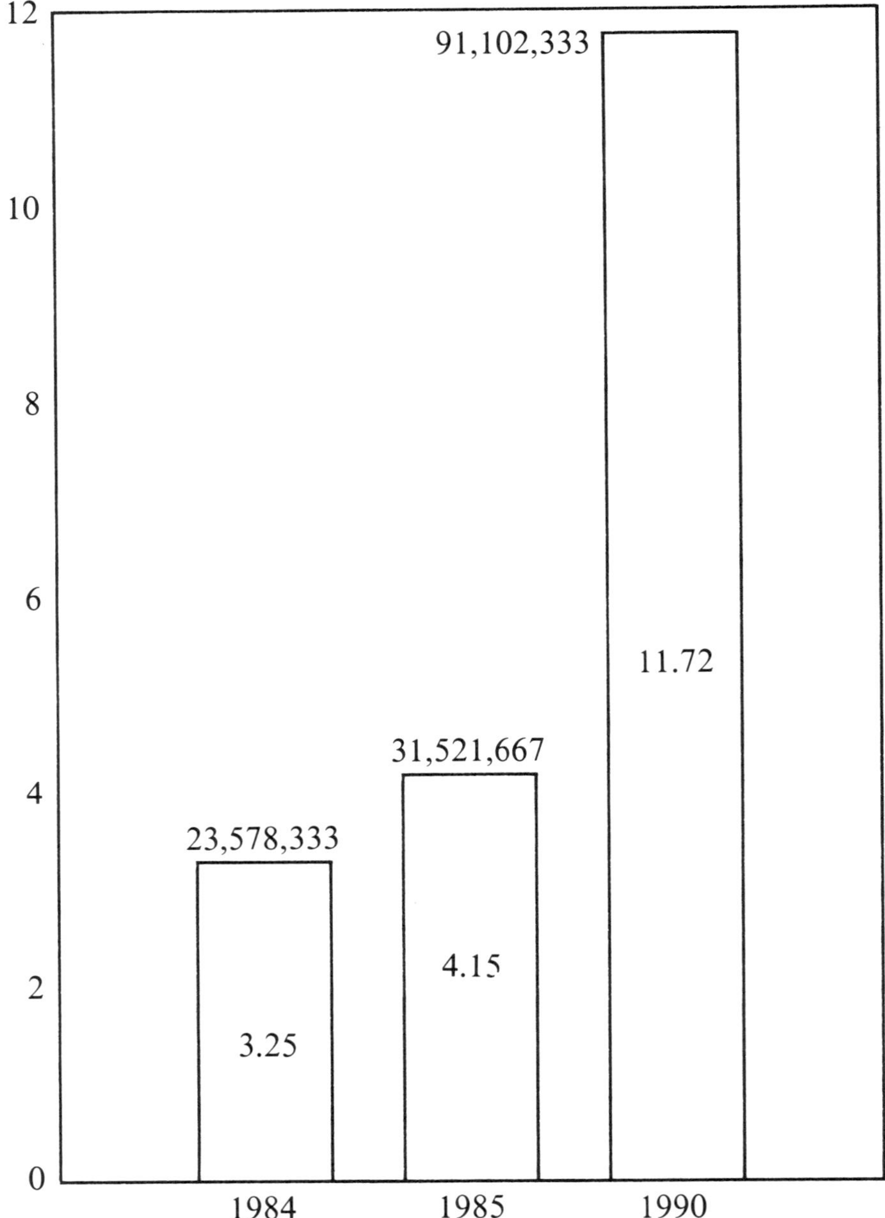

COPYRIGHT 1985 INTERNATIONAL DATA CORP.

* LAN all-types includes PC LANs and terminal/system LANs.
**Workstations refers to CRT-type terminals and business/scientific
personal computers.

Courtesy International Data Corporation

Table 14

PC LAN CONNECTIONS AS A PERCENT OF TOTAL PCS INSTALLED WORLDWIDE/BUSINESS AND SCIENTIFIC PCS

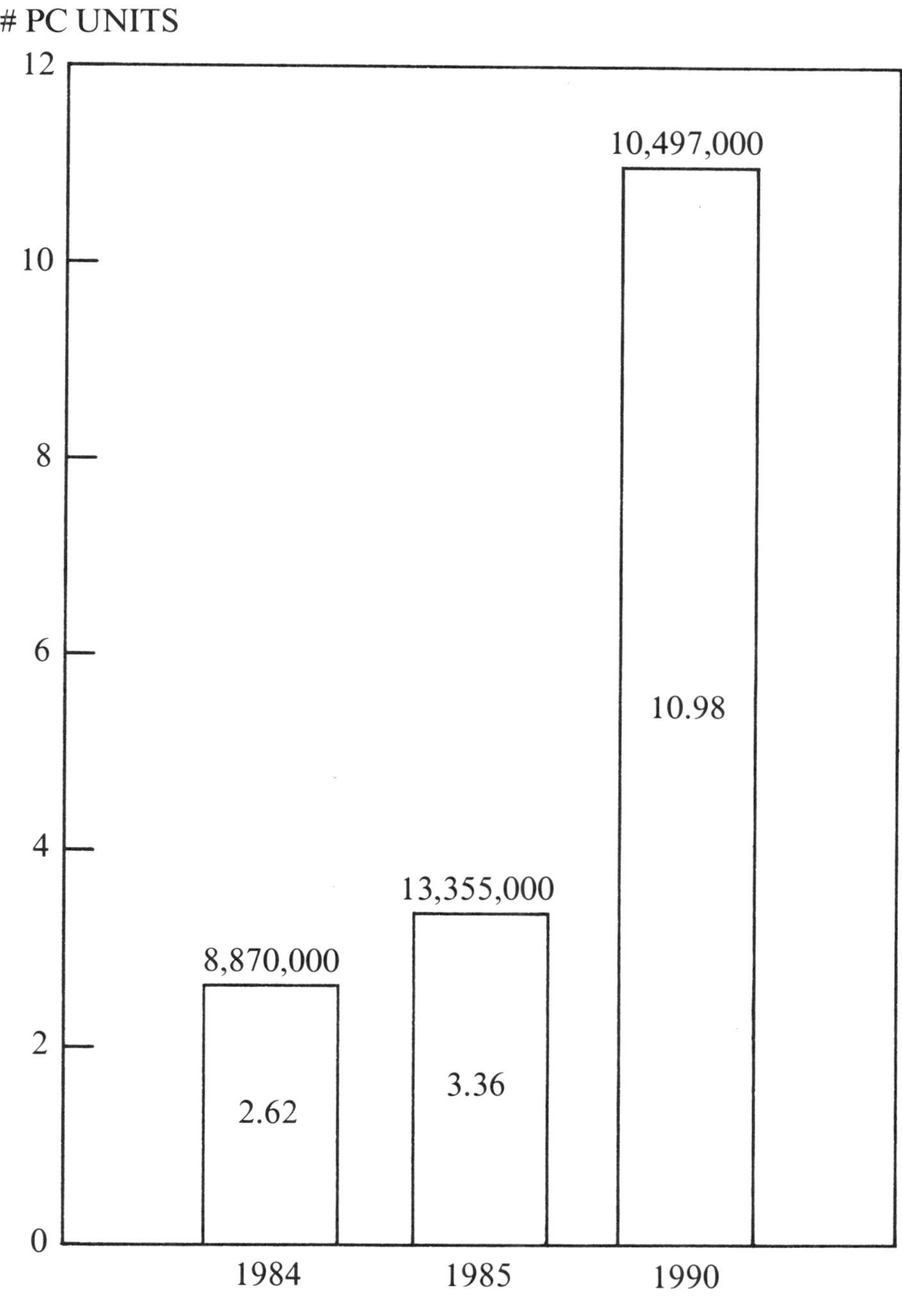

COPYRIGHT 1985 INTERNATIONAL DATA CORP.

Courtesy International Data Corporation

Table 15

TERMINAL/SYSTEMS LAN WORKSTATION CONNECTIONS AS A PERCENT OF TOTAL WORKSTATION* INSTALLED WORLDWIDE

WORKSTATION UNITS

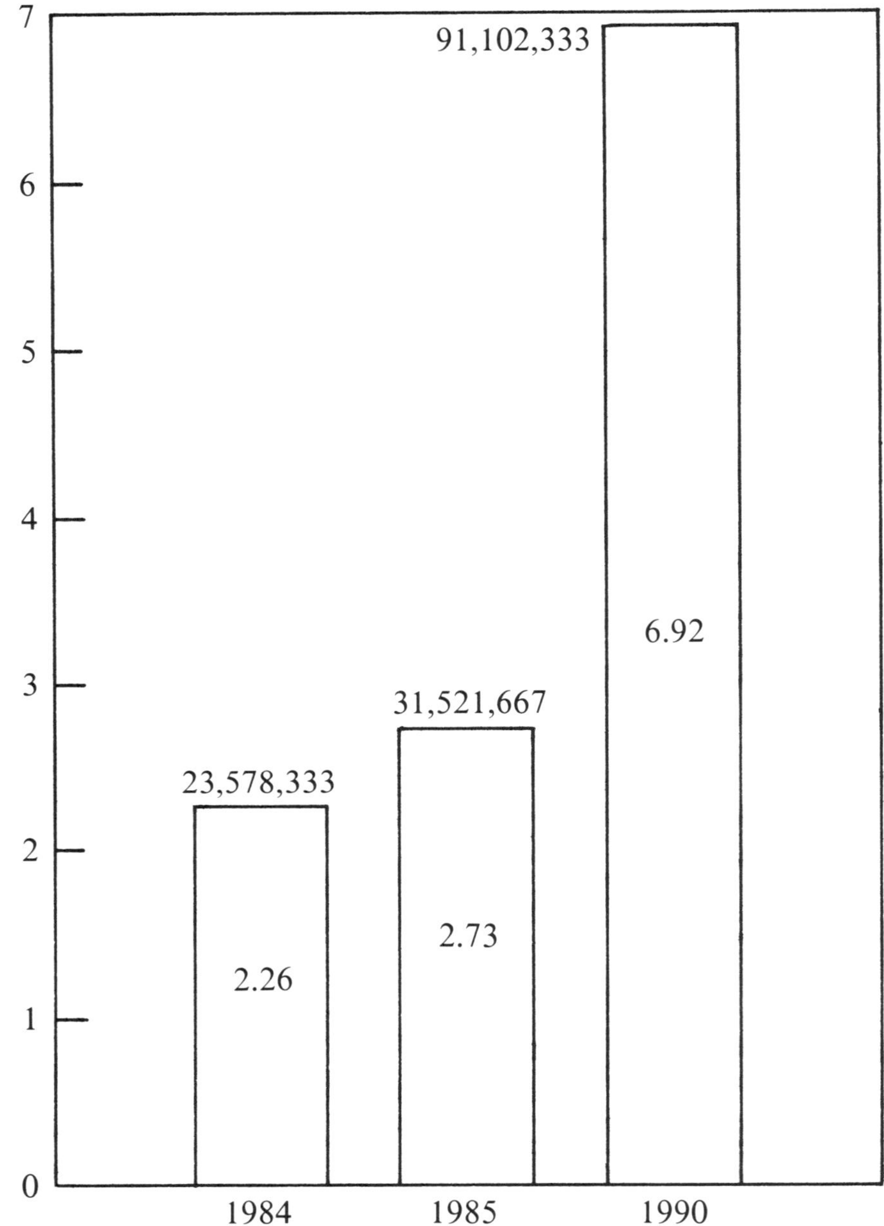

*Workstations refers to CRT-type terminals and business/scientific personal computers.

Courtesy International Data Corporation

Table of Contents

**Order your copy today by completing the attached order form and returning it
with your payment, or by calling TOLL FREE (800) 722-9000. Call today!**

LOCALNET '85 ORDER FORM

P

Yes! I need LOCALNET '85. Please send me _______ copy(ies) at $189 each (plus $4.50 shipping and handling).
   Maryland residents, please add 5% sales tax.
☐ Payment enclosed.   ☐ Please charge my: ☐ VISA   ☐ MasterCard   ☐ American Express

Card No. ____ Exp. Date _______________

Signature ____
   ☐ Please bill me/my company. (I understand the book will be shipped upon receipt of payment.)

Name ____

Title ____

Company ____

Address ____

City _____________________ State _____________ Zip __________

Phone (_____)_____________________________

Return to: Phillips Publishing, Inc., 7811 Montrose Road, Potomac, MD 20854

Is your business in bypass? If so, do you know...

Who is using DTS? How is DTS being used? Where is DTS being used? Are you competitive? Are you reaching your markets? How can you tell?

Find out in The First DTS Market Survey

Volume I of the Bypass Opportunities Series

© 1986 by Phillips Publishing, Inc.

Bypassing the telephone company is blossoming into a $3 billion industry . . . 25% of all large businesses bypass and that number will rise to 50% by 1987. You, the bypass provider, have begun to target your market and scramble for a competitive position.

Now you can take advantage of a valuable new marketing information series that will help you thrive and survive in this competitive new bypass environment. Phillips Publishing, the leading publisher of telecommunications information, brings you the first in a comprehensive series of bypass surveys on digital termination systems (DTS) . . . private microwave . . . fiber optics, satellite . . . and more.

The *First DTS Market Survey* is a complete study of the DTS market. You find out *who* is using DTS. *How* DTS is being used. *Where* DTS is being used. *Why* DTS being used.

THE FIRST DTS MARKET SURVEY—
A Valuable Marketing Tool

The *First DTS Market Survey* is your marketing information source on DTS bypass today. We've compiled, categorized, and published detailed marketing data from 80% of the DTS bypass providers currently on the air. What you get are 540 pages of figures you can put to good use in every phase of your marketing and strategic plan-

ning . . . broken down by company size and by SMSA, and augmented by maps and charts.

Read them. Analyze them. And you'll come away with some startling insights into the nature of the bypass industry—and into the future. The *First DTS Market Survey* will help you:

- Discover profitable DTS market segments to target your sales efforts
- Identify potential DTS users by type of business
- Uncover lucrative service offerings
- Understand better the needs of your current DTS customers
- Assess strengths and growth potential of bypass industry
- Find out how much bypass diversification contributes to total revenues of DTS vendors
- Locate potentially profitable geographical areas of the country
- Understand the implications of potential FCC regulation on your market
- Discover lucrative DTS service mixes

No other volume gives you the figures you need to answer the toughest questions on how you're doing. And no other volume gives you figures you need to determine where you're going.

PHILLIPS PUBLISHING • 7811 MONTROSE ROAD • POTOMAC MARYLAND 20854

WHO IS USING DTS TO BYPASS TODAY

The *First DTS Market Survey* will pinpoint for you who the major users are and what they are doing:

- What new customer bases are emerging and what are their current needs
- What are the needs of your current users
- Why users are choosing DTS over other popular bypass technologies like fiber and satellite
- Where DTS is being used

WHO IS PROVIDING DTS SERVICES NOW?

What is your competition doing? How do your sales revenues compare to other companies'? How great are your expectations compared with your competition's? The *First DTS Market Survey* will give you information on your competitors and more including . . .

- What services and options are DTS providers giving to telecommunications managers and which ones are the most profitable
- What marketing techniques are being used to sell DTS, and which ones are most successful
- Which user markets generate the most revenues and which ones are the most profitable
- Which bypass services contribute the most to the bottomline
- What percentage of DTS providers' business is in other bypass technologies
- How much use of hybrid networks is there among large users

SPECIAL FEATURES

The *First DTS Market Survey* is designed to make it easy for you to access and find the data you need, quickly and efficiently.

All of the data is cross-tabulated by key areas including:

- by user
- by potential user
- by planned user
- by company size
- by geographical location

You also get tables and charts that illustrate the *important* data that will affect your decisions and strategies in the bypass market.

Until now, DTS providers have not been able to fully define their marketplace and market niches. Until now, the DTS industry has been working within a vacuum—with little or no information on prospective markets, growth potential and competition.

Now, for the first time, there is one volume to bridge the gap—the *First DTS Market Survey*—to bring you the information you need to make quicker and more profitable decisions.

THIS NEW PUBLICATION IS <u>NOW</u> AVAILABLE

The moment this remarkable new publication left the press, it was snapped up by those eager to get a really complete picture of DTS and bypass services.

Now you, too, can take advantage of this new publication and all it has to offer. Its 540 pages are filled with all of the facts, figures, charts, tables and cross-tabulations you need to make intelligent decisions in this ever-changing market.

Simply return the attached order form and we'll rush your copy of the *First DTS Market Survey* the moment payment is received. For faster service, call toll-free (800) 722-9000; please have your credit card handy. If you'd like to receive your *First DTS Market Survey* <u>tomorrow</u>, we'll be glad to ship it to you overnight! So, call today.

The FIRST DTS MARKET SURVEY Order Form

☐ **Yes.** I need the *First DTS Market Survey.* Please send _____ copy(ies) at $297 each and rush them to me via U.P.S. (Maryland residents, please add 5% sales tax).

☐ Check enclosed for $ _____. (Please add $4.50 for shipping and handling.)

☐ Bill me. My Survey(s) will be shipped upon receipt of payment.

☐ Bill my company. P.O. # _____. My survey(s) will be shipped upon receipt of payment.

☐ Charge:

☐ VISA   ☐ MasterCard   ☐ American Express

Card number _____
Expiration date: _____
MC Interbank No. _____
Signature _____

Or, call TOLL FREE
800-722-9000

Name _____

Company _____ Title _____

Address _____

City _____ State _____ Zip _____

Phone (_____) _____

Please return to: **The First DTS Market Survey**
Phillips Publishing, Inc.
7811 Montrose Road
Potomac, MD 20854

DT47

PHILLIPS PUBLISHING • 7811 MONTROSE ROAD • POTOMAC MARYLAND 20854